Mysterious Revelation

*An Examination of the Philosophy
of St. Mark's Gospel*

Mysterious Revelation

An Examination of the Philosophy

of St. Mark's Gospel

BY T. A. BURKILL

Cornell University Press

ITHACA, NEW YORK

CORNELL UNIVERSITY PRESS

First published 1963

This work has been brought to publication with
the assistance of a grant from the Ford Foundation.

Library of Congress Catalog Card Number: 63-11306

PRINTED IN THE UNITED STATES OF AMERICA

BY VAIL-BALLOU PRESS, INC.

T. S. B. and S. A. B.
my father and mother
in memoriam

Preface

IN the production of this work I have been greatly helped by
the counsel and encouragement of many teachers and friends,
more particularly the late Professors M. Goguel of Paris, R. H.
Lightfoot of Oxford, and T. W. Manson of Manchester; Professors H. J. Cadbury of Harvard, W. Eltester of Tübingen,
E. Schweizer of Zürich, Morton Smith of Columbia, and P.
Vielhauer of Bonn; and Dr. P. Winter of London.

Thanks are also due to my colleagues here at Cornell, Professors H. Caplan, J. Hutton, and I. Rabinowitz, for advice in the
later stages; and to my wife, for her unfailing assistance.

Certain sections have already appeared in various periodicals,
and for permission to reproduce these I am indebted to Pro-
fessors M. Black (St. Andrews) and W. Eltester (Tübingen),
Principal L. A. Garrard (Oxford), Professors A. Guillaumont
(Paris) and J. Munck (Aarhus), the late Professor R. Pettazzoni
(Rome), and Professors B. Reicke (Basel), W. C. van Unnik
(Bilthoven), and J. H. Waszink (Leiden), editors respectively
of *New Testament Studies, Die Zeitschrift für die neutesta-*

mentliche Wissenschaft, The Hibbert Journal, La Revue de l'histoire des religions, Studia Theologica, Numen, Theologische Zeitschrift, Novum Testamentum, and *Vigiliae Christianae.*

T. A. B.

Goldwin Smith Hall
Cornell University
Ithaca, New York
Whitsuntide, 1962

Contents

Preface   vii

Abbreviations   xi

Introduction   1

Part One: The Secret Fact of the Messiahship

1 St. Mark's Preface   9

  Supplementary Note A: A Numerical Typology?   24

2 Evidence of the Fact in Word and Deed   28

3 Miracles and Miracle Stories   41

4 The Injunctions to Silence   62

  Supplementary Note B: Concerning Mark 5:7, 18–20   86

5 Parables and the Secret   96

6 Hostility and the Secret   117

Part Two: The Mysterious Meaning of the Secret Fact

7 The Confession and the Transfiguration   145

  Supplementary Note C: The Exegesis of Mark 9:1   165

8 A Meaning that is Not Understood   168

9 Strain on the Secret   188

ix

Contents

Supplementary Note D: Secrecy and History 210

10 Realization of the Mysterious Meaning 218

Supplementary Note E: Galilee and Jerusalem 252

11 The Last Supper 258

12 The Trial of Jesus 280

Supplementary Note F: The Competence of the Sanhedrin 300

Conclusion 319

Select Bibliography 325

Index 333

x

Abbreviations

C.B.	*The Cambridge Bible for Schools and Colleges*
E.T.	English Translation
Ex.T.	*The Expository Times*
H.T.R.	*The Harvard Theological Review*
I.C.C.	*The International Critical Commentary*
J.B.L.	*The Journal of Biblical Literature*
J.T.S.	*The Journal of Theological Studies*
L.H.B.	Lietzmann's *Handbuch zum Neuen Testament*
L.K.T.	Lietzmann's *Kleine Texte für theologische und philologische Vorlesungen und Übungen*
M.K.E.K.	Meyer's *Kritisch-exegetischer Kommentar über das Neue Testament*
M.N.T.	*The Moffatt New Testament Commentary*
N.C.H.S.	*A New Commentary on Holy Scripture including the Apocrypha* (edited by C. Gore and others)
R.H.R.	*La Revue de l'histoire des religions*
S.-B.	Strack and Billerbeck: *Kommentar zum Neuen Testament aus Talmud und Midrasch*

Abbreviations

S.B.A.	*Sitzungsberichte der königlichen preussischen Akademie der Wissenschaften*
T.R.	*Theologische Rundschau*
T.W.N.T.	*Theologisches Wörterbuch zum Neuen Testament* (edited by G. Kittel)
W.Comm.	*Westminster Commentaries*
Z.A.T.W.	*Die Zeitschrift für die alttestamentliche Wissenschaft*
Z.N.T.W.	*Die Zeitschrift für die neutestamentliche Wissenschaft*

Mysterious Revelation

An Examination of the Philosophy
of St. Mark's Gospel

Introduction

ST. MARK'S gospel is essentially a soteriological document in
which history is subservient to theology. It was written because
of the surpassing religious importance attached to the person of
Jesus of Nazareth, and the traditions it assembles were themselves
prized in the early Christian communities for the sake of the
religious significance which they were believed to possess. As a
member of the apostolic church, the evangelist holds that Jesus
fulfills the messianic hopes of the prophets of the Old Testament,
and in the course of his work he repeatedly reminds his readers
of the divine character of his hero. Thus in the prologue of the
gospel the testimony of the God-sent forerunner receives explicit confirmation in the declaration of the heavenly voice at
the baptism, and in the subsequent narrative even the demons
corroborate the witness from heaven by giving expression to
their supernatural knowledge of their conqueror's real status
and office. For St. Mark, we may safely say, there is but one
sufficient ground or explanation of the words and deeds of the
Master, namely, the fact that he is the Messiah and stands in a
unique filial relationship to God. In the evangelist's view, it is

in virtue of his messianic status that Jesus overcomes the temptation of Satan in the wilderness, that he teaches with authority and not as the scribes, that he performs miracles, thereby vanquishing the power of the demons, that he dies on a cross and rises from the dead after three days, and that he will come again to judge humanity and finally to establish the kingdom of God with great power and glory.

Of course the evangelist is fully aware that the people among whom Jesus ministered did not share his own religious convictions. As a matter of plain historical fact, they utterly failed to recognize the Messiahship of Jesus; and St. Mark evidently seeks to meet this difficulty—a difficulty which would almost inevitably arise in any attempt to present a connected account of the ministry in terms of the apostolic faith—by maintaining that the Master's true status was a preordained secret.[1] Jesus was

---

[1] A few remarks ought perhaps to be made here concerning R. Bultmann's hypothesis (*Z.N.T.W.*, XIX [1920], 165ff.; *Die Geschichte der synoptischen Tradition*, p. 371; *Theology of the New Testament*, I, 26ff.—cf. Wrede, *Das Messiasgeheimnis*, pp. 207ff.) that St. Mark's doctrine of the secret is really a concealment of the fact that the belief in the Messiahship of Jesus was a consequence of the experiences of the risen Lord: (1) The hypothesis seems to have little or no direct bearing on St. Mark's own interpretation, for the second evangelist manifestly believed that Jesus was and claimed to be the Messiah. (2) Rom. 1:4, which should perhaps be understood in the light of Phil. 2:5ff., scarcely implies that Jesus did not claim to be the Messiah. (3) As is shown by Romans 9–11, the Lord's rejection by his own people raised a problem for the apostolic church; but St. Paul nowhere refers to a conflict between the church's doctrine of the Messiahship and the Lord's claims on his own behalf. (4) John 2:22 and 12:16, which seem to reflect the fourth evangelist's doctrine concerning the Spirit of Truth (cf. John 16:13), can hardly be taken to supply evidence regarding the supposed original significance of St. Mark's doctrine of the secret. (5) In his penetrating criticism of R. Otto's *Reich Gottes und Menschensohn*, Bultmann himself seems to imply that the question whether Jesus actually claimed to be the Son of Man should be approached by a critical consideration of the synoptic "Son of Man" sayings, not of St. Mark's doctrine of the secret (*T.R.*, N.S., IX [1937], 25f.). And it must be recog-

not received as the Messiah, and the evangelist holds that it was divinely intended that he should not be so received. Hence he represents Jesus as deliberately concealing the truth about himself from the people by enjoining the demons to silence and by addressing the multitude in the cryptology of parables. At Caesarea Philippi, however, the messianic secret is revealed to a chosen few. In a moment of inspiration and in the presence of his fellow disciples, Peter confesses that Jesus is the Messiah. Thus the fact of the Messiahship is made known to a select group of human beings, and the members of the group are at once enjoined to guard the secrecy of their newly acquired knowledge. The disciples now see that the words and deeds of their Master are the words and deeds of the Messiah, and they are therefore in a position to receive special instruction in the deep spiritual significance of the secret. But they soon show themselves to be quite unprepared for such instruction. The essential meaning of the Messiahship—its fateful implications for the

---

nized that in such sayings as Mark 8:38; Matt. 19:28; and Luke 12:8—which may well belong to the earliest stratum of the gospel tradition—the Lord seems to distinguish himself as "I" from the Son of Man. Thus it is possible that Jesus simply believed in a correspondence of ethical principle between his own ministry and the mission of the awaited Son of Man, and that such correspondence was transformed into a relation of substantial and personal identity as a result of the resurrection-christophanies. (For the various possible meanings of the expression "Son of Man," see my note in *Ex. T., LVI* [1944–45], 305f.) On the other hand, in an important paper "Gottesreich und Menschensohn in der Verkündigung Jesu" (*Festschrift für Günther Dehn*, pp. 51ff.) P. Vielhauer maintains that the synoptic sayings concerning the coming of the Son of Man are secondary to those concerning the coming of the kingdom of God: Jesus envisaged an imminent and unmediated intervention of God's rule, the interpretation in terms of the eschatological Son of Man being a more concrete mode of representation which originated in the apostolic communities. See my article "The Hidden Son of Man in St. Mark's Gospel" in *Z.N.T.W.*, LII (1961), 189ff., which includes a critical appreciation of E. Sjöberg's work *Der verborgene Menschensohn in den Evangelien* (Lund, 1955); and cf. below. Supplementary Note D.

Master himself and its ethical implications for all who would be his followers—is a heavenly mystery which persistently eludes their grasp. Apparently it is not until their Master has been raised from the dead that they come to understand the mysterious meaning of the messianic secret; for St. Mark seems to hold that Jesus' resurrection means the end of the predetermined period of secrecy and obscurity and the beginning of the predetermined period of enlightenment, in which the gospel of the Messiah is openly proclaimed to the world with understanding and confidence.

Accordingly, although St. Mark is concerned to delineate the earthly life of Jesus, his whole method of treating his subject is very different from what would be normally expected of a modern biographer. The gospel was composed for the edification of believers, not for the furtherance of the cause of historical research. The evangelist shows little or no interest in proximate causes and he offers neither a history of the Master's upbringing nor a psychology of his inner feelings and reactions. Indeed, the Jesus of St. Mark's representation could owe nothing essential to his human ancestry and education, since what he is and what he does are simply the consequences of his divine origin and nature.[2] It follows, therefore, that a right understanding of the gospel calls for a sustained effort on the part of the exegete to appreciate the evangelist's point of view and to identify the questions which he is seeking to answer.[3] In the performance of his task the exegete is fortunate to have at his disposal the canonical epistles of St. Paul and other writings of the New Testament, for these can provide him with valuable first-hand evidence of the beliefs and problems of the apostolic

[2] Cf. J. Weiss, *Primitive Christianity*, II, 699.

[3] Cf. R. G. Collingwood's admonition: "Never think you understand any statement made by a philosopher until you have decided, with the utmost possible accuracy, what the question is to which he means it for an answer" (*An Autobiography*, p. 74). It is legitimate to say that St. Mark sets forth a religious philosophy of history.

4

church. Admittedly St. Mark's gospel largely consists of traditional material which may be ultimately based on the reports of eyewitnesses, but this does not exclude the possibility that the arrangement of the material may be to a considerable extent determined by the doctrinal position of the evangelist. A priori there is no reason for assuming that St. Mark was more of a historian in the academic sense than the other synoptists, and we have only to compare St. Matthew's gospel with St. Luke's in order to see how the same material could be used in the service of different modes of christological interpretation. One may regret that our earliest gospel is not an essay in scientific biography, but the real occasion for such regret can never be removed by constantly trying to make the gospel provide the answers to historical questions of our own formulation which would scarcely have occurred to the evangelist himself. The primary duty of the exegete is to elucidate the gospel as it stands, not as he thinks it ought to be, and questions concerning the supposed original settings of the incidents and sayings it contains, however fascinating, should be regarded as matters of secondary importance.

The evangelist's treatment of his subject—essentially a religious one, the Messiahship of Jesus, the content of the apostolic gospel—resolves itself into the exposition of two central themes, namely, the secret fact of the messianic status of Jesus and the (1) mysterious meaning of that fact. Broadly, the first of these two (2) themes dominates the earlier part of the gospel and the second dominates the later part. For, prior to his account of Peter's confession, the evangelist is mainly concerned to represent the words and deeds of Jesus as esoteric manifestations of the secret fact of the Messiahship; and, after his account of the confession, the evangelist is mainly concerned to show how the fact of the Messiahship mysteriously meant that Jesus had to endure the shame of crucifixion in the fulfillment of his redemptive mission in the world. It is not to be assumed, however, that St. Mark's exposition of the two themes is characterized by perfect logical coherence. He was perhaps the first writer who sought to supply the church's increasing need for a comprehensive account of the ministry of Jesus in terms of the apostolic faith, and, in view of the magnitude of such an undertaking, it is not surprising to find that the various parts of his gospel hang together somewhat loosely. As we hope to show in the course of the subsequent discussions, conflicting motifs are continually competing for dominance in the evangelist's mind, and this considerably weakens the formative power of his thought to weld the multifarious traditions he presents into a consistent pattern of ideas.[4]

[4] Sustained application of the form-critical method has made it clear that the whole question of motivation in the gospels (which may be conscious or unconscious, above or below the surface) is as complicated as it is important, a truth admirably elucidated by H J. Cadbury in his essays, "Rebuttal, a Submerged Motive in the Gospels" (*Quantalacumque: Studies presented to Kirsopp Lake,* pp. 99ff.) and "Mixed Motives in the Gospels" (*Proceedings of the American Philosophical Society,* XCV [1951], 117ff.); cf. his survey of current issues in N.T. studies (*Harvard Divinity School Bulletin,* XIX [1953–54], 49ff.). The complication is due partly to the fact that normally any particular item of the tradition, prior to its being taken up into a gospel, would have had an independent life history, in the course of which it may have served more than one Christian interest whose traces were left behind; and partly to the fact that the synoptists, who had their own dominant motives, utilized the units they selected from the tradition without bringing them into thoroughgoing conformity with a unitary scheme. Even the fourth evangelist, who deals with the tradition in a much more radical fashion than his synoptic predecessors, does not achieve perfect consistency; thus his concern to emphasize the superiority of Jesus to John the Baptist (John 5:31ff.) seems to run counter to his interest in John the Baptist as one sent from God to point out or bear witness to the Word made flesh (John 1:6ff.).

PART ONE

The Secret Fact
of the Messiahship

I

St. Mark's Preface

ST. MARK opens his account of the Lord's public ministry in 1:14–15 where Jesus comes into Galilee proclaiming the glad tidings that the time is fulfilled and that the kingdom of God is at hand. In the thirteen verses which precede this eschatological announcement the evangelist introduces his readers to the central figure of his narrative.[1] He does this, however, not by presenting a historical explanation of the Master's origin and upbringing, but by referring briefly to the mission of John the Baptist, the messianic forerunner promised in the scriptures. As is shown by the superscription—"The beginning [2] of the gospel [3] of Jesus,

---

[1] C. H. Turner (*N.C.H.S.*, pt. 3, p. 53) considers that in v. 14 the reading of Cod. Sin. (μετὰ δέ) is preferable to that of B and D (καὶ μετά) since St Mark uses δέ at the beginning of a paragraph to denote some large new departure in his narrative; here it emphasizes the commencement of the public ministry.

[2] The word "beginning" may here refer to the mission of John the Baptist (God begins his redemptive action in the Messiah by sending the promised forerunner) or to the ministry of Jesus (the Messiah's incarnate life is the prelude to his final manifestation in glory). All English translations of the Hebrew and Greek texts of the Bible cited in this work are the author's own unless otherwise stated.

[3] Presumably, the "gospel" here is not the gospel proclaimed by Jesus,

the Messiah, the Son of God" (v. 1)—St. Mark's primary concern is to delineate the historical content of the apostolic message of salvation. Indeed, the superscription affords an indication of the general plan of the work, for Peter's acknowledgment
of the Messiahship of his Master in 8:29 has its Gentile counterpart in 15:39 where the centurion testifies to the divine Sonship of Jesus. Accordingly, there is a good presumptive reason
for assuming that the expression "Son of God" in the first verse
is a genuine part of the text of the gospel; and as the text of the
Codex Sinaiticus may be based on that of the papyri which Origen took with him from Alexandria to Palestine, the two chief
witnesses for the omission of the expression (the Codex Sinaiticus and Origen) are perhaps only one. It may be supposed also
that accidental omission would be especially easy in this case,
for sacred names were frequently subjected to abbreviation.[4]

It is eminently appropriate that the superscription should be
immediately followed, in verses 2–3, by a citation of two passages of scripture, since it was largely by trying to show that
the career of Jesus was in accordance with the prophecies of
the Old Testament that the apostolic church sought to demonstrate the validity of its belief in the Messiahship of the Master.
Of the two quotations only the second is drawn from the book
of Isaiah (40:3), the first being from Mal. 3:1, which reads:

Behold, I send my messenger and he shall prepare the way before
me; and the Lord whom you seek shall suddenly come to his temple;
and the messenger of the covenant whom you delight in, behold,
he comes, says Yahweh of hosts.

But St. Mark reproduces the first part of this passage in a modified form:

---

but the gospel concerning Jesus proclaimed by the apostolic church; cf.
J. Weiss, *Primitive Christianity*, II, 691. For current Jewish ideas con-
cerning the kingdom of God and the Messiah, see *The Beginnings of
Christianity*, eds. F. J. Foakes-Jackson and K. Lake, I, 269ff., 346ff.

[4] Cf. Turner, *op. cit.*, pt. 3, pp. 50f.

Behold, I send my messenger before your face, who shall prepare your way.

It is possible that the passage was cited in this form through the influence of the LXX version of Exod. 23:20—

And, behold, I send my messenger before your face that he may guard you in the way.

The words "before you," which are added in some authorities at the end of verse 2 were probably introduced by a copyist who had Matt. 11:10 in mind (cf. Luke 7:27). We gather from verses 4–5 that St. Mark intends "my messenger" (v. 2) and "the voice of one crying in the wilderness" (v. 3) to refer to John, who lives in the wilderness on a diet of locusts and wild honey and who announces the coming of one mightier than he, the latchet of whose shoes he is not worthy to stoop down and unloose. On the other hand, in Mal. 3:1 the messenger is the herald of God's sudden coming in judgment, and in Isa. 40:3 it is the way of God that is to be prepared in the wilderness for the return of the exiles; in neither passage is there any mention of the Messiah. It is possible, therefore, that the substitution of the second for the first person in St. Mark's citation of Mal. 3:1 is really an adaptation of the prophecy to a messianic eschatology; it is possible also that the evangelist construes "the way of the Lord" in the second quotation to denote the way of the Lord Jesus.[5]

Malachi evidently identifies the eschatological messenger with Elijah redivivus, for in Mal. 3:23 (E.T., 4:5) he writes:

Behold, I will send you Elijah the prophet before the great and terrible day of Yahweh comes.

---

[5] But it must be observed that the title κύριος ("lord") is not used of Jesus elsewhere in St. Mark's gospel, save in 7:28, where, however, it probably means nothing more than "sir" (cf. John 12:21).

The same kind of doctrine is evinced in Ecclus. 48:1ff. (cf. Sib. Or. 5:187ff., IV Esd. 6:26ff.) and, as is indicated in Mark 9:11ff., the belief was current among the Jews during the first century A.D. that the advent of the Messiah must be preceded by the return of Elijah. The last-mentioned passage also serves to show that St. Mark seeks to defend the fundamental belief of the church by maintaining that John the Baptist is the expected Elijah-forerunner of the Messiah.[6] In his prologue, however, the evangelist does not actually mention Elijah, and the words "with camel's hair and a girdle of skin about his loins" (v. 6), which are ultimately derived from the description of Elijah in II Kings 1:8, do not occur in D (where the reading is simply "with a leathern covering") and were probably brought into St. Mark's text from Matt. 3:4.

Accordingly, the evangelist does not appreciate the mission of John for its own sake, but only in so far as it is the divinely ordained prelude to the saving action of God in the earthly life of Jesus the Messiah. As in the sermons preserved in the Acts of the Apostles, the gospel of Jesus of Nazareth begins with or is introduced by John's proclamation of a baptism of repentance to the people of Israel (see Acts 1:22; 10:37; 13:24). Moreover, St. Mark makes no attempt to explain how John came to his knowledge and estimate of the person to whom he bears witness; he merely informs his readers that the baptizer announces the coming of a mightier one who will baptize the people not with water, but with the Holy Spirit (v. 8). By means of this distinction the evangelist evidently seeks to emphasize and define the superiority of Jesus to his appointed precursor; John knows only of a water-baptism which is the seal of repentance for the remission of sins, but Jesus is informed by the essential power of God and confers the charismata of the Spirit (cf. I Cor. 12:

---

[6] Cf. *Tryph.* 8, 49, 110, where Justin deals with a Jewish objection which is based on the doctrine that the veritable Messiah has to be anointed and proclaimed as such by Elijah.

1ff.) upon all who accept him for what he truly is—the Messiah, the Son of God.

Wellhausen sees in this contrast between the two baptisms a difference in ceremonial practice; in his view, it is a reflection of earliest Christian custom before the church had adopted the rite of initiation by water-baptism:

The baptism with Spirit is baptism without water, that is, it is not really baptism at all but a substitute for it through something better, through the bestowal of the Spirit which appears as the distinctive feature of the activity of Jesus. Water and Spirit here stand in exclusive opposition. Later, matters were so adjusted that there arose a Christian baptism with water and Spirit. The truth is that the Christian community did not take over the rite of baptism from the disciples of John until after the Master's death.[7]

But even if this conjecture is correct, it does not necessarily follow that St. Mark himself understands the contrast in a mutually exclusive sense. Further, in verses 9ff. Jesus receives the Spirit on his baptism with water at the hands of John, and such a representation recalls the doctrine concerning Christian baptism which comes to expression in the Acts of the Apostles. According to this doctrine, baptism with water and baptism with the Holy Spirit stand in closest association with each other; and what differentiates the church's baptism with water from the baptism of John is the conferment of the Spirit which properly accompanies it. Thus in Acts 8:14ff. certain Samaritans are baptized as Christians and the bestowal of the Spirit is delayed, but it is felt that their baptism is not really completed until the Spirit has been conferred upon them; in Acts 10:44ff. as soon as Peter sees that the Spirit has descended upon the people whom he addresses in the house of Cornelius, he concludes that they ought to be baptized forthwith (see Acts 1:5; 11:16f.); and in Acts 19:1ff. some twelve men in Ephesus have submitted themselves to John's

[7] See *Das Evangelium Marci*, p. 5 (author's translation).

baptism, but they know nothing of the bestowal of the Holy Spirit; when, however, they have been baptized into the name of the Lord Jesus, they at once receive the gift of the Spirit and are able to speak with tongues and to prophesy. Thus, in view of the descent of the Spirit in Mark 1:10, St. Mark may understand the baptism of Jesus as the prototype, so to speak, of Christian baptism, in which case it is unlikely that he takes the baptism with the Holy Spirit in verse 8 to exclude baptism with water.[8]

A question which naturally arises at this point concerns John 1:21, where the Baptist openly denies that he is Elijah. Why should the fourth evangelist reject the doctrine upheld by St. Mark, and after him by St. Matthew, that John is Elijah come to life again as the forerunner of the Messiah? In any attempt to answer this difficult question it is important to bear in mind that the belief in the return of Elijah as the messianic forerunner was far from being universally accepted among the Jews

---

[8] In Matt. 3:11 and Luke 3:16 the contrast is between baptism with water, on the one hand, and baptism with the Holy Spirit and with fire, on the other; and it has been conjectured (as, for example, by T. W. Manson in *The Mission and Message of Jesus*, pp. 332f.) that the contrast was originally between baptism with water and baptism with fire. On this view, John's baptism was really not the preliminary to something better, but the last chance of escaping something very much worse, the coming judgment; and the reference to baptism with the Holy Spirit is to be understood as part of the church's adaptation of John's teaching to its doctrine that the Baptist was Christ's appointed forerunner; for the use of "fire" as a symbol of God's condemnation of the wicked, see Isa. 66:15f., Ps. Sol. 15:6ff. On the other hand, it is possible that the words "with fire" were added in Matt. 3:11 and Luke 3:16 to represent the sanctifying activity of the Spirit; cf. Acts 2:3, where "tongues as of fire" appear as signs of the Spirit's descent upon the assembly. In Jewish thought fire, like water, is a means of purification; and in Bab. San. 39a R. Abbahu infers from Num. 31:23 that purification is essentially by fire, not by water, since it is only things destructible by fire which are to go through the water; see S.-B., I, 121f. For an account of the Jewish baptism of proselytes, to which John's baptism has been compared, see G. F. Moore, *Judaism*, I, 332ff.

14

of the period.[9] In Mal. 3:23 (E.T., 4:5) and Ecclus. 48:1ff. Elijah prepares the way for God himself, and there is no reference to the Messiah. In pseudepigraphical literature no special part is assigned to Elijah in the last days, his place being taken by others. In rabbinic eschatology there are no less than three different Elijah doctrines: (1) Elijah is a Gadite who prepares the way for God and is the redeemer of Israel. (2) Elijah is a Benjamite who precedes the Messiah and announces the good news of his coming. (3) Elijah is a Levite who acts as the high priest in the messianic age. Thus there was nothing approaching doctrinal uniformity in Jewish expectation regarding the part to be played by Elijah in the last days. And if it may be supposed that the fourth evangelist knew something of the variety of conflicting opinions on the matter, one can perhaps more easily understand why he should discount the objection raised by those adversaries who claimed that the Messiah ought to be preceded by Elijah redivivus. It is also important to bear in mind that the mutual relations between church and synagogue tended to deteriorate with the passage of time and that in the fourth gospel the Jews appear as the agreed enemies of Jesus. Indeed, in John 8:44-45, the Lord alludes to the Jews as offspring of the devil and as inveterate liars who are completely blind to the truth:

You are of your father the devil and it is your will to do what your father desires. He was a murderer from the beginning and stood not in the truth because there is no truth in him. . . . But because I speak the truth you do not believe me.

This statement affords some indication of the kind of feeling which in certain quarters followed on the failure of the early defenders of the Christian faith, despite all their efforts, to convince the Messiah's own people of the truth of the gospel proclaimed by the church. Accordingly, since the fourth evangelist

[9] Cf. Manson, *op. cit.*, pp. 361f. and S.-B., IV, 779ff.

holds that the Jewish opponents of Christianity are so corrupt as to be devoid of insight into divine truth, it is not altogether unnatural that he should ascribe no importance to the objection from the Jewish side that Jesus ought to have been proclaimed as Messiah by Elijah redivivus.

To return to St. Mark's preface: in the three verses (9–11) which follow John's announcement of the coming of "the mightier one" the readers of the gospel are permitted to know that Jesus, before the commencement of the ministry, is armed with the divine Spirit and acknowledged as the beloved or unique Son of God. The witness of the forerunner is confirmed by a testimony from heaven. It is reported that Jesus comes from Nazareth of Galilee and is baptized by John in the Jordan, that as soon as he rises out of the water he sees the heavens cleft and the Spirit coming down upon him like a dove, and that a voice from heaven addresses him in the following terms:

You are my only Son; [10] in you I am well pleased.

It may be assumed that in these three verses the evangelist has his readers primarily in mind, for Jesus alone sees the heavens cleft and the dovelike descent of the Spirit and it is to him alone that the utterance of the voice is addressed. At the transfiguration, on the other hand, the three disciples who go up the mountain with Jesus are evidently aware of the cloud and it is to them that the voice speaks (9:7). As we shall see more clearly at a later stage, this contrast has an important bearing upon the general question of St. Mark's method of presenting his subject matter.

It is noteworthy that the heavenly voice [11] communicates

[10] For the view that the word ἀγαπητός in 1:11; 9:7; and 12:6 should be translated "only" rather than "beloved," see Turner in *op. cit.*, pt. 3, pp. 52f. For another view, see P. Winter's article regarding "the only begotten Son" in *Die Zeitschrift für Religions- und Geistesgeschichte*, V (1953), 335ff.

[11] Cf. the rabbinic conception of the "daughter of voice" as the medium

no commission to perform a specified task or to preach a specified message; it simply makes the twofold affirmation that Jesus is God's unique Son and that God takes pleasure in him. Nevertheless, this expression of divine approval was probably intended to have reference to the soteriological work which the Lord accomplishes in the course of his earthly career; if this is so, we may assume that God here recognizes the competence of Jesus for the fulfillment of the messianic task to which he is ordained. Accordingly, it is natural that the descent of the Spirit should be associated with the declaration of the heavenly voice, for from very early times it had been believed that a person who was anointed as God's chosen representative on earth was thereby endowed with the divine Spirit which gave him supernormal powers. Thus, according to I Sam. 16:13, when David was anointed as king over Israel by Samuel, the Spirit of Yahweh came mightily upon him from that day forward. And, as we should expect, it was believed that the person who would reign as the Messiah in the golden age of the future would be inspired, though in a much larger measure than any king who had hitherto reigned over Israel, with the Spirit of God which in Isa. 11:2 is alluded to as the spirit of wisdom and understanding, the spirit of counsel and might, the spirit of knowledge and of the fear of Yahweh. Moreover, St. Mark's wording of the heavenly pronouncement is reminiscent of Ps. 2:7 and Isa. 42:1; and it is interesting to find that in the latter passage the Servant, whom God has chosen and in whom his soul takes pleasure, has been endowed with the divine Spirit.

The mention of the dove in verse 10 has given rise to much speculation.[12] Thus Gunkel and Gressmann think of the story

by which God still communicated with men after the cessation of prophecy; see S.-B., I, 125ff., and Moore, *op. cit.*, I, 421f.

[12] For references to relevant literature, see R. Bultmann, *Die Geschichte der synoptischen Tradition*, pp. 264ff., and P. Guénin, *Y-a-t-il eu conflit entre Jean-Baptiste et Jésus?* pp. 130ff.

of the baptism of Jesus as a *Königsberufungs-Sage* and seek to explain the reference to the dove in terms of the ancient mythological motif of the election of a king by means of a bird which is used to choose one out of a number of aspirants to the throne. Gressmann also sees in the figure a reminiscence of the goddess, worshipped in Babylonia as Ishtar and in Syria as Atargatis, who was represented in the form of a dove and who had particularly close connections with the monarchy. Various parallels from biblical literature have been suggested; von Baer, for example, considers that the figure is to be understood in the light of Gen. 8:8ff., where a dove appears as the messenger of the new age of grace and promise which follows on a period of judgment. But perhaps the most plausible suggestion is that made by Bultmann, who holds that the dove in St. Mark's story simply symbolizes the divine power which takes possession of the messianic King; [13] and in support of this hypothesis he notices that both in Persia and in Egypt the supernatural potency of kings was represented in the form of a bird which (at least in Persian representations) was sometimes a dove, and that in the Targum the expression "the voice of the turtle-dove" (Cant. 2:12) is interpreted as "the voice of the Holy Spirit." It must be observed, however, that there is only very slight probability that the dove was understood as a symbol of the Holy Spirit in rabbinical literature.[14] On the other hand, the rabbis not infrequently refer to the dove as a symbol of the community of Israel, and it is possible that this kind of association also may have been present to the mind of the evangelist in his account of the baptism. For, as the Messiah, Jesus is the founder and representative of the new Israel according to the Spirit, and perhaps it is

[13] That St. Mark could construe the designation "Son of God" as a title for the messianic King seems to be shown in the passion narrative where the high priest's question in 14:61 ("Are you the Messiah, the Son of the Blessed?") corresponds to the procurator's question in 15:2 ("Are you the King of the Jews?"); cf. below, Chapter 12.

[14] Cf. S.-B., I, 123ff.

in this capacity that in verses 12–13 he withstands the temptation in the wilderness, thereby demonstrating the superiority of the new Israel to the children of Israel according to the flesh who succumbed to such temptation prior to their entrance into the promised land.

Although St. Mark may sometimes regard the Son of God as the King of the Jews (cf. 15:1ff.), it ought not to be assumed that, in the evangelist's judgment, the divine Sonship of Jesus is dependent upon his messianic status and function in history. In other words, as we understand the matter, the evangelist does not hold that Jesus becomes the Son of God when he is chosen to appear in the flesh as the Messiah, but takes it for granted that the Lord's unique filial relation to God is the transcendental presupposition of the eschatological and soteriological work which he accomplishes on earth. On the other hand, Wellhausen is of the opinion that St. Mark's story implies that Jesus is actually adopted as the Son of God at his baptism: he goes down into the water as an ordinary man and he comes up out of it as the Son of God.[15] Such an interpretation, however, evidently neglects the fact that the first clause of the heavenly pronouncement has its verb in the present tense of the indicative mood, whereas the second clause has its verb in the aorist indicative. And, as Stonehouse has maintained, this contrast suggests the possibility that the first clause concerns an eternal and essential relationship and that the second clause concerns a past choice for the performance of a particular function in history. Admittedly, it may be that in oriental legal parlance the expression "You are my beloved son" is a formula of adoption which means "You shall be my beloved son." [16] But, for an understanding

---

[15] See Wellhausen, *op. cit.*, p. 7. For an instructive criticism of Wellhausen's interpretation, cf. N. B. Stonehouse, *The Witness of Matthew and Mark to Christ*, pp. 16ff., and for the notion of the Messiah's pre-existence in St. Mark's gospel, cf. the article by G. H. Boobyer in *Ex. T.*, LI (1939–40), pp. 393f.

[16] Cf. M. Dibelius, *From Tradition to Gospel*, p. 272.

of St. Mark's thought on the question, it seems to be much more relevant to compare the pronouncement made by the voice from the cloud at the transfiguration:

This is my only Son; listen to him [9:7].

In this utterance the first clause appears to provide the immutable ground or reason for the second; it is because their Master is God's only Son that the three disciples are exhorted to pay heed to his words. And so it is, we submit, in the case of the heavenly pronouncement at the baptism; the first clause provides the immutable ground or reason for the second; it is in virtue of the Lord's unchanging filial status that God has recognized his competence for the fulfillment of the Messiah's work on earth. Accordingly, there seems to be no more justification for holding that Jesus becomes the Son of God at the baptism than there is for holding that he becomes the Son of God at the transfiguration. If we may so express it, Jesus always has it in him to be the Messiah, and therefore the descent of the Spirit and the declaration of the voice from heaven do not affect the Lord's essential status, but are to be understood merely as signs of the fact that he is properly equipped for his redemptive mission in the world.[17]

St. Mark brings his preface to a conclusion in verses 12–13 with what appears to be a theologically significant account of the Messiah's temptation in the wilderness.[18] The story is remarkable alike for its brevity and simplicity. In four short statements we learn that the Spirit drives Jesus into the wilderness, that he remains there for forty days tempted by Satan, that he is in

[17] Various conjectures have been made with regard to the reading of D etc. in Luke 3:22 ("You are my Son; this day have I begotten you"). One possibility is that it is due to a copyist who, in his anxiety to bring the wording of the heavenly pronouncement into exact agreement with Ps. 2:7, overlooked the adoptionism which such a modification would introduce into the text of the gospel.

[18] Cf. R. H. Lightfoot, *History and Interpretation*, pp. 65f.

the company of wild beasts, and that angels minister to his needs. As we have already suggested, the story may have been meant to recall the forty years of temptation in the wilderness to which the children of Israel were subjected prior to their entrance into the promised land. Like them, the Lord may receive supernatural sustenance; but unlike them, as the representative of the new Israel, he enjoys the unqualified approval of God. It ought also to be noticed that in popular belief of the time the wilderness was a favorite haunt of evil spirits, and hence it was only natural that the lord of the demons should be represented as making his appearance there. Presumably Jesus encounters the Baptist by the southern fords of the Jordan (see 1:5); but now he is transported to a remote part of the wilderness, which is apparently the home of wild animals and unfrequented by men, and so he is put to trial by Satan in a scene which is devoid of the presence of human witnesses. For it is not fitting that the eyes of the world should behold the personal struggle in which, as the story doubtless implies. Jesus triumphs over the prince of the demons and thereby gives proof (to the readers of the gospel) that he is indeed the Messiah who is destined to inaugurate the new era of salvation promised by God in the scriptures.

The view that St. Mark construes the story of the temptation in an eschatological sense seems to receive weighty confirmation in verses 14–15, where, after John has been delivered up,[19] Jesus

[19] That is, as we gather from Mark 6:17ff., he was put into prison by Herod Antipas. According to Mark 6:17ff., John was arrested by Antipas because he protested against the latter's illegal (cf. Lev. 18:16) marriage with Herodias the wife of his brother Philip (the tetrarch of Trachonitis); on the other hand, in *Ant.* 18, 5, 2 Josephus states that John was arrested and put to death because Antipas suspected him as the potential leader of a revolutionary movement. Perhaps, in reality, both reasons were involved. It should also be noticed that, according to *Ant.* 18, 5, 4 Salome the daughter of Herodias, and not Herodias herself, was the wife of Philip (the tetrarch of Trachonitis). It is not impossible that there is a reflection of Jezebel's attitude to Elijah in the portrayal of Herodias in Mark 6:17ff.

comes into Galilee proclaiming that the time is fulfilled and that the kingdom of God is at hand, and exhorting his hearers to repent and to believe in the good news. This preaching, in all probability, should be taken to mean that "this age" is passing away and that "the age to come" (prophesied in the scriptures) is already dawning,[20] the result being that those who repent and believe in the gospel may now enjoy something of that blessedness which was expected to characterize the life of the redeemed in the consummated kingdom. If this is so, the opening of the Galilean ministry, according to St. Mark's interpretation, signifies the beginning of the end of the old world order, and perhaps the Baptist must disappear from the scene before the work of the ministry begins, because, as the last representative of the old dispensation of the law and the prophets (see Matt. 11:11–13; 13:16–17), he stands outside the era of salvation.[21] Furthermore, it was commonly believed among the Jews of the

[20] For the significance of the distinction between the two ages in rabbinic eschatology, cf. S.-B., I, 178ff.

[21] On the other hand, according to the fourth evangelist, Jesus opens his ministry before the imprisonment of the Baptist; cf. John 3:24. M. Goguel (*The Life of Jesus*, pp. 271ff.) is of the opinion that in John 3:25 the text of the source material had "with those of Jesus" (O. Holtzmann) or "with Jesus" (Baldensperger) instead of "with a Jew"; and he goes on to argue that, in actual fact, Jesus, having worked for a time in association with the Baptist, eventually left him as a result of a controversy with him concerning the efficacy of baptism as a means of purification. However this may be, the fourth evangelist evidently does not subscribe to the doctrine, which may be evinced in St. Mark's gospel, that the Baptist's work must cease before the Messiah's work can begin. There does not seem to be sufficient evidence for the hypothesis (cf. J. Steinmann, *Saint John the Baptist and the Desert Tradition*; J. Daniélou, *The Dead Sea Scrolls and Primitive Christianity*, pp. 15ff.) that the Baptist broke away from the Qumran community and that Jesus adopted his teaching, which was "apocalyptic and therefore monastic" (Steinmann, *op. cit.*, pp. 174f.). Important differences exist between the New Testament representations of Johannite and Christian baptism, on the one hand, and Qumran baptismal rites, on the other; cf. M. Black, *The Scrolls and Christian Origins*, pp. 97f., 113ff., 168.

period that the triumphant inauguration of the Messianic age would be immediately preceded by a supreme conflict with the forces of evil.[22] When verses 12–13 are read in the light of this common expectation, the temptation seems to possess an eschatological significance as the required prelude to the Lord's announcement of the good news that the time is fulfilled and that the kingdom of God has drawn near.[23]

[22] Cf. Moore, *op. cit.*, II, 36off.

[23] H. Gunkel (*Zum religionsgeschichtlichen Verständnis des Neuen Testaments*, pp. 7of.) suggests that the temptation story may owe something to the ancient idea of a great conflict among the gods for the domination of the world; he also draws attention to the stories of the temptations of Zoroaster and Gautama. Another suggestion (see F. Spitta in *Z.N.T.W.*, VI [1904], 323ff.) is that the story evinces the motif of paradise regained—man and beast again live together in peace—see T. Naph. 8.

SUPPLEMENTARY NOTE A: A NUMERICAL TYPOLOGY?

A. M. Farrer rightly insists that St. Mark, so far from being a mere colorless compiler of impersonal anecdotes, is a living Christian mind of singular power and penetration, and that we should be docile enough to listen to what he has to say, without interposing premature questions based upon our modern ideas of historical inquiry.[1] On the other hand, St. Mark scarcely dominates his materials to the extent supposed by Farrer, and power of thought in this connection should not be equated with dexterity in the manipulation and arrangement of traditional narratives according to the dictates of a preconceived numerical architectonic of a typological character. Indeed, the results of Farrer's own analysis of St. Mark's unfolding thought go to confirm the view that the evangelist's mind is not sufficiently settled in any particular philosophico-theological position to enable him to set forth a wholly self-consistent representative synthesis of the available traditions concerning the ministry of Jesus.[2]

In Farrer's opinion, St. Mark begins his synthetic construction with the dominical symbol "twelve apostles for twelve tribes" and makes of it the framework of a gospel by the addition of two equivalent twelves—"twelve loaves (as though of shewbread) intended for thousands (as it were tribes)" and "twelve healings (recorded in detail) of particular persons (as it were twelve children of Israel)." So in the first three chapters of the gospel Farrer sees an equivalence between the calling of

[1] See *A Study in St. Mark*, p. 7.
[2] Cf. his paper "Loaves and Thousands" (*J.T.S.*, n.s., IV [1953], 1ff. and his later publication *St. Matthew and St. Mark*, which considerably modify the conclusions arrived at in *A Study in St. Mark*.

disciples and the healing of invalids: five persons are called and five are healed. After the fifth healing the twelvefold apostolate is instituted (3:13–18), and this is taken to imply that seven more people should be healed to maintain the parallelism between calling and healing, a parallelism reflected in the saying, "Those who are well have no need of a physician, but those who are ill; I came not to call righteous people, but sinners" (2:17). The feeding theme is introduced in 6:35–44 in the account of the first miracle of the loaves: five loaves are distributed among five thousands; and, in accordance with the requirements of the architectonic, this is taken to imply that seven thousands have still to receive their loaves.

Prima facie the formal parallelism of the second story of miraculous feeding (8: 1–10) with the first story promises to complete the pattern, the remaining seven loaves being distributed. But there are two paradoxical features—the remainders are not measured in large baskets (6:43; 8:19) but in ordinary baskets (8:8; 8:20) and only four thousands (not the required seven) are fed. Farrer explains the reduction in the size of the measures by assuming that, in St. Mark's view, the Gentiles—represented by the Syrophoenician woman and her daughter—have been allowed a quota of the crumbs from the children's table (7:24–28); and he explains the four thousands by arguing that the evangelist's theological ideas do not allow the feeding of the twelve to reach its formal completion before the last supper takes place (14:17ff.). On the ground that five persons are healed in the first three chapters, Farrer also holds that the account of the feeding of the five thousands marks the point where the feeding-series catches up with the healing-series. In the next four chapters four persons are healed (discounting the case of the Syrophoenician, who is non-Jewish), and four thousands are fed at the beginning of the eighth chapter. So there are three thousands still to be fed and three persons still to be healed. The three healings are duly narrated in what follows, but the feeding of the remaining three thousands is never separately dealt with in view of the final feeding of the whole twelvefold group at the last supper.

This short statement is long enough to show that Farrer displays much ingenuity in his attempt to establish the thesis that St. Mark's gospel is constructed on the framework of an arithmetico-symbolical architectonic. But his arguments not infrequently appear to be little else than flagrant examples of special pleading, and we find it hard to avoid the conclusion that if the evangelist really had been seriously concerned to set forth the traditions he selects in accordance with the demands of a numerical pattern or set of patterns, he would have made this much more evident in his work. The correspondences which Farrer discovers sometimes seem to promise well at first sight and then, like phantoms, they vanish in the light of careful investigation. Thus Levi is not a Gentile, though he is taken to be the one left out of the twelvefold apostolate,[3] corresponding to the one loaf (8:14) for the Gentiles (as is supposed) and to the one (as is supposed) healing of a Gentile (7:24–30). Morover the failure of the evangelist to follow up the story of the feeding of the four thousands with an account of a feeding of the required three does not seem to be covered by the narrative of the last supper, in which there is no reference to thousands.

The four men called to be disciples in the first chapter of the gospel are included in the twelvefold apostolate established in the third chapter, but there is no recapitulation of four, or any figurative trace of such, either in the healing-narratives or in the feeding-narratives. In the case of the latter series five thousands are followed by four, making nine—where we would expect four—to be taken up and completed in a twelvefold collective feeding. Also, the first miracle of the loaves does not strictly mark the point where the healings of the sick are caught

[3] St. Matthew takes the Levi of Mark 2:14 to be a member of the apostolate (see Matt. 9:9; 10:3).

up with, for prior to 6:35 eight healings, not five, are described in separate narratives. But why so much emphasis upon separate narratives? On more than one occasion St. Mark is at pains to point out that Jesus heals many more people than those to whose cure a special story is devoted (cf. 1:34, 39; 3:10; 6:5; etc.). And as for the nationality of the persons healed, we cannot be sure that the Gerasene demoniac and the deaf-mute are Jewish, it being reported that Jesus meets both these men while journeying outside Jewish territory (see 5:1; 7:31). Furthermore, if the evangelist were in fact so enthusiastic about numerical patterning as Farrer contends, why are the fishes of the miracles of the loaves (6:41; 8:7) allowed to remain outside the range of the arithmetical symbolism? And why does he write "five thousand *men*" in 6:44 and "*about* four thousands" in 8:9? Perhaps the mention of *men* signifies that more than five thousands are fed (cf. Matt. 14:21), and does not the small word *about* mean that the numeral it qualifies is not to be taken as a precise indication of the number of persons who took part in the feast? Again, if the *crumbs* in the saying attributed to the Syrophoenician woman are deliberately intended to correspond to the *fragments* gathered after the feedings (6:43; 8:8; 8:19; 8:20), why are different words employed in the two cases?

Thus while St. Mark's thinking is informed and sustained by a theology of salvation, it is unlikely that he adapts the traditions he selects on the basis of a typological scheme such as Farrer contemplates.

2

Evidence of the Fact
in Word and Deed

AFTER the imprisonment of John the Baptist (Mark 1:14), Jesus is able to make his public appearance in Galilee preaching the gospel of God or of the kingdom of God.[1] For the way has been duly prepared. The Elijah-forerunner has performed his appointed task; the voice from heaven has confirmed that "the stronger one" is God's unique Son; and Jesus has proved his fitness for the messianic work before him by overcoming the temptation of Satan in the wilderness. The glad announcement which can now be made is evidently tantamount to the gospel proclaimed by the apostolic church; Jesus is the Messiah, the Son of God, in whom the hopes of Israel and the longings of all peoples find their veritable realization.[2] The long-awaited moment has at last arrived—the moment which marks the transition from the age of promise to the age of fulfillment. To use language derived from St. Paul's epistle to the Galatians, the

[1] In 1:14 the reading "the gospel of the kingdom of God" is not quite so well attested as "the gospel of God" (for the latter expression, cf. Rom. 1:1; 15:16; II Cor. 11:7; I Thess. 2:8f.).

[2] The verb "to preach" is used with "the gospel" in 13:10 and 14:9, where the reference in each case is clearly to the gospel preached by the apostolic church.

fullness of time has come since God has sent forth his Son for the salvation of the world (Gal. 4:4). It is true that in 1:14–15 there is no direct reference to the real status of him who makes the glad announcement, but (as will be shown in the course of subsequent discussions) this is only because, in St. Mark's view, the true nature of the Lord is a secret which cannot yet be made known to men. If he were not the Messiah, the gospel could not be preached. The Messiahship of Jesus, that is to say, is the *sine qua non* of the good news that the time of fulfillment has come. Thus, although the people to whom Jesus preaches are unaware of the true nature of his status, it may now be declared that the fateful hour is striking and that God's rule is being finally established in the world. For, in the eyes of believing readers (who know the secret), the kingdom of God is no longer merely an eventuality to be anticipated, but a reality whose charismatic power continually manifests itself in the words and deeds of the prophet from Nazareth.

In 1:15b Jesus concludes his brief announcement of the glad tidings by calling upon his hearers to repent and believe in the gospel, and this reminds us of the similar appeals which occur in early Christian preaching as it is set forth in the Acts of the Apostles (see Acts 5:31; 11:18; 20:21). But invitations to repentance and faith do not seem to be altogether in place at the opening of St. Mark's account of the Galilean ministry, since, according to the general conception of the messianic secret, the people are not in a position to make the required response to the gospel. It must be observed, however, that incongruity of this kind is a constantly recurring feature of the document with which we are concerned. Thus from time to time the evangelist apparently expects the disciples to see Jesus from his own point of view and uses language which implies that they ought to understand him as he understands him.[3] Doubtless, judged by modern biographical standards, such a mode of representation is

[3] For further discussion of this matter, see below, Chapter 5.

seriously at fault. But when it is considered in the light of the writer's ardent religious faith, it is seen as a means of bringing out what is presupposed to be the true appreciation of the person and office of Jesus.

It may be felt that the glad announcement itself also entails an incongruity, since in certain other passages, such as 9:1; 13:7; 14:25; 14:62,[4] the coming of the kingdom with power is still an object of anticipation. But it is unlikely that there is any real inconsistency in this connection for, although the evangelist holds that the appearance of Jesus in Galilee signifies the inauguration of the age of fulfillment, he does not necessarily take the view that the new order has thereby reached its consummation. Admittedly, the eschatological affirmation of 1:15 could hardly have been made within the sphere of Jewish thought, where it was expected that the coming of the days of the Messiah would be heralded by some tremendous disturbance in external nature—"a sign from heaven" (see 8:11; I Cor. 1:22). And R. Jose (*c.* 150 A.D.) even went so far as to say that a person who pretends to forecast or calculate the date of the termination of the present world order has no part in the age to come.[5] Nevertheless, St. Mark's eschatological scheme makes room for such ideas as these, though their applicability is, as it were, postponed from the time of the kingdom's inauguration to the time of its grand consummation. Thus in 13:24-27 the occurrence of startling portents in the universe is the immediate prelude to the glorious appearance of the Son of Man; and in 13:31-32 neither the angels nor the Son but only the Father is aware of the time when heaven and earth shall pass away. If we may follow the line of thought suggested by the parables of growth in 4:26-32 (the seed grows secretly and the size of a grain of mustard seed is incommensurate with that of the full-grown tree), the evangelist's general conception would seem to be that the earthly

---

[4] Regarding the exegesis of 9:1, see below, Supplementary Note C.
[5] Cf. S.-B., I, 671.

ministry is related to the ultimate triumph of the kingdom as ✓ seedtime to harvest. Thus the preparation of the ground for the sowing of the seed corresponds to the work of the old dispensation which comes to an end with the mission of John the Baptist; and just as the silent forces of nature are potent enough to bring the sown seed to fruition, so the divine forces, which are operating (without any cosmic cataclysm) in and through Jesus of Nazareth and his small company of disciples, are a sure guarantee that the ministry will have its glorious fulfillment at the parousia of the Son of Man.

In St. Mark's estimation, then, Jesus exemplifies the kingdom of God upon earth: he is the Messiah and his messianic authority is evident in all his words and deeds. This is brought out in two passages which follow the glad announcement in 1:16–20, where the brothers Simon and Andrew and the brothers James and John suddenly become disciples of Jesus.[6] Perhaps these two pericopes were introduced at the present juncture because disciples were required from the outset of the ministry as witnesses of the historical content of the apostolic message of salvation.[7] Thus in Acts 1:21–22 it is emphasized that the person who is elected to take the place of Judas in the apostleship must be drawn from the circle of those who have followed Jesus from the time of the baptism of John, and according to Acts 10:39 Peter is careful to point out that he is counted among those who have witnessed *all* the things which Jesus did in the country of the Jews and in Jerusalem. However this may be, in the first of the two stories before us Jesus confronts Simon and

---

[6] Cf. 2:14; 3:13–19. Simon Peter, James, and John are represented as the leading disciples. They stand in a more intimate relation to the Master than the rest. They are the only disciples who witness the raising of the little girl (5:37; 5:40); they alone are present at the transfiguration (9:2); they alone go forward with Jesus in Gethsemane (14:33). But Andrew is present with them to hear the great eschatological discourse (13:3).

[7] Cf. E. Lohmeyer, *Das Evangelium des Markus*, pp. 28f., 31.

Andrew and suddenly issues a command ("Come after me and I will make you to become fishers of men!") [8] whose abruptness is reminiscent of a military order, whereupon the two brothers immediately leave their fishing nets and follow him. Accordingly, as Bultmann has remarked,[9] the evangelist here seems to set forth an ideal scene which represents in the symbolism of a single moment what must have really been the result of a more or less prolonged process of development; and it suggests that the divine call is at the basis of genuine Christian discipleship and overrules the claims of the old way of life and the demands of all worldly relationships. In the second of the two stories no command is directly reported, but the response of the sons of Zebedee is just as immediate as that of Simon and Andrew: they at once leave their father in the ship with the hired servants and go after the Lord. In each case, therefore, the compelling might of the word of Jesus receives a remarkable illustration. The fishermen follow, but not merely as pupils might follow a rabbi,[10] for it is the Messiah who has spoken to them and his word is equivalent to the word of God himself. He has the power radically to transform their lives, and their response to his call means their active participation in the soteriological work of the age of fulfillment.

In the following section, which extends from 1:21 to 1:39, St. Mark brings out certain characteristic features of the Galilean ministry by delineating what appears to be meant as a typi-

[8] For the expression "fishers of men," cf. Jer. 16:16 where, however, the men are "caught" that they may be punished by God, not that they may be saved.

[9] See *Die Geschichte der synoptischen Tradition*, p. 60.

[10] Cf. S.-B., I, 187f. The conjecture (see T. W. Manson, *The Teaching of Jesus*, pp. 237ff.) that Jesus preferred *shewilyā'* ("apprentice") to *talmīdhā'* ("student") scarcely seems to have sufficient warrant. *Shewilyā'* is not found in the Palestinian Talmud, and the Syriac versions have *talmīdhā'* for μαθητής; also, St. Luke in 14:26f. may have simply wished to make the statement "is not worthy of me" (perhaps Q—cf. Matt. 10:37f.) more specific.

cal day of the Lord's activities: in verses 21–28 Jesus teaches
in the synagogue at Capernaum on the sabbath and exorcises
an unclean spirit, with the result that the people are amazed and
his fame spreads throughout all the region of Galilee round
about; in verses 29–31, accompanied by James and John, he enters the house of Simon and Andrew and cures the mother of
Simon's wife who is suffering from a fever; in verses 32–34 the
whole town gathers at the door of the house after sunset (which
marks the end of the sabbath), and he heals many of their ills
and drives out many demons; in verses 35–39 he rises at an early
hour the next morning in order to pray in a lonely place and,
on being discovered by Peter and others, he declares that they
should go to the neighboring towns so that he may preach there
also and that it was for this purpose that he came forth.

The first of these four pericopes (vv. 21–28) seems to show
signs of having been subjected to editorial treatment by the evangelist, who is seeking to give a general impression of the effect
produced by the words and deeds of the Lord. It does not possess
the wealth of detail which is characteristic of the typical miracle
story, but one may perhaps conjecture that verses 23–26 constitute the remainder of such a story; in this central part of the
pericope the confession of the unclean spirit (v. 24) and the
injunction to silence (v. 25) evidently have a special significance
for the evangelist (cf. 1:34; 3:11f.). It is possible that the supposed original story began with some such brief introduction as
"On the sabbath he went into a synagogue and a man there with
an unclean spirit . . ." [11] and that verse 27 (to "What is this?")
belonged to its conclusion. Typical features of exorcism sto-

---

[11] The word "immediately" occurs no less than nine times in 1:12–43.
Turner (*N.C.H.S.*, pt. 3, p. 52) describes St. Mark's persistent use of this
word as the oddest mannerism of his gospel. He observes that to some
extent the other evangelists replace it by "behold" (which St. Mark never
employs in narrative) and thinks that St. Mark's frequent use of it is
meant to suggest something of the strain and pressure of the Lord's work
during the ministry.

ries [12] are to be detected in the passage: the demon is disturbed on sensing the presence of its formidable opponent (vv. 23f.); there is the utterance of the potent word by the exorcist (v. 25); the success of the action is demonstrated by the convulsion and the loud cry which mark the demon's exit (v. 26); and the extraordinary character of the deed is emphasized by the reference to the amazement of the spectators (v. 27).

The evangelist appears to have complicated the introduction and the conclusion of the underlying story partly by bringing it into connection with the framework of a larger narrative and partly by introducing the additional motif of the teaching with authority.[13] The same motif is exemplified in the existing form of the chorus in verse 27 ("a new teaching with authority!"). The indefinite plural subject "they" in verse 21a refers back to verses 16–20 and is clearly intended to signify Jesus and his newly acquired disciples. But in verse 21b there is a sudden change to the singular "he," which points forward to the central figure of verses 22ff., where Jesus plays the dual role of teacher and miracle worker; nevertheless, we are to assume that the Lord is accompanied by his four disciples when he goes into the synagogue, as is clear from verse 29. In verses 21b–22, although the context implies that a particular situation is being described, the plural "on the sabbaths" and the imperfect tenses of the finite verbs suggest that the evangelist is seeking to characterize the work of the ministry in a general way. The same tendency to generalize is evinced in verses 27b–28, for the reference to a plurality of unclean spirits conveys the impression that Jesus has already performed a number of exorcisms in the presence of the public, and in the supplementary conclusion of verse 28 the evangelist is anxious to stress that the Lord wins widespread fame because of his miraculous deeds.

---

[12] Cf. below, Chapter 3.

[13] In the first gospel this motif is introduced at the end of the sermon on the mount (Matt. 7:28f.).

Thus in verses 21–28 Jesus is represented as the plenipotentiary of God. He enters the synagogue and teaches with such authority that he astonishes the congregation; unlike the scribes, he does not base his pronouncements on the tradition of the elders, but gives utterance to divine truth as the envoy of God invested with full powers.[14] He communicates directly the instructions of the Father, on whose behalf he has come into the world (cf. John 8:28). It should be noticed, however, that in the New Testament, the word "authority" is normally used not of teaching, but of the power disclosed in miraculous works (cf., for example, 6:7), and therefore the idea may be present in verses 22 and 27 that Jesus is an eschatological prophet who, like the two witnesses of Rev. 11:3ff., is endowed with such power.[15] In any case, there can scarcely be any doubt regarding the main point which the evangelist wishes to make. The same divine potency as that revealed in the Lord's mighty deeds is revealed in his words, or, to express the matter otherwise, he not only acts but also speaks as the Messiah, the Son of God; and yet those who listen to his teaching do not recognize his true status. They feel that there is something unusually authoritative about his teaching, but their knowledge goes no

[14] Cf. S.-B., I, 470. D. Daube (*J.T.S.*, XXXIX [1938], 45ff.) thinks that the phrases "was teaching them as having authority and not as the scribes" and "a new teaching with authority" in vv. 22 and 27 respectively may well belong to the oral tradition; and he argues that a satisfactory explanation of the word "authority" as used in these phrases can be reached by considering the language of the rabbinic sources: (1) The word ἐξουσία may correspond to the Hebrew *rēshūth* in its technical sense of authority to lay down binding decisions. (2) The "scribes" in v. 22 may be inferior teachers who are not entitled to introduce fresh rules. (3) In v. 27 the meaning may be that Jesus gives a new doctrine based on *rēshūth* or as if it were based on *rēshūth*. Daube seeks to render this suggestion plausible by showing that the institution of *rēshūth* goes back to the time of Jesus, that inferior teachers as such are called *sōpherīm* at that period, and that conceptions analogous to "a new teaching with authority" occur in talmudic literature.

[15] Cf. Lohmeyer, *op. cit.*, pp. 35f.

further than this (cf. 6:2f.). Accordingly, when the unclean spirit gives voice to its recognition of the Lord's identity, a foil is provided for the people's failure to discover the mystery. The demon at once perceives that Jesus has come in order to destroy the satanic kingdom of which it is a representative.[16] And on the utterance of the exorcist's potent command, the correctness of the demon's testimony finds striking confirmation: the unclean spirit makes futile agitations, forces a loud inarticulate cry, and forthwith leaves its victim. Nevertheless, although the demon knows that the Messiah's coming means the doom of the principalities of Satan (this particular duel being but a localized manifestation of a conflict which is destined to have cosmic dimensions), the people who witness the miracle are moved only to amazement and to vague questioning among themselves.

In verses 29–31 the mention of Simon, Andrew, James, and John recalls verses 16–20. The account of the healing of the mother of Simon's wife is very brief; as is frequently the case in miracle stories of this category, supernatural power is apparently transmitted by bodily contact between physician and patient ("and he came and took her by the hand"), and evidence of the woman's recovery is furnished by the notice at the end ("and she ministered to them"). The evangelist again seems to be generalizing in verses 32–34 (cf. 3:7–12; 6:53–56). The comment of verse 34c is of special interest, since it appears to indicate that, in St. Mark's view, precautions are deliberately taken to prevent the knowledge of the demons from becoming public property. In the fourth and last pericope of the section (vv. 35–39) it is noteworthy that Jesus prays in solitude (cf. 6:46; 14:32) and that Simon is already acting as the spokesman of his colleagues (cf. esp. 8:29). It is possible that the words "to this end I came forth" in verse 38 are correctly interpreted in St. Luke's

---

[16] For the expression "the Holy One of God" in v. 24, cf. the wording of Peter's confession in John 6:69; and for the notion of the final destruction of demonic powers, cf. Isa. 24:22–23; T. Lev. 18; En. 69:27.

"for this purpose I was sent" (Luke 4:43), for it has already been suggested in verse 35 that Jesus leaves the house in order to pray in a lonely place. That is to say, the ἐξῆλθον ("I came forth") of verse 38 seems to bear the same kind of meaning as the ἦλθες ("Have you come?") of the demon's confession in verse 24 and corresponds to the ἦλθον ("I came") and to the ἦλθεν ("came") in the sayings of 2:17 and 10:45 respectively. If this is so, the last clause of verse 38 signifies that it is part of the divine purpose for which the Messiah came into the world (from God) that he should preach in other towns (besides Capernaum) as a missionary of the gospel.

The account of the cleansing of the leper, which follows in 1:40–45, may be meant to form a connecting link between the preceding pericopes and the series of controversy stories presented in 2:1–3:6.[17] The miracle is introduced without any mention of time or place and no spectators are referred to. It affords further evidence of the Lord's messianic status which, in spite of its secret character, must perforce manifest itself in the form of a miracle worker's great fame (v. 45). The story displays certain characteristic traits of popular accounts of miraculous healings—the communication of health-giving power by physical contact (v. 41), the potent word of the physician (v. 41), and the demonstration of success (v. 44). It may be noted that, according to a rabbinic opinion, it was as difficult to cleanse a leper as to bring a dead person to life again.[18] And it should be borne in mind that in Jewish thought leprosy was very closely associated with the notion of ceremonial uncleanness; as a safeguard against contagion, the leper was segregated from society, and before he could regain his normal place in the life of the community he had to be declared clean in the legally authorized manner (see Lev. 13f.) Thus the cleansing of a leper was a ceremonial process conducted by a priestly supervisor; but the verb "to cleanse" was also used in a medical sense of the

[17] Cf. below, Chapters 4 and 6.   [18] Cf. S.-B., IV, 745.

curing of the disease, and Luke 17:15 (but not in D and certain other authorities) is the only passage in the synoptic gospels where the verb "to heal" refers to the removal of leprosy.

In verse 40 the words καὶ γονυπετῶν ("and kneeling") do not appear in B and D, and perhaps they were omitted in these two authorities either because they were considered to be redundant or because they were felt to express rather too violent an emotion on the part of the leper; a similar omission is made in the Matthaean and Lukan renderings of 10:17.[19] A much-discussed variant occurs in the following verse, where D (supported by two old Latin MSS) has ὀργισθείς ("moved with anger") instead of σπλαγχνισθείς ("moved with pity"); and seeing that the D reading is the more difficult of the two, it may well be the correct one. The modification may have been made because no reason could be assigned for anger in this case; that is, the ὀργισθείς was not understood. Another possibility is that the modification was made for christological reasons (anger was incompatible with the high dignity of Jesus), and support for this hypothesis may be found in the fact that St. Matthew and St. Luke do not include the μετ' ὀργῆς ("with anger") in their renderings of 3:5 (cf. Matt. 12:13; Luke 6:10). It should also be observed that there is nothing corresponding to the ὀργισθείς / σπλαγχνισθείς of verse 41 or to the ἐμβριμησάμενος (which signifies angry displeasure) of verse 43 in the Matthaean and Lukan parallels (Matt. 8:2–4; Luke 5:12–16), though otherwise they follow the wording of St. Mark's story fairly closely.

But if the D reading in verse 41 is correct, the question arises why St. Mark should represent Jesus as being angry in the situation described. One possibility is that it is simply the anger of a transcendent and divine personage on being troubled by the misery and weakness of mortal men (cf. 9:19). Another possibility is that the anger is occasioned by the suggestion that Jesus, although he has the power to cure leprosy, may not be

---

[19] Cf. Turner, *op cit.*, p. 56.

willing to exercise it in this particular case. On the whole, however, the most plausible explanation seems to be that the Lord is provoked to anger because the suppliant is contravening the law, firstly, by moving freely among healthy people and, secondly, by making a request which may be taken to imply that an unauthorized person is competent to cleanse a leper in the complete and official sense. In verse 44 Jesus is represented as acting in conformity with the law, for his instructions appear to mean that the man is not to regard himself as clean (and therefore is not to speak of the cure to anyone) before the official pronouncement has been made by the priestly authority. Thus the story seems to evince an apologetic motive: St. Mark wishes to make it plain early in his work that the conflict with the Jewish religious leaders, which is about to be illustrated in the controversy stories of the following section, really arises not from any disrespect for the law on the part of Jesus (cf. 7:10–13; 12:28–34), but from the evil residing in the hearts of his opponents.[20]

With regard to the injunction to silence in verse 44 St. Mark probably construes it in the sense of his theory of the messianic secret, and it has even been argued that he actually interpolated verse 43 and the words "See that you say nothing to any man, but" of verse 44 into the text of the story as he received it.[21] The last verse of the pericope (v. 45) is apparently a supplementary conclusion composed by the evangelist and designed

---

[20] Cf. R. H. Lightfoot, *History and Interpretation*, pp. 108f. In his later work (*The Gospel Message of St. Mark*, p. 26) Lightfoot argues that the story was given its present position in the gospel to bring out the surpassing nature of the salvation made available by Jesus: the passage is to be understood in the light of Rom. 8:3, for the law of Moses, while providing for the ritual purification of leprosy, indicates no method for the actual purging of the disease. This argument, however, is not a very forceful one: according to contemporary Jewish belief, men of God under the Mosaic dispensation *could* cure leprosy (cf. II Kings 5:1ff.).

[21] See Bultmann, *op. cit.*, p. 227. Cf. below, Chapter 4.

to give a general impression of the widespread fame of the Lord (cf. 1:28). It shows how, despite the injunctions to silence (1:25; 1:34; 1:44), the fact of the Messiahship must needs make its presence publicly felt if only by winning for Jesus a great reputation as a worker of miraculous deeds.[22]

[22] Cf. 5:20; 7:36; Matt. 9:31. Two objections may be raised against the view that 1:45 bears a true analogy to 7:36: (1) The expression "the word" does not mean "the story of the incident" elsewhere in the gospel. (2) There is an awkward change of subject when we pass to the consequential clause. Thus it is not impossible that the first word of v. 45 (ὁ) refers to Jesus, not to his patient. The Lord goes forth and publishes the word (cf. 4:14; 4:33; 8:32) and meets with such a response that he has to resort to lonely places for some days (cf. 2:1); nevertheless, he is sought out and people come to him from every quarter.

3

Miracles and Miracle Stories

IN his presentation of the life of Jesus as the earthly career of ✓
the Messiah, St. Mark makes liberal use of wonder stories. Such
stories appear to have circulated widely in the primitive Christian
communities and to have constituted an important category of
the church's traditions concerning the life of its founder. The
evangelist therefore does not deviate from the prevailing Christian attitude when he lays emphasis on the miraculous element
in the Lord's ministry. He shares the apostolic conviction that
the Messiahship is made manifest in the wonders which Jesus
performs; in St. Mark's estimation, as in that of the church generally, Jesus' miraculous deeds are proof of his divine origin
and evidence of his supernatural power. This conception was
an essential factor in the exposition of the apostolic gospel of
the crucified Messiah.[1] There was nothing incomparable about
the mere fact of Jesus' crucifixion as such; no doubt many
worthy men had suffered martyrdom on a Roman cross. But
those who bore witness to the apostolic faith discerned in the
crucifixion of Jesus a supreme act of divine condescension and

[1] Cf. J. R. Seeley, *Ecce Homo*, pt. 1, ch. 5.

voluntary humiliation, and it was this discernment which was the creative condition of the gospel they proclaimed. He who, as the Messiah of God, was endowed with transcendent might, yet came not to be served, but to serve and to give his life for the redemption of sinful humanity (cf. Mark 10:45); or, to use phraseology derived from St. Paul, he who was essentially divine emptied himself, took the form of a servant, and became obedient even to the death of the cross (cf. Phil. 2:5ff.). Thus the apostolic doctrine of the Messiah's humiliation presupposed the belief that Jesus possessed supernatural power which he exercised not for his own private ends, but only in the interest of human salvation. As we have already noticed, however, although St. Mark holds that the miracles of Jesus are expressions of his messianic authority, he takes the view that they could not be recognized as such by the people who witnessed them. But before we proceed to examine in greater detail the way in which the evangelist's conception of the messianic secret affects his representation of Jesus as a worker of miracles, certain questions of a more general nature need to be considered.

In any attempt to determine the significance of the miraculous in primitive Christian thought it is of first importance that modern ideas on the matter should be carefully distinguished from the ancient outlook. An investigation of primitive religion indicates that from earliest times the notion of miracle has been very closely associated with the feeling of unfamiliarity or unusualness. Etymological research in different languages suggests that a miraculous happening is primarily a happening which is in some sense of an extraordinary character; and both anthropological and psychological studies have shown that it is a deep-seated habit of the human mind to make a broad distinction within the field of experience between ordinary and extraordinary occurrences. The former tend to be taken for granted, whereas the latter seem to require special explanation; and it appears to be a primitive tendency of the mind to explain an extraordinary occurrence by referring it to some kind of mysterious power which has chosen to invade the world of ordinary experience and to interfere with the normal course of events. In this way an unusual event becomes miraculous in the sense of bearing witness to the action of a supernatural power. It is at once a δύναμις ("power" or "mighty work") and a σημεῖον ("sign"), since it is pregnant with extraordinary potency and testifies to the immediate presence of an agency from a transcendent sphere. The coming of the transcendent power presents itself as something arbitrary or capricious, and the natural psychological reaction is one of suspended activity in face of the unknown and the unpredictable. Thus, besides giving rise to numinous feelings of awe and wonder, the miraculous frequently has a paralyzing effect on the mind.[2]

When the notion is understood in this light, it is seen that there is no such thing as a purely objective miracle; an unusual occurrence only becomes miraculous (that is, a sign of the presence of a supernatural agency) through the aid of some measure of intellectual interpretation on the part of the experiencing subject. And the subjectivity of the miraculous is just as palpable when the term is understood in a modern sense and taken to indicate an event which is out of harmony with or inexplicable by the scientifically ascertained laws of nature. The employment of the word "ascertained" in this definition clearly brings out the subjective character of the notion defined; the miraculous is relative to what the subject knows about the ways in which nature behaves. Accordingly, an objective miracle could not truly be said to exist unless one were already acquainted with all natural causes and with all the possible modes of their manifold operations. And when it is asserted that an event which is scientifically inexplicable results from the inter-

---

[2] There are anticipations of this kind of experience in early childhood and in the life of animals; cf. J. Sully, *Studies of Childhood*, pp. 205f., and C. Lloyd Morgan, *Animal Life and Intelligence*, p. 339.

vention of a supernatural agency, still more subjective interpretation is introduced. For in this case it is not only held that the miraculous occurrence is inexplicable on the basis of ascertained laws of nature; it is also implied that the occurrence, while being comprehensible when construed as the effect of a supernatural cause, cannot be understood by ascribing it to any association of purely natural causes, whether known or unknown.

If, then, the miraculous necessarily involves intellectual interpretation on the part of the experiencing mind, the miraculous subject matter of religious documents belongs to the realm of human beliefs rather than to that of so-called facts as they are commonly disclosed in sense perception. It is true, of course, that wonder stories, such as those included in the gospels, deal with objective facts of perceptual experience. But the stories were neither composed nor preserved for the sake of the perceptible facts they relate, as, for example, a particular instance of the removal of a disease or of the cessation of a storm. As they are presented in the narratives, such facts are charged with religious significance; and they were narrated only for the sake of the theological interpretation which they were believed to require. It is therefore erroneous to suppose that the aim of historical investigation should be to seek out the unadulterated facts—in contradistinction to the beliefs with which they are united in the narratives—with a view to the presentation of an alternative mode of explanation designed to prove more acceptable to the modern scientific mentality. Indeed, one may doubt whether any solid ground of pure fact could be arrived at by an analysis of any particular story of this category. If we take, for example, the account of the stilling of the storm in Mark 4:35–41, the historian is hardly in a position to affirm that a storm actually ceased with surprising suddenness while Jesus and his disciples were on the water, and that this unadulterated fact, really due to some atmospheric phenomenon, was misinterpreted by those who witnessed it and ascribed to the agency of a supernatural cause. Moreover, quite apart from this difficulty of discovering particular instances of pure fact, such a procedure could not offer a genuine historical explanation of the miraculous subject matter of the narratives. As we have seen, that subject matter is conditioned by beliefs, and beliefs are elucidated not by being dismissed, but by being considered on the background of the world of ideas to which they properly belong.

The mentality which prevailed in the eastern empire during the first century A.D. did not make the hard and fast distinctions to which the modern mind is accustomed, and men resorted more readily to the notion of supernatural causation. What we understand by the scientific attitude may have been foreshadowed in the schools among Stoics, skeptics, and medical practitioners who swore allegiance to the ideals of the Hippocratic oath, but, generally, ancient thought does not exemplify that interest in the abstract and the impersonal which is necessary for the systematic observation of the working of natural causes. The primitive division of phenomena into the categories of the usual and of the unusual still profoundly affected man's understanding of the world, and, judged by scientific standards, this is an extremely inexact method of differentiating the multifarious items of experience. Any kind of object, independently of its intrinsic properties, could be included in the category of the unusual and ascribed to a transcendent cause, provided that the manner of its presentation was not expected by the experiencing subject. The mind tended to pass lightly over the distinction between the animate and the inanimate worlds, and nonliving things, as well as animals and human beings, were frequently thought to be acting under the direct influence of a supernatural agency. Also, an occurrence might be unusual to one person, but not to another; and it was partly because of the vagueness of the notion of the unusual, and partly because of the imperfection of contemporary knowledge concerning natural processes, that there was ample room for the free exercise of the imagination in the interpretation of phenomena and the assignment of their causal conditions. What is deemed to be invalid or fantastic is dependent upon the criteria of truth which the judging mind adopts, and those criteria are largely determined by the intellectual atmosphere of the prevailing culture. Hence if prevalent ideas familiarize the mind with the notion of supernatural causation and supply no precise means of determining the occasions for its proper employment, much scope is afforded for the unfettered display of personal preferences and imaginative idiosyncracies in historical explanations. Indeed, as historians have often observed, when one considers the mentality of the age, one cannot but be impressed by the relative sobriety of the accounts of the miraculous contained in the canonical gospels.

But it is not sufficient merely to state that the evident predilection for the notion of supernatural causation in ancient explanations of outstanding phenomena was due to the inadequacy of contemporary knowledge concerning natural processes. This inadequacy was itself conditioned by what appears to have been a widespread feeling that proximate causes, as we understand them, are trivialities and not veritable causes at all. The idea of cause appears to have taken its rise in the personal transactions of the individual with his environment, and in primitive thought the activities of other entities tend to be construed after the analogy of the subject's own acts of volition. Experience presupposes that the individual subject, who is acted upon by the outer world, acts upon the surrounding conditions of his existence in response to their manifold demands; and it seems that from the early dawning of conscious experience the subject is aware (however vaguely) of himself as at once patient and agent, as at once effect and cause. Others affect him and he affects others. Thus the actions and reactions of entities generally are wont to be interpreted in terms of the dynamic interrelations between the subject and his environment, and causation is most readily understood anthropomorphically as effectual ✓ action informed by a purpose. When therefore the habitual behavior of entities is disturbed by some unusual phenomenon, the unsophisticated mind is prone to seek an explanation not in the impersonal conception of a particular concurrence of proximate causes as such, but by resorting to the teleological notion of a transcendent being (or beings) who has decided for some purpose to interfere with the usual course of events. The transcendent being may be thought good or evil according to the character of the occurrence which calls for an explanation; but on certain occasions a painful or injurious occurrence could be ascribed to the intervention of a beneficent being as, for example, when it is adjudged to be a punishment inflicted on men for their offences against divine laws.

It was in accordance with the tendency to elaborate and systematize such primitive notions that in Jewish thought during the closing centuries of the pre-Christian era there arose the dualistic doctrine of an evil spiritual kingdom in conflict with the kingdom of God.[3] In the developed form of this cosmology the numerous supernatural beings of early Semitic belief are swept into the service of one or other of the two opposing forces which are continually striving against each other for the domination of man and the universe in which he lives. Each of the transcendent kingdoms is organized after the manner of an oriental state (a conception which probably shows the influence of Zoroastrian ideas) and has a supreme commander who stands at the head of a vast hierarchy of subordinates and directs the strategic operations of his hosts. The archdemon, who is in command of the evil kingdom, has several names assigned to him—Satan, Mastema, Beelzebul (or Beelzebub), Beliar, Asmodaeus (the last of Persian derivation). The

---

[3] Cf. T. W. Manson, *The Teaching of Jesus*, pp. 152ff., E. Meyer, *Ursprung und Anfänge des Christentums*, II, 95ff., S.-B., IV, 501ff., E. Klostermann, *Das Markusevangelium*, pp. 14ff.

agents of Satan are also designated in different ways: שֵׁד is the usual rabbinic term and corresponds to the Greek δαιμόνιον; among other terms are: רוח רעה / πνεῦμα πονηρόν / "evil spirit" and רוח טומאה / πνεῦμα ἀκάθαρτόν / "unclean spirit."

Various traditions regarding the origin of the demons were in circulation. One of these is based on the myth contained in Gen. 6:1ff., which describes the birth of giants as the result of the illicit unions between the sons of God and the daughters of men. A midrashic expansion of the story explains that when the giants died their spirits became the demons who soon began their work of corrupting mankind. But eventually, after pleadings by Noah (who was later entrusted with special medical knowledge) and counterpleadings by Mastema, God decided to imprison nine-tenths of the demons, as he had previously imprisoned their angelic progenitors, and thus limited their nefarious activities by leaving only a tenth of their complement under the effective command of Satan (Jub. 10:1ff.). According to another tradition, the demons are incompleted creations of God; toward the end of the sixth day of the cosmogonical week God was in process of creating them but had not time to provide them with bodies, owing to the advent of the sabbath.[4] A hypothesis which has the support of Josephus sets forth the view that the demons are the spirits of the wicked dead who enter into living people and kill them unless power to ward off the evil invaders can be obtained.[5] Nevertheless, although Satan's demonic agents are essentially incorporeal, they are by no means devoid of all physical properties. They are sometimes thought to be equipped with wings or to be sufficiently like human beings to eat and drink and to reproduce their kind. They are generally invisible, but in certain circumstances they may appear in human or some other form. Their activities are not confined to particular regions of the world or to particular times of the day. They inhabit both the earth and the atmosphere and

[4] Cf. S.-B., IV, 506.   [5] See *Bell.* 7, 6, 3.

can inflict harm on men at any hour; yet they have their favorite haunts, such as wastes and ruins, places ritually unclean (cemeteries, sewers, unwashed hands, and so on), pools of water, and the vicinity of certain trees and shrubs; and they are particularly dangerous during the hours of darkness. Human troubles of all sorts could be ascribed to demonic action.[6] Evil spirits spoil man's material possessions; they corrupt his soul by inciting him to sin and undermine the health of mind and body by causing diseases of every kind. Indeed, the last-mentioned view was so familiar among the rabbis that they frequently refer to an illness in terms of the evil spirit which is supposed to cause it.

But though the demons belong to the kingdom of Satan, they may act in the service of God on certain occasions by executing divine judgment on the wicked; and this is a clear indication that the dualism of the general cosmological theory was not carried through with perfect logical consistency. Jewish monotheistic conviction (a legacy of the great prophets) required that God should be regarded as the sole creator and the sole ruler of the universe and thus precluded the possibility of the development of an absolute metaphysical dualism. It is true that the demons are usually referred to as though they were autonomous beings freely acting according to their own evil designs; but as soon as the matter is considered in relation to first principles, it is seen that the demons can perform their work only because God allows them to do so. Whatever authority Satan and his hosts may have exercised in the world since the days of Enoch (when men began to serve false gods), it is, in the last resort, authority derived from God, the one disposer of all power, whose omnipotence will be finally proved in the messianic age by the total destruction of the kingdom of evil. Thus the whole scheme is fundamentally teleological in the sense that its essential category of explanation is provided by the conception of purpose. God's will is the ultimate ground of

[6] Cf. S.-B. IV, 507ff., 521ff.

the universe and his sovereign purpose presides over the entire course of cosmic history. But among God's creatures are certain beings (angelic and human) who are endowed with the capacity to choose between right and wrong and to pursue purposes which run counter to the moral demands of the creator. And it was thought that the sufferings and misfortunes of common experience arise from particular instances of the misuse of such freedom because, in virtue of a divinely constituted principle of retribution, sin brings baneful consequences in its train; and so, for example, it could be explained that the demons owe their existence to the lapse of the angels and that they began to afflict man on account of his waywardness.

These considerations, then, afford some indication of the world of ideas in which Christianity originated and elaborated its own distinctive doctrine. Not that the Jews of the period subscribed to a carefully defined and completed system of official cosmology. But there were certain commonly accepted beliefs of wide application which exercised control over thought and determined the general character of the prevailing outlook on the world. Furthermore, despite the exclusivism of the Jews and the uniqueness of their ethical monotheism, their ways of thinking were not unaffected by the cultural traditions of other nations. We have already referred to the infiltration of ideas from Persian sources into the Jewish tradition. But in the first century of the Christian era the interaction of cultures had become much more extensive and complicated. Greek was now the general language of commerce and of civilization in the eastern empire, and the imperial government had established an order which facilitated travel. The consequence was that ideas could be diffused over wide areas with remarkable rapidity, and this stimulated the development of Hellenistic culture—that strange amalgam of beliefs and practices derived from primitive magic, Greek philosophy, Orphic religion, Babylonian astrology, doctrines from Egypt and Persia.[7] Jewish religion, too, made its

[7] Cf. E. Bevan, *Hellenism and Christianity*, pp. 91ff.

contribution to this comprehensive syncretism especially through the synagogues of the dispersion and the translation of its sacred literature into Greek.[8] Thus there came to be a certain community of ideas among the peoples inhabiting the eastern Mediterranean region. It is true that Judaism, thanks largely to the spirit of Pharisaism, was not greatly affected by the welter of Hellenistic doctrines. But on the level of popular thought, and to a greater degree in the dispersion, beliefs were current among the Jews which had also found currency in the surrounding world of Hellenistic civilization.

Thus the belief that demons cause human ills was prevalent among Jews and Gentiles alike, and with it went a number of associated ideas concerning the practical means of resisting and overcoming demonic power. It was generally assumed that such power could not be successfully dealt with by man's efforts alone without the aid of a divine being whose power was held to be greater than that of the demons. An assumption of this kind underlies St. Paul's words in Eph. 6:10ff., where he exhorts his readers to be strong in the strength of the Lord on the ground that their struggles are not against flesh and blood, but against the world rulers of this darkness, the spiritual hosts of wickedness in the heavenly places. The apostle here interprets the conception in a strictly ethical sense; the required divine power is made available through the practice of a virtuous life or through the personal fulfillment of God's moral demands. But in popular thought it was more commonly supposed that supernatural assistance against the demons is to be gained by a special knowledge of occult truths or by mysterious magical practices.[9] On these premises, therefore, whether its methods are magical or purely ethical, the art of healing has to do with the supernatural,

---

[8] Cf. Meyer, *op. cit.*, II, 353ff.

[9] The notion that the fulfillment of God's moral commands affords protection against the demons is found in rabbinical writings; but it is also thought that amulets and incantations are effective. See S.-B., IV, 527ff.

and any successful application of the art to a particular case is a miracle, that is, an act which bears witness to the presence of the transcendent power of a divine being who operates through the physician and removes the demonic cause of the disease. Such a mode of interpretation is evinced in the gospel stories of rapid healings as well as in miracle tales from non-Christian sources. Hence these gospel stories belong to a category of literature which extends beyond the bounds of Christianity; and while it is important to notice their peculiarities, it is equally important to define the nature of their more general category by bringing to light the fundamental beliefs which they presuppose and to identify the motifs and the stylistic features which they regularly share with other stories of the same category.

The last-mentioned task has been systematically undertaken by the so-called form critics,[10] and Dibelius' studies led him to think that the following nine pericopes in St. Mark's gospel are typical wonder stories or "Novellen" as he calls them: 1:40–45 (the leper); 4:35–41 (the storm); 5:1–20 (the Gerasene[11] demoniac); 5:21–43 (the raising of the little girl[12] and the woman with the issue); 6:35–44 (the feeding of the five[13]

---

[10] See esp. Dibelius, *From Tradition to Gospel*, pp. 70ff.; Bultmann, *Die Geschichte der synoptischen Tradition*, pp. 223ff.

[11] Turner (*N.C.H.S.*, pt. 3, p. 66) thinks that the readings *Gergesenes* and *Gadarenes* in Mark 5:1 are later emendations of St. Mark's improbable *Gerasenes*, Gerasa being thirty miles southeast from the south end of the Sea of Galilee. Originally the story (cf. 5:14) may have given no place name; cf. Dibelius, *op. cit.*, p. 73, n. 1.

[12] In Mark 5:22 the words "Jairus by name" are omitted from D. They may have been introduced into the Markan text by a copyist who had Luke 8:41 in mind. The name "Jairus" does not appear in the Matthaean parallel (Matt. 9:18). Cf. Bultmann, *op. cit.*, pp. 230, 256f.

[13] "The story of the feeding of the 4,000, Mark 8, 1–9, . . . must be understood as a shortening. . . . Dependence of this form of the narrative upon the Tale of the feeding of the 5,000 is probable. . . . It is also quite possible that the evangelist himself, finding that different numbers in regard to the miracle were in circulation, put together a second form

thousand); 6:45–52 (the walking on the sea); 7:32–37 (the deaf-mute); 8:22–26 (the blind man at Bethsaida); and 9:14–29 (the epileptic boy with a dumb spirit). Dibelius distinguishes the Novellen from the "paradigms," that is, model stories which culminate in an important pronouncement of Jesus; the former are concerned with Jesus the wonder worker, the latter with Jesus the teacher. There are also formal differences to be taken into consideration. The Novellen have a greater wealth of descriptive detail than the paradigms and are less dignified in general tone. When their subject is a case of miraculous healing they usually include a description of the illness, an account of the technique of the cure and a demonstration of the patient's restoration to health.

In making his selection of the nine Novellen from St. Mark's gospel Dibelius gives full weight to the stylistic characteristics of the stories, and this accounts for his exclusion of brief reports (such as Mark 1:29–31, the curing of Peter's mother-in-law) and of secondary compositions (such as Mark 8:1–9, the feeding of the four thousand), and for the great variety of his selected stories with respect to subject matter. Thus the story of the blind man at Bethsaida makes no mention of the cause of blindness (demonic or otherwise), whereas the story of the Gerasene demoniac describes an exorcism. Three of these nine Novellen have nothing to do with the art of healing, namely, the accounts of the stilling of the storm, the feeding of the five thousand, and the walking on the sea. The subjects of this class of story are often designated as nature miracles in contradistinction to healing miracles. But the story of the walking on the sea is very different in character from the reports of the stilling of the storm and the miracle of the loaves; it deals with something that is apparitional, and the supernatural action works upon the person of the miracle worker himself as in the

of the story to include the numbers" (Dibelius, *op. cit.*, p. 78, n. 1). Cf. Mark 8:14–21.

case of the transfiguration or of the resurrection appearances. Also, the account of the stilling of the storm with its "muzzling" —πεφίμωσο (Mark 4:39; compare the φιμώθητι—"be muzzled"— of Mark 1:25) seems to be a form of exorcism story; the wind is rebuked as though it were a storm demon which has taken possession of the sea for a time. Again, a Novelle is a typical miracle story partly because its main purpose is to stress the miraculous character of the action described. But in the report of the cleansing of the leper, while the miracle motif is present, it appears to be subordinated to the apologetic purpose of showing that Jesus acts in conformity with the law of Moses; [14] and the story shows no pleasurable interest in the detailed description of trivial matters. Thus one may hold that there is as much (if not more) reason for excluding this story from a list of Novellen as there is for excluding such a story as that contained in Mark 1:23–27.

Dibelius does not deny the importance of considering the content of the stories and he frequently discusses their themes. But he tends to put the emphasis upon stylistic criteria, and as a result he leaves us with a list of Novellen which, in the interests of clarity, need to be classified according to the basic ideas which they represent. As we have already suggested, a miracle story in the broadest sense is that category of narrative (oral or written) which relates an unusual or striking event for the sake of the supernatural explanation it is assumed to require; and this kind of explanation is found in the notion of a transcendent being who invades the sphere of ordinary experience and causes the unusual event in question. Different stories represent the mode of such supernatural action in different ways, and the main classes of miracle story may be conveniently discriminated from this point of view. Thus the action may or may not occur through human mediation. The resurrection, for example, evidently took place by the direct action of God (see Gal. 1:1;

[14] See above, Chapter 2.

Acts 3:24), whereas in the typical miracle stories of the gospels divine power is mediated through the person of Jesus. It should be observed, however, that in primitive Christianity, as well as in the wider world of Hellenistic religion, there was a tendency to merge the idea of mediation into that of identity, so that miraculous deeds could be related of an individual not merely to show that he was an instrument of a transcendent power but to prove that he was really a divine being.[15] Still, provided this point is kept in mind, it may be stated that the Novellen usually belong to the class of miracle stories which represent divine action in terms of human mediation. Again, mediated or unmediated supernatural action may or may not be represented as removing what is held to be the demonic cause of a baneful effect. Hence we arrive at the distinction between exorcism and nonexorcism classes of story and, if we differentiate healing miracles from nature miracles, each of these two classes is seen to be composed of two subclasses. Thus the story of the Gerasene demoniac and the story of the stilling of the storm represent the subclasses of the exorcism class, and the story of the woman with the issue and the story of the feeding of the five thousand represent the subclasses of the nonexorcism class. It is interesting to notice that in 1:34; 3:10–11 and 6:13 the second evangelist himself apparently desires to bring out the distinction between stories of exorcism and stories of other kinds of miraculous healing. That these three passages are of St. Mark's own composition can scarcely be doubted. They all belong to summarizing sections of the gospel. In 1:34 and 3:7–12 we are presented with general statements concerning the Lord's ministry, and in 6:12–13 the account of the sending forth of the twelve is brought to a conclusion with a summary description of their missionary activities. In the evangelist's view, therefore, it may be that some illnesses are cured by applying methods of exorcism, while others call for a different mode of treatment;

[15] Cf. Dibelius, *op. cit.*, pp. 96f.

and perhaps this means that diseases fall into two classes, namely, those which are occasioned by demon possession and those which have other causes. But the data are not sufficient to allow of anything more than a tentative judgment on the matter. From Mark 9:17–18; 9:20–22 and 9:25 we gather that the evangelist could regard very different kinds of affliction, like dumbness, deafness, and epilepsy, as being caused by a single unclean spirit. At first sight the story of the deaf-mute does not seem to involve the demon pathology but, as Deissmann showed,[16] the expression "the bond of his tongue was loosed" (Mark 7:35) is probably not figurative but means that the patient was liberated from the fetters of the demon responsible for his ailment.

At this point certain salient features of the Novellen should be mentioned.[17] The greatness of the miracle, and thereby the greatness of the miracle worker, is frequently stressed by reporting the gravity or long duration of the illness or the failure of others to cure it. The same kind of motif can be detected in the story of the raising of the little girl, where the people laugh Jesus to scorn on his suggestion that the child is really asleep;[18] that is (as in some of the Epidaurus reports), the miracle is made more impressive by being set on the background of the people's scornful skepticism. Sometimes the actual process of healing is represented as though it were too sacred a thing to be witnessed by the general public (see Mark 5:40; 7:33; 8:23). The retention of Semitic formulas in Mark 5:41 and 7:34 illustrates the widespread belief in the special efficacy of esoteric utterances

[16] See his *Light from the Ancient East*, pp. 306ff.

[17] For detailed references to Jewish and Hellenistic miracle literature, see Bultmann, *op. cit.*, pp. 236ff., 247ff.

[18] Mark 5:39f. The idea behind Jesus' assertion is not that he is more capable than the other people of distinguishing apparent death from real death, for he has not yet visited the child. The meaning is rather that he, being already aware of the miracle he is about to perform, can regard the child's state of death as a temporary condition like sleep. Some argue that the story is dependent on that related in Acts 9:36–43 (the raising of Tabitha).

composed of foreign or incomprehensible words.[19] And formulas of this sort, like the piece of advice preserved in Mark 9:29, may have been handed down for the purpose of offering practical guidance to Christian exorcists. We learn from Josephus that Jewish exorcists were in the habit of using incantations which were believed to have been handed down from King Solomon,[20] and this may well have a parallel in the Christian tradition. Other noteworthy features include the notion of transmission of power by contact, the idea of access to authority and control over an individual by the knowledge of his name, the gesture of laying on the hand, the use of saliva as a medicament, the act of looking up to heaven, and the heaving of sighs. It is typical for a Novelle to have its conclusion in the narration of something which served as a demonstration of the reality of the miracle. Thus in Mark 5:13 it is shown that the many demons have left the Gerasene by an account of their entrance into the swine, and in Mark 5:43 we are probably meant to understand that an individual who has really been restored to life (and is no longer a mere shade or spirit) must have material nourishment (cf. Luke 24:41–43). But sometimes, as in the case of certain paradigms, a Novelle is rounded off with a collective exclamation on the part of the spectators who have been stirred by the wonder worker's supernatural deed.

The Novellen of the gospels, then, are primarily concerned with Jesus the thaumaturge, and in them religious faith is represented in the form of implicit confidence in the power of Jesus to perform miraculous deeds. As suggested at the beginning of the present chapter, such confidence was bound up with the fundamental apostolic doctrine of the Messiah's voluntary humiliation. He who was crucified was the Messiah, and evidence of his divine power was to be found in his supernatural works. Hence the Novellen, which dealt with those works, had an im-

[19] Cf. Lucian's ῥῆσις βαρβαρική (*Philopseudes*, 9) and S.-B., IV, 532f.
[20] See *Ant.* 8, 2, 5.

portant doctrinal service to fulfill in the life of the primitive church. But they had also a more directly practical part to play, for the apostolic church cultivated the art of healing and had its miracle workers (cf. I Cor. 12:28). The Novellen depicted the master healer at work, offered advice on specific points of technique and, above all, emphasized the importance of confidence in the effective power of the divinely appointed miracle worker. But it is not to be supposed that the Novellen consider the inner attitude of the patients of Jesus and represent their faith in his power as though it were a psychological prerequisite for his performance of healing miracles. For example, in Mark 5:36 the ruler of the synagogue is exhorted to believe, but there can be no question of the attitude of the patient, as she is already dead; and in Mark 9:23 it is the father of the epileptic boy, not the boy himself, who is told that all things are possible to him who believes. In the Novellen, that is to say, the miracles of Jesus appear to be necessary expressions of his real nature; he radiates supernatural power almost as the sun radiates light, and while confidence is due to him, it is not an external condition which makes his mighty deeds possible. Nevertheless, in the church's actual practice of the arts of miracle working, one may assume that such confidence was found to be a requirement for their successful application. Where there was no faith in the validity of the church's claims and methods, Christian miracle workers would meet with little success; and within the apostolic communities themselves there would be a tendency for miracles to increase in proportion to the intensity of the prevailing faith in their possibility. Hence sayings which stressed the importance of faith would have a practical value in the life of the apostolic church, and this helps to account for the preservation of such sayings, not only in the Novellen but elsewhere in the gospels. Furthermore, these considerations may shed light on the meaning of Mark 6:5-6. This passage (Jesus could do no mighty work) has been taken to be early and historically trustworthy on the ground that it conflicts with the dominant belief (exemplified by the Novellen) in the sovereign character of Jesus' power to perform miracles. But apart from the question of the earliness or the lateness of the report, it is hard to think that it was preserved in the gospel traditions as an expression of the relative impotence of Jesus. Rather, it would serve to emphasize the unbelief in Jesus' compatriots, which precluded them from receiving the blessings enjoyed by believers. Thus it appears that Mark 6:5–6 is not concerned with the supernatural power of Jesus as such, but is meant to illustrate the privations which result from unbelief. Perhaps the reference is specifically to Jewish lack of faith, in which case the present form of the report may owe something to the disappointing experience of Christian missionaries in their unsuccessful work among the Jews.[21]

It is not unlikely that in certain instances the apostolic communities actually took over miracle motifs, and even entire Novellen, from non-Christian sources and with minor modifications applied them to Jesus. For miracle stories of various kinds circulated widely in the surrounding world.[22] It was generally thought that religion should offer health to the body as well as salvation to the soul; and, according to current Jewish expectation, when the days of the Messiah came miracles would be performed, sickness and death would cease to exist, and the power of the demons would be finally broken.[23] But the influence of external conditions of this sort on the development of the gospel traditions can easily be exaggerated. The church as St. Paul knew it was already composed of charismatic communities which ascribed their transcendent power and inspira-

[21] Cf. A. Fridrichsen, *Le problème du miracle*, pp. 51ff., and below, Chapter 6.

[22] Cf. A. Deissmann, *op. cit.*, pp. 393f.

[23] Cf. Isa. 61:1; 4 Ezra 13, 50 ("And then shall he show them very many wonders"); T. Zeb. 9:8 ("And healing and compassion shall be in his wings. He shall redeem all the captivity of the sons of men and Beliar"); and S.-B., I, 593ff.

tion to the person of Jesus the Messiah; and the belief that Jesus worked miracles finds expression not only in the Novellen but also in the paradigms and in various sayings and parables preserved in Q. Such a society with such an orientation could not have arisen so rapidly by a mere process of borrowing ideas from external sources, but must have had its historical origin in the fact that Jesus had actually performed wonderful deeds which were taken as evidence of his supernatural power or, to use Otto's terminology,[24] as signs of the present operation of the inbreaking kingdom.

Accordingly, there does not seem to be any good reason for doubting that Jesus met with considerable success as a worker of miraculous cures, or that in a general way the Novellen of the gospels have a credible historical foundation. *Wunderheilungen* take place at Lourdes even today more or less as they used to take place at ancient Epidaurus. Recent investigations have shown that the mind exercises great power over bodily processes and that a patient's confidence in the means of cure to which he resorts is an important factor in the restoration of his health. Where such confidence is present, the mind is suggestible to ideas of health; on acceptance these ideas tend to become dynamic convictions acting in the patient as an agency making for his recovery. In this way (without the employment of any medicament) remarkable cures can be effected, especially in cases of psychogenic disease. Admittedly, psychological methods of healing are not always successful even in cases that are fairly obviously psychogenic; but they are much less likely to be successful if they are applied to physiogenic cases. It is also important to notice that followers of any particular exponent of the art of spiritual healing have a natural tendency to report his successes and to neglect his failures. Hence on general grounds one would expect the basic stratum of any collec-

[24] See *The Kingdom of God and the Son of Man*, pp. 80, 106, and *passim*.

tion of reports of miraculous healing to be composed for the most part of stories which deal with psychogenic diseases. As far as the illnesses mentioned in the gospel stories are concerned, it seems that all of them can be nervously or psychically conditioned.[25] Thus under the head of demon possession could come schizophrenia and various forms of obsession. Hemorrhages in women can be induced by hysteria; blindness, deafness, and dumbness are not infrequently psychogenic; and it appears that there is a rare form of leprosy (vitiligo) which is nervously occasioned.[26] On the whole, therefore, it seems reasonable to suppose, in the first place, that noteworthy successes in treating cases of psychogenic illness generally constitute the factual basis of a miracle worker's reputation and, in the second place, that the reports of such successes generally provide the nucleus of a collection which tends to expand in the course of time, partly through the inclusion of stories of a different type—such as stories of nature miracles, for example.[27]

[25] Cf. F. Fenner, *Die Krankheit im Neuen Testament*, pp. 42ff.

[26] Cf. Otto, *op. cit.*, pp. 346f., E. R. Micklem, *Miracles and the New Psychology*, pp. 43ff.

[27] Two works to which attention should be called in this general connection are S. V. McCasland, *By the Finger of Gods*, and R. M. Grant, *Miracle and Natural Law in Graeco-Roman and Early Christian Thought*. For an instructive psychological interpretation of a notable modern case of demon possession, see A. Huxley, *The Devils of Loudun*. P. Carrington holds that there is no justification for "the notion that Jesus accepted popular views about demon possession" (*According to Mark*, p. 80). But if Jesus did not share such views, it is strange indeed that his words and actions, as they are represented in the synoptic traditions, should be so obviously calculated to strengthen and promote them. For the view that *Ephphatha* in Mark 7:34 represents Hebrew (not Aramaic), see the article by I. Rabinowitz in *Z.N.T.W.*, LIII (1962), 229ff.

4

The Injunctions to Silence

ST. MARK holds that the miracles of Jesus disclose his messianic status and authority and thus bear witness to the fundamental truth of the apostolic creed. The importance which the evangelist attaches to evidence of this kind is shown by the liberal use he makes of wonder stories in his narrative, and especially by the way in which he emphasizes that the demons recognize the real nature of their conqueror. Nevertheless, in spite of their evidential value, neither the miracles themselves nor the confessions of the demons exercise any discernible influence upon the insight of the people among whom Jesus works. For, in St. Mark's representation, the time has not yet come for the open proclamation of the gospel of the Messiahship, and so the miracles of Jesus are set forth not as public manifestations of the truth but as esoteric indications of a secret fact.

Accordingly, in the first main section of the gospel (1:14–8:26), which covers the greater part of the ministry, the knowledge of the demons stands in remarkable contrast to the ignorance of men. Being endowed with supernatural insight, the demons are able to apprehend the secret which cannot yet be made known to flesh and blood. Thus in the synagogue at Capernaum the man with an unclean spirit cries out:

What have we to do with you, Jesus of Nazareth? You have come to destroy us.[1] I know[2] you who you are, the Holy One of God [1:24].

This passage should be compared with 5:6–7, where the Gerasene demoniac, seeing Jesus from afar, runs and does obeisance to him and cries out with a loud voice:

What have I to do with you, Jesus Son of God the Most High? I adjure you by God, do not torment me.

Each of these addresses occurs as an incident in a particular case of exorcism, and perhaps St. Mark is in each instance simply transmitting traditional material. It is true that the first-mentioned address appears in a passage (1:21–28) which seems to show signs of having been subjected to editorial treatment. But, as we have previously suggested, verses 23–26, 27a, and 27c (?) may well be remnants of a Novelle which was already current before the evangelist undertook his work.[3]

Nevertheless, it is made apparent in two passages of a different character, 1:32–34 and 3:7–12, that St. Mark himself is anxious to draw the reader's attention to the secret knowledge of the demons. In the first of these passages, it will be recalled, "the whole city" gathers round the door of Simon's house and Jesus cures many of their ills and expels many demons; the last clause (v. 34c) reads:

---

[1] This clause does not seem to be a question. Since the demon knows who Jesus really is, we may presume that it also knows the purpose of his coming.

[2] The reading οἴδαμεν—"we know"—(Cod. Sin., Origen, Eusebius, etc.) is probably due to a copyist who wished to bring the original form of the verb into agreement with the plural ἡμῖν. The demon apparently speaks on behalf of the whole kingdom of demons.

[3] See above, Chapter 2.

And he did not permit the demons to speak, because they knew him.[4]

In the second passage Jesus and his disciples retire to the seaside; a large multitude of people, drawn from widely separated areas, is present, and a little boat is made ready for use in case the thronging of the crowd should become unbearable (see 4:1); Jesus heals many and the sick press upon him in their eagerness to receive health-giving power by touching him (5:25; 6:56). The passage concludes with the words:

And the unclean spirits when they beheld him fell down before him and cried, saying, You are the Son of God. And he charged them much that they should not make him manifest.

Accordingly, in 1:32–34 and 3:7–12, as in 6:54–56, we are presented with summary descriptions of the activities of Jesus. The evangelist is apparently seeking to give some idea of the success of the healing ministry as a whole, and with this end in view he generalizes from the particular incidents related in current stories. Admittedly, specific occasions are described; thus in 1:32–34 it is the end of the sabbath and a crowd has gathered before Simon's house, and in 3:7–12 Jesus withdraws to the seashore and a multitude follows him. But in each case the particularities of the specific situation described subserve the writer's purpose of conveying a general impression and provide an appropriate setting for a summary statement. It seems, therefore, that the imperfect tenses in 1:34c and 3:11–12 should be taken seriously and that we should translate as follows:

And he would not permit [that is, habitually] the demons to speak, because they knew him.

---

[4] Some ancient authorities (including B) have "to be Christ" after "they knew him." These additional words, though justifiable exegetically, were probably introduced into the Markan text by a scribe who had the Lukan parallel in mind (Luke 4:41).

And the unclean spirits whenever they beheld him used to fall down before him and would cry, saying, You are the Son of God. But he would charge them much that they should not make him manifest.

Two objections to this interpretation may be made on grounds of style. In the first place, it may be pointed out that ὅταν in St. Mark's gospel usually means "when" (not "whenever"). Thus Turner observes [5] that in fourteen instances out of twenty repeated action is quite excluded, and he cites 9:9; 13:14; and 14:25 as containing good examples. In each of these three passages, however, the accompanying verb is in the subjunctive mood, and the reference is to a future event—the resurrection of the Son of Man in 9:9, the abomination of desolation in 13:14, and the drinking of the fruit of the vine in the kingdom of God in 14:25. On the other hand, apart from 3:11, ὅταν does not occur in the gospel with a verb in the imperfect tense of the indicative mood, though in 11:19 and in 11:25 (reading στήκετε, not στήκητε [B] or στῆτε [ℵ]) it appears with an aorist indicative and with a present indicative respectively. Its meaning in 11:19 may be, and in 11:25 must be "whenever." Hence one may reasonably suppose that its meaning is "whenever" in 3:11. In the second place, it may be objected that St. Mark uses imperfect and aorist tenses indifferently. Thus in 6:54–56 there are eight finite verbs in the indicative mood, of which four are in the aorist and four in the imperfect tense; they occur as follows: aorist (περιέδραμον), aorist (ἤρξαντο), imperfect (ἤκουον), imperfect (εἰσεπορεύετο), aorist (ἐτίθεσαν), imperfect (παρεκάλουν), aorist (ἤψαντο), imperfect (ἐσῴζοντο). Nevertheless, it seems significant that in 1:34 and in 3:7–12 St. Mark should cease to put the main verbs in the aorist tense when he comes to refer to the injunctions to silence. Thus the verb of 1:34a (ἐθεράπευσεν) and the verb of 1:34b (ἐξέβαλεν) are in the aorist indicative,

[5] See *N.C.H.S.*, pt. 3, p. 60.

whereas the introductory verb of 1:34c ($\H{\eta}\phi\iota\epsilon\nu$) is in the imperfect indicative; and in 3:7–12 the main verbs of verses 7–10 are all in the aorist indicative ($\mathring{\alpha}\nu\epsilon\chi\acute\omega\rho\eta\sigma\epsilon\nu$—$\mathring{\eta}\kappa o\lambda o\acute\upsilon\theta\eta\sigma\epsilon\nu$—$\mathring{\eta}\lambda\theta o\nu$—$\epsilon\mathring\iota\pi\epsilon\nu$—$\mathring\epsilon\theta\epsilon\rho\acute\alpha\pi\epsilon\upsilon\sigma\epsilon\nu$), whereas in 3:11–12 the main verbs are all in the imperfect indicative ($\mathring\epsilon\theta\epsilon\acute\omega\rho o\upsilon\nu$—$\pi\rho o\sigma\acute\epsilon\pi\iota\pi\tau o\nu$—$\mathring\epsilon\kappa\rho\alpha\zeta o\nu$—$\mathring\epsilon\pi\epsilon\tau\acute\iota\mu\alpha$). This parallelism, we suggest, is not fortuitous but rather is due to the design of the evangelist, who feels that the imperfect tense is more appropriate than the aorist in a statement whose general import he wishes to emphasize. For, while he does not employ the tenses with the precision of a writer in classical Greek, it would be rash to assume that the original distinction between the aorist and the imperfect in no way affects his manner of writing. And even with respect to 6:54–56 it is not impossible that he introduces the imperfects partly because he desires to use a particular situation as the basis for a characterization of the success of the healing ministry in general.

The demons, then, are aware of the real nature of Jesus, and in virtue of their knowledge they are able to perform a function in the first main section of the gospel which corresponds to that performed by the heavenly voice in the preface. They can give articulate expression to the truth and thus provide a mode of supernatural testimony to the reality of the Messiahship. Their confessions are made all the more impressive through being set on the background of man's failure to perceive the truth. On being confronted by Jesus, the demons at once acknowledge his Messiahship, whereas the human beings who witness his words and works are moved only to amazement or to surprised questionings among themselves. The typical reaction of the public finds illustration in such passages as the following:

And they were all amazed insomuch that they questioned among themselves, saying, What is this? A new teaching with authority! He commands even the unclean spirits and they obey him. And the report of him went out immediately everywhere into all the region of Galilee round about [1:27f.].

And he arose and immediately took up his bed and went out before them all, insomuch that they were all amazed and glorified God, saying, We never saw the like of it! [2:12].

The response of the disciples betrays no deeper insight than that of the multitude, and is characterized in the following passages from the stories of the stilling of the storm and of the raising of the little girl:

And they feared exceedingly and said one to another, Who then is this, that even the wind and the sea obey him? [4:41].

And immediately the little girl arose. . . . And they were amazed immediately with great amazement [5:42].

Thus even a demonstration of the Master's power to restore the dead to life is not sufficient to bring even his most intimate disciples to an acknowledgment of the secret of his person.

This contrast between the knowledge of the demons and the ignorance of human beings is maintained until the occasion of Peter's confession at Caesarea Philippi (8:29). After this event, apart from a passing reference in 9:20 to the agitation of a demon which indicates that it senses its conqueror, St. Mark makes no further mention of the knowledge of the demons. Henceforth, the contrast is rather between the disciples, who now enjoy divine [6] knowledge of their Master's Messiahship, and the uninitiated multitude who remain in a state of ignorance. Thus, from 8:29 onwards, St. Mark comes to adopt a point of view which is more analogous to that of the fourth evangelist. For, in St. John's gospel, the demons do not appear at all; there is only one evil power, Satan or the prince of this world, and only the disciples confess that Jesus is the Messiah and they, as representatives of believers, stand in contrast to the Jews, the typical

---

[6] Cf. I Cor. 12:3 ("No man can say, Jesus is Lord, but in the Holy Spirit").

opponents of Jesus, who are blind to the truth.[7] It must be noticed, however, that the disciples in the second gospel are never so truly representative of the elect as they are in the fourth gospel. In St. Mark's view, the disciples to the end of the ministry are incapable of comprehending the essential significance of their Master's Messiahship.

But the manifest failure of men to recognize the truth is not to be understood as a frustration of the purpose of Jesus. On the contrary, according to St. Mark's interpretation, it is actually a fulfillment of that purpose. The Lord deliberately intends that men should not discover his divine status and accept him for what he really is—the Messiah, the Son of God. Hence he takes precautions to prevent the knowledge of the demons from being disseminated among the people to whom he ministers. He enjoins the demons to silence; and, similarly, immediately after Peter's confession, he imposes the same injunction to silence upon his disciples:

And he charged them that they should tell no man of him [8:30].

The charge is reiterated a week later (9:2) while Jesus, accompanied by Peter, James, and John, is descending the mountain on which the transfiguration has just taken place; but on this occasion it is indicated that they are to guard the secret only for a limited period of time:

And as they were coming down from the mountain, he charged them that they should tell no man what things they had seen, save when the Son of Man should have risen from the dead [9:9].

Thus it is apparent that, according to the evangelist's interpretation, it was the will of Jesus that the saving truth of his Mes-

[7] Cf. John 6:68f. (the confession of Simon Peter); John 20:28 (the confession of Thomas which, however, takes place in the presence of the *risen* Jesus). In John 8:44 it is stated that it is the will of the Jews to act according to the desires of their father, the devil, who has no truth in him.

siahship should not be openly proclaimed to the world prior to his resurrection.

This conception of the messianic secret would follow as a natural consequence from St. Mark's fundamental conviction that the whole career of Jesus is a fulfillment of the saving purpose of God. On the one hand, he upholds the apostolic belief that Jesus is the Messiah whose coming was foretold in the scriptures and whose divine status was revealed in all his words and works. On the other hand, he holds as a matter of historical fact that Jesus was not recognized as the Messiah by his own nation, but was rejected and even handed over to the Gentiles to be crucified. Hence, by resorting to the conception of the secret, St. Mark is able to maintain the apostolic belief in the Messiahship without denying the plain facts of the historical traditions. Jesus, the Messiah of the church's gospel, was not accepted as such by his own people because his messianic nature was a divinely appointed secret, that is, something concealed from the multitude as a direct result of the Lord's deliberate intention. Thus, so far from being a contravention of the divine purpose, the nonacceptance of Jesus is seen to be a requirement of God's predetermined plan of salvation.

But it would be erroneous to suppose that St. Mark carries out the idea of the secret with perfect consistency. We notice, for example, that there is considerable strain on the secret in the story of the triumphal entry (11:7–10), while in 14:62 Jesus even acknowledges before the sanhedrin that he is the Son of Man who is destined to appear at the right hand of the Power and is coming with the clouds of heaven. Other passages which may be mentioned in this connection are: 2:1–12 and 2:23–28, where Jesus publicly refers to himself as the Son of Man; 10:46–52, where blind Bartimaeus addresses Jesus as the Son of David; and 12:1–12, where the enemies of Jesus realize that the parable of the wicked husbandmen is spoken against them. In these passages (which will have more detailed consideration in later chapters) the public are allowed to receive a revelation which, according to the requirement of secrecy, should be reserved for the chosen disciples. With respect to 14:62, we may assume that Jesus is represented as making an open confession to his Messiahship partly because the evangelist wishes to show that it is the Jewish leaders who carry the burden of guilt for the crime of the crucifixion; they condemn Jesus not in ignorance, but with a full knowledge of his claims. The same kind of motive may also be involved in 12:12. But, taken as a whole, the six passages we have mentioned suggest that a deeper tendency is at work. It is as though the evangelist's confidence in the eschatological manifestation of the Messiah were pressing for characterization (with varying degrees of success) in his portrayal of the incarnate life. A similar impression is conveyed by the story of the transfiguration, although in this case the objective sphere of divine revelation is not permitted to extend beyond the circle of the elect. According to the doctrine of the secret, complete manifestation of the Messiah's heavenly glory belongs to the future, so that the lowliness and the sufferings of the Lord's earthly career are of the nature of a prelude to his parousia in triumph as the Son of Man. And such, so it seems, is the point of view which St. Mark usually takes. But in the particular passages under consideration the revelation of the fact of the Messiahship is in some measure de-reserved, so that once again, though this time in a more general sense, it may be said that to a greater or less extent St. Mark comes to adopt a position which is more analogous to that of the fourth evangelist. For, according to St. John, the incarnation is not a concealment but an open revelation of the Messiah's true nature (to which, however, the enemies of Jesus are blind), and even the hour of the passion may be referred to in terms of exaltation or glorification.[8]

[8] Cf. John 1:14; 12:23; 12:32. Another group of passages which causes difficulty in relation to St. Mark's doctrine of the secret includes Mark

It appears, then, that in the first main section of St. Mark's gospel the demons, unlike human beings, are aware of the fact of the Messiahship and that Jesus enjoins the demons to silence in order to prevent their supernatural knowledge from being disseminated among the people to whom he ministers. That the evangelist understands 1:24–25 in this fashion would seem to be shown by his comments in 1:34c and 3:11–12, especially when these passages are considered in the light of 8:30 and 9:9. Accordingly, as Wrede maintained,[9] the idea of the secret in St. Mark's gospel is essentially a theological mode of representation, and hence it is not to be adjudged by the application of biographical standards. Thus the scene of 1:23ff. is set in the synagogue at Capernaum on a sabbath day; a congregation has apparently assembled for divine service; suddenly a man with an unclean spirit appears, and addressing Jesus cries out that he is the Holy One of God, whereupon Jesus utters a potent command; to the amazement of all who are present, the demon is at once expelled from the man. Now, if the question were raised, one would naturally say that the members of the congregation could hardly fail to hear the demon's address; for the possessed is in the synagogue and cries out aloud. Nevertheless, St. Mark himself construes the injunction to silence in the sense of a command to secrecy, and therefore takes it for granted that the congregation does not hear what the demon says to Jesus. In other words, on the evangelist's interpretation the story is not convincing; the injunction to silence comes too late, since the secret has already been divulged. This consideration, however, only serves to indicate that St. Mark does not see the situation in this perspective. His concern is not so much with the niceties of credible historical description as with the problem raised by the

1:15b; 4:13; 4:40; 7:18; and 8:14–21, where the evangelist evidently expects the disciples or the public to make the same kind of response to Jesus as that which he himself makes. Cf. below, Chapter 5.

[9] See *Das Messiasgeheimnis*, p. 66.

nonacceptance of Jesus. Confronted by this urgent theological problem, he seeks to make it plain to his readers that the demons are aware of Jesus' identity and that precautions are taken to prevent their knowledge from being noised abroad in human society. But since he is not a biographer in the modern meaning of the term, the question of the audibility of the demon's address in 1:24 does not occur to him.

On the other hand, the fact that a congregation is present when the possessed cries out affords some confirmation for our presumption that in 1:23ff. (as distinct from 1:34 and 3:11f.) the evangelist is not creating a new narrative, but for the most part is transmitting traditional material derived from a Novelle already in circulation. Despite its brevity, the passage certainly exemplifies several motifs which are characteristic of the category of exorcism stories, as is shown in the following enumeration:

1. Vv. 23f.   The demon is disturbed on sensing its conqueror. Cf. Lucian, *Apokeruttomenos*, 6 ("But if she sees any physician and only hears that he is one, she is especially incited against him"). Cf. also, Mark 9:20. In Acts 19:16 the demon even provokes its victim to attack and overpower the would-be exorcists.

2. Vv. 23f.   The demon speaks through the person it possesses. Cf. Lucian, *Philopseudes*, 16 ("The patient himself is silent, but the demon answers in Greek or in the language of whatever foreign country he comes from"). Philostratus, *Vita Ap.*, 3:38 ("The demon discovered himself [spoke out] using my child as an actor").

3. V. 24.   The demon knows the power of the exorcist. Cf. *Altorientalische Texte* (ed. H. Gressmann), pp. 78f. ("The evil spirit says to the Egyptian god who is brought to the patient, You come in peace, great god, you who destroy the evil spirits"). See also R. Reitzenstein, *Hellenistische Wundererzählungen*, 124, and Bultmann, *Die Geschichte der synoptischen Tradition*, p. 239.

4. V. 24. The demon seeks to gain access to apotropaic power by using its opponent's name. Cf. Mark 5:7; Acts 16:17. Cf. Josephus, *Ant.* 8, 2, 5 for the use of Solomon's name by the Jewish exorcist Eleazar; in Lucian, *Philopseudes*, 10, reference is made to the belief that cures can be effected through sacred names. Cf. also Mark 9:38; Acts 3:6. Thus the device of naming the name could be employed in attack (by the exorcist) and in self-defence (by the demon).

5. V. 25. The verb φιμοῦν (lit. "to muzzle") is a characteristic expression for binding (καταδεῖν) the demon. Cf. E. Rhode, *Psyche*, pp. 603f. In Mark 4:39 (πεφίμωσο) the reference seems to be to the binding of the demon of the storm. For a modern parallel, cf. the words of Blumhardt (*Briefliche Äusserungen aus Bad Boll*): "I never permit the demons to speak. I command them to be silent" (cited by R. Otto, *The Kingdom of God and the Son of Man*, p. 349, cf. p. 346, n. 2).

6. V. 25. Ἔξελθε ἐξ αὐτοῦ. Cf. ἔξελθε ἀπὸ τοῦ Δ—κοι—, line 3013, leaf 33, the Great Magical Papyrus (Paris), reproduced by A. Deissmann, *Light from the Ancient East*, p. 251 (cf. p. 256, n. 1). Exactly the same formula as that in the papyrus occurs in Luke 4:35 (which has ἀπό instead of St. Mark's ἐκ). For the Hebrew equivalent, cf. S.-B., I, 760 (אצ).

7. V. 27. The spectators are amazed at the miracle. Cf. Mark 2:12; 5:16; 7:37; Philostratus, *Vita Ap.*, 4:20 ("They clapped their hands in wonder"). For the use of ἅπαντες in this connection, cf. Mark 2:12; Acts 9:35; and for the use of ἐθαμβήθησαν ("they were amazed"), cf. Luke 5:9; Acts 3:10 (θάμβος—"amazement").

Thus it appears that the principal elements of 1:23ff. may be explained as characteristic features of a typical miracle story which St. Mark reproduces in abbreviated form and with its introduction and conclusion adapted to the requirements of its context in the gospel. But in this case the address of the demon (v. 24) and the injunction to silence (v. 25) have a meaning within the framework of the story itself and quite independently of the evangelist's doctrine of the messianic secret. Hence we must now seek to determine that earlier meaning on the lines just indicated in our general survey of the narrative's typical motifs.

The parallels suggest that the injunction to silence in its original significance has nothing to do with the idea of concealing a mystery; the verb φιμοῦν ("to muzzle") seems to have been commonly employed in incantations as a technical term for binding a demon and thus subduing it to the will of the exorcist. As an angry dog is rendered harmless when it is muzzled and can no longer bark, so a demon's hostile power is broken when it is brought to silence. But though composed of quasi-technical expressions, Jesus' command is remarkable alike for its simplicity and its brevity. Unlike the demon, Jesus does not make an elaborate declaration; his supernatural power is such that he needs no sacred name, no mysterious formula, and no expression of special gnosis. He commands only that the demon should end its speech and leave its victim. He speaks as the plenipotentiary of God; and as he speaks, so it comes to pass. For the demon's cry in verse 26 does not signify disobedience to the injunction to silence. On the contrary, like the accompanying convulsive movements, it serves only to show that the demon is already reduced to a state of impotence; the creature's nefarious strength utterly fails before the invincible might of him whose coming is destined to seal the doom of Satan's kingdom. Jesus utters the authoritative word and the demon can do no more than make futile (if violent) agitations and force an inarticulate cry prior to taking its abrupt departure like a fugitive thief dispossessed of his spoils (cf. Mark 9:26).

With respect to the demon's address in verse 24, the parallels suggest that it would be originally intended not as a confession, but as a weapon of defense or instrument of apotropaic power. The unclean spirit is evidently disturbed on sensing the menace of impending disaster, and raises its voice to defend itself against its opponent who threatens to launch an attack. Fridrichsen, however, objected to an exegesis of this kind on the ground that the demon's utterance is too elaborate to be used as a mere instrument of self-defense.[10] He thinks that such a moment of supreme danger is hardly a fitting occasion for a prolix address. Hence, while not denying that the apotropaic motif may have been present in the first instance, he contends that the address as it now stands was elaborated (apparently before the story came into St. Mark's hands) for the apologetic purpose of protecting Jesus against the calumny of those who declared that he was in league with Beelzebul, the prince of the demons (see Mark 3:22ff.; Matt. 12:24ff.; Luke 11:15ff.). In their perversity some of the human enemies of Jesus allege that he is an agent of Satan, but the unclean spirit knows that he is the Holy One of God and subverts the allegation by proclaiming the truth to the world. As Fridrichsen himself puts it:

Comment peut-on parler de l'alliance et du secours de Beelzeboul, quand les Esprits eux-mêmes appellent Jésus le Saint de Dieu? [11]

Thus in verse 24 we are presented with a form of early Christian apologetics in which the falsity of the Beelzebul charge is exposed by the demons themselves. The spirit's address is a confession designed to give proof of the divine character of the source whence Jesus derives the supernatural power to perform his miraculous deeds.

But while the unclean spirit undoubtedly gives expression to the truth concerning Jesus, there does not seem to be sufficient warrant for the suggestion that its confession in verse 24 was deliberately framed with a view to refuting the Beelzebul charge. The Beelzebul controversy is dealt with in Mark 3:22ff. and in Matt. 12:24ff./Luke 11:15ff., but in neither case is there any reference to the confessions of the demons. Moreover, the argument that the address of verse 24 is too prolix to be used by

[10] *Le problème du miracle*, pp. 78f.   [11] See *op. cit.*, p. 79.

the demon as a mere instrument of self-defence against the impending onslaught of the exorcist, is far from convincing. The address includes but three concise clauses, and if these are read as though they were meant to have apotropaic significance, the two affirmations which follow on the opening question are seen to increase the effectiveness of the utterance as a defensive weapon. Neither assertion is superfluous. The demon knows the divine purpose of Jesus' coming and the divine character of his status; and by giving full expression to its knowledge it seeks to ward off the threatened offensive of its dangerous opponent. The remainder of the story shows the utter futility of its defensive efforts and thus brings out the absolute nature of the authority of Jesus; his compulsive power is such that he can break down the strongest forms of demonic resistance by the utterance of the simplest commands.

That the whole address is a formula of defense and an integral part of the story in its original form has been persuasively argued by O. Bauernfeind in his monograph on the utterances of the demons in St. Mark's gospel.[12] The opening question, so it appears, is not a free construction, but is formed after the analogy of the question given in I Kings 17:18 (LXX, III Kings), where the widow of Zarephath would drive away the terrible man of God, Elijah, who, she thinks, has brought disaster upon her household:

What have I to do with you, man of God? You have come in to me to bring my offences to remembrance and to slay my son!

Philo expressly refers to these words in an interesting passage,[13] and the way in which he utilizes them suggests that the widow's utterance may have served as the model for a current apotropaic formula. The passage reads:

To return to the book of Kings. Every mind that is about to be widowed and bereft of evils says to the prophet, Man of God, you

---

[12] *Die Worte der Dämonen im Markusevangelium*, pp. 3ff., 29ff., 68f.
[13] See *Immut.* 29.

have come in to me to bring my iniquity and my sin to remembrance.

As in Mark 1:24, the individual who speaks is under the influence of a supernatural power, though in this case the power is
not demonic but divine. The mind is conscious of its self-identity
and yet, as Philo goes on to explain in what follows the quotation
above, it is in a state of God-sent frenzy. For the divine Logos,
the interpreter and prophet of God, has just entered the soul and
is bringing it to newness of life. But the divinely inspired process
of spiritual regeneration induces the painful recollection of past
sins and the mind seems to be inclined (if only temporarily)
to resist the power of the indwelling Logos, which it addresses
partly in terms of an utterance whose apotropaic significance
was perhaps widely known.[14] If this is so, the words τί ἐμοὶ
καὶ σοί (which lay special emphasis on the motif of self-defence)
may have been omitted because the mind's desire to drive away
its heavenly visitor is not firmly established; the wish is checked
and finally overruled by the knowledge that the presence of the
Logos is really something to be prized beyond all else.

[14] This explanation differs from that proposed by Bauernfeind (*op. cit.*,
pp. 5–10), who thinks that the mind greets the Logos with an address
of welcome. He takes the view that the widow's utterance had become
the scriptural prototype of a current apotropaic formula, but he proceeds to argue that when Philo took it over he radically modified its
meaning. That is to say, in Philo's passage an instrument of self-defence
has become an address of welcome; but Bauernfeind allows that the formula is not entirely deprived of its apotropaic significance, since the mind
seeks to ward off the evil influence of its past sins. Such an explanation,
however, seems to be unduly complicated. Bauernfeind's further suggestion (p. 12) that the demon of Mark 1:24 may be identifying itself
with the widow is not acceptable in view of the plurals ἡμῖν and ἡμᾶς,
which seem to indicate that it identifies itself with all the members of
its kind. And there appears to be no real warrant for his more general
suggestion that the self-identification of the demon in Mark 1:24 should
be taken to correspond to the self-identification of Simon, the false
prophet of Samaria (pp. 1–3, 10–13; cf. Acts 8:9ff., Origen, *c. Celsum*, 7,
9, and John 8:48). There would be a real analogy between the two cases
only if the possessed of Mark 1:24 sought to gain power of compulsion
over Jesus by identifying himself with the possessing demon.

It appears, then, that in the address of Mark 1:24 the demon attempts to overcome the menacing onslaught of the exorcist and may be resorting to a current apotropaic formula of scriptural derivation. The demons were masters of the magical arts,[15] and, as we learn from such a story as the Q account of the temptations (Matt. 4:1ff./Luke 4:1ff.), the prince of the demons was well versed in the scriptures! And the "I know" clause with which the address is concluded may have originally belonged to the same circle of ideas as the formula apparently utilized in the earlier part of the address. At all events, statements of a similar character occur in the incantations of extant Hellenistic magical papyri. The following passages are taken from a magical papyrus of the fourth or fifth century,[16] now in the British Museum:

[I know] your name which was received in heaven, I know your forms. . . .

I know your foreign names and your true name. . . .

I know you, Hermes, who you are and whence you are. . . .

The resemblance of this last example to Mark 1:24c is particularly striking. As we have already maintained, however, St. Mark himself construes the address of verse 24 in the sense of his idea of the messianic secret. In his interpretation, that is to say, what seems to have been originally intended as an apotropaic utterance becomes a confession or mode of supernatural witness to the Messiahship; and the formula for binding the demon in verse 25 becomes an injunction to secrecy.[17]

---

[15] Cf. Bauernfeind, *op. cit.*, pp. 12f.

[16] No. 122; see Bauernfeind, *op. cit.*, pp. 14f., and R. Reitzenstein, *Poimandres*, p. 20.

[17] Bauernfeind would object to this exegesis (*op. cit.*, esp. pp. 76ff.; cf. pp. 56ff.—re Mark 3:11f.—where, however, the discussion is somewhat discursive and obscure). If we understand him aright, Bauernfeind's

Injunctions to Silence

Besides the injunctions to silence imposed upon the demons, there are, in the first main section of the gospel, four passages, namely, 1:44; 5:43; 7:36; 8:26, where human beings are enjoined to keep silence, in each instance concerning a miracle which Jesus has just performed. The injunction is disobeyed in 1:45 (if the first word of the verse refers to the patient) and in 7:36 (cf. 5:20?). But this disobedience is not to be taken literally as an actual frustration of the purpose of Jesus. The idea is rather that the Lord's real nature necessarily expresses itself

principal contention in this connection is that St. Mark would not attach importance to the testimony of the demons since in the cosmological dualism of primitive Christianity the essential function of the demons is to wage total war against the kingdom which Jesus represents. They are not yet subdued to the will of God, and their hostility is so great that they could in no wise be brought into the service of the Messiah. The kingdom of God and the kingdom of Satan are diametrically opposed to each other, and representatives of the latter kingdom would not be given a role in the gospel which might have been played by angels and which corresponds to the role assigned to the heavenly voice in 1:11 and 9:7. The charge that Jesus is aided by Beelzebul is vigorously opposed in 3:22ff. Also, the demons, being agents of Satan, are instruments of falsity and do not know the truth (cf. John 8:48). In Jas. 2:19f. the demons believe and are terrified, but their faith is valueless because it does not issue in works. But to interpret the demons' recognition of Jesus' true nature as a form of supernatural witness to the Messiahship does not necessarily detract from their hostility or in any way incapacitate them for the waging of a total war. In knowing that Jesus comes as Messiah the demons know that the doom of the kingdom of Satan is near, yet their knowledge, so far from mitigating the violence of the conflict between the two kingdoms, apparently intensifies it by inciting the demons to make a final and supreme effort in desperation. Doubtless agents of Satan are inherently evil and represent falsity. But to stress the point that even the demons are forced to testify to the truth in this particular case only sets in stronger light (a) the reality of the Messiahship and (b) the ignorance of men. The truth about Jesus has such compelling power that the demons, despite their evil nature, cannot but acknowledge it; yet men do not know it and (for the present) are not meant to know it. Jas. 2:19 seems to presuppose that the demons know the truth of faith; the demons' utterances bear witness to the truth, but not their deeds!

if only in the form of a miracle worker's widespread fame. In St. Mark's interpretation, the miraculous deeds of Jesus are the deeds not of an ordinary miracle worker but of the Messiah himself; and in view of the fact that the miracles were not construed in this sense by the public that witnessed them, the evangelist maintains that it was part of the divine plan of salvation that they should not have been properly understood. It was a direct consequence of God's predetermined purpose that the people should not appreciate the miracles of Jesus as manifestations of his messianic dignity; and hence the Lord deliberately takes precautions to prevent his miraculous works from disclosing his real status and enjoins silence upon the witnesses of his mighty deeds.

As Dibelius has pointed out,[18] it is important to distinguish the injunctions to silence of 5:43, 7:36, and 8:26 from the secrecy which belongs to the miraculous processes described in the stories to which the injunctions are attached. Thus we learn from 5:37 and 5:40 that only the three most intimate disciples and the child's parents are allowed to witness the raising of the little girl; the injunction comes almost at the end of the story in verse 43a:

And he charged them much that no one should know it.

In the concluding clause (v. 43b) Jesus requests that the little girl be given something to eat—a feature which was perhaps introduced by the evangelist who wished to supply additional evidence for the success of the miracle. Again, in the story of the healing of the deaf-mute, the medical operations are not permitted to begin before the patient has been taken aside from the multitude privately (7:33). The story is rounded off with a notice which has all the appearance of being a generalizing comment of the evangelist; it reads:

[18] See *From Tradition to Gospel*, pp. 73, 94.

And he charged them [that is, presumably, the multitude], that they should tell no one; but the more he charged them, the more exceedingly they made it public. And they were astonished beyond measure, saying, He has done all things well; he causes even the deaf to hear and the dumb to speak [vv. 36f.].

Finally, in the report concerning the blind man of Bethsaida, we are informed (8:23) that Jesus takes the patient by the hand and restores his sight outside the village; the report ends with the injunction to silence in verse 26:

And he sent him away to his home, saying, Tell it to no one in the village.[19]

The secrecy which is attached to the miraculous processes in these three cases may be due to the influence of the notion that divine action should be concealed from the profane eyes of the public;[20] the same motif is exemplified in popular wonder stories of widely separated cultures. On the other hand, in each of the three instances, the almost stereotyped injunction to silence does not seem to constitute an integral part of the preceding story (which has already reached a characteristic conclusion in the demonstration of the success of the miracle) and is evidently a

[19] Turner supports this (k) reading; see *N.C.H.S.*, pt. 3, pp. 78, 727f. Turner observes that St. Mark uses εἰς habitually for "in" as well as "into" (cf. 1:9), and scholars were tempted to adapt his phrases to grammatical rule by inserting or substituting some part of the verb "come" or "enter" (B has done this, for instance, in 1:21, 39; 8:26), or else by changing εἰς (with acc.) to ἐν (with dat.) as B does in 2:1. The Latin evidence does not help us to decide between two Greek prepositions since early translators rendered such details of the Greek into the idiom of their own language; but in 8:26, the only texts to give one verb only, and that the right one—"Tell it to no one (into the village)"—are the Codex Bobiensis (k) and one other Old Latin MS.

[20] Cf. Mark 9:25a (in 9:29 the recipe against the deaf and dumb spirit is passed on esoterically); Acts 9:40; I Kings 17:19. For references to nonbiblical stories, see Bultmann, *op. cit.*, p. 239, n. 4. This secrecy is not involved in such stories as Mark 1:23ff.; 2:1ff.; 3:1ff.

supplementary notice appended by the evangelist himself. In the injunctions of 5:43 and 7:36, as in 8:15 and 9:9, the verb διαστέλλεσθαι ("to charge strictly") is used; and in 8:26 it appears that εἰς ("into") is employed with the meaning of ἐν ("in"), as in 1:9 and 2:1 (reading εἰς οἶκον with D and other authorities). The injunction is disobeyed in 7:36, so that the miraculous deeds of Jesus are proclaimed seemingly against his will. One may perhaps be permitted to compare 1:45 and 5:20; but a surer parallel is to be found in 7:24b:

And he went into a house and desired no one to know it; and he could not be concealed.

As we have already suggested, the idea is not that Jesus was actually frustrated, but that his real nature was such that he could not escape winning a great reputation as a performer of miracles. Although it is not reported that the injunctions of 5:43 and 8:26 were disobeyed, it would be practically impossible to carry them out, for the little girl and the blind man could hardly be expected to spend the rest of their days in hiding. The difficulty is particularly acute in the case of the little girl; the funeral arrangements have been made, the mourners have already assembled in the house (5:38b) and are aware that the child is dead when Jesus enters the room where the corpse lies. But St. Mark does not consider the matter in this aspect, any more than he considers the historical difficulty caused by the audibility of the demon's confession in 1:24.

It is probable that the injunction to silence of 1:44 is also to be interpreted in the light of St. Mark's conception of the messianic secret; and it may be argued that the evangelist actually interpolated verse 43 and the words ὅρα μηδενὶ μηδὲν εἴπῃς, ἀλλά ("see you say nothing to anyone, but") of verse 44 into the text of the story of the cleansing of the leper as he received it.[21]

---

[21] Cf. Bultmann, *op. cit.*, p. 227. Carrington writes of 1:40–45: "It contains the first of the famous commands to keep silence, which are most

On the other hand, one would have thought that the doctrine of the secret itself would hardly require the employment of such forceful language as that used in verse 43, for even if the ἐμβριμησάμενος is allowed to have the meaning "having given strict orders" (cf. Matt. 9:30), the ἐξέβαλεν ("cast out") seems to express an affective violence which accords well with the emotional tone already given to the story by the ὀργισθείς ("moved to anger") in verse 41. Thus it is not unlikely that verse 43 was included in the story before it came into St. Mark's hands and, if this is so, we may infer on a priori grounds that the words ὅρα μηδενὶ μηδὲν εἴπῃς, ἀλλά were also included in the pre-Markan form of the story. For when orders are given in a mood of angry irritation, they usually contain a negative command, that is, a prohibition of the action (whether actual or possible) which occasions the speaker's irritation. Accordingly, we should assume that, with the exception of verse 45, St. Mark is transmitting the text of the story substantially in the form in which he found it, and hence that verse 43 and the interdiction of verse 44 (like the injunction to silence of 1:25) have a significance which is independent of the evangelist's doctrine of the secret.

Seeing that no spectators are mentioned in the story, one could suggest that the original idea behind verses 43–44a is that the nature of the cure is a holy thing which must on no account be profaned by being disclosed to the public. But this story does not refer to any mysterious technique (such as that described in 7:32ff. or 8:22f.) and no special medical formula or prescription (such as that of 9:29) is given. An alternative possibility is

---

naturally explained by the simple suggestion that Jesus did not like this kind of publicity" (*According to Mark*, p. 55). But why should the injunctions to silence of vv. 25 and 34 of the same chapter not be "famous"? And if the Jesus of St. Mark's representation does not like publicity, why is it that in the next pericope (2:1ff.) he stages a public demonstration of his capacity to forgive sins by performing a miraculous healing?

that Jesus does not advertise his miraculous powers after the manner of the ordinary wonder worker.[22] But neither this nor the preceding suggestion seems to offer a satisfactory explanation of the emotional agitation evinced in verse 43, which in all probability has a cause similar to that of the ὀργισθείς in verse 41.[23] Jesus is displeased with the leper because he has not complied with the provisions of the law of Moses; and the continued displeasure of verse 43 is perhaps occasioned by the thought that the man will further contravene the law by associating with healthy people and informing them of the cure (or cleansing)

---

[22] Cf. Fridrichsen. *op. cit.*, pp. 77ff., where it is argued that the injunctions to silence in 1:44; 5:43; 7:36 and 8:26 are not from St. Mark's hand, but were already present in the tradition and were meant to defend Jesus against the charge of being a magician in league with Beelzebul. Jesus was not a charlatan of the stamp of Lucian's Alexander: "Quand on le représentait comme un sorcier de grande envergure, on répondait du côté chrétien que toute réclame lui était étrangère. Au lieu de s'attacher ceux qu'il avait guéris, au lieu de les faire marcher devant son char triomphal, au lieu de faire publier sa gloire par eux, il les a jeté dehors et leur commandé sévèrement de se taire. C'est donc l'extrême opposé des pratiques du thaumaturge ordinaire" (p. 81). It should be noticed, however, that in Mark 3:22ff., while it is denied that Jesus is a miracle worker who is in any sort of alliance with the prince of the demons, there is no mention of the common characteristics of miracle workers, such as their enthusiasm for self-advertisement; and that in the parallel in Matt. 12:15ff. the reticence of Jesus is simply given a scriptural warrant by a citation (in v. 19) of Isa. 42:2 ("He shall not strive nor cry aloud; neither shall any one hear his voice in the streets"). Nevertheless, despite the indirect nature of the evidence, it is not impossible that both evangelists were to some extent influenced by a desire to bring out a contrast between Jesus and the ordinary thaumaturge. Attention ought also to be drawn in this connection to the fact that St. Mark's mode of representation seems partly to have been determined by a concern to show that Jesus was really innocent of all seditious messianic activity; although his words and works greatly impressed the public, so far from seeking to arouse excitement among the people, he did his utmost to check it (see R. H. Lightfoot, *The Gospel Message of St. Mark*, pp. 37, 46).

[23] Cf. above, Chapter 2.

before he is officially pronounced clean by the competent authority. Hence Jesus is represented as brusquely casting the man forth and forbidding him to have any social intercourse prior to the pronouncement of the priest's verdict. The legal procedure will then be "a testimony to them" in the double sense that it affords official proof of the reality or completeness of the cure and witnesses to Jesus' respect for the law. In St. Mark's interpretation, however, the injunction to silence of verse 44 may also serve as a theological explanation of the people's failure to understand the Lord's miraculous deeds as disclosures of his messianic status.

SUPPLEMENTARY NOTE B: CONCERNING
MARK 5:7, 18–20

The story of the Gerasene demoniac (Mark 5:1–20) shows little sympathy for the swine and their Gentile owners and, as Wellhausen suggested, it is perhaps a tale which was originally told of a Jewish exorcist in a foreign country and subsequently adapted and applied to Jesus. However this may be, the story is the most elaborate Novelle preserved in the gospels,[1] and it exemplifies several typical motifs, the most important of which may be set forth as follows:

1. Vv. 2, 6.   The exorcist is confronted by the demoniac.

2. Vv. 2–5.   An unclean place, such as a cemetery, is a fitting resort for one possessed by an unclean spirit.

3. Vv. 3–5.   The gravity and danger of the patient's illness is emphasized.

4. V. 7.   The demon senses the exorcist and by giving expression to its knowledge of his person seeks to defend itself against the impending attack.

5. V. 8.   The exorcist utters the potent command.

6. V. 9.   To secure knowledge of the demon's name is to gain access to power over it.

7. V. 10.   The demon requests its conqueror to grant it a special concession.

8. Vv. 11f.   The request is made more definite and the exorcist complies.

---

[1] For a detailed discussion of the story, see Bauernfeind, *Die Worte der Dämonen im Markusevangelium*, pp. 23ff., 34ff., 69ff. For the typical motifs, see the list and the many references in Bultmann, *Die Geschichte der synoptischen Tradition*, pp. 236ff.

9. V. 13. The reality of the exorcism finds overt demonstration in the stampede of the swine.

10. V. 13. The motif of the outwitted devil may be present. Contrary to the legion's expectations, the desire expressed in the request of v. 10 is not fulfilled; the demons are cheated out of a permanent lodging in the district.

11. V. 15. The success of the miracle receives further demonstration; the patient is now seated, clothed and in his right mind.

12. Vv. 14–20. The miracle makes a great impression upon the inhabitants of the region.

a) Vv. 14–17. The herdsmen flee and recount what has happened in town and country. The people are so afraid of a miracle worker who possesses such tremendous supernatural power that they beseech Jesus to leave their neighborhood.

b) Vv. 18–20. The reaction of the patient stands in contrast to the fear of his fellow countrymen. He wishes to accompany Jesus, presumably, as a disciple (cf. 3:14a). But Jesus orders him to go to his home and tell his folk how the Lord has shown mercy to him; and he departs and to the amazement of all he proceeds to proclaim what Jesus has done for him.

Thus, adjudging the matter in a general way, the story may well have circulated in the apostolic communities as an account of the way in which Jesus won fame in a foreign land. Its main themes are characteristic features of the category of Novellen, and the mode of their presentation is such that they seem to find their their natural explanation within the framework of the story itself. In this case St. Mark is evidently reproducing a current Novelle with a high degree of faithfulness, and no part of the narrative as it now stands appears to bear a direct reference to any particular element in the wider context of the gospel. Even verse 1, with its mention of the country of the Gerasenes (see the mention of Decapolis in verse 20), does not need to be regarded as editorial, establishing a connection with what precedes, for it may only make definite the general implication of verses 11ff. that the scene is set in non-Jewish territory.

It would appear that the demon's address of verse 7 plays the same kind of role in the story as that played by the address of 1:24 in the story of the exorcism in the synagogue at Capernaum; the demon senses the identity of its dangerous opponent and raises its voice to defend itself against him.[2] The two addresses resemble each other in certain noteworthy respects:

1. The first five words are the same in both addresses, save that 1:24 has the first person plural ($\dot{\eta}\mu\hat{\iota}\nu$) instead of the first person singular ($\dot{\epsilon}\mu o\acute{\iota}$). This slight difference makes it improbable that there is any direct dependence of one passage on the other; for the first person singular of verse 7 would hardly have been changed to the first person plural in 1:24, the context of which contains no suggestion of there being a plurality of possessing demons; and, inversely, the first person plural of 1:24 would hardly have been changed to the first person singular in verse 7, where the possessing demon is legion. The relationship between the two opening clauses would seem to be one of common dependence upon a current apotropaic formula which was derived from the widow's utterance given in I Kings 17:18.

2. The demon is aware of the exorcist's divine origin and nature. The designation $v\dot{\iota}\dot{\epsilon}$ $\tauo\hat{v}$ $\theta\epsilono\hat{v}$ $\tauo\hat{v}$ $\dot{v}\psi\acute{\iota}\sigma\tauov$ ("O Son of God the Most High") of verse 7 corresponds to the designation $\dot{o}$ $\ddot{a}\gamma\iotaos$ $\tauo\hat{v}$ $\theta\epsilono\hat{v}$ ("The Holy One of God") of 1:24. In the LXX the word $\ddot{v}\psi\iota\sigma\tauos$ ("most high") is employed to translate the Hebrew word עֶלְיוֹן. As a title for God the word is not uncommon in the Old Testament, and apparently in Hellenistic Judaism, which tended to be syncretistic.[3] But it is not frequently used of God in the New Testament, where it appears only in

---

[2] Cf. above, Chapter 4.

[3] Cf. E. Klostermann, *Das Markusevangelium*, p. 49.

passages with an Old Testament coloring and in utterances of demons—the present case (cf. the parallel in Luke 8:28 [D], τί ἐμοὶ καὶ σοὶ υἱὲ τοῦ ὑψίστου) and Acts 16:17. Perhaps, as Bauernfeind suggests,[4] the term as a title for God had polytheistic and magical associations.

3. The demon knows that the appearance of Jesus omens ill for agents of Satan such as itself. The verb βασανίσῃς ("torment") corresponds to the verb ἀπολέσαι ("destroy") of 1:24, and for its use in this connection, cf. its employment by the φάσμα in Philostratus, *Vita Ap.* 4, 25.[5]

It seems then, that the demon's address of verse 7 would be originally understood as an utterance made in self-defence; but, as in the case of 1:24, St. Mark probably takes it to be a confession which bears witness to the truth of the Messiahship of Jesus. In the present instance, however, the address is not immediately followed by an injunction to silence, but this is not altogether surprising. For, in the first place, if the evangelist (who has already made his general position clear in 1:24f., 1:34 and 3:11f.) is not interfering with the text of the story as it came to him, it may be observed that the technical use of the verb φιμοῦν ("to muzzle") in the imperative mood was no universal and necessary requirement in Greek incantations. And, in the second place, even if the evangelist is interfering with the text and is actually responsible for the interpolation of verse 8, he may have felt that the insertion of a φιμώθητι ("be muzzled"; cf. 1:25) or a πεφίμωσο ("be muzzled"; cf. 4:39) would have been singularly inappropriate here in view of the subsequent conversation which takes place between the legion and its conqueror.[6]

---

[4] *Ibid.*, p. 24.

[5] Cf. the Greek incantations (in which ὁρκίζω or ἐξορκίζω—"I adjure"—is used) cited by Bauernfeind, *op. cit.*, pp. 24ff. Perhaps the last clause of the address of v. 7 should be rendered: "Jesus, you Son of the Most High God, I adjure you by God . . ."

[6] Various suggestions have been made concerning v. 8; three possibili-

With respect to verses 18–20 it is often argued that they constitute the whole or part of a secondary ending to the story. One view [7] is that the story had its original conclusion in verse 15, which establishes the reality and completeness of the cure and mentions the fear of the witnesses. Verses 16–17 supply the motive for bringing Jesus back to the other side of the sea, where the greatest of the miracles reported in 4:35–5:43 (the raising of the little girl) is to be performed. Verses 18–20 represent a further addition to the section and have a symbolical meaning which is connected with the preceding story of the stilling of the storm. Late in the day (cf. I Cor. 10:11b) Jesus, that is, the gospel borne by the disciples (4:36) in the boat of the church, crosses from Jewish to Gentile soil. The voyage is difficult and dangerous (4:37–40), and the problem of the person of Jesus makes itself acutely felt (4:41). A landing having been made on the other side, the power of Jesus is made manifest, and the question arises whether those who have been thus drawn within its orbit should attach themselves to the original

---

ties may be mentioned here: (1) V. 8 originally stood before v. 7 and perhaps instead of v. 6, which partly repeats what is reported in v. 2 (the exorcist is confronted by the demon). The position of v. 8 was modified because the demon did not immediately obey the command. But in this case, why was not the command simply omitted? Cf. Bauernfeind, *op. cit.*, pp. 48ff. The προσεκύνησεν ("he bowed down") of v. 6 does not seem to be a magical device for the avoidance of eye meeting eye (*ibid.*, pp. 52f.); rather it brings out the demon's recognition of Jesus' utter superiority in power. (2) V. 8 did not appear in the original form of the story, but was added by the evangelist (or by an earlier or later editor) who felt that such a story should properly contain such a command (cf. 3:30). (3) V. 8 stands in its original position. Jesus is so powerful that the demon at once senses that it must now leave its victim. An explicit command is not really necessary; it comes as an afterthought and is put in the form of a subordinate clause. Cf. Lohmeyer, *Das Evangelium des Markus*, pp. 95f. This last possibility seems to us to be the most acceptable one; the story as a whole shows delight in the narration of subordinate details.

[7] See R. H. Lightfoot, *History and Interpretation*, pp. 88ff.

Jewish-Christian community (5:18; cf. 3:14a). The answer is given in the negative; Gentiles are to remain as Gentiles among their own people, there making known the boundless mercy of Israel's God that is conferred through Jesus. Thus the man's action in 5:20 is in accordance with the command set forth in the preceding verse; the God of Israel is glorified when Jesus is proclaimed (cf. Rom. 15:9–12).

An alternative possibility [8] is to regard verses 18–20 as a supplementary conclusion which is to be understood after the manner of 7:36 (cf. 1:45; Matt. 9:30f.); Jesus is proclaimed apparently against his will. There is a contrast between the command of verse 19 and the action of verse 20; in verse 19 the healed man is told to go to his folk at *home* and to tell them of the great mercy which *God* (ὁ Κύριος—"the Lord") has shown to him; the word οἶκος ("house") denotes a place of concealment from the public elsewhere in the gospel (cf. 7:17a; 7:24b; 8:26a). But the man goes about *Decapolis* proclaiming the benefits which *Jesus* has bestowed upon him. Thus Jesus will not permit one who is aware of the secret of his Messiahship to return with him into Jewish territory; and he imposes an injunction to secrecy upon the healed man by bidding him to go to his home and to tell his people of the mercy of God, not of the person of his healer; but the healed man disobeys the command and the result is that, despite the repeated injunctions to silence, Jesus wins fame as a miracle worker.

This exegesis, however, is open to certain weighty objections:

1. The contrast between verses 19 and 20 is not a formal one; verse 20 begins with καί, not with ὁ δέ (cf. 1:45a; 7:36b).

2. The word οἶκος ("house") does not always denote a place of retreat from the multitude (cf. 3:20).

[8] See Wrede, *Das Messiasgeheimnis*, pp. 140f., Dibelius, *From Tradition to Gospel*, pp. 74, 87. Dibelius thinks that the story has its original ending in v. 17 (not v. 15), only vv. 18–20 being due to St. Mark.

3. The expression ὁ Κύριος ("the Lord") in verse 19 does not seem to stand in any sort of opposition to the expression ὁ Ἰησοῦς ("Jesus") in verse 20; Jesus is the mediator of God's saving mercy.

4. The healed man is not necessarily aware of Jesus' Messiahship. The confession of verse 7 is made by the demon, not by its victim.

Accordingly, there are good grounds for holding that St. Mark did not compose verses 18–20 in order to convey the meaning set forth in the exegesis under consideration. If he had appended verses 18–20 to the story with such a meaning in view, he would surely have made his point more explicit. And if verses 18–20 form the original conclusion of the story, it cannot be maintained with any degree of certainty that he would understand them in the sense suggested.

Furthermore, there does not seem to be any real necessity for taking verse 15 to be the original conclusion of the story. The people's request that Jesus should leave their borders (v. 17) follows naturally from their fear of him (v. 15). And the healed man's desire to accompany Jesus (v. 18) stands in remarkable contrast to the attitude of his compatriots; it serves to indicate that Jesus is really not one who is to be merely feared. The people generally are disturbed by the presence of an exorcist who possesses such tremendous supernatural power, but the healed man responds with gratitude; he learns to see in the miracle of his cure a signal manifestation of the saving mercy of God (v. 19) and he proceeds to proclaim it as such in Decapolis (v. 20). Admittedly, the ending of the story is relatively prolonged and detailed; but the same may be said of other parts of this Novelle. For example, in verses 2–6 the tombs, where the demoniac has his habitation,[9] are referred to no less than three

[9] Subterranean burial chambers are still to be found on the eastern side of the Sea of Galilee (so Lagrange; cf. Lohmeyer, *op. cit.*, p. 94, n. 3).

times; the impossibility of restraining the man is elaborately described; [10] and the possessed meets the exorcist twice (vv. 2, 6).

Bauernfeind also sees in verses 19–20 the original climax of the story,[11] but he connects their meaning in an unusual way with the request of the legion in verse 10.[12] Since Wellhausen made the suggestion, it has often been thought that the story evinces the old motif of the devil which has been outwitted:

1. In verse 9 the demons boast about their great numbers and unwittingly betray their name, thus delivering themselves into the hands of their opponent.

2. The demons desire to remain in the district (v. 10); but they elect to enter the swine (v. 12) and thereby deprive themselves of a lodging in the district (v. 13).

Bauernfeind, however, maintains that the demons are not so stupid as this exegesis would suggest:

1. Jesus may be so powerful that the demons can do no other than answer the question of verse 9a.

2. The story does not concern itself with the ultimate fate of the demons (as distinct from their new hosts). There is no mention of the underworld as there is in Luke 8:31.

3. In verse 13 the demons control the swine as they have previously controlled their human victim.

But Bauernfeind proceeds to argue from the third consideration that the demons actually cause the swine to stampede in order

---

[10] Notice the three infinitives following the διά in v. 4.

[11] See *op. cit.*, pp. 38ff.

[12] For parallels to this request, see Bultmann, *op. cit.*, p. 239. Properly a *legion* in the Roman army numbered about six thousand infantry; it was a loan-word in Aramaic as well as in Greek; cf. S.-B., II, 9. The many demons can be referred to as a single being because they are in common possession of the same victim. It may be that the use of the term *legion* in this context betrays anti-Roman feeling—a rare phenomenon in the gospels; cf. P. Winter, *On the Trial of Jesus*, p. 129.

to incite the people against Jesus by making him responsible for the loss of the animals. In other words, it is not the demons that are deceived by the exorcist; on the contrary, it is the exorcist who is deceived by the demons. He complies with their apparently innocent request to remain in the district and permits them to enter the swine. The result is that Jesus himself is compelled to leave the district. Nevertheless, the situation is finally saved by the healed man who remains in the region and proclaims the great things which Jesus has done for him. This interpretation, however, is unacceptable on several grounds:

1. The story presupposes that Jesus' might is irresistible. Even the defensive address of verse 7 only brings out the legion's weakness; it adjures the Son of God in the name of God! Bauernfeind himself holds that the question of verse 9 is one which the demons are forced to answer (*op. cit.*, pp. 46f.). Thus the Jesus of this story is hardly one capable of being deceived by the demons.

2. The story contains no suggestion that Jesus had any intention of remaining in the country of the Gerasenes.

3. The story does not state that the people wish Jesus to leave their district specifically because they hold him responsible for the destruction of the swine.

4. It is probable that the stampede of the swine serves simply as a demonstration of the reality of the exorcism [13] and that neither the original teller of the story nor the evangelist would consider the question of the relation between the stampede and the motives of the possessing demons. The most that one could reasonably say on the latter point would be that the wild action of the animals is an expression of the impotent rage of the demons.

Accordingly, we are led to believe that verses 18–20 constituted an integral part of the Novelle as St. Mark received it. The verses

[13] Cf. Dibelius, *op. cit.*, pp. 87ff.

have no direct bearing on the evangelist's doctrine of the messianic secret. They continue to expound the theme introduced at verse 15 (the impression produced by the miracle upon the people), and they indicate that Jesus is not to be regarded merely as a strange and terrifying wonder worker. The story would circulate in the primitive communities as an account of the way in which Jesus won fame in a foreign land, and it is not impossible that the action of the healed man at the end would be seen as a sort of anticipation of the work of the apostolic missionaries. As Fridrichsen put it:

Ces paroles de Jésus [v. 19] sont la voix du *missionaire* qui se sert du miracle pour propager la foi. Il en était du Christianisme primitif comme de toute autre oeuvre missionaire, la propagande se faisait en grande partie par la *famille;* quand quelqu'un avait fait l'expérience des bienfaits de la nouvelle religion, cet évènement exerçait une large influence parmi les parents et ceux qui habitaient la même maison.[14]

[14] *Le problème du miracle*, p. 82.

5

Parables and the Secret

ACCORDING to St. Mark's fundamental doctrine, the Messiahship of Jesus is a fact, yet a fact which may not be openly proclaimed to the world until the Son of Man has risen again from the dead. It is for this reason, as we have seen, that the demons are enjoined to silence, since they with their powers of supernatural insight are able to perceive the truth which is veiled from mortal eyes. And it is for the same reason, as we learn from 4:10ff., that Jesus addresses the multitude in parables. For in the evangelist's interpretation (and contrary to normal expectations) the parables of Jesus are not meant to make plain the essential content of the message of salvation, but to obscure it; they are a means of guarding the mystery or secret of the kingdom of God. Such is the most natural meaning of the text as it stands in 4:10ff., and the various attempts which have been made to obtain a different interpretation arise from a failure to appreciate the evangelist's doctrinal point of view. One may conjecture that behind the present text there is a saying of Jesus which had a different import and which was worked over by the evangelist for theological reasons; but of the meaning of the

passage as it now exists there can be no reasonable doubt, and
it is with the significance of the gospel as it is, not as he thinks
it ought to be, that the exegete is primarily concerned.

Apart from the eschatological discourse in 13:3–37, the section in which St. Mark expounds his theory of the function of
the parables (4:1–34) is the longest section in the gospel that is
entirely concerned with the Lord's teaching. The three parables
it contains—the sower (vv. 3–8), the seed growing secretly
(vv. 26–29) and the mustard seed (vv. 30–32)—are not intended
to give an exhaustive account of the teaching, but are presented
as particular illustrations of its general character; verses 2 and
33 imply that the evangelist has selected them from a larger collection. All three deal with the phenomenon of growth in nature and suggest that the great spiritual harvest of the kingdom
will most certainly come despite the lowliness of its beginnings
in the ministry of Jesus. Perhaps it was because of their message
of confidence in the ultimate triumph of the kingdom that
St. Mark selected them and chose to insert them here, for in
the two previous chapters Jesus is for the most part engaged in
conflict with his opponents, who in 3:6 conspire to bring about
his destruction and in 3:22 go so far as to declare that he is
possessed by Beelzebul, the prince of the demons. Although the
people generally do not realize it, the mysterious forces of the
Almighty are at work on the side of the little group of disciples gathered round their Master, and their cause must finally
prevail.

The opening verse of the section was probably composed by
the evangelist to provide an appropriate setting for the teaching in the general framework of the gospel; it seems to refer
back to 3:9, where Jesus requests that a small boat be held in
readiness so that he can put out to sea should the crush of the
thronging crowd become too great; and this verse occurs in a
pericope (3:7–12) apparently written by St. Mark as a summary account of the nature and the effect of the Lord's activi-

ties in Galilee. The immediate introduction to the parable of the
sower in verse 2 may have already existed in the evangelist's
source; it should be compared with the words "and he said,"
which in verses 26 and 30 introduce the parables of the seed
growing secretly and of the mustard seed. It is possible that the
explanation of the parable of the sower (vv. 13–20) was also
included in the source, for verse 13 presupposes that the disciples
have asked for the meaning of this particular parable, whereas
in verse 10 they inquire about the significance of parabolical
teaching in general and receive the required reply in verses
11–12.[1] With its emphasis on the things which prevent the word
from coming to its proper fruition, the explanation makes the
parable more obviously an exhortation to be on one's guard
against the ill effect of tribulation, anxiety, and the like. Assuming that this explanation was found in the source, St. Mark
probably modified the original question by substituting the
plural "the parables" for the singular "the parable" (v. 10); he
may also have added the words "when he was alone" and was
perhaps responsible for appending "with the twelve" to "they
that were about him." If this is so, the source, with its particular question and with its distinction between the parable and
the explanation, would afford the evangelist with a good opportunity for setting forth his general doctrine concerning the
significance of the Lord's teaching in parables.

The explanation of the parable of the sower is followed in
verses 21–25 by a group of sayings continuing the private instruction to the disciples. These traditional sayings, assembled
perhaps by St. Mark himself, evidently give further expression

---

[1] In his article concerning public pronouncement and private explanation in the gospels (*Ex. T.*, LVII [1945-46], 175ff.) D. Daube gives
some rabbinic analogies which exemplify the three characteristics: (1)
a pronouncement by the master for public consumption, (2) a question
by the disciples after the departure of the outsiders, (3) an explanation
of the public pronouncement given by the master to the disciples in
response to their inquiry.

to the general theory expounded in verses 11–12. Whatever meanings may have originally been attached to them, in their present context they can refer only to the secret of the kingdom granted to the disciples but withheld from the multitude. They indicate that one day the veil will be uplifted and the secret ✓ will be made manifest to the world; at a later stage (9:9) we gather that the great disclosure will not be made before the Son of Man is risen from the dead. But in the meantime the disciples are to be on the alert, for more truth is yet to be imparted to them; to him who has more shall be given. But with verse 25 this private instruction comes to an abrupt end, since in verse 26 Jesus is once again speaking in parables to the multitude. At this point it seems as though St. Mark has temporarily lost sight of the situation, otherwise he would have introduced the parable of the seed growing secretly with some such notice as that to be found in 8:34a. An alternative view is that he regards the two parables in 4:26–32 as further explications of the parable of the sower. But this exegesis is probably incorrect, for the explanation of verses 13–20 is self-contained and gives the impression of being complete in itself; also, the words "with many such parables" in verse 33 most naturally refer to the seed growing secretly and to the mustard seed as well as to the sower; and, finally, it is suggested in verses 35–36 that Jesus has *just* been speaking to the multitude (and not to the disciples alone), whom he now leaves by crossing the sea. In verses 33–34, with which this relatively extensive section of teaching closes, the evangelist again refers back to the general doctrine of verses 11–12.

The significance of verses 10–12 has been the subject of much controversy, and they must now be examined in detail; they read:

And when he was alone they that were about him with the twelve asked him about the parables. And he said to them, To you is given the mystery of the kingdom of God, but to those who are without all things are done in parables in order that

seeing they may see and not perceive,
and hearing they may hear and not understand,
lest they should turn back and it be forgiven them.

In this passage St. Mark makes a sharply defined distinction between the disciples, who are entrusted with the mystery of the kingdom, and the uninitiated masses, who are permitted only to hear the teaching in parables. The saving truth of the gospel is hidden behind the parables from the profane eyes of the general public, but the divine secret is granted to the favored company of the elect. The parables are designed to conceal the truth from the multitude; and they are obscure in themselves. To be understood they must be accompanied by special clarifications such as the explanation of the parable of the sower given in verses 13–20. That the evangelist regards the parables as being of the nature of riddles which require solutions is made clear in the generalizing comment of verses 33–34:

And with many such parables he spoke the word to them as they were able to hear it; and without a parable he did not speak to them; but privately to his own disciples he explained all things.

Thus truth which lies in the form of parables is truth concealed; [2] and it is revealed only to those who are privileged to belong to the fellowship of the disciples.

St. Mark's conception is therefore opposed to the common supposition that the parable, as a concrete representation of its subject matter, is designed as a means of facilitating comprehension. That he should come to think of the nature of parabolical discourse in this way, though surprising to us at first sight, would be a natural consequence of his doctrine of the messianic secret. The true import of the Lord's teaching, as well as of his mighty works, was concealed from the multitude, and since the

[2] For this notion see Justin, *Tryph.* 52; *Ep. Barn.* 17, 2, cited in Wrede, *Das Messiasgeheimnis*, p. 63, n. 1.

teaching preserved in the tradition was to a large extent in parabolical form, it would come to be assumed that this form must have been chosen for the set purpose of screening the truth. Moreover, it is evident that the parables were handed down and circulated in the churches isolated from their original contexts, with the result that the question of their precise significance would not infrequently become a debatable matter.[3] For a parable would normally be spoken in response to a particular situation which would exercise control over the meaning and limit the application. But with the loss of such contextual control much greater scope would be afforded for the contemplation of alternative possibilities in the way of interpretation, and adapted meanings would be supplied under the pressure of prevailing needs and purposes. Thus standards of interpretation would establish themselves pragmatically; and perhaps under the influence of primitive notions associated with epiphanies and greatly emphasized in the mystery religions, it would be felt that the right standards could be known only by the initiated few as distinct from the unchristian public outside. With regard to the parable of the sower, for example, was it originally intended to comfort the disciples—not all work for the kingdom fails, though some of its efforts may seem to be futile? Or was it a warning to the people against the disastrous consequences of indifference to the word of God? Or was it simply a statement of theological fact [4]—some will be saved and others lost? The explanation of the parable which follows in verses 14ff. limits

---

[3] Cf. Bultmann, *Die Geschichte der synoptischen Tradition*, pp. 216f. In the course of his penetrating criticisms of V. Taylor's commentary on St. Mark's gospel Morton Smith observes: "Whether or not Jesus intended the parables to conceal the true purport of his teaching, there has certainly been enough disagreement about their meaning to make defensible the opinion that they are deliberately obscure" (see *H.T.R.*, XLVIII [1955], 31).

[4] Wellhausen (*Das Evangelium Marci*, p. 34) conjectures that Jesus was reflecting on the effects of his own teaching.

the meaning and it is granted only to the disciples. Besides showing the influence of an allegorizing tendency, it is more definitely
hortatory than the parable itself; it exhorts the reader not to be
like those who fail to make the right response to the word and
to be on his guard against the evils to which they succumb.

In St. Mark's view, however, over and above the secret meanings concealed in the particular parables, there is the fundamental secret which is common to them all, since, as it seems,
it concerns the person of him who composes the parables. Admittedly, the evangelist offers no formal explanation of what
precisely he understands by the mystery of the kingdom of
God. He assumes that his meaning is clear as, indeed, it is when
the passage is considered in the light of the doctrine of the book
as a whole.[5] He is referring to the truth disclosed by the heavenly voice at the baptism—the truth hitherto unrecognized by
mortals, but known to the demons—that Jesus is the Messiah,
the Son of God; and the passage may be said to point forward
to 8:27ff., where Peter, as the representative of the elect, confesses that his Master is the Messiah and where the disciples are
at once forbidden to divulge their newly acquired knowledge
of the truth.

It appears, therefore, that St. Mark in 4:11 is not thinking of
the kingdom of God in any abstract sense, whether as a future
or as a present reality, but of the kingdom as it is embodied in
the person of Jesus the Messiah. In other words, the reference is
to the saving message of the apostolic preaching or the essential
content of the Christian gospel; the phrase "the kingdom of
God" has similar significance in Acts 1:3, for example, where
"speaking the things concerning the kingdom of God" means
"preaching the gospel" (cf. Acts 8:12; 19:8). "Those who are
without or outside" are accordingly those who cannot accept
the good news of the Messiahship of Jesus, which the apostolic
preachers proclaim to the world. They are outside, not literally,

[5] Cf. Wrede, *op cit.*, pp. 57ff.

102

but rather in the sense of being uninitiated into the Christian mystery of salvation. That such is the meaning is indicated in 4:10, where, while it is stated that Jesus is alone, there is no report of his having entered a house or other building. The multitude, being addressed in parables, are prevented from knowing the mystery of God, the secret which, according to Col. 2:2–3, is none other than "Messiah in whom are hidden all the treasures of wisdom and knowledge" (Col. 1:25ff.). They are strangers to the essential truth of the church's message and, in consequence, are excluded from the blessings enjoyed within the fellowship of the Christian communities.

But it is important to notice that, according to St. Mark's doctrine, the distinction between the uninitiated public and the disciples is by no means an absolute one, for to the end of the book the latter fail to understand the mystery with which they are entrusted. Despite all the esoteric instruction which the elect are privileged to receive, they show no signs of making progress in the way of understanding. Although they continue to witness the mighty works performed by Jesus, they do not see in them a disclosure of the Messiah's power. Even after Peter's confession of the Messiahship in 8:27ff., the real significance of the secret still eludes their grasp. That which is hidden for the purpose of being made manifest must remain hidden for the time being; as we learn from 9:9, full manifestation can only come when the Son of Man is raised from the dead. Thus it is not to be thought that an impassable gulf separates the favored few from the multitude of outsiders for, prior to the resurrection, the elect may adumbrate but cannot fully represent those who possess the light of the apostolic faith.

The incapacity of the disciples is brought out by the questions of 4:13, which follow immediately after the intimation of their sacred privilege:

And he says to them. Do you not understand this parable? and how will you understand all the parables?

Having asked these two questions Jesus proceeds to give the explanation of the parable of the sower. Perhaps the questions already existed in St. Mark's source, the evangelist himself, as we have previously suggested, being responsible for the insertion of verses 11–12. However this may be, in their present context the questions evidently contain a rebuke. They imply that those who are permitted to stand behind the screen of parabolical obscurity and who are favored with the mystery of the kingdom ought to apprehend the meaning of this particular parable since this particular meaning is easier to understand than the fundamental secret which is involved in them all. But on the basis of St. Mark's doctrine we know that the disciples are not yet in a position to understand the mystery, as the illumination bestowed by the resurrection appearances still belongs to the future. The passage thus presents us with a historical difficulty, the situation being such that the disciples are expected to understand something which, by the very nature of things, they are precluded from understanding.

It is probable, however, that the evangelist was unaware of this problem, for his attitude was quite different from that of a modern historian. Doubtless, from the historical point of view, the situation is as intolerable as the factual implication of 5:43, for example, where those who witness the miracle of the little girl's revival are forbidden to make known what they have seen. Accordingly, as in the case of 5:43, if exegesis is to do justice to the evangelist, the questions of 4:13 must be interpreted in the light of the writer's theological conviction and religious purpose. St. Mark is persuaded that the Messiahship, though a secret, is a fact, and he intends his readers to understand this truth. For those who have ears to hear and eyes to see, the parables, no less than the mighty works of Jesus, manifest his divine Sonship; and therefore, when the evangelist allows the disciples to be rebuked for not perceiving the reality which the parables disclose, he is drawing the attention of his readers to the fact of the Messiahship, which, while being clear to them, was not yet comprehended by the disciples. From St. Mark's own standpoint, the Messiahship is an obvious fact, an open secret constantly being revealed in the Lord's words and works; and it is this view which asserts itself in the questions of 4:13 and makes a demand of the disciples for insight similar to his own and, it may be added, to that of his readers. The evangelist's perspective being the correct one, the disciples ought to perceive what he perceives!

The same kind of demand is made in a similar fashion elsewhere in the gospel. Thus in the account of the stilling of the storm, when calm has been miraculously restored, Jesus at once turns to his disciples and asks them:

Why are you fearful? have you not yet faith? [4:40].

The evangelist himself has the necessary faith which enables him to apprehend the miracle as a disclosure of the Lord's messianic power, and the questions put to the disciples are an indication that the real character of the miracle is only understood when it is perceived in this particular aspect. Men ought to recognize the truth wherever it is to be found, and therefore the disciples ought to have the faith by which the truth in this case can be recognized. But the disciples merely continue to be greatly afraid and say one to another:

Who then is this, that even the wind and the sea obey him?

a rhetorical question to which the reader is expected to supply the obvious answer:

He is Messiah, the Son of God.

A closer parallel to the questions of 4:13 is provided in 7:18, where St. Mark is again concerned with the secret meaning contained in a parable—this time, the parable about what defiles a man. The parable is given in 7:15. Jesus enters a house away from the multitude, and his disciples ask him for an explanation of the parable in verse 17 (v. 16 is omitted by many ancient authorities and is probably a later interpolation); in verse 18 Jesus asks the disciples why they are thus without understanding also, that is, like the multitude; and in verses 18b–23 the explanation of the parable is presented. It will be noticed that these four sections closely correspond to the parts of 4:3–20, where, excluding verses 9 and 11–12, we have the parable of the sower in verses 3–8, the disciples' request for an explanation in verse 10, the rebuke of the disciples implied in the questions of verse 13, and the explanation of the parable in verses 14–20. No less than five further questions of the same character as those of 4:13 occur in 8:13–21, the passage which concerns the secret significance of the miracles of the loaves. Jesus and his disciples are crossing the sea and, according to 8:14, they have forgotten to take bread, though they have one loaf in the boat with them. In verse 15 Jesus issues a warning against the leaven of the Pharisees and the leaven of Herod, and it seems to have no logical connection either with what precedes or with what follows. Perhaps it was a traditional saying which found its way into this context through the association of ideas; it was felt to be appropriate that a saying which mentioned leaven should introduce a conversation about bread.[6] Despite the fact that there is one loaf with them in the boat, the disciples (in v. 16) begin to reason one with another because they have no bread, apparently misunderstanding the saying about the leaven; and Jesus pro-

---

[6] In 9:49f. there is a little group of sayings concerning salt, which also may have been brought together through the association of ideas. The Lord's warning (without any reference to Herod) appears in a different context in Luke 12:1, where the leaven of the Pharisees is taken to denote their hypocrisy; in Matt. 16:12 the warning is against the teaching of the Pharisees and Sadducees. We know that in rabbinical literature the term "leaven" was used to symbolize the evil disposition in human nature (cf. S.-B., I, 728f.), and this may provide the clue to its original meaning in the Lord's warning.

ceeds to rebuke them for their obtuseness by asking the questions which follow in verses 17–18.

Why do you reason because you have no bread? Do you not yet perceive, neither understand? Have you your heart hardened? *Though you have eyes, do you not see, and though you have ears, do you not hear?*

He then reminds them of the two miraculous feedings and ends the conversation by again asking:

Do you not yet understand?

Thus the disciples ought to see the secret significance of the miracles of the loaves; that is to say, they ought to understand what the evangelist apparently means his readers to understand, namely, that Jesus is none other than the Messiah and Lord, whose presence is discerned at the church's sacramental meals of fellowship and who imparts spiritual food for the nourishment of the souls of the elect. To use terminology derived from John 6:22ff., he is the bread of life which comes down from heaven and the one true loaf that is with the disciples in the ship.[7]

---

[7] In his article in *J.T.S.*, n.s., III (1952), 161ff., G. H. Boobyer contends that St. Mark does not regard the miracles of the loaves as prefigurements of the eucharist. Among his arguments are: (1) Expressions such as εὐχαριστεῖν ("to give thanks") and κλᾶν ἄρτον ("to break bread") were not yet technical terms of eucharistic practice. (2) In I Cor. 10:1ff., St. Paul associates the eucharist with the manna received by the Israelites in the wilderness, but St. Mark connects the miracles of the loaves with the leaven of the Pharisees and of Herod (8:15). (3) The multitudes fed, not accepting Jesus as the Messiah, were not suitable for admittance to a eucharist or even to a symbolical enactment of one. (4) For St. Mark, wine as well as bread was an essential element of the eucharist (cf. 14:22ff.). (5) The abundance of food stressed in 8:14ff. does not fit in happily with St. Mark's idea of the eucharist as depicted in 14:22ff. (6) In John 6:27 the fourth evangelist contrasts the temporal bread of the miracle with the eternal bread of the eucharist. (7) As Lohmeyer suggested, the leaven of the Pharisees and of Herod in Mark

Accordingly, in St. Mark's representation of the matter, the disciples are not so sharply distinguished from the uninitiated multitude as 4:11–12 might lead us to suppose; the mystery of the kingdom may be granted to the disciples, but they are unable to understand it. On the other hand, in St. Matthew's gospel the disciples fully comprehend the secret meanings of the parables; as we read in 13:51:

Have you understood all these things? They say to him, Yes.

Whereas the multitude is blind, the disciples see. It is true that in 13:18–23 the disciples are given the explanation of the parable

---

8:15 probably refers to possessive Jewish nationalism, a religious and political aspiration shared by both Pharisees and Herodians, who would keep the vineyard (12:7) and the bread (7:27) for themselves; the disciples are to beware of such exclusivism; the children's bread is to be shared with the Gentiles, for the Messiah can supply more than enough spiritual food for all nations. We agree with Boobyer in his positive thesis, summarized under the last heading, but hold that he errs in his complete rejection of the view that St. Mark connected the miracles of the loaves with the eucharist: (1) Terms such as εὐχαριστεῖν, though not technical, *were* associated with the eucharist. (2) St. Mark could have made the connection in question without being acquainted with I Cor. 10:1ff. (3) The multitudes certainly do not make ideal communicants, but the same could be said of the company that gathered with Jesus in the upper room; in St. Mark's view, prior to the resurrection, the disciples can only imperfectly represent the elect. (4) Though wine is not mentioned in connection with the miracles of the loaves, the word "bread" could on occasion cover both elements of the sacrament; it would seem that in John 6:48ff. "I am the bread of life" means "I am the bread and wine of life." (5) Though there is no reference to an abundance of food in Mark 14:17ff., an abundance is doubtless taken for granted in a spiritual sense. (6) The contrast between the temporal or physical and the eternal or spiritual is applicable to the eucharist itself; and St. Mark in 8:14ff. applies the distinction to the miracles of the loaves. We conclude therefore that St. Mark does associate the miracles of the loaves with the eucharist; but, as is generally the case with the philosophical notion of anticipation, the prefigurements are imperfect in the sense that they lack certain qualities possessed by the actuality they prefigure.

of the sower (cf. 13:36–43; 15:15–20) and that in 8:26 and in 16:8 the disciples are rebuked for having insufficient faith. Nevertheless, they more truly represent God's chosen than they do in St. Mark's portrayal, and in 13:10–18 (the parallel to Mark 4:10–13) their eyes and ears are called "blessed" because they see and hear the things which many prophets and righteous men vainly aspired to apprehend. To them it is given *to know* the mystery or mysteries [8] of the kingdom of Heaven, and, as Matt. 13:51 seems to imply, they can generally grasp the meanings of the parables without the aid of special instruction. But it would be erroneous to think that, in St. Matthew's view, the meaning of a parable lies on the surface or that the method of teaching in parables is employed in order to facilitate apprehension of the truth. Admittedly, the fact of the Messiahship is not concealed from the general public to the extent that it is in St. Mark's gospel, but the parables are hardly a means of its manifestation. Although they may contain truths which have been hidden from the foundation of the world (Matt. 13:35), those truths are not revealed save to the few who are endowed with special insight, that is, to the disciples. Indeed, it appears from Matt. 13:12–13 that parables are inflicted upon the public in order to remove what little capacity they have, presumably, by putting them into a state of mental confusion.[9] Because they are dull-witted they are addressed in parables, and this has the effect of making them still more obtuse; but the disciples, since

[8] Although most witnesses support the plural "the mysteries" in Matt. 13:11, it is possible that this reading is the result of assimilation to Luke 8:10, which also has the infinitive "to know." In the latter passage the expression "the mysteries" seems to refer simply to the secret meanings of the parables.

[9] This view is supported by the position of the parables in St. Matthew's scheme of rearrangement in Matt. 5–13; just as the Lord restricts his miraculous activities among his own people for their unbelief (Matt. 13:58), so he addresses the public in parables as a punishment for their unresponsiveness; cf. below, Chapter 6, n. 47.

they are generally capable of seeing through the parables, are favored with further powers of insight into the truth. Thus, in an important sense, St. Matthew's standpoint approaches that of St. John: the Messiah of apostolic belief is made manifest to the world in the person of Jesus of Nazareth, but human understanding is so perverse that he who is revealed passes unrecognized by the majority of men.[10]

St. Mark, too, is facing the problem set by the failure of men to recognize the Messiahship and in 4:11–12 he offers a partial solution. Jesus was not accepted for what he really was because the truth was hidden from the multitude by the teaching in parables, and it was part of the divine purpose that the Messiahship should be concealed in this way. Jesus deliberately chose to address the people in parables for the purpose of preventing them from knowing his real nature; or, to express the same doctrine in different language, it was predetermined in God's plan of salvation that the parables should guard the mystery of the kingdom. This is the point of the quotation of Isa. 6:9–10, a passage which seems to have been frequently employed in early Christian apologetics to explain the rejection of the gospel by the Jews (cf. John 12:37ff.; Acts 28:25ff.). Thus, when a sustained attempt is made to appreciate the thought of the evangelist, it is seen that verses 11–12, so far from being an absurdity or a piece of historical nonsense,[11] are meant to express an important theological truth; it is only when the chapter is treated as though it were an essay in objective biographical statement that these verses cause difficulty.

An objection which is sometimes made against the natural meaning of verses 11–12 is that it stands in conflict with such sayings as that in 4:21 and more particularly with the teaching

---

[10] This doctrine is not altogether absent from St. Mark's gospel; it seems to be implied in such passages as 2:1–12; 2:23–28; 12:1–12; 14:62.

[11] For this phrase, see T. W. Manson's essay in *Studies in the Gospels* (ed. D. E. Nineham), p. 220.

of the parable of the sower.[12] The lamp is not screened but placed on the stand, and the seeds fall on the bad as well as on the good ground. As we have already suggested, however, when verse 21 is read in conjunction with verse 22, the implication seems to be that the lamp *is* hidden, though only for a limited period. It is concealed in order that it should be made manifest on some future occasion. With respect to the parable of the sower, the explanation given in verses 15–20 shows that St. Mark takes it to be primarily an indication of various evils which hinder different types of hearer from making the right response to the preaching of the word, and when construed in this sense it does not contradict the doctrine that the parables guard the mystery. This doctrine is concerned with something more specific, namely, the divine purpose evinced in the Lord's method of speaking to the multitude in parables. And it does not imply that the parables are meaningless; they contain a meaning, but the meaning cannot be grasped by hearers who are without the necessary insight. In St. Mark's view, those who belong to the multitude are hearers of this kind and they could be described in terms of one or other of the three classes who, in the explanation of the parable of the sower, fail to bring the word to its proper fruition.

Thus, from one point of view, it may be said that the multitude does not respond to the word because their spiritual capacities are marred through evil influences, or, from another point of view, that the parables conceal the truth from the multitude by holding a meaning which they cannot apprehend. In verses 11–12, however, St. Mark is not content to state the fact of the multitude's insensibility to the secret, since he wishes to refer their nonacceptance of the Messiahship to the divine purpose. He therefore affirms not merely that the parables hide the truth from the multitude, but that they are actually intended to do so, and this affirmation, while going beyond what is indicated

[12] Cf. C. G. Montefiore, *The Synoptic Gospels*, I, 101f.

in the explanation of the sower parable, does not contradict it. The conception of purpose is introduced, whereas in relation to the parable of the sower this conception does not seem to have been present to the mind of the evangelist. It is true, of course, that a sower sows his seed in order to obtain as large a harvest as possible. But such an observation is hardly relevant to the discussion, for in verses 11–12 St. Mark is dealing with the purpose of God, which, in this particular instance, happens to coincide with that of the preacher of the word. Moreover, although the sower may normally seek a maximum harvest, the fact remains that some of the seeds generally fail to come to fruition; and it may be presumed that the evangelist, with his strong monotheistic faith in the sovereignty of God, would, in the last resort, regard this fact as a consequence and not as a frustration of God's overruling purpose.

Generally, when exception is taken to verses 11–12, objections seem to be raised on the subjective ground that Jesus could not possibly have intended the simple imagery of his parables to conceal the essential truth of his message from the people. And if this prepossession is discounted, as it should be by the exegete who seeks to appreciate the evangelist's position, it is seen that the various proposals which have been made for emending the passage, are left with very insecure support.

These proposals may be conveniently divided into two classes, namely, those which concern the translation and those which concern the Greek text. A typical example from the first class is the suggestion that the ἵνα in this context should be translated "because" and the μήποτε "perhaps." From such passages as John 8:56 and Matt. 25:9 it is argued that these translations are linguistically permissible; also, St. Matthew may have understood St. Mark's ἵνα in a causal sense, since in 13:13 he replaces it by ὅτι. The meaning would then be that the multitude are taught in parables because of their dull-mindedness, and the purpose of their being so addressed is to make it easier for them to understand the message which Jesus proclaims. But even if we allow two unusual translations in so short a passage, the question remains: Why does the evangelist persist in stating that Jesus explains the parables privately to his disciples? If the parables are deliberately designed to facilitate understanding on the part of the dull-minded multitude, surely those to whom the mystery is granted would hardly stand in such need of special elucidations. A further suggestion is that the ἵνα should be construed in a consequential sense, the meaning being that the multitude's failure to comprehend the truth is the result but not the purpose of Jesus' teaching in parables.[13]

In connection with this proposal a reference is generally made to a tendency of the Hebrew mind to represent the inevitable consequence of an action as though it were the purpose of the action. Thus in Isa. 6:9–10, the passage quoted by St. Mark in verse 12, the prophet is apparently called to preach to the people to the end that they should not repent! Perhaps the writer is in a pessimistic mood and is convinced that the people are so wicked that no success will attend his work, or, as Buchanan Gray suggested,[14] the form of the commission may reflect the discouraging effect on Isaiah of years of fruitless warning. Thus, on the assumption that the words are not ironical, the anticipated or experienced consequence of Isaiah's preaching is here presented as though it were actually God's original intention when he called him to undertake his prophetic task.

But it is illegitimate to conclude from such considerations as these that Isaiah's mode of expression does not correspond to his personal conviction or belief. Indeed, in so far as the prophet believed in the divine nature of his vocation, he would regard his prophetic mission and all that it obviously entailed as being

---

[13] Cf. H. Pernot, *Etudes sur la langue des évangiles*, pp. 90f.

[14] *Isaiah 1–39* (I.C.C.), p. 101. Cf. C. F. Kent, *Sermons, Epistles and Apocalypses of Israel's Prophets*, p. 108; and J. Skinner, *Isaiah 1–39* (C.B.), p. 47.

in accordance with God's predetermined purpose. Similarly with regard to Mark 4:11–12, if the evangelist holds that the Lord's parabolical teaching does not meet with the hoped-for response and the people remain unrepentant, he would not take this negative result to be, in an ultimate sense, contrary to the will of God. For the fundamental presupposition of his gospel is that Jesus is the Messiah whose life and work are a fulfillment of God's plan of salvation; and his faith would require him to affirm that the unrepentance which follows as the negative consequence of Jesus' teaching, must have been provided for in God's inscrutable purpose.

A proposal of the second type is made by T. W. Manson, who contends that the ἵνα is a mistranslation of the Aramaic ד, which has several uses, and in the present case should have been rendered by the relative pronoun οἵ.[15] In support of this view it is argued that St. Mark's quotation from Isa. 6:9–10 follows the Targum, with which it agrees, against the Hebrew and against the LXX, by having the verbs in the third rather than in the second person, and by preferring "forgive" to "heal" at the end. The principal difference is that, whereas St. Mark has a final, the Targum has a relative, form, and the divergence is accounted for by supposing that St. Mark's version arises from a misunderstanding of the Targum as a result of the ambiguity of the ד. Thus the following translation is arrived at:

To you is given the secret of the kingdom of God; but all things come in parables to those outside, who
> see indeed but do not know
> and hear indeed but do not understand,
> lest they should repent and receive forgiveness.

In this translation the quotation from Isa. 6:9–10 is introduced not as an explanation of the purpose of the teaching in parables

---

[15] See *The Teaching of Jesus*, pp. 74ff.

but as a definition of the people outside: they are those who hear the parables, yet fail to understand them. This means, however, that Jesus is asked one question and offers the answer to another, for in verse 10 the disciples do not ask for information concerning the multitude outside, but make inquiries about the significance of the parables. And even as a definition the proposed rendering is not altogether satisfactory, since it would serve equally well as a definition of the disciples who, no less than the multitude, are unable to grasp the meaning of the parables. Also, the μήποτε ("lest") still seems to imply that the hearers are not meant to understand and to repent; and the further suggestion that it indicates a factual condition or a hoped-for contingency—the last clause amounting to a new sentence which ought to be translated "For if they did, they would repent. . . ." or "Perhaps they may yet repent. . . ."—gives the impression of being somewhat forced.

Thus there appears to be no cogent reason for modifying the existing text or the ordinary translation of verses 11–12. The natural meaning accords with ideas expressed elsewhere in the gospel, and in the passage may be discerned an attempt to explain the nonacceptance of the Messiahship; the true nature of Jesus was a secret, and the parables were a divinely appointed means of concealing the truth from his audience. St. Mark is therefore meeting the same kind of problem as that with which St. Paul deals in Rom. 9–11, but whereas the evangelist here takes the view that the multitude are prevented from knowing the mystery through the Lord's parabolical mode of speech, St. Paul maintains that God actually dulls the faculties of the Jewish people. As we read in Rom. 11:5–8:

Even so then at the present time also there is a remnant according to the election of grace. But if it is by grace, it is no longer of works; otherwise grace is grace no more. What then? What Israel seek, this they did not obtain; but the election obtained it and the rest were hardened; as it is written:

God gave them a spirit of insensibility,
eyes that they should not see
and ears that they should not hear,
to this very day.

Thus, in spite of their differences in standpoint, both thinkers agree that the failure of the people to recognize the Messiahship, or, to employ Loisy's words, *l'échec de l'évangile auprès des juifs* [16] was, in the last resort, neither a freak of chance nor even an outcome of human volition, but a provision of God's sovereign purpose.[17]

[16] See *Les évangiles synoptiques*, I, 741. Morton Smith detects a difference of motive, but the same theory, in vv. 11f. and v. 34; to use his own words, "In Mk. 4, 11f. the concern is to explain the rejection by the Jews, in 4, 34 to discredit outside teachers and justify the disciples' claim to a monopoly of the true, secret doctrine" (*H.T.R.*, XLVIII [1955], 31). The latter motive (which became extremely influential during the second century in the church's conflict with Gnosticism) may well affect St. Mark's thinking to a certain extent, but it does not seem to have the same fundamental importance as the concern to explain the rejection. Similarly, the desire to bring out a contrast between Jesus and the ordinary miracle-worker appears to have a subsidiary part to play in connection with the injunctions to silence. Cf. above, Chapter 4, n. 22.

[17] There is a reminiscence of St. Mark's theory of the parables in John 16:25, though here the word παροιμία ("figure") is used, and it is the disciples, not the general public, from whom the truth is in some sense hidden; as with St. Mark, the concealment is only temporary. But St. John's usual view is that the Messiahship is openly revealed in the world, yet men generally, as it were blinded by the light, cannot see its transcendent glory (cf. John 1:9ff.); and even the disciples cannot fully appreciate its wealth of meaning till the Spirit of Truth leads them into all truth (cf. John 16:13).

6

Hostility and the Secret

ST. MARK'S attitude to the Jewish nation is somewhat complicated and could not be adequately characterized in a simple, unqualified statement. Thus while he may believe that the Jews [1] enjoy the God-given prerogative of being the first among men to have the gospel addressed to them [2] and even that the heathen can only have the opportunity of knowing the way of salvation after the Messiah has actually been rejected by his own people,[3] yet he seems to take the view that Jesus in some meas-

[1] In the second gospel, apart from the five instances of the title "the King of the Jews" (15:2, 9, 12, 18, 26), the actual expression "the Jews" occurs only once, in a passage (7:3f.) which is probably an editorial notice (and therefore relatively late) and which has a context whose subject matter is polemical. On the other hand, the expression occurs about seventy times in the fourth gospel, where the Jews, appearing as the agreed enemies of Jesus, play much the same role as that played by the hierarchs in the synoptic gospels.

[2] Cf. 7:27, which perhaps implies that the bread of life must needs be offered to Israel before it can be dispensed among the Gentiles.

[3] Cf. 15:39, where a representative of the non-Jewish world testifies to the truth of the gospel after the Jews have done as they pleased with Jesus.

ure anticipates the work of the church's mission to the Gentiles. For in 5:1ff. the Lord passes into heathen territory and, in consequence of the marvelous cure which he performs there, his fame as a mediator of the mercy of God is spread abroad among the inhabitants of Decapolis; and in 7:24ff. he journeys as far north as the region of Tyre and effects a miraculous exorcism from a distance on the daughter of a Syrophoenician woman. It may be unfair to take the children's bread and throw it to the dogs, but there is no good reason why the latter should not eat of the crumbs which are left under the children's table.[4]

Moreover, in any attempt to understand St. Mark's thought on the Jewish question it is important to bear in mind that the mutual relations between Judaism and Christianity tended to deteriorate with the passage of time. When the gospel was being written, the apostolic message was meeting with wide acceptance in the non-Jewish world, but the Jews for the most part continued to show themselves unwilling to respond to its appeal. St. Paul seems to have regarded the recalcitrance of his own nation as a temporary state of affairs, and even toward the end of his career he could still look forward to the day when all Israel would be saved (Rom. 11:25ff.). But the apostle's hope of a conciliation was not to find fulfillment. Anti-Jewish feeling within the church became more intense and, on the Jewish side, the opinion could have been expressed in certain influential circles that the affirmation of the Messiahship of Jesus was in itself an offence sufficiently serious to merit the infliction of a capital sentence.[5] Accordingly, St. Mark, despite his doctrine of

---

[4] Cf. 7:28f. For the conception of the necessary precedence of the Jews, see Rom. 1:16 (where, however, the "first" is omitted in B and G); Rom. 2:9–10; Acts 13:46. St. Mark may have held that just as the Messiah comes to the Jews and is rejected by them before a Gentile can make the Christian confession of faith, so the word of God must first be spoken to the Jews and be rejected by them before the apostolic missionaries are able to turn their attention to the Gentiles.

[5] Cf. below, Chapter 12 and Supplementary Note F, n. 4.

the divine necessity of the passion, seeks to show that the Jews as represented by their leaders of the period are to be held morally responsible for the most terrible crime of rejecting the only Son of God who came among men solely for the purpose of serving and redeeming them.[6]

It is true that St. Mark, unlike the author of the fourth gospel (cf. John 20:30f.), nowhere gives open expression to his sympathies and, save in 13:14, he does not address his readers directly. But there can be little doubt regarding the general nature of the constituency for which the gospel is intended. It is evidently a limited constituency, in which the names of Alexander and Rufus, the sons of Simon of Cyrene, are well known,[7] and in it the validity of the Christian standpoint is taken for granted. Thus the evangelist assumes that the conflict with the Jewish authorities arises from the evil thoughts and malicious scheming of the scribes and others (see 2:6–8; 3:6; 12:13; 14:1), not as a result of any design or wrong on the part of Jesus. Even Pilate is aware of the innocence of him who is called King of the Jews, and knows that the chief priests have delivered him up because they are envious of him (cf. 15:10ff.). Jesus fulfills a divine commission, and hence he does not wish to subvert the God-given law of Moses, but carefully complies with its requirements (see 1:44; 7:9–13; 12:28–34). In so far as the moral and spiritual principles he enunciates are at variance with the enact-

---

[6] See 10:45. In the account of the crucifixion the incident of the rending of the temple veil (15:38) may be partly meant as a form of testimony to the divine nature of Jesus, in which case it provides a Jewish parallel (in addition to that of 8:29) to the testimony of the natural world (15:33) and to that of the Gentile world (15:39). This Jewish testimony, however, unlike its Gentile counterpart, may not be given by a human being because of the evangelist's belief in the culpability of the Jews for the crucifixion; the temple here seems to symbolize the Jewish religious ideal, from which the people themselves have fallen short; cf. 8:29, where Peter represents the true Israel.

[7] See 15:21. The other synoptists leave out the allusion to Alexander and Rufus; see Matt. 27:32; Luke 23:26.

ments of the law as these are commonly understood, his teaching is securely founded upon a deeper appreciation of the true meaning of the scriptures and of the divine will. He shows, for example, that it was only on account of man's hardness of heart that the law made provision for a husband's possible desire to divorce his wife: and a mere concession to the weakness of human nature should not be construed as a direct expression of God's will for men (10:1ff.). In the evangelist's judgment, therefore, it is really the scribes and Pharisees who make void the word of God by maintaining a tradition of purely human invention, which perverts the real significance of scriptural statements; [8] and, similarly, it is the Sadducees who are seriously at fault in their hermeneutics when they fail to realize that the God of the patriarchs is the God not of the dead but of the living (12:26f.). The standard of inward purity which Jesus propounds and explains (7:14ff.) is more fundamental in God's sight, so it is implied, than all the rules for ceremonial cleanness, for, as was revealed to the prophet Isaiah, a people may honor God with their lips, that is, to all outward seeming, while their heart is far from him (7:1ff.). In fact, the correct attitude to the law—and any sensible scribe perforce recognizes it—is determined by the regulative principle involved in the two commandments of love to God and love to one's neighbor, practical adherence to which is of far greater religious importance than the offering of all the holocausts and sacrifices ever prescribed (12:28ff.).

Furthermore, seeing that the conception of divine retribution played an essential part in the thought of the apostolic church, it is not surprising to find certain passages in which St. Mark betrays the conviction that Israel has already sealed its own

---

[8] See 7:8–13. For the evangelist's conception of the scribal tradition as a purely human artifice which really obscures the will of God, cf. the purely human thoughts of Peter in the rebuke of 8:33 which, from a historical and subordinate standpoint, prevent him from comprehending the meaning of Messiahship in God's real intention.

doom by rejecting the Messiah.[9] Thus the story of the withering
of the fig tree, the earlier and later parts of which are separated
by the account of the cleansing of the temple,[10] would seem to
symbolize the terrible fate which must inevitably befall the
Jewish nation.[11] Israel stands under the curse of the Messiah and
therefore of God himself [12] because it has failed to bring forth
the fruit [13] which one would naturally have expected of a

[9] The doctrine of divine retribution (cf. 8:38; 9:41–48; 10:28–31, etc.),
which received great emphasis in the prophetic religion of the Old Testament, was derived by Christianity from Judaism. St. Paul puts it succinctly in the familiar words: "Whatsoever a man soweth, that shall he
also reap" (Gal. 6:7). The expression "the wrath of God" is frequently
used of God's reaction to sin (cf. Rom. 1:18, etc.). St. Paul already applies the principle to the Jews for killing the Lord Jesus and the prophets
and for driving out the apostolic preachers (I Thess. 2:14–16). But
with the widening of the breach between church and synagogue, there
was a natural tendency for this idea to become increasingly prominent
(cf. Matt. 27:25; John 8:24; 9:35–41).

[10] See 11:12–25. St. Mark shows a predilection for such intercalations.
Sometimes the intercalation seems simply to signify a lapse of time, as in
the story of the raising of the little girl (5:21–24, 35–43), which is
divided into two parts by the account of the healing of the woman
with an issue (5:25–34). But in other instances a parallel seems to be
intended, as in the story dealing with Jesus' relatives (3:20–21, 31–35),
which is divided by the account of the Beelzebul controversy (3:22–30),
and as in the present case of the story concerning the fig tree (11:12–14;
19–25), which is divided by the account of the cleansing of the temple
(11:15–18). A contrast is set forth in 14:1–11: the devotion of the
woman who anoints Jesus' head (14:3–9) is presented on a sinister
background of malicious scheming (14:1–2, 10–11). The story of the
mission of the twelve is divided into two parts (6:7–13, 30) by the narrative regarding the attitude of Herod and the death of the Baptist
(6:14–29); in this case the intercalation is perhaps meant to allow for
the time required for the completion of the mission and also to draw a
contrast between a certain measure of popular success and the danger
of opposition in high political circles.

[11] Cf. the unproductive fig tree of the parable in Luke 13:6–9.

[12] Conversely, certain authorities on the Jewish side seem to have
considered that Jesus was cursed, hence the mode of his death; cf. Gal.
3:10–14.

[13] For the metaphorical use of the imagery of the tree and its fruit

privileged people; but, as is suggested by the intercalation (11:15–18), this condemnation is also the historical ground of the shameful end of the Messiah himself. For Jesus' violent, but legitimate (11:17), censure of the Jews for their misuse of the temple is presented as the immediate occasion of the fateful decision which leads directly to the arrest and crucifixion (11:18). Thus the evangelist appears to have a significant parallel in mind: Jesus condemns the nation to which he belongs, and this very condemnation brings about his own death as well as the ruin of the Jewish people. The death of the Messiah, that is to say, involves the destruction of Israel, and, from another point of view, the destruction of Israel involves the death of the Messiah.[14] Again, in the parable of 12:1ff. the wicked husbandmen refuse to deliver the fruit which is rightly demanded of them and eventually they go so far as to murder the landlord's beloved or only son; the result is that the landlord destroys his faithless tenants and confides the vineyard to the care of others. Thus the defection of God's chosen people means their own perdition, and yet it redounds to the benefit of the rest of mankind. The Gentiles inherit the promises; thanks to the disobedience of the Jews, they are now able to enjoy the mercy of God (cf. Rom. 11:30).

Accordingly, if the foregoing considerations are sound, it is part of St. Mark's doctrinal purpose to make it plain to his readers that the ill-will of the Lord's own countrymen was the determining factor behind the crucifixion, and hence that the burden of guilt for this gross injustice is to be borne by a people whose God-given privileges only serve to make their conduct

---

to signify the moral agent and his conduct, cf. the sayings in Matt. 3:8–10/Luke 3:8–9; Matt. 7:15ff.

[14] The evangelist's capacity to combine a theological doctrine of predestination with a lively belief in the reality of moral responsibility seems to be reflected in the story of the fig tree; though it is not the season for figs (11:13c), yet the tree is cursed for its fruitlessness.

the more reprehensible. Such a motif, however, naturally gives rise to a certain inconsistency in the evangelist's treatment of his material. For, in so far as he is concerned to emphasize the culpability of the Jews, he tends to contravene the requirement of his more general doctrine of the messianic secret by allowing the real nature of Jesus to come out, as it were, into the light of day. Consequently, in St. Mark's representation, Jesus does not always address the public in the cryptology of parables, as he is said to do in 4:34a, and he does not always seek to perform his miracles in private, as he does, for example, in 5:40; 7:33 and 8:23. On the contrary, in certain passages the fact of the Messiahship is to a greater or less extent exposed to public view, and so it may be maintained that the Jews are in an inexcusable position, having perpetrated their crime not in ignorance, but with a cognizance of that for which Jesus stands (cf. Rom. 1:20). Thus in 2:1–3:6,[15] where we are presented with a series of five controversy stories,[16] Jesus shows little indication of de-

[15] The stories of this section may have already been collected and edited before St. Mark wrote; and it is not impossible that the similar stories of 12:13–44 were derived from the same (written) source, for 3:6 and 12:13 are the only passages in the work which mention the Herodians. The stories of both sections deal with questions of Jewish religious thought and practice, and it may be noted that in each of the sections one or two isolated sayings of the Lord are included (2:21–22; 12:38–40) in addition to the paradigms. The conversation of 12:28–34, however, may have been introduced by St. Mark himself in order to show that Jesus did not really violate the law (cf. 1:40–45). Perhaps 3:6 (which may have replaced the original conclusion of the isolated paradigm) is due to the postulated pre-Markan compiler who wished to draw attention to the ultimate issue of the conflict; and in the supposed source 12:13 (without "of the Pharisees and of the Herodians") would be the immediate sequel of 3:6.

[16] If St. Mark does not take 2:13f. to be integral to 2:15–17, there are six stories in this section, but still only five controversy stories. We may assume that v. 13 is editorial (perhaps due to St. Mark himself); it introduces the call of Levi which, like the call related in 1:16–20, takes place at the seaside. It may be that the saying of the Lord in v. 17 originally justified the call of v. 14, vv. 15–16a having been added by the

siring to shun the multitude, and in this respect the section stands in remarkable contrast to what immediately precedes (1:14–45) and follows (3:7–19). It includes no confession by a demon and no injunction to silence. Indeed, Jesus performs two miraculous healings in the presence of his opponents (2:1–12; 3:1–6); he publicly speaks of the purpose of his mission (2:17), tacitly identifies himself with the Son of Man (2:10; 2:28), and uses language which implies that the time is coming when he will be no longer with his disciples (2:19b–20; cf. 3:6).

It must not be thought, however, that the section under consideration is wholly devoid of connection with the preceding narrative. In the first place, there does not seem to be any real inconsistency between 1:45 and 2:1–2, for the evangelist probably does not intend the μηκέτι ("no longer") of 1:45 to be

---

evangelist. The opposition objected to Jesus' association with publicans, but instead of "associate" they say "eat" (with reference to the laws of cleanness), and the evangelist provides an appropriate background by supposing a meal (cf. Dibelius, *From Tradition to Gospel*, p. 64, n. 1). But this would seem to leave vv. 14 and 16b without satisfactory connection, and perhaps vv. 13f. should be understood on the same lines as 1:16–20, as a self-contained story with its own lesson. Also, St. Mark shows a liking for series of three: thus he presents three parables in 4:1–34, three predictions of the passion in 8:27–10:52, three miracle stories in 4:35–5:43 (if 5:21–43 may be taken as a single story) after the relatively prolonged teaching of 4:1–34, and three miracle stories in 7:24–8:10 after the relatively prolonged teaching of 7:1–23. Hence the evangelist may well regard the section as made up of six stories: the first three (2:1–17) concern sins and sinners, the second three (2:18–3:6) concern Jewish religious customs; words and deeds of the Lord give the church's answers to the questions involved (cf. Lohmeyer, *Das Evangelium des Markus*, p. 49). Perhaps 2:17 once circulated as an isolated saying, vv. 15f. having been composed to supply it with a particular occasion. It is historically unlikely that the scribes of the Pharisees would have been present at such a meal. Rather, they are introduced as the agreed enemies of Jesus. The apostolic church would see in the paradigm a justification of its own mixed membership, and the table fellowship would probably be taken as signifying fellowship in general. The disciples are questioned presumably as the representatives of the Christian communities concerned (cf. Bultmann, *Die Geschichte der synoptischen Tradition*, p. 16).

taken in an absolutely strict sense, any more than he means by the μηκέτι χωρεῖν ("no longer room") of 2:2 that the house could not possibly contain one more person; and in 2:1 he does not report that Jesus goes "openly" into Capernaum. Actually, 2:1–2 may imply that Jesus is still being pursued by the people (cf. 1:37; 1:45), since he is in a house (perhaps that of Simon; cf. 1:29) and the multitude evidently resorts to him there, though this time in order to hear his preaching of the word; and as we gather from such passages as 7:17 and 7:24, the evangelist sometimes uses the term "house" to denote a place of retreat from the public.[17] In the second place, the preceding narrative shows how Jesus established a reputation in the region of Galilee both as a teacher and as a worker of miracles and how he gained the allegiance of some; hence in 2:1ff. the evangelist is able to assume that the Lord is already being accompanied by a more or less permanent body of disciples.[18] In the third place, the story of the cleansing of the leper (1:40–45) seems to have a reference forward to 2:1ff., as well as a reference backward to 1:14–39.[19] It takes up the theme of what precedes, in that it emphasizes the essential power of Jesus,

---

[17] The question of the extent to which St. Mark himself may be responsible for 2:1f. constitutes a delicate problem. The anacoluthon in 2:1 suggests that the words "it was reported that he was at home" may have been part of the story's introduction as the evangelist found it; and v. 4 seems to presuppose an earlier notice setting the scene in a house. But vv. 1a, 2 may well be due to St. Mark. Like St. John, he shows a fondness for πάλιν ("again"; 2:1a); he employs it as a very unemphatic connecting link, and hence 2:1; 2:13 and 3:1 do not necessarily refer back to 1:21a; 1:16; and 1:21b respectively (cf. Turner in *J.T.S.*, XXIX [1928], 283ff.). For "he spoke the word to them" (2:2c), cf. 8:32a. It may also be noted here that the impersonal plural (2:3) occurs over twenty times in St. Mark's work; the other synoptists usually alter it by inserting a definite subject or (especially St. Luke) by substituting the passive voice (cf. Turner in *J.T.S.*, XXV [1924], 378ff.).

[18] The term "disciples" first occurs in 2:15.

[19] Cf. above, Chapter 2. The first evangelist apparently attaches special importance to this story, for it appears at the head of his selection of ten miracle stories presented in Matt. 8f.

which is such that, despite his aversion to any form of self-advertisement, he wins widespread fame as a worker of miraculous healings (cf. 1:44 with 1:25; 1:34, and 1:45 with 1:28; 1:35). The miracle described, in fact, affords a particularly striking illustration of the Lord's supernatural authority, and the story perhaps contains a suggestion of his superiority to the law. For the latter may provide rules for detecting leprosy and methods for removing the ensuing defilement, but it supplies no recipe for the cure of the disease (cf. Rom. 8:3). Also, unlike Naaman in the scriptural story, this man is not required to wash himself seven times in the river Jordan (see II Kings 5:10); Jesus' touch and word alone are sufficient to effect an instantaneous cure. But besides having a significant connection with what is related in the foregoing narrative, the story seems to have an important bearing on the controversies which follow, as we have already suggested. For in 1:44 Jesus is apparently concerned that the man should not regard himself as clean before the priest has pronounced his verdict. Thus, by placing the story in its present context, the evangelist probably means to imply that Jesus respects the law and hence that he is not the guilty party in the conflict about to be delineated.[20]

The first of the controversy stories—the account of the healing of the paralytic (2:1–12)—is of special interest, because it is the only passage in the gospel which concerns the right to forgive sins.[21] While the evangelist apparently holds that all the miraculous deeds of Jesus provide evidence of his supernatural power, in this case it is explicitly stated (v. 10) that the miracle

[20] Since Jesus touches the leper (1:41), it may be thought that he does not comply with the law; otherwise he would have taken measures to remove his own defilement. But Jesus is the agent in the story and healing power would pass from him to the patient (cf. 5:30). Presumably, such a conception would exclude the idea of a passage of defilement from the patient to Jesus.

[21] Cf. Luke 7:48, where Jesus assures the woman who anoints his feet that her sins are forgiven.

is performed in order that the seated scribes [22] may come to acknowledge the Son of Man's authority on earth to forgive sins. And it is not altogether unfitting that this particular question should be dealt with at the present stage, since, according to 1:4, the appointed forerunner has announced a baptism of repentance unto remission of sins. It is noteworthy, however, that the question of forgiveness appears only in verses 5b–10, which form the central part of the story before us; and it seems likely, as Loisy maintained, that these verses are an interpolation. Without them the story is a Novelle, not a controversy story at all, and so we may presume that the interpolation had already been made before St. Mark undertook his work. The faith of the paralytic and of those who carry him is shown by the action described in verse 4 [23] and is recognized by Jesus in verse 5a, while verses 11–12 evince three characteristic motifs of miracle stories, namely, the potent command of the healer, the demonstration of the success of the miracle, and the amazement of the spectators. The impression produced on the hostile scribes finds no mention, for they would hardly be included among those who glorify God in verse 12, and we are perhaps meant to take it for granted that they are temporarily put to silence (cf. 3:4). The parenthesis with its awkward change of subject in the address of verses 10–11 is quite understandable on the assumption that verse 10 is the ending of an interpolation and

---

[22] Cf. 1:22, where the Lord's mode of teaching is contrasted with that of the scribes. It is unlikely that the scribes here remain seated out of disrespect, since in 3:31–35 the true family of the Messiah is represented in the form of a seated audience. On the other hand, in the first gospel no one sits in the presence of Jesus, save when he hangs on the cross (Matt. 27:36)—and of course at meals (Matt. 15:35).

[23] Wellhausen conjectured that "they uncovered the roof" rests on a misunderstanding of an Aramaic original meaning "they brought him up to the roof." H. Jahnow (*Z.N.T.W.*, XXIV [1925], 155ff.) suggests that originally the men would go into the house by way of the roof in order to prevent the demon from becoming aware of the proper entrance; but cf. the article by S. Krauss in *Z.N.T.W.*, XXV (1926), 307ff.

that verse 11 was once the immediate continuation of verse 5a.[24]

In view of St. Mark's doctrine of the secret, one may be tempted to argue with Wellhausen and others that the expression "the Son of Man" in verse 10 (and in verse 28 of the same chapter) refers not to the speaker as such, but to humanity in general.[25] But there does not seem to be sufficient justification for this exegesis, for there is ample evidence that the evangelist

[24] H. Pernot (*Ex. T.*, XXXVIII [1926–27], p. 106) suggests that the ἵνα in v. 10 is used in a sense which it has in modern Greek, and that the translation should run: " 'Well, you will see that the Son of Man has power on earth to forgive sins.' He says to the paralytic, 'I say to you, Arise. . . .' " D. S. Sharp (*Ex. T.*, XXXVIII, 428f.) questions the validity of this interpretation, and translates as follows: " 'But know assuredly that the Son of Man has authority to forgive sins on earth.' He says to the paralytic. . . ." By this rendering Sharp claims to avoid an awkward parenthesis, and for the use of ἵνα with the subjunctive as a virtual imperative, he compares 5:23 and refers to J. H. Moulton and G. Milligan, *Vocabulary of the Greek Testament,* pt. 4, p. 305a (3). In our view, however, there is no need to take the ἵνα in any other than its usual sense. The disjointed construction is due to the interpolation. Neither Pernot nor Sharp succeeds in eliminating abruptness from the passage.

[25] For a defence of this interpretation, see *The Beginnings of Christianity* (eds. F. J. Foakes-Jackson and K. Lake), I, 378f. It may be noticed here that apart from 2:10 and 28, the expression "the Son of Man" does not occur before Peter's confession (8:29). After 8:29 it is used twelve times and in seven of these instances (8:31; 9:12; 9:31; 10:33; 14:21, twice; 14:41) the necessity of the Son of Man's suffering is brought out. Of the remaining five instances, three (8:38; 13:26; 14:62) are concerned with the parousia, one (9:9) with the resurrection, and one (10:45) with the redemptive purpose of the incarnate life. On the other hand, St. Matthew and St. Luke use the expression more freely than St. Mark of the whole course of the Lord's earthly career (cf. for example, Matt. 11:19; Luke 9:58). For the view that Jesus, as in Dan. 7:13, used the expression in a collective sense with reference to the community of the saints of the Most High, see T. W. Manson, *The Teaching of Jesus,* pp. 211ff., and *The Servant-Messiah,* pp. 72ff., and for the view that there was a radical opposition in current Jewish expectation between the eschatology of the Son of Man and the eschatology of the Messiah, see J. Héring, *Le royaume de Dieu et sa venue,* pp. 75ff., and below, Chapter 9, n. 34.

does not work out his theory of the messianic secret with strict logical consistency.[26] Thus in 12:12, for example, the hierarchs evidently understand the meaning of a parable in which Jesus really alludes to himself as God's beloved or only Son; and in 14:62 the Master makes a public acknowledgment of his Messiahship and confidently informs his judges that they shall see the Son of Man coming with the clouds of heaven. It would appear, indeed, that St. Mark is not wholly satisfied with his doctrine of the secret and that he is feeling his way after a mode of representation analogous to that of the fourth evangelist. Moreover, whatever the supposed original significance of 2:10 and 2:28 may be, there is reason for thinking that St. Mark and his readers would be interested not so much in the right of men generally to forgive sins as in the right of the church to perform such action. For according to the tradition preserved in Matt. 18:18 (cf. Matt. 16:19) and in John 20:23 the Lord conferred upon his followers the authority to forgive sins; and hence it was only natural that attempts should have been made within the church to prove that the Lord himself possessed authority of that kind, especially in view of the Jewish objection that it was blasphemous to ascribe the power to forgive sins to any one other than God.[27]

In St. Mark's story the main contention is that the Messiah's power to heal is a sure sign or token of his power to forgive sins, and this evidently presupposes the popular belief in a causal connection between sin and human affliction.[28] For the idea behind the declaration of forgiveness in verse 5b appears to be that a person who heals thereby removes the moral causes of illness and

[26] Cf. above, Chapter 5; below, Chapters 8, 9, and 10.

[27] In rabbinic literature, while it is assumed that the messianic community will be delivered from sin, the right to forgive sins is never ascribed to the Messiah; this is a right which belongs exclusively to God; cf. S.-B., I, 495.

[28] For this belief, cf. above, Chapter 3.

is therefore able to forgive sins. It must be admitted, however, that such a line of argument would be of doubtful apologetical value. Thus while the assertion that human sins cause human afflictions undoubtedly contains a considerable measure of truth, there is no warrant for assuming that every case of illness is the result of sin committed by the patient. As Jesus seems to recognize in Luke 13:1ff., the suffering of the innocent is as much a fact of common experience as the operation of a principle of moral retribution. Also, the proof of the power to forgive sins by reference to the power to heal is an argument which could be applied to any miracle worker independently of his moral character. It betrays a tendency to subordinate ethical qualities to thaumaturgical powers; and we may safely say that if such a tendency had prevailed in the church, Christianity would have rapidly degenerated into a mere technique of magic. But thanks to the spiritual discernment of St. Paul and others, the danger was averted, and generally the church aspired after "the greater gifts" and followed "a still more excellent way" in its fundamental valuations.[29]

Accordingly, it is not surprising to find that Jesus in John 9:1ff. disapproves of the popular belief that any assignable case of illness is due either to the sin of the sufferer himself or to that of his parents; and, as Fridrichsen pointed out,[30] it may be that the Lord really disapproves of the belief implied in verse 10 of

[29] Cf. I Cor. 12:31. The sayings in Matt. 7:22–23 and Luke 10:20 seem to be directed against members of the church who were prone to exaggerate the importance of miracle working; and perhaps the account of the temptations of Jesus in Matt. 4:1ff./Luke 4:1ff. should be understood in a similar sense; cf. Fridrichsen, *Le problème du miracle*, pp. 84ff., 94ff. St. Paul could sometimes refer to his own deeds of power as signs of his apostolic authority (II Cor. 12:12); but he would not regard them as his sole title to such authority.

[30] See *op. cit.*, pp. 90ff. Of course Jesus, as he is represented by the fourth evangelist, does not deny that illness is sometimes due to the sin of the sufferer; cf. John 5:14.

St. Mark's story that the power to heal constitutes a convincing proof of the spiritual authority to forgive sins. Such an interpretation turns on the significance attributed to the counterquestion in verse 9.[31] One possibility is that a declaration of forgiveness is easier than a declaration of healing, since the efficacy of the former is unverifiable, whereas the latter should issue in an observable effect on the patient;[32] and Jesus is represented as naïvely assuming that anyone would necessarily supply such an answer to the question. On this exegesis, however, one would have expected a καί or an οὖν, rather than a δέ, to mark the connection between verses 9 and 10, for the δέ in verse 10 suggests that the two verses may stand in opposition to each other. If this is so, since verse 10 implies that the miraculous healing (being the basis of the proof) is more difficult than the forgiveness of sins, the question in verse 9 must be ironical and have the contrary sense that forgiveness is really the more difficult of the two actions, although the scribes think otherwise—perhaps as a result of the way in which the question is framed, it being of the nature of a trap, like the counterquestion in 11:30.

Thus verse 9 may be an interpolation within an interpolation, introduced by St. Mark himself, who is averse to the implications of the story as he receives it. In his view, the argument from the act of healing to the act of forgiveness is an argument from less to more, and yet, seeing that some believers are wont to reason in this way, he allows the story to have a place in his gospel as a mode of demonstration which meets a demand that has won popularity in certain circles. On such an interpretation, therefore, the passage would afford an illustration of the conservative character of the evangelist's manner of dealing with the tradition; in spite of personal disapproval, he does not reject the story,

---

[31] The counterquestion is characteristic of controversy stories; see 3: 4; 11:30; 12:37. For rabbinic parallels, cf. Bultmann, *op. cit.*, pp. 43ff.
[32] Cf. Klostermann, *Das Markusevangelium*, p. 23.

but accommodates it to his own higher point of view by inserting the subtle counterquestion of verse 9, which has an inner as
well as an outer meaning.[33]

The story of the healing of the paralytic is followed by the
brief account of the call of Levi the son of Alphaeus [34] and the
controversy story regarding the Master's association with publicans and sinners (2:15–17). All three narratives deal with sins
or sinners, and perhaps they were first brought together for this
reason. With the exception of the two sayings in 2:21–22 (which
may be meant to emphasize the necessity of the separation of
Christianity from Judaism) and the editorial notice in 3:6, the
rest of the section is composed of three controversy stories concerning Jewish religious customs. The first of these (2:18–20),
which is apparently intended as a justification of the Christian
practice of fasting on Fridays, provides a further illustration of

[33] G. H. Boobyer (*H.T.R.*, XLVII [1954], 115ff.) contends that the
only significant editorial adaptation in the story is the interpolation
(made by the evangelist himself or by a previous editor) of v. 10a—"But
that you may know that the Son of Man has power on earth to forgive
sins"—and the omission of a small conjunctive expression before the
clause, "he says to the paralytic" (v. 10b). Boobyer thinks that v. 10a is
addressed not to the scribes but to the Christian readers of the gospel,
and that 2:28 (cf. 7:3) might be understood along the same lines. This
exegesis, however, offers no satisfactory explanation of the "all" in v. 12,
which, in view of the persistent hostility of the scribes in St. Mark's
gospel, can scarcely be accounted for by being regarded simply as "an
excusable and fairly obvious overstatement" (*ibid.*, p. 119). Moreover,
the evangelist does not apply his theory of the messianic secret with
the high degree of consistency supposed (*ibid.*, pp. 118f.). Also, failing
to recognize the importance of the counterquestion in v. 9, Boobyer
commits the evangelist to a precarious piece of apologetics without sufficient consideration; cf. also H. A. Guy, *The Origin of the Gospel of
Mark*, pp. 87f.

[34] See 2:13f. This man is not referred to again in the gospel; thus,
unlike the first evangelist (Matt. 9:9) but like the third evangelist (Luke
5:27), St. Mark apparently does not identify him with the Matthew
mentioned in the list of the twelve (3:18). It has been conjectured that
he was a brother of James, the son of Alphaeus.

the conservative character of the tradition; for, in the words
of Dibelius, "although the need was felt of justifying fasting,
it was preserved in a saying of Jesus really of a contrary tendency." [35] The two remaining stories afford warrant for the Christian position in the matter of sabbath observance: in 2:23–28
scripture is cited to show that one may work on the sabbath
for the purpose of satisfying the physical need for food,[36] while

[35] See *op. cit.*, p. 66. The original saying seems to be preserved in v.
19a, vv. 19b–20 (which presuppose the passion) being a secondary composition appended after the church had adopted the practice of fasting.
Bultmann (*op. cit.*, pp. 17f.) sees the original form of the story in vv.
18b–19a; he thinks that the story in this form was a construction (based
on the traditional saying of v. 19a) made in the *Urgemeinde* when the
question of the relation between Christianity and the Baptist sect was a
matter of immediate interest; in this case, it would be assumed in the
Urgemeinde that "the bridegroom" remained with "the sons of the bride-
chamber" after the crucifixion. As a parallel to v. 19a, Bultmann cites
the Indian proverb: "Who eats gruel on the day of rejoicing?" (*ibid.*, p.
107, n. 1). The figure of the wedding feast is sometimes used of the days
of the Messiah in rabbinic writings; cf. S.-B., I, 517. Although the law
does not require that certain days of the week should be regularly kept
as fast days, it seems that certain enthusiastic Pharisees established the
practice of fasting on Monday and Thursday of each week as a special
act of piety, and the church eventually took over the custom of fasting
twice a week, but altered the days to Wednesday and Friday; cf. Luke
18:12; *Didachē*, 8, 1; *Ap. Constitutions*, 7, 23, 1; for other references, see T. W. Manson, *The Mission and Message of Jesus*, p. 603;
G. F. Moore, *Judaism*, II, 260. Even if St. Mark, following a supposed
lectionary scheme, intended 2:18–22 to be read at the midwinter
Tammuz celebration (and this is extremely doubtful; see W. D. Davies
in *The Background of the New Testament and its Eschatology*, pp.
124ff.), there would still be no justification for Carrington's hypothesis
(see his *According to Mark*, p. 69) that Jesus, a generation earlier, took
an active part in the popular Tammuz celebrations and actually played
the role of the bridegroom in a Jewish adaptation of the fertility cultus.

[36] It was unlawful to pluck standing corn on the sabbath, since such
action was regarded as a form of harvest labor; cf. S.-B., I, 615ff. For
the view that the story originally ended at v. 26, see Bultmann, *op. cit.*,
pp. 14f. According to I Sam. 21:1ff., it was Ahimelech, not Abiathar (v.
26), who gave David the shewbread. It may be, however, that the phrase
ἐπὶ ᾿Αβιαθὰρ ἀρχιερέως should be rendered "at the passage of scripture

in 3:1–5 the practice of healing on the sabbath is defended by means of a counterquestion which has the immediate effect of silencing the critics.[37] With the notice of the coalition between

---

concerning (or entitled) Abiathar the high priest," for in Mark 12:26 ἐπὶ τοῦ βάτου evidently means "at the passage of scripture concerning (or entitled) the Bush" (see the note by J. W. Wenham in *J.T.S.*, n.s., I [1950], 156).

[37] Actually, the probable answer of the Pharisees would have been: it is good to heal on the sabbath only when the patient is dangerously ill (cf. S.-B., I, 623). But attention should be called to the interesting notes on Mark 2:1–3:6 in the third appendix of H. Riesenfeld's *Jésus transfiguré* (pp. 318ff.). The author agrees with J. Jeremias (*Jesus als Weltvollender*, pp. 21ff.) that 2:18–22 should be understood eschatologically (the messianic age having come, fasting is no longer practiced), and he goes on to argue that the next two pericopes should be understood in the same kind of sense. In 2:23ff. Jesus does not speak as a rabbi against rabbis—rather the conduct of the disciples in plucking (and eating) the ears of corn prefigures the great sabbath of the messianic epoch; the old sabbath has been replaced, a point which the Pharisees do not grasp; the ears of corn symbolize the eschatological and eucharistic bread, and David, as prototype of the Messiah, performs an action which anticipates the Christian communion. Similarly, in 3:1ff. we have not really a legalistic dispute—the point is rather that the old sabbath has been replaced by the new one of the messianic age; in the Aramaic behind the phrase "to do good on the sabbath" there may have been a play on words, the expression "the good day" having come to be used for the sabbath, and so the original meaning could have been that "doing good" (a messianic motif) is the proper way to celebrate "the good day" of the messianic epoch. Riesenfeld further suggests that 2:13–17 represents the eschatological meal as well as the eucharist, and he connects 2:1–12 (which he considers to be all of a piece) with the rite of baptism, a rite involving the remission of sins and, like miraculous healing, requiring faith. It seems unlikely, however, that the evangelist himself attached an eschatological meaning to 2:18ff., 2:23ff., and 3:1ff. It is not impossible that 2:19a was originally meant in an eschatological sense, and that such a significance was largely removed when the qualification in verses 19b–20 was added. Riesenfeld's proposals are of more doubtful worth as far as 2:23ff. and 3:1ff. are concerned, the usual interpretations in this case being in accord with the teaching of Jesus as it is expressed in such passages as 7:1ff. and 12:28ff., where the moral is exalted above the ceremonial; in 12:18ff. Jesus does not contemplate the

the religious and the civil authorities in 3:6,[38] this first series of controversy stories is brought to a conclusion; by informing the reader that the authorities conspire to do away with Jesus, the remark really points forward to the final outcome of the conflict which is to be described in detail in the passion narrative.

Next come two generalizing passages, probably composed by the evangelist himself as a foil to the preceding controversies. In 3:7–12 Jesus is again by the sea,[39] and so great is his reputation that a large multitude of people, drawn from such widely separated places as Jerusalem and Sidon, resort to him there; nevertheless, the messianic secret is carefully guarded (vv. 11–12). In 3:13–19 Jesus ascends a mountain (cf. Matt. 28:16) and selects a body of twelve men (a list of whose names is appended) that they might accompany him and that he might send them forth to preach and to have authority to exorcize demons.[40]

---

abolition of the institution of marriage until the general resurrection of the dead (which may presumably coincide with the parousia) and perhaps he did not envisage the supersession of the institution of the sabbath until the same date. It is quite possible that St. Mark read 2:13ff. in the light of the eucharist, but Riesenfeld's suggestions with respect to 2:1ff. do not appear to carry very much weight, the element of faith providing too slender a connecting link to warrant the introduction of the notion of baptism into the exegesis of the pericope. Cf. P. Winter, *On the Trial of Jesus*, pp. 118–119, where it is maintained that the Markan controversy stories are largely retrojections of ecclesiastical controversies into the life of Jesus; and cf. F. W. Beare's treatment of Mark 2:23ff. in *J.B.L.*, LXXIX (1960), 130ff.

[38] In Lohmeyer's judgment (*op. cit.*, p. 67) it is historically unlikely that Pharisees would have deigned to form a coalition with supporters of the house of Herod, which was generally regarded among the Jews as a foreign dynasty; he thinks that the pro-Pharisaic policy of Agrippa I (d. 44 A.D.) may have first suggested the idea of such a coalition. But cf. Winter, *op. cit.*, pp. 127ff.

[39] With the exception of the special case of 6:1ff., Jesus does not again appear inside a synagogue in St. Mark's gospel.

[40] Carrington (*op. cit.*, p. 29) states that in St. Mark's gospel Jesus "is inseparable from the fellowship or household of the Twelve, which he forms around him and to which he commits everything." This state-

Seeing that in the course of time the content of their preaching is to become the gospel of Jesus, the Messiah, the Son of God, we may assume that the evangelist construes the appointment of the twelve to represent the foundation of the Christian church. Hence it is not unnatural that he should return to the theme of opposition in the passage which immediately follows,[41] for at the time of writing the Jewish people, to whom Jesus primarily addressed himself, had proved themselves to be the most intransigent antagonists of the gospel proclaimed by the apostolic church. But now the conflict becomes more bitter than hitherto, because it assumes a wholly personal character. Jesus belonged to Israel and fulfilled the messianic hopes of the prophets, yet he was rejected by the religious leaders of Israel. To employ the phraseology of the fourth evangelist, the Messiah came to his own, and they that were his own did not receive him (cf. John 1:11); and such seems to be the poignant reflection of St. Mark in the passage under consideration. By intercalating a story [42]

ment is false. In 14:10f., Judas reduces the twelve to eleven, and in 14:50 the remaining eleven all forsake Jesus at the arrest.

[41] Mark 3:20–35. This passage stands in noteworthy contrast to 3:7–19 where: (1) the scene is set by the sea and then on a mountain; (2) people come from a wide area and Jesus chooses the twelve; (3) the demons acknowledge Jesus' divine Sonship; and (4) Jesus frees the possessed. But in 3:20–35: (1) the scene is set in a house; (2) Jesus' mother and his brothers come from their home (cf. 6:3, which may imply that only his sisters are still at home) and the scribes come from Jerusalem; (3) it is alleged that Jesus is an agent of Beelzebul; and (4) Jesus himself is said to be possessed.

[42] Mark 3, 22–30. The basis of this story may be preserved in vv. 22b–26 (the objection and the twofold answer). Perhaps it was once preceded by a miracle story (cf. Matt. 12:22/Luke 11:14) which St. Mark did not require in view of vv. 9–12. V. 22a (cf. the indefinite subject τινες in Luke 11:15) may be partly due to the evangelist, and v. 30 wholly so. Possibly vv. 27–29 were originally two isolated traditional sayings of Jesus. (Cf. Bultmann, *op. cit.*, pp. 10ff.). The reply (vv. 23–26), unlike the objection (v. 22b), presupposes a consistent moral dualism between the forces of Satan and the forces of God; v. 22b is an indication that popular demonological thought sometimes worked on the prin-

between the earlier and the later part of another,[43] he suggests
a significant parallel between the kinsfolk of Jesus, who declare
that he is beside himself (v. 21) and apparently seek to prevent
him from continuing his work (vv. 21, 31), and the scribes from
Jerusalem, who ascribe his extraordinary powers to the inspiration of Beelzebul, the prince of the demons (v. 22). On the other
hand, when the matter is considered in a broader perspective, it
is seen that the blindness and the hostility of Jesus' physical relatives serve to bring out the real nature of the Messiah's family;
those who are truly related to him belong to the spiritual community in which the will of God is performed.[44]

The next two chapters contain material of a different character: in 4:1–34, besides offering an explanation of the nonacceptance of Jesus as the Messiah, St. Mark sets forth three
parables of growth which evince his unfailing confidence in the
ultimate triumph of the kingdom of God over all the opposing
forces of evil; and in 4:35–5:43, by presenting a series of three [45]
miracle stories, he supplies further evidence of the supernatural
power which Jesus uses for the benefit of men. But the theme
of opposition recurs at the beginning of chapter six, directly after
the account of the raising of the little girl,[46] in the story of the

---

ciple of "no honour among thieves" (cf. Fridrichsen, *op. cit.*, pp. 71ff.,
and above, Chapter 3).

[43] Mark 3:20f., 31–35. The D reading in v. 21, which makes vv. 20f.
an independent story, was probably due to a copyist who could not wait
for the continuation in vv. 31–35. Vv. 21, 35 seem to belong to the original basis of the story. Vv. 31–34 may be a secondary construction providing a concrete representation (in the form of an attentive audience)
of those who do the will of God. Perhaps v. 20 is partly due to St. Mark
himself. Cf. Bultmann, *op. cit.* pp. 28f.

[44] Vv. 33–35. Whereas the mother and the brothers of Jesus stand outside (v. 31), the multitude is seated within the house (vv. 20a, 32) and
represents the true family of the Messiah (v. 34); cf. the favorable appeal to the multitude in 8:34a.

[45] In St. Mark's view, 5:21–43 may be a single story; cf. above, n. 16.

[46] It is noteworthy that in the fourth gospel the decision to put Jesus
to death (11:53) follows on the seventh and greatest sign (the raising of

rejection of Jesus in his native place or *patris* (6:1–6), and this story is immediately followed by the account of the mission of the twelve (6:7–13:30) with its intercalated reports concerning Herod's mistaken opinion of Jesus (6:14–16) and the death of John the Baptist (vv. 17–29). Thus the arrangement of the traditions at the present juncture (the end of the narrative of a settled ministry in Galilee) suggests that the evangelist again wishes to indicate in advance the shape of things to come.[47] He seems to regard the story of Jesus' rejection in the *patris* [48] as a

---

Lazarus), in which the Messiah is revealed as the resurrection and the life (11:25).

[47] Lightfoot (*History and Interpretation*, pp. 182ff.) points out that all the synoptists attach special importance to the story of the rejection in the *patris*. In Matt. 13:53–58, as in Mark 6:1–6, the incident is seen in its tragic aspect. St. Matthew places the story at the end of his great scheme of rearrangement in Matt. 5–13 and thereby makes the incident the climax of the Galilean ministry. But he depicts Jesus as deliberately restricting his miracles among his own people in consequence of their unbelief (Matt. 13:58), and this gives the story a sternness which it does not possess in St. Mark's gospel. On the other hand, St. Luke is more concerned with the glad reception of the gospel by the Gentile than with the tragedy of its rejection by the Jew. He places the story of the rejection in the *patris* at the outset of his account of the ministry (Luke 4:16–30) and presents the incident as though it were foreseen and inevitable from the beginning. Thus St. Luke does not see the story in its tragic aspect. Whatever opposition may be offered at this point can only result in an extension of the field of the ministry.

[48] Certain interesting problems are raised by 6:1–6: (1) In v. 3a the reading "Is not this the carpenter, the son of Mary . . . ?" is surprising in view of (*a*) the fact that it does not mention Joseph, (*b*) Origen's statement (*c. Celsum*, 6, 36) that the gospels nowhere describe Jesus as a carpenter. Hence the original reading may be: ὁ τοῦ τέκτονος υἱὸς καὶ Μαρίας ("the son of the carpenter and of Mary"; Fam. 13 etc.), which was altered in the interests of the doctrine of the virgin birth. But the reference to Jesus as the son of Mary may have been meant as an insult (cf. Lightfoot, *op. cit.*, pp. 187f.), and it should be noticed that the text in Matt. 13:55 and Luke 4:22 has not been altered in the interests of the doctrine mentioned. (2) It is not till we come to v. 3a (v. 3c, if the reading of Fam. 13 is correct) that there is any sign of hostility on the part of the congregation; v. 2 reads as though Jesus were meeting with

representation on a small scale of the final rejection of the Messiah by his own nation, an act which resulted in the crucifixion and the subsequent world-wide mission of the apostolic church.

St. Mark probably takes the ἐσκανδαλίζοντο ("they were scandalized") in verse 3c (cf. I Cor. 1:23; Rom. 9:33) and the ἀπιστίαν ("unbelief") in verse 6 (cf. Rom. 3:3; 11:20) to symbolize the Jewish attitude to the apostolic belief in the crucified Messiah, in which case he again contravenes the strict requirements of his doctrine of the messianic secret. But verses 5–6 involve a further difficulty, for verse 5a seems to be contradicted by verse 5b. It is possible, therefore, that the original conclusion was without verse 5b, and it would be meant not as an indication of the impotence of Jesus in face of the disrespect of his compatriots, but as an impressive illustration of the baneful consequences of unbelief: those who do not show the respect and honor which are due to the divine prophet, necessarily preclude themselves from receiving the marvelous blessings which he can bestow upon them. If this is so, verse 5b may have been added by St. Mark (Matt. 13:58 seems to presuppose a Markan text which included verse 5b) who mistook verses 5a and 6 to signify that Jesus was completely frustrated by the hostility of his own people; by interpolating verse 5b he transforms a complete failure into a partial one. But on the assumption that St. Mark misinterpreted verses 5a, 6 in this way, the οὐκ ἐδύνατο ("he could not") in verse 5a would come into conflict with the belief in the

great success (cf. 1:21–28—Jesus' first appearance in a synagogue). (3) The story culminates in the general pronouncement of v. 4, which shows a striking resemblance to the first part of the saying preserved in the Oxyrhynchus papyri: "A prophet is not acceptable in his *patris*, neither does a physician perform cures on those who know him" (*Ox. log.* 6, ed. Grenfell and Hunt). V. 5a may be a translation into a dramatic form of the second part of this saying. Thus it has been conjectured that a story of success has been transformed into a story of failure under the influence of the disappointing experience of the church in its missionary work among the Jews, aided by a traditional saying of the Lord. Cf. Bultmann, *op. cit.*, pp. 30f.

sovereign might of the Messiah, which is evident elsewhere in the gospel, and hence he ought to have adopted some such ending as Matt. 13:58, where the words οὐκ ἐδύνατο do not appear. Accordingly, it seems more satisfactory to suppose that St. Mark did not misunderstand verses 5a, 6 in the manner suggested, and that he introduced verse 5b in order to make room for the fact that a few Jews responded to the gospel proclaimed by the apostolic church.

After the brief account of the return of the apostles in 6:30 [49] comes a further series of three pericopes dealing with the supernatural power of Jesus and showing his extraordinary adequacy in situations to which the disciples are quite unequal. In 6:31–44, being moved with compassion, he multiplies a few loaves and fishes and feeds a multitude of five thousand men; in 6:45–52 he compels his disciples to cross the sea alone, and when a contrary wind distresses them he comes to their aid by miraculously walking on the water; and in 6:53–56, having taken to the shore, his presence in Gennesaret is soon made widely known, and he proceeds to achieve more fame as a worker of marvelous healings.[50] But the evangelist again takes up the theme of opposition in 7:1–23, a composite passage in which Jesus enunciates the principle of inward purity over against the Pharisaic doctrine of ceremonial cleanness. This relatively prolonged section of controversy is characteristically followed by yet another series of

[49] Mark 6:30 is the only passage in St. Mark's gospel where the word "apostle" is used. In 6:31–7:37 and 8:1–26 the evangelist seems to be reproducing two parallel cycles of the same tradition. Thus: (1) 6:31–44 (feeding of five thousand)/ 8:1–9 (feeding of four thousand); (2) 6:45–52 (walking on the sea)—no parallel in chapter 8; (3) 6:53–56 (crossing to Gennesaret)/8:10 (crossing to Dalmanutha); (4) 7:1–23 (conflict with Pharisees)/8:11f. (conflict with Pharisees); (5) 7:24–30 (Syrophoenician woman—conversation about the bread of the children)/ 8:13–21 (conversation about bread); (6) 7:31–37 (healing of a deafmute)/8:22–26 (healing of a blind man).

[50] In 6:54–56 we have a generalizing summary probably composed by St. Mark; cf, such passages as 1:45; 3:7–12; 3:20; 6:31–33; 7:36f.

three stories which afford further demonstration of the supernatural power of Jesus. In 7:24–30 [51] he holds a conversation
with a Syrophoenician woman and expels a demon from her
daughter by miraculous action from a distance; in 7:31–37, having passed through the region of Decapolis, he cures a man who
is suffering from deafness and a speech impediment; and in 8:1–9,
again being moved with compassion, he multiplies a few loaves
and small fishes and feeds a multitude of about four thousand
people. Nevertheless, despite such impressive manifestations of
the supernatural power of Jesus, neither his opponents nor even

[51] St. Mark himself may have brought this story into its present context, for its similarity to 8:13–21 (the alleged parallel in the second cycle
of tradition) is very slight. The story is appropriately placed seeing that
the doctrine of ceremonial cleanness has just been repudiated; cf. Acts
10:28. The "yes" (v. 28), which is omitted in D, Fam. 13 etc., may have
crept into the Markan text from the parallel in Matt. 15:27; it does not
occur elsewhere in St. Mark's gospel. The "lord" (v. 28) probably should
be translated "sir" (cf. John 4:49, R.V.). The three later evangelists
often put the word (no doubt with the meaning "Lord") into the mouth
of the disciples addressing Jesus. St. Luke and St. John also often use
"the Lord" in narrative. But St. Mark never uses "the Lord" in narrative
and never uses the vocative except here (cf. Turner in *N.C.H.S.*, pt.
3, p. 76). He may take the word to refer to Jesus in 1:3 (a scriptural
quotation); cf. 12:35–37. B. H. Streeter (*The Four Gospels*, p. 260) sees
an earlier form of the story in Matt. 15:21–28, and Bussmann (*Synoptische Studien*, I, 49ff.) argues that the story did not appear in the
first edition of St. Mark's gospel. On the other hand, the saying in Matt.
15:24 (which certainly has a primitive ring about it) may be based on
Matt. 10:6, and Matt. 15:28 seems to be secondary to Mark 7:29f. Admittedly, Mark 7:27a weakens the argument for the position taken in
Mark 7:27b; but St. Matthew perhaps omitted it precisely for this reason. There is hardly sufficient evidence for the view that, in the light
of Mark 7:27a, the first miracle of the loaves should be understood as
a feeding of Jews, and the second as a feeding of Gentiles. The Q
story in Matt. 8:5–13/Luke 7:1–10 closely resembles Mark 7:24–30;
these are the only two stories in the synoptic gospels which concern
miraculous action from a distance, and in each Jesus is surprised by the
utterance of a Gentile who pleads on behalf of his or her child or
slave; for some interesting comments on these stories, see P. Winter:
op. cit., pp. 4, 139.

his disciples are able to discern the real nature of his person and office. Thus in 8:11–12 the Pharisees reveal their ignorance by demanding of him a sign from heaven,[52] and in 8:13–21 the disciples betray their complete failure to grasp the mysterious significance of the miracles of the loaves. But the healing of the blind man in 8:22–26 seems to foreshadow the enlightenment of the disciples, related in the following pericope, which marks the opening of the second main section of the gospel.

[52] Cf. I Cor. 1:22. In Lohmeyer's view (*op. cit.*, p. 156), the point is that the Pharisees are unaware of the secret that only God can give signs. St. Mark refers to the miracles of Jesus not as "signs" but as "powers." On the other hand, it should be noted that, according to 13:22, the false messiahs and the false prophets will work signs and wonders. St. Mark evidently holds that the cosmic disturbances or signs, which current Jewish expectation commonly associated with the advent of the days of the Messiah, are to take place in connection with the parousia of the Son of Man; cf. 13:4; 13:24ff. Mark 8:12 is not inconsistent with 13:30 if we may assume that "this generation" in 13:30 signifies the second generation of Christians (Jesus is speaking privately to four disciples; cf. 13:3ff.) rather than the first, the reference being to a time when only a minority of Jesus' contemporaries would still be alive: cf. 9:1.

PART TWO

The Mysterious Meaning

of the Secret Fact

7

The Confession
and the Transfiguration

THE story of Peter's acknowledgment of the fact of the Messiahship (8:27ff.) constitutes a turning point in St. Mark's representation of the earthly life of the Lord. For hitherto, although Jesus' messianic dignity has constantly revealed itself in authoritative word and miraculous deed, human beings have failed to recognize it. But now a decisive change takes place. The disciples become aware of the mystery of their Master's greatness, and thus the evangelist is able to introduce them (and the readers of the gospel) to an elucidation of the fateful significance of the Messiahship and its implications, not only for Jesus himself, but for all who would be his followers. Hence it is with the Master's deeper instruction of his disciples in the essential meaning of his status and office that the second main section of the gospel, which extends from 8:27 to 10:52, is primarily concerned. During the Galilean ministry the multitude have been the chief recipients of the teaching, but now they are relegated to the background and the disciples come to the fore; Jesus discloses the fundamental truth esoterically within the fellowship of the elect. Thus the ministry becomes a more distinctly private affair; and the word "multitude" (which occurs twenty-two times prior to 8:27) appears in only four of the seventeen constituent pericopes of the second edition (8:34ff.; 9:14ff.; 10:1ff.; 10:46ff.). Moreover, with the disciples' discovery of the messianic secret, the contrast between supernatural knowledge and human ignorance of the truth, a notable characteristic of St. Mark's account of the Galilean ministry, to some extent falls away; and in consequence there is no longer the same call for the inclusion of transcendent modes of attestation to the Messiahship. Admittedly, the truth of Peter's confession receives divine confirmation in the utterance of the voice from the cloud on the mount of the transfiguration (9:7). But there are no further references to the supernatural knowledge of the demons, and only on two occasions in this section is Jesus allowed to give demonstration of his power to work miracles—in healing the boy with a deaf and dumb spirit (9:14ff.) and in healing blind Bartimaeus (10:46ff.); and it is arguable that the story of the latter miracle should not be regarded as belonging exclusively to the second section of the gospel, since it seems to bear a special relation to the account of the triumphal entry, which follows in 11:1ff.

In 8:27ff. it is reported that Jesus and his disciples proceed, evidently from Bethsaida (8:22), into the villages of Caesarea Philippi,[1] and as they journey[2] the Master asks:

Who do men say that I am?

[1] This town was the ancient Paneas, situated some twenty-five miles to the north of the Sea of Galilee, near the springs of the Jordan and close to the southwestern slope of Mount Hermon; it was rebuilt by the tetrarch Philip in honor of Caesar Augustus (see Josephus, *Ant.* 18, 2, 1). Bultmann (*Z.N.T.W.*, XIX [1920], 169; cf. *Die Geschichte der synoptischen Tradition*, pp. 275ff.) holds that v. 27a is the conclusion of the preceding pericope; he compares the story of the Syrophoenician woman (7:24ff.), which in his view also has a topographical notice at the end (v. 31) as well as at the beginning (v. 24a). But whether or not the tradition associated the confession with Caesarea Philippi, St. Mark himself evidently localizes it in the region of the town, and this may be significant: Jesus is first revealed to men as Messiah in the neighborhood

The disciples reply that some say that he is John the Baptist, and others, Elijah; but others, one of the prophets. Jesus does not declare that these various opinions are erroneous; [3] he simply asks a further question:

But who do you say that I am?

to which Peter, acting as the spokesman of the whole body of his colleagues, answers:

You are the Messiah.[4]

Jesus does not express any satisfaction with Peter for this reply, but (just as he has previously enjoined the demons to keep si-

of a heathen city beyond Galilee of the Gentiles. Bultmann's main thesis in this connection is that the story of the confession is a *Glaubenslegende* (cf. Dibelius, *From Tradition to Gospel*, p. 115); that is, Peter's experience of the risen Lord (held to constitute the creative basis of the Christian faith) is thrown back into the heart of the ministry; and for the original conclusion of the legend (thought to be retained in Matt. 16:17–19) has been substituted a polemic (vv. 32f.) against Jewish Christianity (represented by Peter) from the standpoint of Hellenistic or Pauline Christianity. This hypothesis is worthy of serious consideration; but whether or not we accept it, it is important to observe that St. Mark's vital belief in the Messiahship, which is continually pressing for expression in his account of the Master's earthly career, now finds a new outlet, though still the truth cannot be openly proclaimed (8:30).

[2] For the phrase "in the way" cf. 9:33–34; 10:17; 10:32.

[3] In v. 28 "John the Baptist" and "Elijah" are in the accusative and go with λέγουσίν σε εἶναι (understood); the first ὅτι belongs to the λέγοντες. The second ὅτι belongs to λέγουσιν (understood); "one of the prophets" (nominative) follows σὺ εἶ (understood). This change in construction from an accusative with an infinitive to a nominative with a finite verb (cf. the δέ after the second ἄλλοι) may reflect a change in meaning: each of the first two opinions mentioned implies that Jesus has a special eschatological significance, whereas, according to the third opinion, he is just an ordinary prophet (cf. Lohmeyer, *Das Evangelium des Markus*, p. 162, n. 2). It is to be observed, however, that there is no such change of construction in 6:14f., where the same popular opinions are given in the same order. In St. Mark's view, all three opinions are alike false; for him, the Baptist is the divinely appointed forerunner of Jesus the Messiah (cf. 9:9ff.).

[4] Following Matt. 16:16, so it seems, some authorities add "the Son of (the living) God."

lence) he strictly charges the disciples that they should tell no one concerning him. Thus the fact of their Master's real nature is revealed to the elect, and this prepares the way for an explanation of the secret significance of that fact in the light of God's sovereign purpose: the Son of Man must suffer many things, be rejected and killed, and after three days rise again from the dead.

Seeing that 8:27 in an important sense is the commencement of a new main section of the gospel, it may have been expected that its introductory conjunction would have been δέ instead of καί. For, as C. H. Turner pointed out,[5] it is evidently St. Mark's practice to use δέ at the beginning of a pericope as an indication of some large new departure in the narrative generally. Unlike the other synoptists, and especially St. Luke, who prefers δέ, he ordinarily commences a new paragraph with καί. Excluding 15:16, which should not be regarded as the beginning of a new paragraph, and taking the reading of the Codex Sinaiticus in 1:14 to be the correct one, there are only four occasions on which St. Mark opens a new paragraph with δέ—1:14; 7:24; 10:32; 14:1—and in each case there is a significant break in the continuity of the gospel story. At 1:14 the account of the ministry commences; at 7:24 Jesus goes to the region of Tyre, leaving Palestine for the first time; at 10:32 Jerusalem is first mentioned as the goal of Jesus' movements; and at 14:1 the story of the ministry proper is over and the passion narrative begins. Accordingly, seeing that the ordinary conjunction καί is used to mark the transition from 8:26 to 8:27, we must be on our guard against overemphasizing the abruptness of the break in the narrative at this point. Although the story of the confession is in a real sense a turning-point in the gospel and opens a new main section of the work, the evangelist probably does not think of it as being without preparation in the preceding narrative.

Considering the matter from the side of topography, there is nothing surprising about the journey from Bethsaida (8:22) to

[5] *J.T.S.*, XXVIII (1927), 152. Cf. above Chapter 1, n. 1.

Caesarea Philippi (8:27). It is only a continuation of an itinerary which has been proceeding for some time mostly outside Galilee. Jesus apparently ceases to conduct a settled ministry in Galilee as early as 6:32, a notice which follows on the mention of Herod Antipas' knowledge of Jesus (6:14ff.), the parenthesis on the death of John the Baptist (6:17ff.), and the brief report concerning the return of the apostles (6:30). He is at Bethsaida in 6:45, in the plain of Gennesaret (south of Capernaum) at 6:53, in the region of Tyre at 7:24, in Decapolis at 7:31, in Dalmanutha or Magedan or Magdala (perhaps the same district as Gennesaret) at 8:10, again at Bethsaida in 8:22, and in the villages of Caesarea Philippi at 8:27. Thus, from a topographical point of view, the transition from 8:26 to 8:27 may be said to be a natural continuation of the preceding narrative.

Moreover, the story of the healing of the blind man in 8:22ff. may have an allegorical connection with the conversation of 8:14ff., on the one hand, and with the conversation of 8:27ff., on the other.[6] In 8:14ff. the disciples' lack of spiritual insight is greatly emphasized. They do not appreciate the mysterious significance of the miracle of the loaves which has been performed on two occasions in their presence. They have forgotten to take bread, and yet they have one loaf with them in the ship; that is, presumably, they are unable to perceive that their Master is none other than the Messiah, the Son of God, who continually imparts the true bread of life to those who are willing to receive it (cf. John 6:22ff.). Though they have eyes, the disciples do not see. They are blind to the spiritual truth; and Jesus closes the conversation with the rhetorical question:

Do you not yet understand?

In 8:22ff. follows the story of the restoration of sight to the blind man. Its successive clauses stand in a noteworthy parallelism to those of 8:27–30, and it may be intended to serve as a

[6] Cf. R. H. Lightfoot, *History and Interpretation*, pp. 90f.

sort of allegorical anticipation of the story of the confession and to symbolize the removal of the disciples' blindness or the opening of their eyes to the fact of the Messiahship. That is to say, a miracle takes place between the conversations of 8:14ff. and 8:27ff., not merely in the literal sense that a blind man receives his physical sight by marvelous means, but also in the deeper sense that the disciples are endowed with sufficient supernatural insight to apprehend the secret of their Master's transcendent greatness.

Accordingly, it would be erroneous to suppose that in 8:27ff. Jesus is meant to question his disciples in order to prove their knowledge and that Peter's confession is the result of a more or less prolonged process of educational development. The first of the two questions is concerned not with the knowledge of the disciples themselves, but with the opinion of men generally; and, seeing that Jesus is aware of the inmost thoughts of men's hearts (cf. 2:8) and that the powers at his disposal are more than a match even for those of the demons (cf. 1:23ff.), it cannot be that he is here represented as an ignorant rabbi who is seeking information from or about his pupils. He knows the answers to the questions before he asks them, and he knows what the answers of the disciples will be. The passage does not confront us with an academic examination that forms the triumphant climax of a period of education, but with a declaration that is preceded and made possible by a miracle or a mysterious act of divine self-disclosure transcending the intellectual processes and capacities of the natural man (cf. Matt. 16:17; I Cor. 12:3). The disciples' answer to the first question shows that people generally do not know the truth concerning Jesus, and their answer to the second question emphasizes the public's ignorance by way of contrast. The elect, whose faculties have been divinely quickened, are permitted to receive the mystery of the kingdom; they are in a position of privilege. But for the mass of men the messianic secret remains a secret and, as is indicated by the injunction to silence in verse 30, is meant to remain a secret. On the other hand, the secret content of the divine revelation is only very imperfectly understood by the disciples, and the distinction between the elect who know and the public who do not know requires extremely careful statement. Sometimes, indeed, it seems as though the disciples still possess no more knowledge of heavenly mysteries than the multitude. Nevertheless, in a supreme moment of inspiration the elect are enabled to perceive the fact that Jesus is the long-awaited Messiah, the promised prophet, priest, or king, whom God has appointed for the eschatological task of establishing his kingdom in righteousness. And on the basis of the disciples' recognition of this fateful fact Jesus can proceed forthwith to expound its significance in relation to his own future career and to that of all his followers. Thus Peter's confession is not the climax of the conversation, but is the starting point and presupposition of the subsequent teaching of verses 31ff. In itself it is an inadequate representation of the truth; hence, instead of congratulating Peter, Jesus goes on to set forth the difficult yet necessary implications of his Messiahship.

In the prophetic instruction of verse 31 it is succinctly explained that the Son of Man, who is tacitly identified with the speaker, must suffer many things and be rejected by the elders and the chief priests and the scribes and be killed and after three days rise again. Similar instruction is repeated with somewhat less detail in 9:31, and with somewhat greater detail in 10:33–34, and it is of interest to notice that in all three passages the title "Son of Man" is used in preference to the title "Messiah," which occurs in Peter's confession. Actually, the latter expression is not employed again in the second section of the gospel, except at 9:41, where (with reference to the disciples who are being addressed) we have the phrase "in name that [that is, because] you are of [that is, belong to] Messiah." Such preference for the title "Son of Man"—which does not appear to have been widely current in Jewish circles as a messianic designation [7]—may be meant to bring out the distinction between the true meaning of Messiahship, as it is exemplified in Jesus, and popular messianic ideas which Peter seems to have in mind (v. 32). Jesus is the veritable Messiah, not the Messiah of common apocalyptic imagination, for his ultimate triumph over evil can only be secured after a preliminary period of suffering and humiliation. The Messiah's reign in power and glory (cf. v. 38) has its necessary prelude in the tragedy of the passion, and the causal necessity involved, although it is worked out in a human life on the stage of human history, is fundamentally not a mode of historical determination. It is neither an accidental concurrence of the forces of circumstance nor the decree of a blind fate which determines the course of Jesus' career, but the will of God as it has been revealed in the scriptures. The small word "must" (δεῖ) is indicative of the overruling purpose of God, and it reflects the apostolic belief that the divine promises recorded in the scriptures have their fulfillment in the shame of the crucifixion as well as in the triumph of the resurrection.[8]

Thus St. Mark makes it clear to his readers that Jesus was in no wise surprised by the people's hostile reaction toward him. Men generally failed to recognize his real nature; they did not receive him as the Messiah, and, in the evangelist's view, it was divinely preordained that they should not so receive him. By enjoining the demons and his disciples to silence and by teaching the multitude in parables, Jesus deliberately concealed the truth from them; and in thus guarding the secret of his Messiahship he was acting in accordance with the will of God. For all that

[7] Cf. S.-B., I, 485ff., 956ff.

[8] The verb δεῖ has the same sort of meaning in 9:11; 13:7; 13:10. It occurs with an explicit reference to scripture in Luke 22:37; 24:44; John 20:9; and Acts 1:16. Cf. the informative article by E. Fascher in the Bultmann *Festschrift* (ed. W. Eltester), pp. 228ff.

he did and all that he suffered ultimately followed from the provisions of God's primordial plan for the redemption of the world, and because Jesus was already acquainted with those provisions, he knew what the future had in store for him, and, more particularly, he knew what awaited him in Jerusalem (cf. 10:33f.). Nevertheless, as we shall see more clearly when we come to deal with the passion narrative, in spite of his doctrine of divine predetermination, the evangelist evidently believes that the representative leaders of the Jewish nation were responsible for the crime of the crucifixion. The mention of the three prominent classes by name—the elders and the chief priests and the scribes—in such a brief prophecy as that of verse 31 stresses the point that all the leading parties in the Jewish community must equally assume responsibility for guilt in rejecting the Son of God (cf. 14:64b). Anti-Jewish feeling may also perhaps be detected in the employment (in the passive voice) of the verb "to kill" (cf. I Thess. 2:15) instead of the intransitive verb "to die," which occurs, for example, in St. Paul's summary statement of belief in I Cor. 15:3 (cf. Rev. 1:18; 2:8) and contains no suggestion that the death of Jesus was a violent one.

In verse 32b, however, Peter shows himself to be quite incapable of understanding his Master's explanation of the secret fact which has just been revealed through the mediation of his own confession. He at once takes Jesus aside and begins to rebuke him apparently for upholding the doctrine that the Son of Man must be rejected and killed. Presumably, he imagines that such suffering and humiliation would be incompatible with the high dignity of Messiahship: Jesus is in error and his error calls for immediate correction. But in verse 33 the situation undergoes a further radical change. Jesus turns about and, seeing his disciples,[9] he rebukes Peter in no uncertain terms:

[9] These words may be meant to indicate that the remonstration takes place before all the disciples.

Get away, Satan! For your thoughts are not those of God, but those of men.[10]

The word "satan" can mean simply "enemy" or "opponent" (cf. I Kings 11:14), but the evangelist is probably thinking of the great tempter, the ruler of the demons.[11] That is to say, Peter presents himself as an agent of the devil in proposing that Jesus should deviate from the appointed path of suffering. It has been divinely ordained that the Messiah is to achieve victory over the forces of evil through the shame of the cross, and hence any suggestion that he should avoid the passion may be construed as a temptation which comes from Satan himself. Moreover, Peter's inability to grasp the eschatological necessity of the Messiah's sufferings betrays the real condition of the disciples' understanding.[12] It is much the same as that of unregenerate human nature. Admittedly, the veil has just been withdrawn from the Messiahship in the presence of the disciples. But their powers of insight are so limited that they remain fundamentally in the same position as the general public, who think that Jesus is John

[10] This is the only passage in the gospel in which ὀπίσω with the genitive is used in the sense of "away from"; elsewhere (cf. 1:17; 1:20; 8:34) it signifies "following after" as a disciple; εἰς τὰ ὀπίσω (without μου) would have been more natural (cf. 13:16; Ps. 6:11). Torrey (*The Four Gospels*, p. 294, note on Matt. 16:23) sees behind the expression a well-known Aramaic idiom which is not "behind *me*" but "behind *yourself*," and means simply "Retreat!"

[11] Cf. 1:13; 3:22; Matt. 4:10. For "Satan" as the Aramaic name for the devil, cf. the words "Abba, Father" (of God) in 14:36; Rom. 8:15; Gal. 4:6. There was a natural tendency in the early church for Greek equivalents to replace such Aramaic expressions, and the fact that the latter are retained to a greater extent in St. Mark's gospel than in the other gospels, is a sign of the relative earliness of his work. Thus he uses "Satan" in 1:13; 3:23; 3:26; 4:15; 8:33, but never "the devil" or "the evil one" (cf. Turner in *N.C.H.S.*, pt. 3, p. 53, note on 1:13). In 3:22 it is explained that Beelzebul or Satan is the ruler of the demons.

[12] For the statement ὅτι οὐ φρονεῖς κτλ., cf. Phil. 2:5; 3:19; 4:2; Col. 3:2. The contrast between God's thoughts and man's is to be found in the Old Testament; cf. Isa. 55:8f.

the Baptist, or Elijah, or one of the prophets. They are unable to penetrate the essential meaning of the secret fact; the significance of the Messiahship is still an inscrutable mystery.

Accordingly, it is not altogether surprising that in 8:34 Jesus should call the multitude to him and address the teaching of 8:34b–9:1 to them as well as to the disciples. For, in the first place, the latter's failure to discern the eschatological necessity of the passion is an occasion, as it were, for extending his court of appeal; and, in the second place, the teaching which is now given concerns the practical implications of faith in his Messiahship for *all* believers. It is true that, if the whole passage is taken as an essay in coherent historical description, the reference to the multitude at this point confronts the exegete with serious difficulties. Thus the context would lead us to suppose that Jesus is being accompanied by his disciples alone; in verse 27 he is traveling with his disciples in a strange country, and there is no suggestion that others are present or that he is conducting a public ministry. Also, even the bare fact of the messianic secret is unknown to the multitude, and yet in the teaching of verses 34bff. Jesus, as the crucified Messiah, is an example to his followers. The evangelist, however, does not see the situation from the strictly historical point of view and, in consequence, he is quite unaware of such difficulties. He simply wishes to impress upon the members of the church or churches for whom he is writing the moral significance of the apostolic faith in the crucified and risen Messiah. And, seeing that the disciples are not yet able to embrace the postresurrection faith and for the present can represent God's elect only in an imperfect or anticipatory way, reference is made at verse 34a to people who stand outside the circle of discipleship. This reference is really from the past to the future, from the obscurity of the period of the earthly ministry to the revelation and enlightenment of the period of the apostolic faith, which begins with the resurrection (cf. 4:21f.; 9:9). In other words, the evangelist is reminding his readers that suffering with the Messiah is a condition of glorification with him (cf. Rom. 8:7). They must be prepared to suffer and even to die for the sake of their faith; and only those who comply with the gospel's stringent demands for self-abnegation will be found worthy of the unspeakable reward which it promises.

At Caesarea Philippi, then, the secret of the kingdom of God, as it is embodied in the person of Jesus, is granted to men of flesh and blood; Peter acknowledges the Messiahship of his Master, and in consequence the disciples are in a position to receive the doctrine of the eschatological necessity of the passion. Such a doctrine, however, is paradoxical in the extreme, and the disciples completely fail to assimilate it. How can it be that one who is empowered to teach with authority and to perform miraculous deeds should be rejected by his people and put to death? St. Mark evidently feels that the situation calls for some convincing demonstration of the reality of the Messiahship, and this is supplied in a remarkable fashion in the story of the transfiguration which follows in 9:2ff. For a fleeting moment the veil of the flesh is withdrawn, and Peter, James, and John are privileged to behold their Master in the heavenly glory which is proper to him as the Messiah, the Son of God. Doubtless, those who enjoy the apostolic faith can discern the Messiahship of Jesus in all his words and works and sufferings, but open manifestation of the glory of his essential nature still belongs to the future, to the day of his parousia as Son of Man at the kingdom's consummation. Nevertheless, even in the midst of the earthly ministry, something of the glory of the parousia may be shown in advance to his three closest disciples; the beatific light may penetrate the obscurity of his humble, human life and actually change his bodily form for a season. Hence in 9:2ff. the Master undergoes a temporary metamorphosis, and once again, as at the baptism (1:11), the divine voice speaks, though on this occasion (9:7), it is the three disciples, not Jesus, who are addressed. Here and now, before the end of the ministry, God

156

himself affixes the seal of divine confirmation to Peter's confession, and provides a final and sufficient guarantee [13] of the valid-

[13] Cf. U. von Wilamowitz-Moellendorf, *Die Verklärung Christi* in *Reden und Vorträge*, II, 290. On the other hand, G. H. Boobyer (*St. Mark and the Transfiguration Story*, p. 76, n. 1) argues that the resurrection was of such importance in St. Mark's thought that he could scarcely have stopped short of an account of it and ended his gospel at 16:8. But several objections may be urged against this view: (1) None of the four evangelists gives an account of the resurrection as such. (2) St. Mark probably considered that the story of the empty tomb in 16:1–8 was sufficient to show that the predictions of it in 8:31; 9:31; 10:34 had been fulfilled. (3) As a proof of the reality of the Messiahship of Jesus an account of a christophany was hardly necessary in view of the confessions of the demons and especially the testimony of God himself at the baptism and at the transfiguration. (4) Though each of the three predictions mentioned has its climax in a reference to the resurrection, almost all the details given concern the passion prelude; and this corresponds to the comparative brevity of the story of the empty tomb in relation to the detailed passion narrative of the two preceding chapters. (5) If the original ending was lost or if the evangelist was prevented from completing his work, why did not the church for which it may have been written supply a suitable conclusion? (cf. R. H. Lightfoot in *J.T.S.*, XLVI [1945], 221ff.). (6) The conclusion of the gospel in 16:1–8 may be abrupt and sketchy, but the same is true of its preface, where St. Mark makes no reference to the birth and upbringing of Jesus. (7) St. Mark could have held that the christophanies more properly belonged to the life of the church than to the earthly ministry, and it was with the latter that he was primarily concerned; and yet if the promise of a reunion in Galilee (14:28; 16:7) refers to certain resurrection appearances there (cf. I Cor. 15:5ff.), he sought to establish a connection between the ministry and the life of the church (cf. below, Supplementary Note E, n. 7.). (8) It is erroneous to imagine that an ending at 16:8 is a stylistic impossibility (see Lightfoot, *Locality and Doctrine*, pp. 10ff.). (9) There are difficulties involved in any attempt to show how the narrative could proceed satisfactorily after 16:8 (cf. the remarks of J. M. Creed in *J.T.S.*, XXXI [1930], 175ff.). (10) The argument that the superscription in 1:1 requires another ending in which Peter acknowledges Jesus as Son of God (cf. Turner in *N.C.H.S.*, pt. 3, p. 124) is not a strong one, for the Jewish confession of 8:29 has its Gentile counterpart in 15:39. Cf. N. B. Stonehouse, *The Witness of Matthew and Mark to Christ*, pp. 86ff.; and Lightfoot, *The Gospel Message of St. Mark*, pp. 80ff.

ity of the apostolic faith in the crucified Messiah. For in the declaration of the voice from the cloud it is expressly acknowledged that Jesus enjoys a unique filial relationship to God. He is God's beloved or only Son; as such he has been elected to perform his messianic role on earth, and as such he is to be heard and obeyed.

Thus the transfiguration story may be said to offer a dramatic demonstration of the glory of Jesus' messianic status. For a brief interval the three disciples are permitted to see the real nature of their Master, which is ordinarily concealed beneath his body of flesh. In one sense, therefore, the scene seems to have a supratemporal significance, since in it the Messiah, who retains his essential identity yesterday and today and forever (cf. Heb. 13:8), is revealed as he truly is. But the scene also seems to possess an eschatological significance [14] and to anticipate in some

[14] Cf. G. Kittel's observation, *T.W.N.T.*, II, 252: "Seine Verklärung ist Vorwegnahme seiner Eschatologie." Cf. also E. Lohmeyer, "Die Verklärung Jesu nach dem Markus-Evangelium," *Z.N.T.W.*, XXI (1922), 185ff., where it is maintained that the transfiguration scene is one of eschatological fulfillment. Lohmeyer considers that the story is composed of two principal elements. The original part is contained in vv. 4f. and 7f. and is to be understood in terms of current Jewish expectations, according to which, at the end of the present age, Moses and Elijah would reappear, Yahweh would again tabernacle with his people, and men would receive true instruction in the torah. In the story Jesus is regarded as the one through whom such eschatological hopes find their realization. Being the Messiah, divinely commissioned to inaugurate the age to come, he is the preeminent figure in history, and his presence guarantees the presence of the new order prophesied in the scriptures. Thus the original part of the story exemplifies characteristic motifs of Jewish eschatological expectation. The second principal element is contained in vv. 2c–3 and represents a later accretion, the motif of metamorphosis being derived from the sphere of Hellenistic religion; cf. the transfiguration of Apuleius on his initiation into the cult of Isis (*Metamorphosis* xi). It should be noticed, however, that Lohmeyer later came to hold that there is no need to regard vv. 2c–3 as a Hellenistic accretion to the original form of the story, for the idea of metamorphosis is to be found in Jewish literature (cf. Ex. 34:29; II Bar. 51:10–12); see

measure the glory to be made manifest to the world at the consummation of the kingdom. Construed in this sense, the story points forward to the day when the Son of Man will come in the glory of his Father with the holy angels (cf. 8:38); it presents us with a transitory preenactment on a small scale of a lasting manifestation which will have cosmic dimensions.

It would appear, then, that if the exegete is to do full justice to St. Mark's account of the transfiguration, he must recognize the dual significance of its symbolism with respect to time. While the scene is a dramatic indication of a triumph in glory which is to follow on the shame and humiliation of the passion, yet its meaning is not exhausted by a future reference of this kind. It is something more than an enacted promise. The voice from the cloud does not declare that Jesus will be the Son of God at some future date, but simply that he *is* the Son of God; and in making this declaration the voice is only repeating what has previously been acknowledged at the baptism, before the commencement of the ministry. In the evangelist's interpretation, that is to say, Jesus begins his saving work as the Messiah, the Son of God. Such is his essential status and such is the one sufficient ground and explanation of his words and deeds. Hence the content of the revelation, or that which is revealed, at the transfiguration, is an unchanging, secret fact—the constant presupposition of Jesus' manifold activities on earth.[15] On the other hand, it re-

his *Das Evangelium des Markus*, p. 174, n. 7. For an interesting discussion of the associations of the transfiguration story with messianic and eschatological motifs involved in the Jewish liturgy, particularly respecting ceremonial enthronement and the feast of tabernacles, see H. Riesenfeld, *Jésus transfiguré*, pp. 265ff.

[15] Cf. J. B. Bernadin, "The Transfiguration," *J.B.L.*, LII (1933), 181ff. The author of this paper maintains that the transfiguration is to be understood as a transitory manifestation of the Messiah's preexistent glory which is generally concealed by Jesus' physical body. He notices (p. 183) that in current apocalyptic literature the Messiah is a supernatural (En. 48:6), heavenly (Sib. Or. 5:414), preexistent (II Bar. 29:3) figure who dwells in God's presence (En. 46, 1ff.) and is God's Son (En. 105:2).

mains that, as an act of revealing, the incident is evidently meant to foreshadow that final act of revealing which is destined to take place at the kingdom's consummation.

Accordingly, St. Mark's account of the transfiguration does not disclose a status which Jesus is to enjoy on a future occasion, whether it be at his resurrection [16] or at his parousia. Such an interpretation would confuse the act with the content of the revelation. Moreover, the story does not seem to have any direct connection with the resurrection.[17] In so far as it has a reference

[16] In Rom. 1:4 it is stated that Jesus was determined to be the Son of God in power, according to the spirit of holiness, by the resurrection from the dead, and this is sometimes thought to support the view that the transfiguration is a picturesque forecast of the resurrection, for at the transfiguration Jesus is designated Son of God. The implication of Rom. 1:4 is that Jesus' post resurrection status is in some sense superior to his previous status. The same idea is also present in Phil. 2:5ff., if the ἁρπαγμόν may be translated "godsend" (cf. Lightfoot, *History and Interpretation*, pp. 212f.); complete equality with God was not a godsend for the preexistent Messiah, but something that he could achieve only by his voluntary humiliation. But St. Mark does not seem to be in agreement with St. Paul on this matter. Rather, his general christological position mediates between that of St. Paul and that of St. John. The fourth evangelist holds that the Lord is unchangingly the divine Logos or Messiah, whose heavenly glory is openly made manifest throughout the days of his flesh; the appearance is, so to speak, perfectly adjusted to the reality of his nature. On the other hand, in St. Mark's view, the appearance is not so adjusted to the reality. That is to say, he seems to agree with St. Paul against St. John that the glory of the Messiah is generally concealed from the world during his earthly life.

[17] For the view that the account of the transfiguration was originally a resurrection story, cf. M. Goguel, "Esquisse d'une interprétation du récit de la transfiguration," *R.H.R.* LXXXI (1920), pp. 145ff.; Bultmann, *op. cit.*, pp. 278ff. Bultmann thinks that the writer of II Pet. 1:17f. still knew the account of the transfiguration as a resurrection story (p. 278, n. 1); but see Boobyer, *op. cit.*, pp. 13ff., 30ff., 43ff., where it is maintained that the author of II Peter, as well as the author of the Ethiopic Apocalypse of Peter, regarded the synoptic transfiguration story as a forecast, not of the resurrection, but of the parousia. The main motif of the transfiguration story may have been originally connected with the early idea of the resurrection as a glorification and have

to the future, it is probably meant to point forward beyond the resurrection to the advent of the Son of Man with great power and glory.[18] Admittedly, the evangelist does not actually employ the term δόξα ("glory") in his description of Jesus' transfigured appearance; but that he is thinking of a change into a form of glory can hardly be doubted, and it is not surprising to find that the term occurs in St. Luke's version of the story (Luke 9:32). St. Mark's report reads as follows:

And after six days [19] Jesus takes Peter and James and John, and leads them up into a high mountain [20] privately by themselves; and he was transfigured before them, and his garments became glistening,[21] very white, such as no fuller on earth can whiten them. . . .

---

owed something to the experiences in which the risen Jesus appeared in radiant form (cf. Acts 9:3f.; II Cor. 3:18). But this does not mean that Mark 9:2ff. was originally a resurrection story. For a psychological study of the resurrection appearances and a consideration of certain modern parallels, see M. Goguel, *La foi à la résurrection de Jésus*, pp. 393ff., a work too little known in this country; cf. his more recent study, *The Birth of Christianity*, pp. 73ff.

[18] Cf. Boobyer, *op. cit.*, pp. 23ff., 67ff.

[19] The precise note of time seems to imply that St. Mark attaches special importance to the transfiguration. Elsewhere in the gospel precise notes of time are found only in the passion narrative, the best parallel to this one being in 14:1—the opening of the passion story (cf. 14:12, 17; 15:1, 25, 33, 34, 42; 16:2). Regarding the *six* days, it may be noticed here that the divine glory remains on Mount Sinai for six days before Moses is received into the cloud (Ex. 24:16), and that the seventh day is a holy day (Ex. 35:2, etc.); cf. B. W. Bacon, "After Six Days," *H.T.R.*, VIII (1915), 94ff. St. Luke has "about eight days" (Luke 9:28).

[20] In Matt 28:16 the risen Jesus appears on a mountain in Galilee; in Rev. 21:10 the seer witnesses the descent of the new Jerusalem from the vantage point of "a great and high mountain." Lohmeyer (*Das Evangelium des Markus*, pp. 174, 180) sees in the localization of the transfiguration on a mountain in Galilee of the Gentiles, a polemic against the official Jewish doctrine that Mount Zion and Jerusalem mark the region of eschatological fulfillment.

[21] B. H. Streeter conjectures that the original reading was: καὶ ἐγένετο στίλβον τὸ πρόσωπον, καὶ τὰ ἱμάτια αὐτοῦ λευκὰ λίαν; the πρόσωπον was perhaps accidently omitted, in which case the readings of fam. θ, k

Not only the "glistening" or "gleaming" character of the appearance but also its being "very white" suggests that the transfiguration is to be understood as a glorification; for, in the New Testament, whenever the adjective "white" is used of clothing, it always refers to the garments of angels (cf. Matt. 28:3; Mark 16:5; John 20:12; Acts 1:10) or to those of the saints who have been glorified in heaven (cf. Rev. 3:4, 5, 18; 4:4; 6:11; 7:9, 13).

Accordingly, it may be assumed that in St. Mark's account of the transfiguration Jesus temporarily appears in a body of that ethereal substance known as "glory," which, according to current Jewish belief, characterizes the essential life of heavenly beings and presents itself in the form of a tenuously material light. Thus "glory" marks the presence of God (cf. Ex. 16:10; Asc. Isa. 10, 16) and that of the angels (cf. T. Lev. 18:5). At the end of the present age the elect will be transformed into glorious beings (cf. II Bar. 51:10ff.); they will shine as the brightness of the firmament (cf. Dan. 12:3) and be invested with garments of a glory that will never fade away (cf. En. 39:7). The Messiah himself will be radiant like the sun and will remove all darkness from under heaven (cf. T. Lev. 18:1ff.). Ideas of the same kind are exemplified in the writings of St. Paul. Thus the Messiah possesses a body of glory in his exalted, heavenly state (cf. Phil. 3:21); he will appear in glory at his second coming (cf. II Thess. 1:9f.), and the faithful will be glorified to participate in the Messiah's final triumph (cf. I Cor. 15:43, 51ff.). In the mind of the apostle, therefore, the notion of glorification as a process of substantial metamorphosis is closely associated with the conception of the Messiah's exaltation and with that of his ultimate victory over the forces of evil.

It is important to observe, however, that while St. Paul apparently regards the Lord's resurrection as tantamount to his

and of Syr. S. and of B represent different solutions of the resulting difficulty; Matt. 17:2 and Luke 9:29 agree in making mention of Jesus' countenance; see *The Four Gospels*, pp. 315f.

glorification, this does not seem to be the view of the second evangelist.[22] From such passages as I Thess. 1:10; Rom. 8:34; Col. 3:1, we may perhaps infer that in the apostle's belief the resurrection of Jesus coincides with his exaltation to heaven in glory and hence that the christophanies are appearances of the exalted Jesus in a glorious form. On the other hand, in the first and third gospels, although the body of the risen Lord possesses certain supernormal powers (cf. Luke 24:36), its properties still seem to be fundamentally physical (cf. Matt. 28:9; Luke 24:43). Thus for St. Matthew and St. Luke, as it seems, the resurrection christophanies are appearances of Jesus in a nonglorified form; and, as we learn from Acts 1:1ff., these appearances occur during a period of forty days after the passion. At the end of this specified period the risen Lord is received into heaven and presumably he is glorified at the same time, for it is stated (Acts 1:11) that his return from heaven will be after the manner of his exaltation. Accordingly, the resurrection body is not, as it is for St. Paul, a glorified body; and in all likelihood St. Mark, too, is at variance with St. Paul on this matter, and, like the other synoptic evangelists, differentiates the Messiah's resurrection from his exaltation and glorification. For, in the first place, the story of the empty tomb, with which St. Mark concludes his gospel, affords no indication of the Lord's glorification. It simply shows that the predictions of the resurrection of the Son of Man in 8:31; 9:31; and 10:34 have been fulfilled; the rolled-back stone mentioned in 16:4 may be taken as evidence of the Lord's departure from the tomb, but hardly of his glorification. In the second place, the term "glory" is used only on three occasions in the gospel (8:38; 10:37; 13:26), and in each case it refers not

---

[22] Cf. Lohmeyer, *Das Evangelium des Markus*, p. 180, n. 1. The christophany related in Acts 9:3ff.; 22:6ff.; 26:12ff. is not, in St. Luke's view, a resurrection appearance as such, since Jesus has already been exalted (Acts 1:9). St. Paul, however, who represents an earlier doctrine, places his own experience of the risen Messiah in the same category as the appearances to Peter and his colleagues (I Cor. 15:5ff.).

to Jesus' resurrection, but to the exalted and glorified state in which the Messiah will appear at the time of the kingdom's consummation.[23]

✓   In the economy of St. Mark's gospel, then, the story of the transfiguration possesses great significance. It provides a dramatic demonstration of the glorious nature which properly belongs to Jesus as the Messiah, the Son of God, and affixes the seal of divine confirmation to Peter's recognition of the messianic secret in 8:29 and to the Master's interpretation of the secret in 8:31. For a few fleeting moments the veil of the flesh is withdrawn and the three disciples are privileged to behold their Master as he really is and as he will be made manifest to the world when he comes in clouds with great power and glory.

[23] In the fourth gospel, as in the first and third gospels, the resurrection body of Jesus has supernormal powers (cf. John 20:19) and yet seems to be fundamentally physical (cf. John 20:20). But it would be incorrect to say that, for St. John, the resurrection christophanies are appearances of Jesus in a nonglorified form, since, according to his interpretation, the incarnation is a revelation, not a concealment, of the Messiah's glory (cf. John 1:14), and he can describe the passion in terms of glorification and exaltation (cf. John 12:23, 32). Perhaps it is because the incarnate Logos is always in a state of open glorification that there is nothing corresponding to Mark 9:2ff. in the fourth gospel. On the other hand, it must be noticed that such a passage as John 20:17 reflects the Lukan distinction between the Messiah's resurrection and his exaltation or ascension.

Note on Mark 9:1

SUPPLEMENTARY NOTE C: THE EXEGESIS
OF MARK 9:1

The interpretation of the story of the transfiguration given in the preceding chapter is corroborated when the story is considered in relation to its immediately preceding context, for the promise of 9:1 also seems to refer to the parousia. It should be noted, however, that C. H. Dodd in his *Parables of the Kingdom*, pp. 53f., and in his article in *Ex.T.*, XLVIII (1936–37), 138ff., argues that 9:1 does not refer to the parousia. He thinks that it should be translated as follows:

There are some of those standing here who will not taste death until they have seen that the Kingdom of God has come with power [ἐληλυθυῖαν ἐν δυνάμει].

Dodd compares the passage with Rom. 1:4, where it is stated that Jesus was appointed Son of God with power (ἐν δυνάμει) by the resurrection from the dead; and, on the ground that St. Mark's gospel may have originated in Rome, he suggests that the idea associated with the phrase "with power" is the same in both documents. He concludes the article with the following words:

The prediction would be fulfilled if it [that is, the Kingdom] came at any time between the utterance of the saying and the moment of perception, whenever that might be. But it is *consistent* with the view that the Kingdom of God actually came in the complex of events ending with the resurrection of Christ, and that the disciples shortly afterwards perceived that this was the case. The story of Pentecost may, in my view, be taken to represent the moment of perception.

But this exegesis is exposed to serious objections, as is shown in the articles by J. Y. Campbell and J. M. Creed in *Ex.T.*,

XLVIII, 91ff., 184f., and in Boobyer's study *St. Mark and the Transfiguration Story*, pp. 58ff. Here the following considerations may be brought against Dodd's interpretation:

1. The word ἰδεῖν is not usually constructed with an accusative and a participle when it has the force which Dodd wishes to ascribe to it in 9:1, namely, "to perceive mentally" or "to recognize"; when it has this sense the fact recognized is normally introduced by a ὅτι.

2. 9:1 should be interpreted in the light of 8:38, which clearly refers to the parousia; 9:1 is partly intended to give some indication of the date of the great event mentioned in 8:38—the parousia will occur within the lifetime of some of those standing by and listening to Jesus.

3. The indication of the date of the parousia in 13:30 is reminiscent of 9:1; in 13:30 it is stated that "this generation shall not pass away until all these things come to pass," and the "all these things" must include the parousia which is mentioned in 13:26.

4. According to 13:26 the coming of the Son of Man in clouds is to be "with great power and glory," and the words "glory" and "power" occur in 8:38 and 9:1; the phrase μετὰ . . . δόξης in 13:26 corresponds to the ἐν τῇ δόξῃ of 8:38, while the phrase μετὰ δυνάμεως in 13:26 corresponds to the ἐν δυνάμει of 9:1; and this double correspondence suggests that all three verses concern the parousia.

5. The first evangelist evidently takes 9:1 to refer to the parousia (see Matt. 16:28).

6. The third evangelist omits the words ἐληλυθυῖαν ἐν δυνάμει in his version of 9:1 (see Luke 9:27), and this may be most readily explained by supposing that he takes 9:1 to refer to the parousia; he does not wish to embarrass Christian readers of the second generation who are still awaiting the arrival of the kingdom of God "with power."

7. In Rom. 1:4 the phrase "with power" is associated with

the Messiah's resurrection, not with his earthly ministry; hence Rom. 1:4 can hardly be cited in support of the view that the kingdom of God came "with power" in the complex of events which *ended* with the resurrection.

8. St. Mark nowhere brings the Messiah's resurrection into explicit connection with "glorification" or "coming with power." Whether or not the evangelist belongs to a church in Rome, his doctrine seems to differ in certain important respects from that of St. Paul.

9. St. Mark appears to hold that the kingdom is coming "with power" throughout the ministry of Jesus, and he may use the perfect, instead of the present, participle in 9:1 to suggest an idea of completeness. Some of those standing by will witness the triumphant consummation of the eschatological process which has its humble beginnings in the earthly life of the Messiah. At the end the kingdom is "with power"; it is no longer *coming* "with power" but has *come* "with power."

8

A Meaning that
is Not Understood

AS a result of Peter's confession at Caesarea Philippi the disciples
are in a position to receive special instruction in the profound
significance of the messianic secret. But they soon show themselves to be quite unable to appreciate such instruction. The
essential meaning of the fact of the Messiahship—its fateful
implications for the Master himself and its moral implications for
all who would be his followers—is a heavenly mystery which
persistently eludes their grasp. Jesus expounds the truth to them
in various ways. In Mark 8:31 they are informed that the Son
of Man must suffer many things and be rejected and killed and
after three days rise again; and similar prophetic instruction is
repeated in 9:31 and again in 10:33–34. In 8:35 they are taught
that whoever loses his life for the gospel's sake will save it, and
in 9:35 that if anyone wishes to be first he must be last and
servant of all (10:43f.). In 10:1ff. they are shown that even the
ordinances of the law are not to be blindly followed, but are to
be carefully adjudged in the light of the highest standards which
scripture exemplifies. In 10:13ff. the presence of the children is
used as an occasion for illustrating that the blessings of the king-

dom are freely given,[1] while in 10:17ff. the incident concerning
the rich man, who alleges that he seeks eternal life, serves as an
opportunity for pointing out that entrance into the kingdom
calls for renunciation and great efforts of will. Nevertheless, despite sustained instruction in such a variety of forms—prophecy
and example, paradox and illustration—the disciples are still, according to St. Mark, utterly incapable of comprehending the
essential significance of the messianic secret.

Thus, after the first prediction of the passion and resurrection
in 8:31, it is reported that Peter takes Jesus aside and begins to
rebuke him, and by so doing only shows that his thoughts are
not those of God, but those of men. The three disciples who
witness the transfiguration are exceedingly afraid, Peter not
knowing what he should answer;[2] and as they descend the

---

[1] Mark 10:15 and 9:37 would each have a more appropriate context
if they were interchanged; for in 9:36 Jesus sets a child in the midst
of the disciples who have just been disputing about personal greatness,
and in 10:13 the disciples rebuke those who bring children to Jesus that
he might touch them; see Turner in *N.C.H.S.*, pt. 3, p. 87.

[2] It seems unlikely that 9:6a finds a rational explanation in 9:6b; each
clause has a γάρ, and the second clause may well be simply a more general statement of what is really affirmed in the first, namely, the fact
that the three disciples are quite unable to grasp the significance of what
is happening. As H. Riesenfeld has insisted (*Jésus transfiguré*, pp.
283ff.), the fear attributed to the disciples by St. Mark (4:41; 5:40;
6:50–51; 9:6, 32; 10:24, 26, 32; and also, 16:5, 8) is always a theological
rather than a psychological phenomenon: "Leur crainte est rapportée
dans l'intention de faire ressortir un manque de foi, l'incapacité de com-
prendre la portée messianique des paroles et des actes de Jésus" (p. 285).
Similarly, the fear of the women in 16:8 is not properly a subjective
reaction to a numinous event, but expresses their failure to understand
what has taken place, Peter and his fellow disciples in Galilee being the
first genuine witnesses of the Messiah's resurrection; in the evangelist's
view, it would seem, a witness in this connection must comprehend that
to which he testifies—hence the notice "they said nothing to anybody"
(16:8b). Riesenfeld further observes that the incapacity of the disciples
in Gethsemane is indicated by *sleep* (not fear), probably because in
this case (14:33) fear and anguish characterize the Messiah himself (*ibid.*,
p. 286, n. 27).

mountain they are unable to understand what Jesus signifies by the resurrection of the Son of Man (9:10), while the disciples who remain on the plain below cannot cure the boy possessed by a deaf and dumb spirit (9:18). Immediately after the second prediction of the passion and resurrection in 9:31, it is noted that the disciples fail to grasp the meaning of the saying and are too afraid to make inquiries. Their failure is made all the more palpable by the dispute on the question of who is the greatest, which follows (9:34), and by their prevention of an outsider [3] from continuing his good work of exorcising demons with the help of Jesus' name (9:38). Later, they wish to send away those who bring little children to their Master (10:13), not realizing that the kingdom of God belongs to such as are of a childlike spirit; and when Jesus informs them of the difficulty with which the wealthy enter into the kingdom of God, they are amazed (10:24), and they are greatly astounded and do not know who can be saved (10:26). Finally, on the occasion of the third prediction of the passion and resurrection in 10:32ff., when they are going up to Jerusalem, it is observed that they are amazed and that those who follow are afraid; and, directly afterwards, James and John make their selfish request for the highest places in the consummated kingdom (10:37). It is clear, therefore, that despite Peter's confession and the remarkable confirmation of its truth at

---

[3] In 9:38 the reading "who follows not *with* us" may be due to a copyist who had Luke 9:49 in mind; that is, ἡμῖν (Cod. Sin., B), not μεθ' ἡμῶν (D, k), is probably the correct reading. At this stage of the gospel St. Mark seems to regard Jesus and the disciples as forming a single group, and never again are the disciples said to follow Jesus, except apparently in 10:32, where Jerusalem is mentioned for the first time as their destination. This exegesis finds support in 8:38, provided that the reading "of me and *mine*" (W, k) is the correct one, as it may well be. Cf. Turner in *J.T.S.*, XXVI (1925), p. 240, and in N.C.H.S., pt. 3, pp. 80, 84. T. W. Manson also favors the reading of W, k, in 8:38; he notes that the only other example of ἐμός in the gospel is in 10:40, where ἐμόν means *"mine"* and that in 13:31 we have οἱ δὲ λόγοι μου, not οἱ ἐμοὶ λόγοι; see his *Teaching of Jesus*, pp. 332f.

the transfiguration, the disciples do not understand what Messiahship really means; and it is interesting to notice that they continue to address Jesus as "rabbi" (9:5; 11:21; 14:45) or "teacher" (4:38; 10:35; 13:1),[4] as if no discovery had been made at Caesarea Philippi.

But though there are no signs of a deepening of the disciples' understanding after 8:29, Peter's confession is of importance because it enables the evangelist to introduce his readers to the fundamental doctrine of the eschatological necessity of the passion. It is true that the ultimate removal of Jesus has previously been implied or suggested in certain passages. Thus in 2:20 we learn that the sons of the bridechamber will begin to fast on the day when the bridegroom is taken away from them; in 6:1ff. the story of the rejection in the *patris* is probably meant to foreshadow the final rejection of Jesus at Jerusalem by his own countrymen; in 8:14ff., where the mysterious significance of the miracles of the loaves is dealt with, there seems to be a veiled reference to the church's celebrations of the last supper, which took place on the night of the betrayal. Moreover, the conception of the overruling predetermination or necessity of the divine purpose permeates the whole of the gospel. The course of Jesus' life is in accordance with the declared will of God, and scripture is cited at 1:2 and at 4:12 in order to give demonstration of this truth. The same kind of thought, as we have seen, really lies behind the repeated injunctions to silence. On the other hand, it is not until we come to 8:31 that the idea of the controlling necessity of the divine purpose is brought into specific connection with the passion, and, as we should expect, this doctrinal synthesis has an especially close association with the further idea of the fulfillment of scriptural promises. For while no great difficulty attaches to the thought of a Messiah who performs mar-

---

[4] Jesus applies "teacher" to himself in 14:14. In the other synoptic gospels the disciples do not address Jesus as "rabbi" or "teacher" save in Matt. 26:49, where, however, Judas is speaking!

velous works and teaches with authority, it is far from easy to understand that Jesus should be rejected and crucified precisely in virtue of the fact of his messianic dignity. Adjudged by all ordinary human standards, such a doctrine is paradoxical in the extreme and makes a pressing demand for attestation in the scriptures, wherein the will of God is held to be revealed. Hence reference to scripture is expressly made in 9:12b and in 12:10 and frequently in the passion narrative itself.

In St. Mark's view, then, the whole career of Jesus is a fulfillment of the purpose of God. Above all, he wishes to emphasize that the shameful climax of the earthly ministry is an integral part of the divine scheme for human redemption; and after 8:29 he can give free expression to this conviction in the form of an explanation of the fact of the Messiahship now made known to the disciples. That such is the evangelist's attitude seems to be indicated in the incidental remark which follows the first prediction of the passion and resurrection:

And he spoke [ἐλάλει] the word [τὸν λόγον] openly and with boldness [παρρησίᾳ] [8:32a].

As in 4:14 the expression τὸν λόγον in this context is practically tantamount to "the gospel," [5] for the notion of the divine necessity of the passion belongs to the heart of the apostolic message of salvation (cf. I Cor. 15:3f.). The main point of the remark is that the essential content of the good news proclaimed by the apostolic preachers, though it is implied throughout the work, is now set forth explicitly for the first time. The significance of the messianic secret is no longer concealed from the disciples. The word is spoken παρρησίᾳ, that is "openly" or "without reserve." [6] But it should be noticed that this interpretation does not exclude

---

[5] Cf. Luke 1:2; Acts 14:25. In the latter passage the verb λαλεῖν is used in conjunction with τὸν λόγον; cf. Mark 2:2; 4:33; Acts 4:29, 31.

[6] Cf. John 7:4, where ἐν παρρησίᾳ is the opposite of ἐν κρυπτῷ, and John 16:25, where παρρησίᾳ is the opposite of ἐν παροιμίαις.

the possibility that the παρρησίᾳ also signifies "with boldness" or "with confidence" (cf. Acts 4:13, 29, 31). The Lord is sure of his ground and speaks of his coming sufferings with the confidence of one who is complete master of the situation, whereas his disciples, without any firm grasp of the truth, are uncertain and dismayed. Perhaps therefore, as Wrede suggested,[7] we should discern a parallel in 10:32, where it is related that Jesus leads the way to Jerusalem; though fully aware of the fate awaiting him there, he goes ahead of his frightened followers apparently with courage and confidence.[8]

In St. Mark's estimation, however, the period of suffering and humiliation is but a transient phase in the working out of God's saving purpose. The passion is, indeed, an eschatological necessity which takes place according to the will of God, and yet it is considered to be a sort of prelude to the Messiah's expected coming with great power and glory. In an important sense, therefore, the earthly ministry is not the sphere of divine revelation, but the appointed antecedent of such revelation. From one point of view, the Lord's self-abnegation is the price which is paid for the imminent triumph of the Son of Man at the parousia; and from another point of view, the days of his flesh cover the period of obscurity which precedes the Messiah's glorious reign

[7] See *Das Messiasgeheimnis*, p. 100.

[8] Following k, Lohmeyer (*Das Evangelium des Markus*, p. 167) takes λαλεῖν, not ἐλάλει, to be the correct reading, thus making v. 32a the last clause of the prediction itself: the risen Son of Man must proclaim the gospel publicly. Lohmeyer draws attention to Luke 24:46f., I Tim. 3:16, and the so-called shorter ending of St. Mark's gospel, and he argues that at an early date the last clause of the prediction in its supposed original form was modified because it was not literally fulfilled. But the k reading may be more satisfactorily accounted for by supposing that it arose from a misunderstanding of παρρησίᾳ, which in the present context means not "publicly" (cf. vv. 30, 34a) but "explicitly and with confidence." Also, the three passages which Lohmeyer mentions hardly provide the parallels required, for in none of them is it stated that the risen Messiah himself proclaims the gospel publicly.

in his exalted, heavenly state. Clearly, this general position bears a close resemblance to St. Paul's conception of the Messiah's superexaltation as the reward of his voluntary self-humiliation (Phil. 2:5ff.). He who was originally in the form of God laid aside his rightful prerogatives, willingly took upon himself the nature of a lowly, human servant, and in his obedience eventually stooped to die even by crucifixion. In fact, the Messiah's assumed human guise was so effective that the rulers of this age [9] did not recognize the mystery of God's wisdom, which was concealed beneath his outer person, for if they had perceived it, they would never have crucified the Lord of glory (I Cor. 2:6ff.). Nevertheless, the sublime condescension, evinced by the Messiah's life of humble service and by his death in utter shame, has proved itself to be the ground of his present supremacy in heaven, the power and glory of which will soon be demonstrated to the world (Phil. 3:20f.). As we have previously observed,[10] however, St. Mark, unlike St. Paul, seems to believe that the Lord remains unchangingly Messiah in essence, although the truth may not be publicly proclaimed before the resurrection (9:9), which must take place three days after the crucifixion; [11] and such proc-

[9] In I Cor. 2:6ff., if the phrase "the rulers of this age" refers to demonic powers, St. Paul is at variance with St. Mark, who holds that the demons *do* recognize the divine nature of Jesus and that it is the Jews (he does not mention the demons in this connection) who are to be held responsible for the crucifixion. But it must be noted that on certain occasions St. Paul, too, can blame the Jews for the death of Jesus (cf. I Thess. 2:14f.).

[10] See above, Chapter 7, n. 16.

[11] Cf. 8:31; 9:31; 10:34. St. Mark prefers "after three days" to "on the third day," though in 14:58 and in 15:29 (where, however, in each case the reference is to Jesus' alleged declaration that he would destroy and rebuild the temple) we have $\delta\iota\grave{\alpha}$ $\tau\rho\iota\hat{\omega}\nu$ $\mathring{\eta}\mu\epsilon\rho\hat{\omega}\nu$ and $\mathring{\epsilon}\nu$ $\tau\rho\iota\sigma\grave{\iota}\nu$ $\mathring{\eta}\mu\acute{\epsilon}\rho\alpha\iota\varsigma$ respectively; cf. the "after six days" of 9:2 and the "after two days" of 14:1. In I Cor. 15:4 the Messiah's resurrection takes place $\tau\hat{\eta}$ $\mathring{\eta}\mu\acute{\epsilon}\rho\alpha$ $\tau\hat{\eta}$ $\tau\rho\acute{\iota}\tau\eta$, and in the New Testament generally this is the usual way of dating the resurrection. Both Jews and Greeks counted in the first day as well as the last when reckoning up an interval, so that "on the third day" could be used in the sense of our "day after tomorrow"; cf. the

lamation will evidently receive its final confirmation at the parousia of the Son of Man (8:38; 13;26; 14:62), the precise date of which is known to none save God alone (13:32).

Thus St. Mark appears to distinguish four principal stages or periods in the historical realization of God's plan of salvation: namely, the period of preparation, which comes to an end with the removal of John the Baptist; the period of Jesus' ministry on earth, which is characterized by suffering and obscurity; the postresurrection period, in which the gospel of the Messiahship is openly proclaimed; and the period of eschatological fulfillment, which will be gloriously inaugurated by the Son of Man at his still-awaited parousia. It is true that the evangelist does not present us with a systematic body of doctrine concerning these periods and the manner of their interconnection. Thus in the three predictions of the passion and resurrection (8:31; 9:31; 10:33f.) he does not make so much as a passing reference to the parousia and, conversely, in the three passages which expressly concern the parousia of the Son of Man (8:38; 13:26; 14:62) there is no mention of the passion or of the resurrection. The evangelist does not offer any elucidation of what precisely he understands by the important doctrine of the necessity of the Messiah's sufferings, and he makes no attempt to explain the nature of the connection between the passion and the parousia, on the one hand, and between the resurrection and the parousia, on the other. The evangelist's position, in fact, has all the appearance of being a tentative one. The various parts of his doctrine

---

French "une quinzaine" for "a fortnight." Also, such passages as Gen. 42:17f. and II Chron. 10:5, 12, show that "after three days" could mean the same as "on the third day." But it must be noted that there are no known instances of this usage in the works of Gentile writers, and this may help to account for the general predominance of "on the third day" in the New Testament as a whole. St. Matthew has "after three days" in 27:63. Cf. Turner in *N.C.H.S.*, pt. 3, pp. 79f. For a full discussion of modern speculations regarding the origin of the doctrine of the Messiah's resurrection on the third day, see Goguel, *La foi à la résurrection de Jésus*, pp. 157ff.

do not form a harmonious and well-defined system of thought. On the contrary, his ideas hang together somewhat loosely, and the work as a whole leaves one with the impression that the writer is really feeling his way after a more adequate and more satisfying statement of the saving truth which the apostolic church discerned in the life and work of its founder.

But there can be little doubt regarding the evangelist's fundamental attitude. Convinced that Jesus is the Messiah, he takes the view that the Lord's humiliation represents the pledge or guarantee of his triumph in glory which is subsequently to be revealed. It is as though the soteriological process were governed by a principle of divine retribution which ultimately effects a reversal of the situation in the period of the earthly ministry. The servant shall be lord and the last shall be first. Because Jesus is the Messiah, he must be rejected before his glory can be made manifest, and those who are truly his followers know that personal self-sacrifice is the prerequisite of their heavenly reward (8:34ff.; 10:17ff.) and that the cause of the church can only be vindicated after it has passed through a period of persecution and direst distress (13:3ff.). The evangelist therefore considers the sufferings of Jesus and the tribulations of the church in the light of the glory which is still to be revealed (cf. Rom. 8:18), and yet, seeing that the glory always comes *after* the humiliation, there is a break or division in the soteriological process. The sufferings and the glory belong to different epochs, and the relationship between them is no more intimate than that which obtains between means and end. They are not brought together in the unity of a single conception as they are, for example, in the fourth gospel, where the idea of the cost of the passion has almost disappeared.[12]

[12] This may be illustrated by comparing St. Mark's account of Jesus' grief in Gethsemane (14:32ff.) with the brief statement in John 12:27. There is no suggestion in John 18:1ff. that Jesus was in distress of soul immediately before his arrest.

Accordingly, St. Mark's thought is essentially bipolar. On the one hand there is the recognition of the fact of suffering, and on the other hand there is the faith in the Messiah's promised supremacy, and these two contrasted elements in St. Mark's total interpretation are never united in an effective synthesis. Moreover, such doctrinal separation has a formal counterpart in the evangelist's arrangement of much of his material. We have already noticed that no reference is made to the parousia in connection with the predictions of 8:31; 9:31; and 10:33–34, but the same point finds ample illustration in other passages. Thus in chapter 8 verses 34b–37 deal with the necessity of self-sacrifice in true discipleship, whereas the last saying in the section (9:1) promises that certain of those present will not taste of death until they see the kingdom of God come with power. The story of the transfiguration in 9:2ff. sets forth the essential glory of the Messiah, but it includes no mention of his coming afflictions.[13] In 10:17–31 verses 17–27 are mainly concerned to point out that self-denial and renunciation are necessary for entrance into the kingdom or the attainment of eternal life, while in verses 29–31 it is the magnitude of the ensuing reward which is emphasized. The eschatological discourse in 13:5ff. has its climax in the prediction of the parousia (v. 26), but it contains no reference to the passion, which is narrated in the next two chapters; verses 5–23 describe the final sufferings of the faithful and the calamities which are to befall the whole of humanity in the last days of the present age, and, although in verse 13b salvation is promised to him who endures to the end (cf. v. 20), it is not till we come to verses 24–27 that the glory of the parousia is portrayed, and in this connection there is no reference to suffering. It may be that the evangelist regards the passion of the Messiah as the archetype, so to speak, of the final afflictions of the faith-

---

[13] In St. Luke's version of the story, on the other hand, Moses and Elijah converse with Jesus concerning the "exodus" which he is about to accomplish in Jerusalem (Luke 9:31).

ful, but the discourse affords no indication of an idea of this kind.[14] Finally, the passion story deals primarily with the Lord's self-humiliation, and it includes only one reference to the ultimate triumph of the Son of Man (14:62), for it seems probable that the promise of a reunion in Galilee after the passion (14:28; cf. 16:7) refers to an appearance, or plurality of appearances, of the risen Jesus, not to the parousia; such, at all events, is the line of interpretation which is adopted by the first evangelist (cf. Matt. 28:7ff., 16ff.).

A further consequence of the bipolarity of St. Mark's thought consists in his persistent refusal to dwell on the sufferings of the Messiah or on the afflictions of the church without drawing the reader's attention to the future in which they are to find their end and justification. Accordingly, although the evangelist is for the most part dealing with events of the past and is setting forth the gospel in its historical aspect, his general attitude in the last resort is prospective rather than retrospective. He evinces something of the undying hope of the primitive church and looks beyond the humiliation and sufferings of the past to the age to come, the age of fruition and revelation. Indeed, one can hardly avoid the impression that the evangelist is interested in the earthly life of the Messiah, with its obscurity, lowliness, and final shame in crucifixion, not for its own sake, but for the sake of the glory which it precedes and makes possible. The ministry of Jesus points forward to the time when that which is made secret comes to light (4:22; 9:9), and in the postresurrection period the saving truth is propagated in the world. But the end is not yet (13:7c). The secret of the Messiahship may now be understood and be publicly proclaimed by the church, but the last, triumphant confirmation of the gospel is still the object of earnest expectation (cf. Rom. 8:18ff.), and of such confirmation the

[14] Of course the teaching of 13:5ff. probably owes something to the Jewish conception of the Messiah's birth pangs (see v. 8c); for the Jewish doctrine, cf. G. F. Moore, *Judaism*, II, 360ff.

tribulations of the elect are a presage and a guarantee (13:24). Furthermore, even the parousia itself, despite the preceding disturbances in nature (13:24f.) and the subsequent convocation of the elect (13:27), is not to be identified with the awaited consummation, but is to be regarded as a preliminary sign thereof (13:29). Thus the evangelist is still looking beyond the events he relates toward a future in which, as he expects, they will have their triumphant climax. Finality continues to elude his grasp.

In St. Mark's view, then, the earthly ministry of the Messiah can hardly be in an unqualified sense the locus of revelation.[15] On the other hand, there is a countertendency at work which militates against the bipolarity of the evangelist's fundamental position and induces him to represent the life of Jesus as the locus of secret revelation. Apparently, he is not wholly satisfied with the doctrine that the humiliation of the Messiah is the means to future triumph and supremacy, and he comes to attach a greater degree of intrinsic importance to the incarnate life than is allowed, for example, in the teaching of St. Paul. The latter shows little interest in the details of Jesus' earthly career; in his estimation it seems to be sufficient to know that the Messiah lived a real human life and that he was actually crucified, such humiliation being understood as the condition of his subsequent exaltation and the pledge of his imminent return in glory. Probably the delay in the arrival of the awaited parousia helped to bring about the new emphasis. But however the change is to be accounted for, there can be no doubt that St. Mark goes some way toward closing the gap between the suffering and the supremacy of the Messiah or toward overcoming the bipolarity of what seems to be his primary position. For he evidently believes that the Lord's Messiahship is an immutable fact and that something of the glory of the exalted Son of Man is already revealed even

[15] This expression is borrowed from Dibelius' penetrating discussion of the christologies of St. Paul and of the evangelists; see his *From Tradition to Gospel*, p. 299.

amid the lowliness and shame of the life of Jesus of Nazareth. But in so far as the church's historical traditions concerning the earthly career of its founder are evaluated from this standpoint, the difficulty raised by the final rejection of Jesus becomes all the more perplexing; and, as explained previously, the evangelist seeks to solve the problem by means of his doctrine of the messianic secret.

St. Mark's conception of the life of Jesus as the locus of secret revelation is remarkably illustrated in the story of the transfiguration (9:2ff.). For a short interval the Master is disclosed to the chosen three in the glory of his real nature and in the form in which he will appear to the world at the parousia. We are thus presented with a scene of eschatological fulfillment; and though it would be unjustifiable to assume that all the main items of the story are severally meant to refer to some feature or other of the final consummation, it seems probable that some of its symbolism should be partly construed in this sense.[16] The presence of Moses and Elijah[17] suggests the idea that the scriptures bear witness to the Messiahship of Jesus, for they may well appear on the scene as the representatives of the law and the prophets of the Old Testament. But it is not unlikely that their presence also has an eschatological significance and that they typify the elect who will be gathered together on the last day (13:27) to take part in the inauguration of the new age.[18] Peter's

[16] The eschatological character of the symbolism appears to be somewhat overemphasized by Boobyer in his *St. Mark and the Transfiguration Story*, pp. 69ff.

[17] In v. 4 Elijah is mentioned before Moses; perhaps this is because Elijah was much in the evangelist's thought at the time (cf. 8:28; 9:11). The natural order is given in v. 5.

[18] In Jewish eschatology of the first century A.D. outstanding figures of Old Testament history are frequently thought to have some part at the consummation, though Moses is less prominent in this connection than one would have expected; the belief in his translation (as distinct from that of Elijah; see II Kings 2:11) seems to be relatively late; cf. S.-B., I, 753ff. A saying (cited in S.-B., I, 757) is attributed to Jochanan

proposal (9:5) to build three tabernacles,[19] one for Jesus, one for Moses, and one for Elijah, evidently rests on a misunderstanding of the significance of the situation (v. 6). His words may be taken to imply that Moses and Elijah stand on an equality with Jesus, in which case the mistake is corrected in verse 7 by the utterance of the voice from the cloud.[20] Jesus is God's unique Son, and his instruction alone is to be obeyed; [21] he is the promised Messiah, the chosen representative of the kingdom of God, and as such he supersedes even the greatest of the prophets and teachers of the old dispensation. But a further motif may be involved. Perhaps Peter does not realize when making his offer that the

---

b. Zakkai (first century A.D.) in which God promises that Moses will return with Elijah at the end; according to S.-B. (I, 756) this saying is of late origin, perhaps even as late as 900 A.D., but Lohmeyer (*Das Evangelium des Markus*, p. 175, n. 4) refuses to follow S.-B. on this point. The Samaritans seem to have expected the return of Moses as the Messiah; cf. Foakes-Jackson and Lake, *The Beginnings of Christianity*, I, 404ff. In the primitive church it was believed that the patriarchs and prophets would participate in the blessings of the consummated Kingdom; cf. Luke 13:28f., Heb. 11:16.

[19] The feast of tabernacles, like the passover, had come to refer to the final deliverance; for the eschatological associations of the idea of dwelling in tabernacles, see Lohmeyer's article in *Z.N.T.W.*, XXI (1922), 191ff. Cf. Rev. 7:15; 21:3. Realized eschatology seems to be reflected in John 1:14; the Messiah already *tabernacles* in his incarnate life. Cf. H. Riesenfeld, *Jésus transfiguré*, pp. 146ff., 265ff.

[20] Following the Syriac version Wellhausen held that the correct reading in v. 7 is αὐτῷ, not αὐτοῖς; the cloud overshadows or envelops Jesus alone. But it seems more likely that αὐτοῖς is the original reading (so Dibelius, *op. cit.*, p. 276, n. 2; Lohmeyer, *Das Evangelium des Markus*, p. 177, n. 1). That is, the cloud envelops the three disciples or, alternatively, all the six persons who take part in the scene; seeing that there is no suggestion that the disciples behold the transfiguration from a distance, the latter alternative is perhaps the more acceptable; the idea behind the Syriac variant may be that the cloud which conceals God's own presence may come into contact only with Jesus, the Son of God.

[21] Cf. Deut. 18:15; Acts 3:22. St. Mark may have Jesus' teaching regarding the necessity of suffering especially in mind; that is the teaching to be attended to and taken to heart.

transfiguration is but a transient anticipation of the glory of the consummated kingdom. He overlooks that the permanent enjoyment of the blessings of the new age, which will be shared by *all* the people of God (cf. 13:27), cannot come to pass until the Master's prophecies regarding the necessity of suffering have been fulfilled.

As they descend the mountain (9:9) the three disciples are informed, as we should expect, that they must tell no one of their experience. But this injunction to silence is of special interest because it is the only one in St. Mark's gospel which explicitly sets a time limit to the period of concealment. The implication is that the fact of Jesus' Messiahship is to be openly proclaimed after the Son of Man has been raised from the dead; in the meantime the secret must be carefully guarded. Moreover, the reference to the resurrection in this connection induces the evangelist to deal with certain interconnected theological problems concerning the mission of John the Baptist, the sufferings of Jesus, and the coming of the kingdom of God.[22]

The construction of the passage (vv. 10–13) is somewhat disjointed, however, and various proposals have been made with a view to making it read more coherently. Indeed, Turner [23] even goes so far as to assert that the passage as it now stands is unintelligible; and he solves the difficulty by supposing that verse 12b has been accidently transposed to a wrong place and should be brought back to its natural position in immediate sequence to verse 10. Another possibility [24] is that verse 12b is an interpolation introduced through the influence of Matt. 17:10–13, where the first evangelist strengthens St. Mark's interpretation of the Jewish doctrine of the forerunner by drawing attention to the

[22] Cf. above, Chapter 1.

[23] See *N.C.H.S.*, pt. 3, p. 82. Turner observes that in 9:10 we should translate "discussing with one another" (cf. 11:31) or "kept . . . to themselves." He also notices that in 9:11 St. Mark uses the indirect for the direct interrogative.

[24] See Bultmann, *Die Geschichte der synoptischen Tradition*, pp. 131f.

analogy between the fate of the Baptist and that of Jesus (Matt. 17:12b) and by explicitly identifying the Baptist with Elijah redivivus (Matt. 17:13). But such proposals as these are purely conjectural, and, on the whole, it seems safer to hold to the integrity of the received text of the passage and to assume that the first evangelist has improved its construction without adding to the ideas it entails. It is true that the passage does not read smoothly, but it appears to be an exaggeration to say that it is unintelligible in its present form. The question regarding the return of Elijah is quite relevant at this point in the narrative.[25] Not only is Elijah mentioned in 8:28 and in 9:4-5 (twice), but in 9:1 Jesus promises that some of those who stand by will not taste of death until they see the arrival of the kingdom in power, and in 9:2ff. there is a remarkable demonstration of the reality of Jesus' messianic status. But if the time of the kingdom's consummation is fast approaching and the Messiah has actually come in the person of Jesus, the question naturally arises: Where is the Elijah forerunner prophesied in the scriptures? The evangelist supplies the answer in verses 12-13. In his judgment the scribes rightly teach that Elijah must come first and restore all things; and he goes on to affirm that Elijah has in fact already come and men have done as they pleased with him, the implication being, so it would seem, that the prophecy concerning the return of Elijah has been fulfilled in the person of John the Baptist.

Before making this affirmation, however, the evangelist apparently wishes to meet a possible objection to his interpretation, and he reminds his readers that, according to the scriptures, the Son of Man suffers many things and is counted for nought. In other words, he holds that the rejection of John does not disqualify him for fulfilling the role of Elijah, any more than the

---

[25] Mark 9:11. As in 4:10; 7:17; 9:28; 10:10; 13:4, the problem faced by the evangelist is set forth as a question put to Jesus by the disciples, his solution being given in Jesus' reply.

rejection of Jesus precludes him from being Messiah. On the contrary, the fact that John is "delivered up" (1:14) only goes to confirm the view that he is the divinely appointed forerunner of the Messiah, for the Messiah himself is also "delivered up" (9:31; 10:33); and as the earthly fate of the latter is in accordance with the declared will of God, so is the earthly fate of the former. Thus the evangelist envisages a certain correspondence between the death of the forerunner and the death of him for whom he prepares the way, and it is interesting to notice that just as the passion story is much more detailed than the preceding narrative of the ministry, so the story of the death of John in 6:17ff. is much more detailed than the account of his mission presented in the preface (1:4ff.).

In 9:14ff. there follows the story of the healing of the boy possessed by a dumb and deaf spirit, and it stands in noteworthy contrast to the story of the transfiguration. The Messiah again appears amid the woes of humanity, and the miracle he performs is made all the more impressive through being set on the background of the disciples' impotence (vv. 18b, 28). The next paragraph contains the second announcement of the passion and resurrection (9:31), and after this comes a series of some seven pericopes which are mainly concerned to bring out the ethical implications of the doctrine of the crucified Messiah. The section includes illustrations of the persistent failure of the disciples to assimilate the truth, frequent references to the great reward which attends the fulfillment of the gospel's rigorous demands, and an exemplification of the need for a deeper understanding of the significance of the law of Moses.[26] In 10:32–34 the evan-

[26] (1) Mark 9:33ff. call for humility. (2) 9:38ff. (cf. Num. 11:26ff.) stress the need for tolerance, sympathy with the weaker, and so on. (3) 10:1ff. deal with the question of marriage and divorce, but it is not wholly true to say that the discussion is disgressive. (In 10:1 the D reading ὁ ὄχλος may well be correct, for St. Mark never elsewhere uses the plural, his usage in this respect being different from that of the other synoptic evangelists. In 10:2 the words προσελθόντες Φαρισαῖοι are

gelist presents the third and most detailed of the predictions of the passion and resurrection,[27] which is followed by the passage concerning the request of the sons of Zebedee (10:35–45) and the story of the healing of blind Bartimaeus (10:46–52). According to the first of these two last-mentioned pericopes, James and John ask for positions of preeminence in the Messiah's "glory" (vv. 35–37), and the ten are moved with indignation (v. 41), presumably because they are jealous of their own dignity and are afraid lest the two brothers should secure some advantage over them. Confronted by such selfish ambition and rivalry, the Master proceeds to make yet another attempt to impress the truth upon the minds of his disciples, this time by means of an antithesis (vv. 42–45). It is pointed out that the way to greatness in the kingdoms of the world is very different from the way to greatness in the kingdom of God as it is exemplified in the career of the Son of Man, who came not to be served, but to serve and to give even his life for the redemption of many.[28]

---

omitted in D, and have probably come in through the influence of the parallel in Matt. 19:3. The later tradition tends to make the subject more definite; cf. 3:2 with Luke 6:7; 5:22 with Luke 8:41; 14:13 with Luke 22:8.). (4) 10:13ff. teach that "entrance into the kingdom" (cf. 9:47) is possible only to him who is willing to receive the kingdom as a little child. (5) 10:17ff. show that the attainment of "eternal life" (cf. 9:43, 45) is conditioned by self-sacrifice. (6) 10:23ff. emphasize the difficulty with which the rich enter the kingdom. (7) 10:28ff. indicate the greatness of the reward which comes of self-abnegation for "the gospel's sake" (cf. 8:35.).

[27] Thus in 10:33f. alone is it stated that the Son of Man will be delivered to the Gentiles.

[28] This is the only explicit reference to redemption in the work. Bultmann (*op. cit.*, p. 23) sees the original form of the pericope in vv. 35–37, 40; he argues that vv. 38f. are a *vaticinium ex eventu* and that vv. 41–45 are an appendix dealing, not with precedence in the coming kingdom but with precedence in the Christian community. This interpretation, however, is unsatisfactory: (1) It is difficult to believe that vv. 35, 37, 40 once circulated as an independent paradigm. (2) The insertion of v. 41 is left without explanation. (3) While vv. 42–45

With this antithesis the teaching of the section comes to an end, but the disciples still show no signs of comprehending its true import, their failure being made the more apparent by the story concerning blind Bartimaeus, which seems to form a connecting link between the second main section of the gospel and the third.[29] Although he does not belong to the privileged circle of the chosen disciples and despite his physical disability, yet the blind man has sufficient insight and faith to address Jesus as the Son of David and to receive healing at his hands.[30]

In the light of the foregoing considerations, then, it seems that in the evangelist's interpretation there is an important correspondence between the multitude's failure to recognize the fact of the Messiahship and the disciples' inability to understand its

---

do not mention a future reward in "glory," it would appear to be assumed that those who adopt the ideal of service are the people destined to participate in the blessings of the consummated kingdom. Accordingly, it seems to be probable that vv. 41–45 belonged to the original paradigm; and if vv. 38–40 are taken to be a unity and v. 41 is seen to be the natural sequel to v. 37, we may reasonably presume that vv. 38–40 were inserted, perhaps after St. Mark had completed his work, in recognition of the martyrdom of James and John. Dibelius (*op. cit.*, p. 51) goes further and conjectures that the paradigm in its earliest form showed no personal interest, the request of vv. 35–37 being made by unnamed disciples. Manson (*The Teaching of Jesus*, pp. 313ff.; cf. p. 294, n. 2) maintains that the words οἱ δοκοῦντες ἄρχειν κτλ should be construed in a sense similar to that of "whoever wishes to become great among you . . . ," and he translates as follows: "You know that those who aspire to rule over the Gentiles subjugate them and the greatest of them rule them despotically. Not so is it among you; but whoever wishes to become greatest among you shall be your servant. And whoever wishes to attain primacy among you shall be the slave of all."

[29] Similarly, the story concerning the healing of the blind man at Bethsaida (8:22–26) seems to establish a connection between the first and second main sections of the gospel; cf. below, Chapter 9.

[30] Cf. the appeal to the multitude in 8:34 after Peter's failure to appreciate the significance of the first prediction of the passion and resurrection, and the reference to the strange exorcist in 9:38ff. after the disciples' disputings about the greatest among them.

meaning. In each case the failure is evidently to be explained as a provision of God's sovereign purpose for the salvation of the world. Jesus is not frustrated by the obtuse reactions of the disciples to his teaching any more than he is frustrated by the indifference or hostility of the public at large. He may continue to instruct the disciples in various ways and on various occasions, but St. Mark leaves us with the impression that it has already been divinely determined that they should not yet comprehend the significance of such instruction. Their spiritual sight is dim, and so it must remain until the Son of Man rises again from the dead, when the period of obscurity will give way to the preordained period of enlightenment in which the messianic secret may be publicly proclaimed for the salvation of humanity. Accordingly, although the disciples cannot understand their Master's instruction at the time of its communication, they can retain it as part of a priceless tradition,[31] and can thus prepare themselves for the propagation of the gospel in the world.

[31] Cf. 8:32a and 9:10 and the use of κρατεῖν in 7:3, 4, 8.

9

Strain on the Secret

THE story of the healing of blind Bartimaeus in 10:46–52 seems to form a connecting link between the second main section of the gospel and the third. This third section extends from 11:1 to 13:37 and constitutes St. Mark's account of the Jerusalem ministry. It stands in noteworthy contrast to the second section, and in a certain measure it is reminiscent of the evangelist's account of the Galilean ministry. Thus it contains no private instruction of the disciples, save in 13:1ff., while in 12:13ff. we are presented with a series of controversy stories which closely resemble those previously encountered in 2:1ff. On the whole, however, a careful consideration shows that the differences between the first main section of the gospel and the third outweigh the similarities. Thus in 11:1ff. there is no proclamation of the good news, no call to repentance, no exorcism, no confession by a demon, and no injunction to silence. There is only one parable, the parable of the wicked husbandmen in 12:1ff., and this, unlike the parables of 4:1ff., is understood by those to whom it is addressed; and there is only one miracle, the cursing of the fig tree in 11:12ff., and this seems to be set forth not so much as a proof of the supernatural power of Jesus but as a symbolical indication of the terrible fate that awaits the Jewish people. The truth is that in 11:1ff. the evangelist is primarily concerned with the theme of opposition, and such a preoccupation is not unnatural, seeing that the section in question immediately precedes the passion narrative presented in 14:1ff.

Moreover, although the theme of unwarranted opposition to Jesus is a constantly recurring feature of St. Mark's account of the Galilean ministry, in 11:1ff. it is delineated in a new aspect. For in these passages Jesus takes the initiative in an unprecedented fashion, the consequence being that the evangelist's doctrine of the secret Messiahship is subjected to great strain. In 11:1–10 Jesus arranges what is clearly intended as a public messianic demonstration; in 11:15–18 he casts out those who profane the temple with their commercial activities; and in 12:1–12 he deliberately provokes his opponents by making an inauspicious utterance against them. Thus the evangelist is apparently seeking to make it plain that the events he relates have a profound significance which is utterly different from their outward show—that he who was despised by his own people and came to a shameful end on a cross is really none other than the heaven-sent Messiah, who entered Jerusalem and cleansed the temple in the fulfillment of God's soteriological purpose; and hence the narratives under consideration read as though the true nature of Jesus is reaching out, so to speak, for some definite form of articulate expression and open acknowledgment, which, however, it cannot yet receive.

It is of interest to notice that the story concerning blind Bartimaeus is immediately preceded by the pericope which deals with the failure of the sons of Zebedee to appreciate the moral implications of the fact of their Master's Messiahship. For on two previous occasions in the second main section of the gospel (8:34; 9:38ff.) favorable reference to outsiders has been made immediately after an exemplification of the disciples' incapacity to understand the significance of the messianic secret. But besides having a backward connection of this kind, the story seems also to have a notable bearing on the account of the triumphal entry which follows. For the blind man addresses Jesus as the Son of David, and hence the story provides a foil to the acclamations of the people in 11:9–10. If this is so, the story of the healing of blind Bartimaeus, like the story of the healing of the blind man at Bethsaida in 8:22–26, forms a connecting link between two main sections of the gospel; and it should be observed that in each instance the following pericope reports the continuation of a journey and has a καί, not a δέ, as its introductory conjunction.[1]

It would appear, then, that in 10:47–48 blind Bartimaeus recognizes the Messiahship of Jesus; and yet there is no indication in the narrative of the way by which he comes to know the secret. One possibility might be that the man is possessed by an unclean spirit which causes his blindness[2] and that it is through the demon's supernatural powers of insight that he is enabled to address Jesus as the Son of David. But this exegesis is unsatisfactory because no demon is mentioned and, in any case, a demon would hardly request an exorcist to come and liberate its own victim. Again, it is unlikely that the "many" in verse 48 are disciples of Jesus engaged in preventing the secret of their Master's status from being divulged; the natural interpretation is that there are members of the general public among those who enjoin Bartimaeus to silence (cf. v. 46). In the light of such considerations, therefore, we may be inclined to agree with Wrede[3] that the passage has nothing to do with the evangelist's doctrine of the messianic secret; in his view, the nearest parallel is in 10:13, where the disciples rebuke those who bring children to Jesus

---

[1] Cf. above, Chapter 7.
[2] Cf. F. Fenner, *Die Krankheit im Neuen Testament*, p. 22; S.-B., IV, 524f.
[3] *Das Messiasgeheimnis*, pp. 278f.

that he might touch them, manifestly because they feel that their Master ought not to be troubled with what is, in their eyes, a triviality.

Basing his argument upon evidence derived from the folklore of the Near East, Bishop considers that the messianic meaning of the title "Son of David" may not be primary.[4] He thinks that Jesus reminded the common people of the great miracle worker, Solomon, and suggests that this is the reason for the blind man's use of the title in 10:47–48. If this view were tenable, the grounds for Wrede's interpretation would be considerably strengthened. But Bishop's argument is not convincing. The significance which may be ascribed to "the Son of David" in current Arabic folklore can hardly be taken as an indication of its significance for the inhabitants of Palestine in the first century of our era. And it is of interest to notice that Josephus, in his eulogy of Solomon's wisdom and skill in the art of exorcism, refers to him simply as "Solomon," not as "the Son of David."[5] On the other hand, we gather from Jewish literature, rabbinic and apocalyptic, that the Davidic ancestry of the Messiah was generally assumed in the eschatological speculations of the period, and that the expression "the Son of David" came to be frequently employed as a messianic designation.[6] Indeed, it seems to have been precisely in virtue of the prevalence of this form of messianic belief in Jewish thought, that the apostolic church attached high value to the doctrine of the Lord's descent from David and eventually sought to demonstrate the validity of the doctrine by elaborating genealogies such as those preserved in Matt. 1:1ff. and Luke 3:23ff. St. Paul holds that Jesus was born of the seed of David according to the flesh (Rom. 1:3); and St. Mark evidently takes the same view, though in 12:35–37 he points out that the Messiah is much greater than David and hence (if full justice is to be done to his

[4] See *Ex. T.*, XLVII (1935–36), 21ff. [5] *Ant.* 8, 2, 5.
[6] Cf. S.-B., I, 11ff., 525.

divine status) he should be designated "the Lord of David" (as in Ps. 110:1), not "the Son of David." [7]

Accordingly, while not denying that there is a recurrence of the motif of 10:13 in 10:47–48, we cannot agree with Wrede that the latter passage is without importance in relation to the evangelist's doctrine of the messianic secret. For, by addressing the miracle worker as the Son of David, the blind man attributes to Jesus a status which in the evangelist's view properly belongs to him, and thus in a surprising fashion the secret comes to the ears of the general public. Perhaps Bartimaeus calls out under the stress of temporary emotional excitement and does not realize the full import of the words he uses; at all events, when he comes near Jesus he addresses him simply as "rabbouni" (v. 51). Nevertheless, for a passing moment, as though by a flash of divine inspiration, the blind man presents the multitude with an opportunity to apprehend and acknowledge the fact of the Messiahship; but the opportunity is not taken. He calls out loudly to the Son of David, yet the bystanders only remonstrate with him and enjoin him to silence, whereupon he shouts out all the more—"Son of David, have pity on me!"—and the people about him do not recognize the significance of his words.[8] Thus St. Mark seems to be anticipating the idea to which the fourth evangelist gives expression in John 9:39: the Lord appears on the scene that those who do not see may see and that those who see may become blind.

[7] Similarly, as Rom. 1:4 shows, St. Paul thinks that it is insufficient merely to state that Jesus was born of the seed of David. Whatever may have been the exact nature of the situation in which the paradigm of 12:35–37 originated, St. Mark's inclusion of it in his work does not imply that he rejects the doctrine of Jesus' Davidic descent, any more than St. Matthew's inclusion of it in his work implies that he rejects the doctrine. Cf. John 7:42, which is not necessarily at variance with Rom. 1:3.

[8] Since Jesus responds to the man's renewed shouting, the story exemplifies the value of persistency; cf. Luke 11:5ff., 18:1ff.

The blindness of those who see receives further illustration in the story of the approach to Jerusalem, which follows in 11:1–10. The evangelist apparently wishes his readers to see what even the disciples did not see at the time—that Jesus entered Jerusalem as the messianic King in fulfillment of the will of God, which is revealed in the scriptures (cf. John 12:16). In verses 1–6 the Master sends two of his disciples into the village opposite them in order to procure the young ass which he requires for the forthcoming demonstration. He knows in advance where and how they will find the animal and that they will not be prevented from taking it away; and he thus appears to be acting in accordance with a transcendent scheme which has already been drawn up even to the minutest detail, as in 14:12–16, where he sends two of his disciples into the city to prepare for the last supper. The mention of the Mount of Olives in verse 1 may be significant, for it seems to have been a popular belief that the Messiah would make his appearance on that eminence.[9] The colt or foal of an ass in verse 2 is reminiscent of the animal referred to in Zech. 9:9, a passage which is actually adduced in St. Matthew's version of the story (Matt. 21:5). The notice that the colt is one upon which no one has ever sat would perhaps be intended to imply that the animal is to be employed for a special religious purpose (cf. Num. 19:2; I Sam. 6:7) or, more specifically, as Bacon suggested,[10] it may be a recollection of the νέον (lit. "new") in the phrase πῶλον νέον, which occurs in the LXX translation of the Zechariah prophecy (cf. also, Luke 23:53b).

In 11:7–10 the two disciples bring the colt to their Master, as he has instructed them, and when they have put their outer garments on it, he seats himself and proceeds to ride toward the gates of the city amid the enthusiastic acclamations of fellow travelers who may have been going up to Jersusalem to celebrate

[9] Cf. Josephus, *Ant.* 20, 8, 6; *Bell.* 2, 13, 5; also, Luke 24:50; Acts 1:12; 21:38. Perhaps the belief took its rise from Zech. 14:4.
[10] See *The Beginnings of the Gospel Story*, p. 159.

the feast of the passover (14:1, 12–16). Many spread their garments on the road, and others strew green branches cut from the fields. Thus Jesus receives a form of ovation which would have befitted a king,[11] and yet there is no explicit acknowledgment of his messianic status in the people's acclamations:

Hosanna!
Blessed is he who comes in the name of the Lord!
Blessed is the coming kingdom of our father David!
Hosanna in the highest!

These words recall Ps. 118:25–26, which read:

O Yahweh, we beseech thee, save [us] now!
O Yahweh, we beseech thee, send now prosperity!
Blessed is he who comes in the name of Yahweh!
We have blessed you from the house of Yahweh.

The Hebrew of the first of these lines runs:

אנא יהוה הושיעה נא

which in the LXX (Ps. 117:25) is rendered as follows:

ὦ Κύριε σῶσον δή.

Hoshianna is really an appeal for help (in certain instances it appears as βοήθησον in the LXX), and was sometimes addressed to God on behalf of the king (cf. Ps. 20:10; E.T., 20:9), but was not always employed with reference to a king; Ps. 118:25a, for example, indicates that it could be used as a general prayer for salvation or divine help. The expression constitutes the first acclamation in St. Mark's account (11:9b) and is repeated in the fourth (v. 10b) with the addition "in the highest." This phrase corresponds to the Hebrew "in the heights," which could mean "from the heavens"—as the poetic parallelism in Ps. 148:1 seems to show.[12] Hence verse 10b may be translated:

[11] Cf. II Kings 9:13; S.-B., I, 844ff.
[12] Cf. C. C. Torrey, *The Four Gospels*, p. 295, note on Matt. 21:9.

Save [us], we beseech thee, from heaven!

Another possibility is that the acclamation is an abbreviated utterance meaning:

Save [us], we beseech thee, [who dwellest] in heaven!

In either case, however, the people are praying that God may inaugurate the era of salvation by an act of his transcendent and omnipotent will. Again, we gather from such passages as Matt. 11:3 or Luke 7:19 and John 11:27 that the expression "he who comes," which occurs in the second acclamation (v. 9c), had messianic associations for the early Christian reader, but here it simply forms part of a customary form of religious greeting; and in Ps. 118:26a the acclamation is used to greet those who come up to the temple to celebrate the feast of tabernacles.[13] The mention of "our father, David" in the third acclamation (v. 10a) provides a significant contrast to the utterances of blind Bartimaeus in the previous pericope. Despite the enthusiasm of their welcome, the people do not realize that the time of fulfillment has already arrived and that the kingdom of God has drawn near (cf. 1:14f.) in the person of him who rides on the colt and who is at once the Son of David and the Son of God.[14]

On the other hand, in the corresponding passages of the three later gospels the Christian conception is set forth clearly and without reservation. Zech. 9:9 is adduced by the fourth evange-

---

[13] As part of the hallel Ps. 118 was also used at the feast of the passover; cp. W. O. E. Oesterley, *A Fresh Approach to the Psalms*, pp. 33ff., 136ff. Pss. 113–118 constituted the hallel. The feast of tabernacles was the new year festival.

[14] In Bab. San. 98a R. Joshua b. Levi (*c.* 250 A.D.) declares that the Son of Man will come in the clouds of heaven (cf. Dan. 7:13) if Israel is worthy of it, but if Israel is unworthy of it, he will come in lowliness and riding on an ass (cf. Zech. 9:9); and Lohmeyer (*Das Evangelium des Markus*, pp. 232f.) conjectures that St. Mark may anticipate the rabbi's doctrine in 11:1–11—the King does not come to Zion in glory because the inhabitants of Jerusalem are unworthy of such a coming.

list (John 12:14f.), as well as by the first (Matt. 21:4f.). And, what is more significant, the royal dignity of Jesus is openly acknowledged in the people's cries of welcome. Thus in Matt. 21:9 the acclamations read:

Hosanna to the Son of David! [15]
Blessed is he who comes in the name of the Lord!
Hosanna in the highest!

In Luke 19:38 they read:

Blessed is he who comes, the King, in the name of the Lord!
In heaven peace and glory in the highest!

And in John 12:13 they read:

Hosanna!
Blessed is he who comes in the name of the Lord, even the King of Israel.[16]

Thus the doctrine of the secret, which is already subjected to great strain in St. Mark's narrative, no longer obtains in the later gospels. The barriers it imposes have been broken down by the urge to represent the earthly life of Jesus directly in terms of the apostolic faith in his Messiahship and hence he can be publicly welcomed, not merely as a pilgrim engaged on a prophetic mission, but as the messianic King whose coming takes place in accordance with the declared will of God.

In 11:11 St. Mark rounds off his account of the approach to Jerusalem with a notice which points forward to the story of the cleansing of the temple. Having entered the city, Jesus goes into the temple and looks round at all things, whereupon, owing to

[15] "Hosanna" seems to be here used as a formula of greeting in much the same way as the German "Heil" is used in "Heil dem König!" The dative is one of advantage: "We pray 'Hosanna' for/on behalf of the Son of David!" But cf. Lightfoot, *The Gospel Message of St. Mark*, p. 62.

[16] It should be noticed that in the fourth gospel, but not in the synoptics, Jesus is acclaimed by people who come out of Jerusalem to meet him; see John 12:12f.

the lateness of the hour, he retires to Bethany with the twelve.[17] It is unlikely that the evangelist here means to depict Jesus as a stranger to Jerusalem who is moved by a natural desire to see the sights of the city.[18] The point is rather that Jesus is Lord of the temple and the God-sent guardian of its sanctity, and hence he must inspect the place to determine whether or not its affairs are being conducted aright. Perhaps the implication of the "all things" is that he acually penetrates those parts of the building to which the ordinary pilgrim could not gain access. At all events, on the following day he acts and teaches in the temple with such transcendent power that he evokes astonishment in all the multitude (11:18c; cf. 1:22) and causes the religious leaders to question him regarding the nature and the source of the authority he exercises (11:27f.).

St. Mark presents the story of the cleansing of the temple in 11:15–19, where it divides the account of the cursing of the fig tree into two separate sections.[19] As was pointed out in Chapter

---

[17] St. Mark does not explain why Jesus leaves the city when evening comes (cf. 11:19; 11:27). In certain parts of the passion narrative it seems to be presupposed that Jesus has his quarters outside Jerusalem, possibly in the vicinity of Bethany, which was at the second milestone from the city and thus more than a mile beyond the Mount of Olives (cf. 14:3, 16, 26). Was it because of the difficulty of securing accommodation in Jerusalem at the time of the passover? Or was it because of the hostility of the Jewish leaders? Perhaps St. Mark takes the latter view (cf. 11:18–19; 14:1–2).

[18] Cf. Loisy, *Les évangiles synoptiques*, II, 268. There is a noteworthy similarity in vv. 11, 15, 27. If, in St. Mark's source, the question regarding Jesus' authority immediately followed the story of the cleansing of the temple, the account of the cursing of the fig tree (vv. 12–14, 20–25) owing its present position to St. Mark, vv. 11, 27 (and 19) are probably based on v. 15, having been composed by the evangelist as connecting links.

[19] Vv. 12–14; 20–25. The view is often taken that this story is based on the parable in Luke 13:6–9. But E. Schwartz (*Z.N.T.W.*, V [1904], 80ff.) thinks that it is an aetiological saga: there was a well-known withered fig tree near Jerusalem, and the tale arose in Christian circles that Jesus had cursed it, the curse to hold good till the parousia, at which

6, by means of this intercalation the evangelist suggests a parallel between the fate of the Messiah and that of the Jewish people; Jesus condemns Israel, and this condemnation brings about his own death as well as the destruction of the nation to which he belongs. The intercalated story falls into four main parts: verses 15–16 concern Jesus' act of cleansing the temple; [20] verse 17 pro-

---

time the tree would come to life again; cf. 13:28f. The gospels contain no other story of the miraculous fulfillment of a curse, but cf. the talmudic saying: "A rabbi's curse takes effect even if there is no real warrant for his utterance of it" (see S.-B., I, 859). The story suggests that Jesus is the Lord of nature; cf. the more general idea that the natural world exists for the service of man (Gen. 1:26ff., Ps. 104:14). It may seem strange that in v. 13 Jesus takes the foliage as an indication of the presence of fruit; but the point lies in the difference between the tree's appearance from a distance and its true condition, which a closer inspection reveals. Again, if it is not the season for figs (v. 13c), why does Jesus expect to find fruit on the tree? It has been suggested that he is looking for winter figs (so S.-B., I, 857). But perhaps v. 13c was added by St. Mark when he placed the story in its present context; for him, the incident takes place sometime (though apparently more than four days) before the passover. Evidently the determinism implied in v. 13c does not detract from the evangelist's belief in moral responsibility. The story may have originally ended at v. 20, vv. 21–25 having been appended by an editor (perhaps pre-Markan) who saw in the miracle an illustration of the importance of faith. The four sayings of the Lord in vv. 22–25 were probably brought together through the association of the ideas of faith and of prayer in v. 24. There are four notices of time in 11:11–12, 19–20, but no more such notices till we come to 14:1. Since the latter refers forward, St. Mark may not mean to restrict the Jerusalem ministry to a period of two days. He can hardly think that the account of the ministry on the third day extends beyond 12:12. Admittedly, he may assume that in 11:1–10 the welcome is given by pilgrims going up to Jerusalem for the celebration of the passover. But, as the passover is not mentioned before 14:1, it still seems unlikely that he regards all the teaching in 11:20–13:37 as the work of a single day; also, 14:49 appears to imply a longer period of teaching in the temple than two days. Accordingly, there are good grounds for holding that the division into days in 11:11–20 has nothing to do with a definite conception of a last week.

[20] Wine, oil, birds, and so on, required for the sacrifices, were sold

vides scriptural warrant for such violent action; in verse 18 the
hostile response of the chief priests and the scribes is set in contrast to the favorable impression which is made on the multitude;
and in verse 19 it is observed that Jesus goes out of the city when
evening comes.[21] In verse 17 part of Isa. 56:7 (LXX) is cited,[22]
while the expression "a den of robbers" seems to be derived from
Jer. 7:11 (LXX), and perhaps the evangelist has other Old
Testament passages in mind, such as Hos. 9:15; Zech. 14:21;

---

in the court of the Gentiles; cf. S.-B., I, 850ff.; Abrahams, *Studies*, 1st ser.,
pp. 83ff. Doves were used in connection with the purification of women
(Lev. 12:8; Luke 2:24f.) and of lepers (Lev. 14:22) and in other connections (Lev. 15:14, 29). The half-shekel tax for the maintenance of
the temple had to be paid in Phoenician money, and perhaps this accounts for the presence of money-changers in the court; cf. S.-B., I,
760ff. Since the tax had to be paid before Nisan 1st and since, according
to Shek. 1:3, the money-changers set up their tables in the temple on
Adar 25th, it has been inferred that the cleansing took place more than
two weeks before the passover: so Branscomb, *The Gospel of Mark*, p.
204. There are rabbinic rulings which prohibit the use of the temple
as a thoroughfare; cf. S.-B., II, 27. It is possible that the Pharisees (or
some of them) opposed the Sadducean priesthood for permitting commercial activity to take place in the temple area: so Klausner, *Jesus of
Nazareth*, pp. 313f.

[21] Vv. 18f. may be due to St. Mark. For v. 18, cf. 1:22 and 11:27. V.
19 prepares for v. 20. The R.V. "every evening" is probably an error,
resulting from the mistaken assumption that St. Mark writes classical
Greek and never uses ὅταν for ὅτε; cf. Turner in *N.C.H.S.*, pt. 3, p. 95,
and above, Chapter 4. Bultmann (*Die Geschichte der synoptischen Tradition*, p. 36) suggests that v. 17 is also due to St. Mark; cf. John 2:17,
where, not Isa. 56:7, but Ps. 69:10 (E.T., 69:9) is adduced. Perhaps St.
Mark takes the "you" in v. 17 to refer to the Jewish nation generally;
but this does not necessarily exclude the possibility that the chief priests
are being accused of making excessive profits out of the commercial
business under their sanction; cf. S.-B., I, 853.

[22] Lohmeyer (*op. cit.*, pp. 236f.) thinks that this appeal to Isa. 56:7
reflects the attitude of the pious folk of the land of Galilee, who regarded the temple as the chief synagogue or house of prayer and who
were inclined to disapprove of the sacrificial cultus. In any case the appeal is made from the standpoint of Christian universalism; cf. Rom.
10:12f.; Gal. 3:8.

Mal. 3:1ff. For it is St. Mark's conviction that the cleansing of the temple occurs in fulfillment of the scriptures and as an integral part of the Messiah's earthly mission. Nevertheless, although the bystanders may be surprised at this extraordinary demonstration of the Lord's authority, they cannot penetrate the mystery of his real status. On the other hand, in St. Matthews's version of the story even the children who are in the temple hail Jesus as the Son of David (Matt. 21:15), so that, as in the case of the triumphal entry, what is only implicit in St. Mark's gospel becomes explicit in St. Matthew's.

In 11:27ff. the chief priests and the scribes and the elders (cf. 8:31) betray their ignorance of the truth by coming to Jesus and questioning him concerning the nature of the authority to which he lays claim.[23] But Jesus refuses to enlighten them. So far from giving a plain answer to a plain question, he asks a counterquestion, which has the immediate effect of putting his opponents into a state of embarrassment. No doubt the evangelist means to imply that the authority of Jesus, like that of the Baptist, comes from God, and yet he refrains from giving open expression to such an idea, inadequate though it is as a repre-

---

[23] St. Mark may have used a source in which 11:28 was the direct continuation of 11:17; cf. John 2:13ff., where the authority question (in a modified form) is occasioned by the cleansing of the temple. It is possible that the story regarding authority once ended with the counterquestion in 11:30. This question seems to presuppose that those who raise the original questions (v. 28) believe in the divine character of John's baptism, whereas vv. 31–33 may have arisen from the recognition that the chief priests and others (v. 27) would not believe in John. Hence, if v. 27 is due to St. Mark, perhaps he is also responsible for vv. 31–33. Presumably, he takes the ταῦτα in v. 28 (twice) to refer to the cleansing of the temple (as in the supposed source). But the content of the counterquestion suggests the possibility that it originally referred to some practice, the validity of which was disputed by followers of the Baptist; cf. Bultmann, *op. cit.*, p. 18, n. 2. In vv. 30f. "heaven" is a pious circumlocution to avoid naming God directly; cf. 14:61f., S.-B., I, 862ff. In v. 32b the ὄντως may have been put in the principal clause for the sake of emphasis; so Klostermann, *Das Markusevangelium*, p. 120.

sentation of his doctrinal position. In 12:1ff., however, the narrative assumes quite a different character. Jesus again takes the initiative and almost deliberately evokes the wrath of his enemies (11:27) by making an ominous utterance against them.[24] He who is to be accused and condemned at the forthcoming trial (14:55ff.) here becomes the accuser and even proceeds to condemn those who are destined to be his judges. In verses 1b–9 he tells the story of the wicked husbandmen,[25] thereby signify-

---

[24] Cf. St. Luke's account of the rejection in the *patris* (Luke 4:16–30), where Jesus' words (vv. 23–27) are seemingly designed to arouse the anger of his compatriots (vv. 28f.)

[25] Two interesting rabbinical parallels are cited in S.-B., I, 874f. For the allegorical meaning of the parable, cf. I Thess. 2:14–16; Matt. 23:34–36/Luke 11:49–51; Matt. 23:37–38/Luke 13:34–35; Acts 7:52–53. The general idea seems to be that the Jews, as represented by their religious leaders, are liable to punishment at the hands of God because they are responsible for rejecting the Messiah and the prophets who were sent before him. The opening words of the parable are evidently based on parts of Isa. 5:1–7, where Israel appears as the vineyard of Yahweh; cf. S.-B., I, 877. In the Old Testament the prophets are frequently referred to as the servants of God; cf. Amos 3:7; Jer. 7:25; Zech. 1:6. The mention of the landlord's beloved or only son (v. 6) recalls the declarations of the heavenly voice at the baptism and at the transfiguration (1:11; 9:7). Some features of the story seem to have no direct bearing on the allegorical meaning, as, for example, the details in v. 1. Certain other features of the story, however, appear to be governed by the allegorical meaning. Thus, what human landlord would have continued to send his servants in such a situation as that depicted in vv. 2–5? But his attitude is understandable when it is taken as a symbol of the long-suffering of God. Again, what human stewards would have supposed that they would come into possession of the estate if they killed the heir (v. 7)? But their argument is understandable when it is construed in terms of the idea that the Jews rejected the Messiah because they selfishly wished to be the sole inheritors of God's covenanted promises. In the earlier part of the story the vineyard appears to represent the Jewish nation, the husbandmen being the national leaders. But in v. 9 the vineyard evidently stands for the God-given privileges of the chosen people. Presumably, the "others" (to whom those privileges are transferred) are the Gentiles; cf. Rom. 11; 11–32; Matt. 8:11–12/Luke 13:28–29. For the question in v. 9a, cf. Isa. 5:4.

ing, so we may infer, that the Messiah will be shamefully put to death, that the Jews responsible for the outrage will be destroyed, and that the sacred trust of the chosen people will be transferred to the new Israel of Christianity; and in verses 10f., by the citation of Ps. 118:22–23,[26] he suggests that the Messiah, despised and rejected on earth, will be finally exalted to a position of preeminence through a marvelous manifestation of God's supernatural power.

On this occasion the method of teaching in parables[27] is not employed, as it is in the evangelist's general interpretation (cf. 4:11f.), for the purpose of concealing the truth from the public. For, according to the observation in verse 12b, the hierarchs perceive that the parable is spoken against them. That is to say, they identify themselves with the wicked husbandmen and, as we learn from verse 12a, they are prevented from immediately fulfilling their role as such only by their fear of the multitude, which is favorably disposed toward Jesus.[28] Thus St. Mark's fundamental belief, which is evidently pressing for explicit recognition in his narrative concerning the triumphal entry and

[26] Exactly as in the LXX rendering (Ps. 117:22f.). Perhaps the psalmist's words were originally meant to refer to Israel, disdained in the present, yet divinely destined to a future of glorious supremacy. In rabbinical literature Ps. 118:22 is taken in various senses, being applied to Abraham, to David, to the Messiah, and the expression "the builders" is sometimes used of the doctors of the law; cf. S.-B., I, 875f. It appears that St. Mark sees in Ps. 118:22 a prophecy of the crucified Messiah's resurrection or exaltation; cf. Acts 4:11; I Pet. 2:7, where the same passage is adduced. The αὕτη in v. 11a (which corresponds to the *z'ōth* in the Hebrew original) refers not to "the head of the corner" (v. 10c), but to the act or process of exaltation; cf. Klostermann, *op. cit.*, p. 123.

[27] The expression "in parables" in v. 1a may be understood in various ways: (1) It is used as an adverb and means simply "parabolically" (cf. 3:23). (2) It indicates that St. Mark presents but one parable from a collection (cf. 4:33). (3) It shows that St. Mark regards vv. 10f. as forming a separate parable (but it should be noted that in v. 12b he uses the noun in the singular).

[28] V. 12 (like v. 1a) is probably due to the evangelist; cf. 11:18. Perhaps 12:12 marks the close of the third day in Jerusalem, as 11:18f. mark the end of the second day.

the cleansing of the temple, here subjects his doctrine of the secret to a strain that it cannot withstand, the result being that there is a temporary disclosure of the fact of the Messiahship outside the circle of the initiated.[29]

The six pericopes set forth in the following section (12:13–44) afford further illustration of the causes of the conflict between the Messiah and the leaders of his own nation. The section is reminiscent of the series of controversy stories presented in 2:1–3:6, and, as previously suggested,[30] it is possible that the evangelist is utilizing the same source in both cases. However this may be, it is clear that St. Mark is again concerned to emphasize the unjustifiable character of the hostility shown by the religious authorities. It is not Jesus but his opponents who misinterpret the scriptures (vv. 24–27), and even a scribe realizes the correctness of the Master's attitude to the law of Moses (vv. 28–34), though, generally speaking, the scribes are thoroughly wicked and liable to God's severest condemnation (vv. 38–40). The section also provides yet another illustration of the evangelist's predilection for series of three in his arrangement of the material,[31] for it falls naturally into two parts, each consisting of three pericopes. The first part (vv. 13–34) exemplifies the sagacity of Jesus by showing how he replies to three difficult questions which are successively brought to him by various representatives of the religious authorities: in verses 13–17 certain Pharisees and Herodians question him regarding the lawfulness of paying tribute to Caesar; in verses 18–27 some of the Sadducees raise a question about marriage in the postresurrection life;[32] and in verses 28–34a one of the scribes questions

[29] Cf. above, Chapters 6 and 8.   [30] See above, Chapter 6, n. 15.
[31] Cf. above, Chapter 6, n. 16.
[32] This story may have once ended at v. 25; vv. 26f. appear to be a supplementary conclusion. Do vv. 24f. imply that in the consummated kingdom man will recover his pristine androgynous character? As P. Winter has shown (*Z.A.T.W.*, LXVIII [1956], 71ff., 264; LXX [1958], 26of.) the interpretation of Gen. 1:27; 5:2, in *Zad. Frags.* col. 4, 11, 20f. and in Mark 10:6 (cf. Matt. 19:4) may involve an underlying concept

him concerning the greatest commandment of the law. These problems are dealt with in such a masterly fashion that, according to the observation in verse 34b, no one ventures to ask him any more questions.[33] The second part of the section (vv. 35–44) represents Jesus as the assailant of his opponents: in verses 35–37 he propounds a question (based on Ps. 110:1) which implies that the scribes are in error, apparently because they hold that the Messiah owes his supernatural authority to physical descent from David;[34] in verses 38–40 he issues a warning against the

of man as created with a bisexual constitution. Cf. *Pseud. Clem. Hom.* 3, 54, 2; II Clem. 12:2; *Gosp. Thomas*, 23; also, cf. Isa. 11:7c, which probably entails the notion that primordial vegetarianism will be reestablished in the *eschaton*.

[33] V. 34b may have been added by the evangelist, who is perhaps also responsible for the present position of vv. 28–34a.

[34] Dibelius, however, thinks that St. Mark has no christological theory in mind when he includes vv. 35–37 in his gospel; that is, he hands down the saying simply as an example of the Lord's critique of scribal learning (see *From Tradition to Gospel*, p. 261). There has been much speculation regarding the original significance of vv. 35–37. One possibility is that Jesus actually disclaimed physical descent from David: he awaited his own glorification as the transcendent Son of Man who would establish God's everlasting kingdom in the heavens: this form of expectation was opposed to the popular belief that the Messiah ben David would come and establish a political kingdom on earth: the anthropic eschatology of Jesus was "messianized" by the apostolic missionaries in their endeavor to convince the Jews that their Lord was the Messiah foretold in the canonical scriptures, and not merely the celestial Man of unorthodox apocalyptic literature; cf. Héring, *Le royaume de Dieu et sa venue*, pp. 87, 95f., 128, 142. But if the two eschatologies were so radically opposed to each other in the teaching of Jesus and in Jewish expectation generally, it is hard to understand how the church could have synthesized them in a brief interval of a few years; St. Paul assumes that Jesus was born of the seed of David in Rom. 1:3. Another possibility is that the argument of vv. 35–37 originated in the church: either it was meant to take the point from Jewish objections to the church's doctrine that Jesus was of Davidic descent, or it was meant to demonstrate that Jesus was the Son of God and not merely the Son of David. The last-mentioned view is taken by Wrede in his *Vorträge und Studien*, pp. 147ff.

scribes, whom he condemns for their ostentation, rapacity, and hypocrisy; and in verses 41–44 he points out that a poor widow's small offering really is of much more value than all the larger gifts of the wealthy.[35] The evangelist sets the scene for these animadversions within the precincts of the temple (v. 35; cf. v. 41a), whereas the stories constituting the preceding triad are left entirely without any notice either of time or of place.

In 13:1ff., as Jesus leaves the temple, his attention is drawn to the magnificence of its buildings, whereupon he declares that the time is coming when not one of its stones shall remain on another without being broken down. This prediction of terrible destruction is construed to have an eschatological significance, and the four closest disciples,[36] as soon as they are alone with Jesus on the Mount of Olives, question him about the time of fulfillment and, more particularly, about the strange events expected to take place as the preliminaries to the end of the existing world order. In response to these inquiries the Master proceeds to give what is by far the longest uninterrupted course of private instruction in St. Mark's gospel.[37] The homily is characteristically composed of three main sections: in verses 5–23 Jesus deals with the birth pangs of the new age, giving some indication of the coming tribulations of the church and of mankind generally and warning his disciples against false messiahs and false prophets who will arise and seek to lead them astray; in verses 24–27 he makes use of scriptural phraseology to delineate the closing

[35] For parallels to this idea in Jewish, Greek and Buddhist literature, see S.-B., II, 45f.; Bultmann, *op. cit.*, pp. 32f.

[36] According to St. Mark, Simon and Andrew, James and John have been disciples for the longest time; see 1:16–20. Andrew is not with the other three at the raising of the little girl (5:37ff.) or at the transfiguration (9:2ff.) and is not associated with them in the Gethsemane scene (14:32ff.), being mentioned only in 1:16; 3:18; and 13:3; in 1:29 the house of Simon and Andrew is referred to.

[37] The parabolical teaching in 4:1ff., it will be recalled, is partly public, partly private.

scene of the eschatological drama, briefly describing the signs of cosmic dissolution, the parousia of the Son of Man, and the convocation of the elect; and in verses 28–37 he emphasizes the need for viligance on the part of all believers by observing that (though the end is near) no one, save God alone, can be sure of the exact day or hour of the Lord's appearing and by issuing the command to watch on no less than three occasions.

Since verses 1–4 are primarily concerned with the destruction of the temple,[38] it is somewhat surprising that this disastrous event is not expressly mentioned in verses 5–37. Admittedly, St. Mark may understand the saying in verse 2 to be an eschatological prophecy and he may take it for granted that the destruction of the temple is included among the calamities predicted in verses 5–23.[39] Even so, one can hardly maintain that the eschatological discourse was actually composed for the setting provided in verses 1–4. It seems rather to be a more or less faithful reproduction of an independent item of the gospel tradition which was perhaps already current in writing when St. Mark undertook his work; and we may reasonably suppose that it would circulate in the early communities as a source of comfort and as a means of encouragement to the faithful in their

[38] It has been argued that the prophecy in v. 2 is an authentic saying of Jesus, since it does not envisage destruction of the temple by fire; cf. Josephus, *Bell.* 6, 4, 5; but, according to *Bell.* 7, 1, 1, the imperial order for the complete demolition of the temple is given after the fire (which would have little effect on the stonework.) For parallels to the prophecy, cf. Mic. 3:12, S.-B., I, 1045; Josephus, *Bell.* 6, 5, 3.

[39] It appears that the expression "the abomination of desolation" (v. 14) was originally used with reference to the profanation of the temple by Antiochus Epiphanes in 168 B.C. (cf. Dan. 9:27; 11:31; 12:11; I Macc. 1:54); much later (40 A.D.), it may have been used of Caligula's attempt to erect his statue in the temple (cf. Josephus, *Ant.* 18, 8, 2); but in v. 14 it is qualified by a masculine participle and probably refers to the Antichrist; cf. II Thess. 2:3f., and the discussion in Rawlinson, *St. Mark*, pp. 187f. It has been suggested that the phrase "where he ought not" (v. 14) is a vague substitute for an earlier reference to the temple which no longer existed when St. Mark wrote; cf. Branscomb, *op. cit.*, p. 233.

trials and perplexities. For the fundamental aim of its author or authors [40] is to show that the period of suffering, through which the church must pass, is but a transient phase in the working out of God's sovereign purpose, which will shortly come to its triumphant and glorious consummation.[41] The fact that St. Mark presents the discourse in the form of private instruction to the four disciples of longest standing at once suggests that he means to set it forth as an application of the Master's teaching to the pressing spiritual needs of his Christian readers. It should be borne in mind, however, that, since the experience of postresurrection enlightenment still belongs to the future, even the most favored of the disciples can represent Christian believers only in an imperfect or anticipatory way. The evangelist seems to be fully aware of the limitations of the four in this connection, for in verse 14 the reader is explicitly referred to [42] and in verse 37 the last of the three adjurations to watchfulness (cf. vv. 33, 35) is expressly addressed not merely to the four, but to all— that is, presumably, to all who read the gospel.[43]

According to St. Mark's arrangement of the material, the

[40] There are various reasons for thinking that the discourse is a composite construction: (1) Parts of the address are in the second person, other parts in the third; cf. v. 14 with v. 26; v. 21 with vv. 20, 22; vv. 24–27 with vv. 28–37. (2) Warning against false messiahs is given in vv. 5–6, and again in vv. 21–23. (3) Such passages as vv. 7–8, 14–20, and 24–27 could have occurred in a Jewish apocalypse, whereas such a passage as vv. 9–11 seems to bear the marks of a Christian origin. (4) In vv. 5–31 there is no suggestion of uncertainty regarding the date of the end, but in vv. 32–37 such uncertainty gives point to the commands to vigilance; indeed, it is possible that vv. 32–37 were appended to the discourse by St. Mark; cf. 14:37–42, and notice that the exhortation to watch is given *three* times (vv. 33, 35, 37.). For a review of modern interpretations, see G. R. Beasley-Murray, *Jesus and the Future.*

[41] The word δεῖ is used in vv. 7 and 10, where it no doubt refers to the controlling necessity of God's overruling will or purpose; cf. above, Chapter 7, n. 8.

[42] In this respect 13:14 is unique in St. Mark's gospel.

[43] Cf. the appeal to the multitude in 8:34a, and above, Chapter 7.

apocalyptic discourse is occasioned by the prophecy of the destruction of the temple (13:2), and this prophecy is eminently suited to its present context; for in the preceding narratives the temple has figured as the principal scene of Jesus' activities (11:11, 15, 27; 12:35), and the evangelist has been concerned to point out that Israel, as represented by its leaders, stands under the condemnation of God and is already doomed to perdition (11:14, 20; 12:9, 40). But what is of much greater importance for the understanding of St. Mark's general mode of thought is the fact that the eschatological discourse is placed immediately before the passion narrative. As we noticed in the foregoing chapter,[44] the discourse itself includes no mention of the Messiah's impending crucifixion, and it seems to treat the afflictions of the elect almost as though they were but the pre-determined means to an expected reward in a glorious future; accordingly, it may be said to exemplify the bipolarity of the evangelist's fundamental doctrinal position. On the other hand, there are two passages in the passion narrative which seem to refer back to the apocalyptic discourse, a fact (among others) which suggests that St. Mark is not completely satisfied with the bipolarity involved in what appears to be his primary position. The passages in question are 14:37–42 and 14:62. The first of these recalls 13:33–37, where the four disciples are enjoined to watch (the charge being given three times,) lest the Lord should come suddenly and find his servants sleeping;[45] and the second

[44] See above, pp. 177ff.

[45] In 13:32 the term "hour" is used of the Messiah's expected manifestation in glory, and when this hour has arrived, presumably there will be no need for vigilance; in 14:41 the term "hour" is used of the Messiah's passion, and now that this hour has arrived the three disciples may apparently sleep on and take their rest; such parallelism suggests that St. Mark is foreshadowing the doctrine of the fourth evangelist, according to which the passion is the "hour" of the Messiah's glorification (John 12:23; 13:1; 17:1). The addition of the words "and pray" after "watch" in 13:33 (as in Cod. Sin. and other authorities) was probably first made by a copyist who had 14:38a in mind.

recalls the prediction of the parousia in 13:26 and is, indeed, the most impressive illustration in the gospel of the persistent tendency to transcend the general conception of the messianic secret and to delineate the earthly life of Jesus directly in terms of the church's belief in the heavenly glory of his essential status.

SUPPLEMENTARY NOTE D: SECRECY AND HISTORY

In his detailed and scholarly commentary *The Gospel According to St. Mark* (1952), V. Taylor evinces a curiously vacillating attitude with respect to the fundamental question of the evangelist's conception of secrecy. While he is not wholly uninfluenced by form-critical investigations, Taylor's basic view would seem to be that St. Mark presents us with what is more or less a plain historical record of the ministry of Jesus. He sometimes seems to be under the impression that the line of approach commended by Wrede in his work *Das Messiasgeheimnis in den Evangelien* (1901) stands or falls with the view that Jesus did not actually claim to be the Messiah,[1] although this is really a hypothesis which is not necessarily bound up with the general contention that St. Mark was *inter alia* greatly concerned to explain why Jesus was not accepted as Messiah by his compatriots during the course of his earthly career. It may well be that the evidence used by Wrede in support of the theory of the secret is not all of a piece and calls for more than one type of explanation. On the other hand, as H. J. Cadbury has reminded us,[2] Wrede by no means neglected the aspect of contradiction in the gospel, though the probability is that he oversimplified matters by referring merely to two opposite motives which failed to cross in the evangelist's thinking, namely, a desire to show that the Messiahship was hidden and a natural inclination to give direct expression to his Christian conviction. As we have seen more than once, subsidiary motives (some of which had come to be submerged) were apparently involved in several instances.[3]

Moreover, it should be borne in mind that we have to rely al-

[1] A matter briefly dealt with above, Introduction, n. 1.

[2] *Proceedings of the American Philosophical Society*, XCV (1951), 120, n. 3.

[3] Cf. above, Introduction, n. 4.

most exclusively on the synoptic gospels for information respecting the mentality of the historical Jesus, and these documents primarily bear witness not to the mind of the Master, but to the interests of the evangelists and to the concerns of the primitive church to which they belonged. The synoptists had their own particular points of view, selecting from the material at their disposal and to a considerable extent arranging the extracts as they thought fit. On occasion they did not hesitate to modify the content of what they received to suit their own purposes in the situations in which they found themselves; also, each constituent item of the tradition would have had a history of its own before coming into the hands of the evangelists. The exegete therefore needs constantly to be on his guard against making dogmatic statements of a psychological nature concerning Jesus of Nazareth. The gospels doubtless offer scattered reflections of his mind, but the fact remains that in a large measure we see him as in a glass darkly and not face to face.

For convenience of exposition we divide our examination of Taylor's position into eight main parts; the parenthetical page numbers refer to his commentary.

1. Taylor cites (pp. 122f.) various arguments which have been put forward against Wrede's theory:

(i) Jesus would not have been regarded as Messiah after the resurrection unless he had been recognized as such during his ministry.

This argument may or may not be true; certainly, it cannot be established a priori. And is there no truth whatsoever in the doctrine of Euhemeros, that the gods were notable men who had come to be venerated as divine after their death?

(ii) The crucifixion is unintelligible unless Jesus was condemned as a messianic pretender.

But may not Jesus have been condemned on a false charge? If he had aroused civic unrest and had spoken of a kingdom that would supersede the Roman empire, his Jewish opponents could easily have trumped up a charge and persuaded the procurator that he was guilty of a capital offence.

(iii) Had Jesus not made claim to Messiahship, the first Christian preachers would not have incurred the odium of proclaiming a crucified Messiah.

But why not? With the belief that Jesus had risen from the dead may have been born in the minds of the preachers the further belief that Jesus was Messiah despite his crucifixion, and this may have been transformed into the doctrine that he was Messiah because of his sacrifice. In making such a mental transition they would be aided by the passion psalms, the conception of the Suffering Servant, the notion that the first-born in Israel must be sacrificed or redeemed,[4] and so on.

(iv) The inscription on the cross, the accounts of Peter's confession, the triumphal entry, the trial before the sanhedrin, all bear witness to the existence of a messianic tension during the ministry.

But the titulus on the cross was perhaps based on a false charge. The story of Peter's confession may have been a projection of the Christian faith into the lowly sphere of the ministry. In the narrative of the entry into Jerusalem the people do not actually ascribe messianic dignity to Jesus; he is hailed merely as one who comes in the name of the Lord. As far as the account of the trial before the sanhedrin is concerned, it is arguable that it may be nothing more than an expansion of the reference to the matutinal conference in 15:1; in any case it is unlikely that any of the disciples would have been present at such a meeting.

Thus it would seem that there is little ground for Taylor's

---

[4] Cf. R. H. Lightfoot, *The Gospel Message of St. Mark*, pp. 57f., and G. Vermes, *Scripture and Tradition in Judaism*, pp. 193ff. Regarding Mark 10:45, see C. K. Barrett's contribution to *New Testament Essays* (ed. A. J. B. Higgins), pp. 1ff.

assertion that the criticisms of Wrede's theory represent "powerful" arguments.

2. After expressing surprise that Wrede's influence should have persisted in scientific investigation of the gospel, Taylor proceeds to make the concession that the idea of the secret, though untenable as Wrede presented it, is of great historical and theological significance. He even goes so far as to declare that it lies behind almost every narrative of the work, and more especially in the healing of the paralytic, the feeding of the five thousand, the entry into Jerusalem, and the trial scenes.

It is difficult to understand why these five narratives should have been singled out in this connection, two of them (the triumphal entry and the Jewish trial) having already been cited as passages which militate against Wrede's theory of the secrecy. Perhaps the evangelist had the idea of messianic secrecy in mind when he presented the miracle of the loaves; but in the story of the healing of the paralytic and the account of the Jewish trial, Jesus is allowed *openly* to refer to himself as the Messiah or Son of Man.

3. Taylor asserts that the idea of the messianic secret was not imposed on the records from without, but is a factor integral to the tradition itself. The Messiahship in the consciousness of Jesus was not so much a matter of status as of action; it was a destiny, and therefore he silences the demoniacs and enjoins the disciples to keep silence until after the resurrection. Although he was already the Messiah, he would not be the Messiah before his destiny was fulfilled.

But the available evidence hardly justifies a statement of this kind. The injunctions to silence mostly occur in passages of an editorial character; and as for those which may reasonably be regarded as belonging to the tradition, St. Mark could have been the first writer to understand them in the sense of the messianic secret. Moreover, Taylor's description of the messianic consciousness of Jesus is extremely obscure. If Jesus was the

Messiah, how could he not be the Messiah at the time when he was speaking to his disciples? Is the meaning simply that he believed that God had chosen him to play the part of Messiah on some future occasion—at the parousia, for instance?

4. Taylor thinks (pp. 123f.) that Jesus' own view of his office is in harmony with St. Mark's christology and soteriology, and this agreement is alleged to be so striking that it must reflect the actual historical situation and cannot be the work of art.

But as Taylor's description of the messianic consciousness of Jesus is presumably a construction based on what are taken to be hints made by St. Mark (no reference is made to Q in this connection), the fact that it agrees with the evangelist's theory of the Messiahship should occasion no surprise. And why should a case of remarkable agreement between the ideas of two individuals be a reflection of fact rather than a production of art?

5. In treating of soteriology in the gospel (p. 124), Taylor argues that, according to St. Mark, the action of Jesus arises out of what he is—the Suffering Servant and the Son of Man.

But does not this contradict the previous contention that the convictions of Jesus agree with the evangelist's doctrine? For Taylor has already asserted that in the view of Jesus himself Messiahship is primarily a matter of action, not of status.

6. In his account of the evangelist's use of the expression "Son of God" (p. 121), Taylor maintains that the evangelist has no theory of the incarnation, though his assumption is that Jesus was *Deus Absconditus*—his deity was concealed behind the human life, but clear to those endowed with the necessary insight.

At this point Taylor comes preciously near the position he is concerned to refute, namely, that according to St. Mark mortal men could not comprehend the real status of Jesus during the ministry. Surprisingly enough, however, Taylor also declares that the evangelist may not have reflected upon christology at all—a statement extremely difficult to accept in view of the fact that the Messiahship of Jesus constitutes the basic theme of the gospel.

7. The unsatisfactoriness of Taylor's position finds further illustration in his comments on specific passages which are of great importance for an understanding of the evangelist's attitude of mind.

(i) Commenting on 5:43 (p. 297), Taylor argues that when Jesus had brought the little girl to life again he told those with him in the room not to report what had taken place because he wished to avoid the embarrassment of publicity for the time being.

But how could such an injunction in such a situation possibly have had the effect alleged to be desired? The mourners and others would have had to be told that no funeral would take place, whereupon an explanation would have been demanded.

(ii) Commenting on 7:36 (pp. 355f.), Taylor surmises that reluctance to have the cure advertised could have been expressed even if the injunction was sure to be disobeyed.

Are we to infer from this that St. Mark believed that the Messiah was frustrated?

(iii) Commenting on 8:12 (p. 363), Taylor asserts that Jesus' refusal to give a sign is here influenced by St. Mark's doctrine that his messianic status was concealed from the people.

But has not Taylor already asserted that the evangelist's view represents the intention of Jesus himself?

(iv) Commenting on 8:26 (p. 373), Taylor declares that, as in the case of 7:36, secrecy could not be ensured, and so the interdiction should be regarded as an editorial note expressing the evangelist's idea of the secret.

In this instance the alleged agreement between St. Mark's view and that of Jesus himself evidently gives way to direct disagreement.

(v) Commenting on 8:30 (p. 377), Taylor explains that Jesus enjoins the disciples to silence in view of the political repercussions which might follow on Peter's acknowledgment of the Messiahship.

On the other hand, in the introduction (p. 123) Taylor seems to be critical of the idea that Jesus enjoined silence in order to avoid possible revolutionary activity on the ground that it suggests that Jesus played for safety. One would have thought that the reasonable course would have been to interpret the prohibition now made to the disciples in the light of the previous injunctions made to the demons (cf. esp. 3:12). As it stands, the interdiction in 8:30 lacks historical credibility; understood as Taylor construes it, the implication would seem to be that Jesus was not sufficiently a master of words to make it clear to his disciples that he meant to have nothing to do with political or militant Messianism.

(vi) Commenting on 9:9–10 (p. 393), Taylor maintains that the injunction made to the three disciples after the transfiguration is quite natural, though he concedes that the time limit may in fact have been less explicitly expressed.

But what would be the point of keeping knowledge of the secret from the other disciples when, according to 8:27ff., the messianic secret had already been given to them? The likelihood is that the injunction follows directly from St. Mark's own philosophy of history.

(vii) Commenting on 11:1ff. (p. 452), Taylor asserts that, though puzzled, the people understand the symbolic action (riding on the colt of an ass) sufficiently well to realize that Jesus is not the Messiah of their hopes.

But would the people have made their enthusiastic acclamations if they had seen that Jesus was not the sort of individual they wanted? Surely the messianic tension in the account of the triumphal entry can best be understood in terms of a conflict of motives in St. Marks' mind.

8. In his exposition of 4:10ff. (pp. 254ff.), Taylor concedes that in St. Mark's view the parables were meant to conceal what

Jesus meant, whereas in fact they were employed to elucidate the teaching.

Once again the alleged agreement between St. Mark's doctrine and the actual intention of Jesus gives way to direct disagreement. Should not this important instance of such lack of accord be brought into relation with the injunctions to silence? [5]

[5] C. E. B. Cranfield's commentary *The Gospel according to Saint Mark* (1959) is open to much the same general kind of criticism as Taylor's work; cf. Winter's observations in the *Theologische Literaturzeitung*, LXXXV (1960), cols. 744ff.

10

Realization of the Mysterious Meaning

ST. MARK'S passion story forms the climax of his gospel, and in a general way the first thirteen chapters may be described as a preparation for it. Thus the death of Jesus is already hinted at in 2:20, where the Pharisees are told that the sons of the bride-chamber will fast when the bridegroom is taken away from them, and in 3:6, where it is observed that the Pharisees and the Herodians take counsel together against Jesus with a view to destroying him. But besides foreshadowings of this kind, the first thirteen chapters set forth certain regulative ideas in the light of which, as the evangelist believes, the reader may be enabled to interpret the passion correctly. Thus the conception of the extraordinary authority of Jesus, which receives great emphasis in the account of the Galilean ministry, helps to make it possible for the reader to understand the passion as a supreme act of divine condescension: Jesus is endowed with supernatural might and he uses it not for the purposes of personal aggrandizement, but solely in the interest of human salvation, finally humbling himself even to the extent of sacrificing his life. Again, passages dealing with controversy, which frequently occur in the account of the Galilean ministry and which become predominant on the account of the Jerusalem ministry, contain indications that Jesus always remains faithful to the true meaning of the scriptures; and in this way the ground is prepared for the interpretation of the crucifixion as the outcome of unwarranted hostility on the part of the religious authorities. But it is the second main section of the gospel which has the most direct and obvious bearing on the passion and its rightful interpretation. For, on the basis of Peter's confession, the Master proceeds to instruct his disciples in the fateful significance of his Messiahship, showing that his coming sufferings and death are the divinely appointed prerequisite of his exaltation as the Son of Man. Thus, in St. Mark's representation, the story of the passion is the story of the historical realization of the essential meaning of the Messiahship—a meaning which is already made known to the reader before the account of the Jerusalem ministry begins; and, although the disciples cannot understand the passion in this light at the time of its occurrence, they are destined so to understand it when, as witnesses of the resurrection, they openly proclaim the gospel to the world.

In an important sense, therefore, the first thirteen chapters of St. Mark's book are a preparation for his passion narrative.[1] Nevertheless, this narrative possesses a self-sufficiency which distinguishes it sharply from the preceding sections, and, indeed, it seems likely that the main outline of the narrative enjoyed an independent existence long before St. Mark undertook to write his gospel. For the most part the narrative moves forward coherently from the report of the plotting of the hierarchs (14:1f.) to its climax in the story of the empty tomb (16:1ff.); and the indications of time and place (which now occur more frequently

---

[1] As W. Marxsen has maintained, the work grew backwards: "The passion-story represents the first text of the tradition concerning Jesus to be fixed in writing. This then grew backwards" (*Der Evangelist Markus*, p. 17).

than in the earlier sections) are often so securely woven into the texture of the narrative that they could not be regarded as editorial connecting links imposed by the evangelist on what were originally isolated items of traditional material. It is true, of course, that some of the constituent elements of the narrative may have once possessed a separate existence: thus the story of the anointing (14:3–9), the account of the preparations for the last supper (14:12–16), and the report of the nocturnal trial (14:55–65) were perhaps first introduced to their present contexts by the evangelist himself. That the passion narrative underwent expansion in this way is indicated by a consideration of the treatment which St. Mark's version of it receives at the hands of the later evangelists: for example, St. Matthew adds the story of Judas' suicide (Matt. 27:3–10), the reference to the dream of Pilate's wife (Matt. 27:19), the scene in which Pilate washes his hands in the presence of the multitude (Matt. 27:24f.); St. Luke adds the report of the trial before Herod (Luke 23:8–12), and so on. But it still remains that a brief account of the principal events (the arrest, the trial, the crucifixion, and the christophanies) probably existed from a very early date. The main outline of the narrative is the same in all the synoptic gospels; and, what is more significant, even the fourth evangelist, who generally takes considerable liberties with the synoptic tradition, faithfully reproduces the fundamental framework of the passion narrative as it appears in the second gospel. Presumably, he is here dealing with a connected tradition which was so old and so firmly established in Christian thought and memory that he is unable to treat it with his usual freedom.

The early establishment of a connected account of the passion could hardly be accounted for by reference to a purely biographical interest on the part of the apostolic communities, for if such an interest had been operative, the relative paucity of the traditions concerning the ministry would be quite inexplicable. Indeed, from a purely biographical point of view, an account of the early life of Jesus would have been much more valuable than a detailed description of the circumstances of his death. It would appear, therefore, that the early establishment of a passion narrative in Christian tradition must have been largely due to the special soteriological significance which the apostolic church attributed to the shameful death of the Messiah.[2] As we gather from I Cor. 15:3-4, the primitive gospel consisted essentially of three fundamental affirmations: that Christ died for our sins according to the scriptures, that he was buried, and that he was raised on the third day according to the scriptures. It is noteworthy, too, that in all the epistles of the New Testament there is not so much as a passing reference either to the mission of John the Baptist or to the Galilean ministry. The passion, on the other hand, is greatly emphasized. St. Paul glories in the cross (Gal. 6:14); he preaches the gospel of a Messiah crucified, which is (in the eyes of believers) the power of God and the wisdom of God (I Cor. 1:23f.), and he regards the cross as the means of reconciling Jews and Gentiles in one body to God (Eph. 2:16) and as the culmination of the Messiah's self-humiliation (Phil. 2:8). According to Heb. 12:2, Jesus is the perfecter of faith who for the joy that was set before him endured the cross, despising shame; and, according to I Pet. 3:18, Christ died for sins, once for all, the righteous for the unrighteous, that he might bring us to God. Moreover, St. Paul seems to construe the crucifixion and the resurrection eschatologically, as a divine pledge or guarantee of the Messiah's expected coming in glory (I Thess. 4:14; I Cor. 11:26), the resurrection of Jesus being an anticipation of the final resurrection of the elect (I Cor. 15:20). Thus the passion and the resurrection appearances were events of such profound importance for the apostolic message of salvation that some account of them would be an almost inevitable accompaniment of the earliest Christian preaching. The protagonists of the new

[2] Cf. Dibelius, *From Tradition to Gospel*, pp. 22f.

faith would be called upon to show how the paradox of the cross was resolved in the triumph of Easter, and how the death of Jesus in shame and humiliation was brought about through the malice of his own people and yet by the determinate counsel and foreknowledge of God (cf. Acts 2:23), whose sovereign will was believed to be already disclosed in the prophecies of the Old Testament.[3]

In St. Mark's passion narrative two principal methods are employed for the purpose of proving that the events recounted really occurred according to the will of God.[4] In the first place, the scriptures are appealed to,[5] and this is done in various ways: thus in 14:27 there is a (not quite accurate) quotation of Zech. 13:7, which is expressly introduced as a scriptural citation; in 15:34 the opening words of the twenty-second psalm are ascribed to Jesus, but without any explicit reference to the fact that they are derived from scripture; in 14:21 there is a general appeal to the scriptures, but no particular passage is adduced;

[3] Cf. above, Chapter 6.

[4] Cf. G. Bertram, *Die Leidensgeschichte Jesu*, p. 42. In St. Mark's view the necessity of the passion is tantamount to its accordance with the scriptures; it may be noticed, for example, that the δεῖ ("must") in 8:31 corresponds to the γέγραπται ("it is written") in 9:12b; cf. above, Chapter 7, n. 8.

[5] It is possible that the scriptures were sometimes appealed to in a general way before a definite passage could be actually adduced. It is also possible that in certain scriptural passages, especially Pss. 22; 31; 69; Isa. 53, the passion was found depicted in advance; and if (as seems likely) these passages were habitually read in the primitive communities, some of the motifs they contain may have found their way into the Christian passion narrative in the process of its formation. On the other hand, it is significant that, despite the LXX rendering of Ps. 22:17 (E.T., 22:16), Luke 24:39 and John 20:24–29 are the only passages in the gospels which suggest that the hands of Jesus were nailed to the cross; for this serves to illustrate the conservative character of the early tradition. Cf. Dibelius, *op. cit.*, pp. 184f., 188f. And creative influence operated *from* the gospel traditions, at least in one instance: the titulus on the cross (Mark 15:26) prompted Christian scribes to alter the wording of Ps. 96:10 (LXX 95:10); see P. Winter, *On the Trial of Jesus*, pp. 108f.

and in 14:61a (cf. 15:5a), although scripture is neither quoted nor mentioned, the motif is reminiscent of Isa. 53:7. In the second place, the precise foreknowledge of Jesus is referred to: thus in 14:8 he speaks of his coming burial; in 14:18 he predicts that one of the twelve will betray him; and in 14:27–31 he announces that all his disciples will be caused to stumble, that he will proceed into Galilee after his resurrection, and that Peter will disown him three times before the cock crows twice. Such foreknowledge does not merely illustrate Jesus' powers of supernatural insight; it also suggests that his earthly destiny has been determined in advance as a provision of God's presiding purpose.[6]

Of course St. Mark believes that the whole career of Jesus was worked out according to the will of God, and we may remind ourselves that the opening words of the gospel are immediately followed by a citation of biblical prophecies (1:2f.) and that the conception of the messianic secret is itself a form of theological predestinarianism (cf. 4:11f.). But it was a matter of special urgency to show that the passion was a fulfillment of the divine will or purpose, since the doctrine of the crucified Messiah was a stumbling block to Jews and foolishness to Gentiles (cf. I Cor. 1:23). Men asked how the shamefulness of the betrayal, the disgrace of the rejection, and the horror of the crucifixion could be compatible with the transcendent dignity of a heaven-sent Messiah; and the exponents of the apostolic faith replied by maintaining that a right appreciation of the prophecies of the Old Testament showed that Jesus' ignominious

[6] Cf. the predictions in 8:31; 9:31; 10:33f. It should be borne in mind that there is one notable limitation to Jesus' prescience: he does not know the exact hour of the parousia (13:32); this limitation would explain the church's lack of precise information on the matter, besides giving point to the ethical demand for vigilance (cf. 13:33–37). For an interesting parallel to Jesus' foresight, cf. Philostratus: *Vita Ap.*, 5:12 ("His prescience was gained not by wizardry, but from what the gods revealed to him").

death was an integral part of his divine mission for the redemption of the world. No doubt those to whom post resurrection christophanies had actually been vouchsafed would feel that their personal experience of the risen Lord was in itself a sufficient guarantee of the validity of their belief in the Messiahship of Jesus; but as soon as they sought to justify the mode of interpretation they gave to their religious experience, they would naturally resort to the scriptures in which (as was assumed by Jews and Christians alike) God's purpose was made known to men of old.[7]

Nevertheless, as is already made clear in the earlier sections of the gospel, although St. Mark believes that the sufferings and death of Jesus were ultimately determined by the will of God, he is none the less convinced that the Jewish people, through the agency of their representative leaders, are to be held responsible for the terrible crime of rejecting the Messiah.[8] Accordingly, in 14:1–2 the passion narrative opens with an account of the plotting of the chief priests and the scribes, who are trying to get hold of Jesus by stratagem and have him put to death. In 14:43 those who accompany Judas at the arrest come from the chief priests and the scribes and the elders. In 14:64 Jesus is unanimously condemned to death on a charge of blasphemy at a special nocturnal session of the sanhedrin. In 15:1ff. the chief priests with the elders and scribes and the whole sanhedrin deliver Jesus up to Pilate, and in the course of the ensuing trial the chief priests make many accusations against him. But Pilate

---

[7] Winter (*op. cit.*, pp. 4f.) notices that in Luke 16:29–31 Moses and the prophets are resorted to in an attempt to weaken the criticism that the argument from the christophanies had not persuaded the people generally. Cf. John 15:24b–25, where, paradoxically enough, the fourth evangelist makes a predestinarianistic appeal to the Old Testament to demonstrate that the Jewish opponents of Jesus are normally free and therefore without excuse for their sin (John 15:22).

[8] The actual expression "the Jews" is used sparingly by St. Mark; see above, Chapter 6, n. 1.

perceives that they are acting from motives of envy and, since it is customary for him (at the time of the feast) to release one prisoner on popular demand, he hopes that the multitude will request him to set Jesus free. The chief priests, however, incite the people to ask for the liberation of a man called Barabbas, who lies in prison apparently on charges of murder and sedition; and consequently, as Pilate wishes to satisfy the multitude, Jesus is delivered up to be crucified.[9]

Accordingly, the narrative makes it clear that it was really through the ill will of his own people that the Messiah was rejected and crucified—an idea which is already to be found in

[9] Apart from the gospels, nothing is known of a custom of releasing a prisoner on popular demand at the feast of the passover; but that representatives of the imperial government sometimes made such releases, seems to be shown by a papyrus of the first century A.D. (see Deissmann, *Light from the Ancient East*, pp. 266f.), according to which a man called Phibion was set free by the prefect, G. Septimus Vegetus, presumably in deference to a popular demand. Possibly, however, the statement in 15:6 is an erroneous inference from the story itself and made (perhaps by St. Mark) to provide the story with an introduction. Rawlinson has conjectured that the tradition arose from a historical coincidence: (1) The multitude (15:8) may have been composed of Barabbas' partisans, who happened to arrive at this point in the proceedings to beg for his release (so E. Meyer, *Ursprung und Anfänge*, I, 195). (2) In the early Caesarean text of Matt. 27:16f. the name "Barabbas" is twice given as "Jesus Barabbas," and this may have been the original reading, which was soon modified because it was thought improper that a criminal should possess the same name as the Lord. Also, the wording of the designation "the man called Barabbas" in Mark 15:7 may imply that St. Mark knew that Barabbas was not his primary name; indeed, it is possible that Mark 15:7, as St. Matthew knew it, had "Jesus who was called Barabbas." (3) Thus the multitude's demand for the release of "Jesus" (that is, Jesus Barabbas) was perhaps mistaken by Pilate as a demonstration of popular sympathy in favor of Jesus of Nazareth, whom he at once offered to release; but the chief priests intervened and made common cause with the partisans of Barabbas, in return for the support of the "Barabbas" party in favor of their own demand for the crucifixion of Jesus of Nazareth. See Rawlinson, *St. Mark*, pp. 227f. For a recent discussion of the whole question, see Winter, *op. cit.*, pp. 91ff.

the writings of St. Paul (cf. I Thess. 2:14–16) and in the early speeches of the Acts of the Apostles (cf. Acts 3:13). Moreover, as is shown by a comparison of the gospels, St. Mark's successors tend increasingly to emphasize the innocence of Jesus, the unwillingness of Pilate, and the guilt of the Jews; thus in Matt. 27:19 the procurator is warned by his wife against condemning this innocent prisoner; in Matt. 27:25 all the people (on their children's behalf as well as their own) openly assume the responsibility which Pilate has just disclaimed; in Luke 23:4, 14, and 22 the procurator makes a threefold declaration of the prisoner's innocence; in John 18:36–37 Jesus makes a relatively prolonged statement before Pilate, and subsequently (John 19:6) Pilate tells the chief priests and the officers to take the prisoner themselves and crucify him as he finds him guilty of no offence; in John 19:11 Jesus makes a second statement before the procurator, whereupon Pilate immediately seeks to release him and is prevented from doing so only by the animated protests of the Jews (John 19:12). Such an anti-Jewish tendency, which comes to its full expression in the apocryphal Acts of Pilate,[10] may be fairly described as a natural outcome of the church's historical situation. For, whereas the gospel was meeting with wide acceptance in the Gentile world, the Jews for the most part were setting themselves in vigorous opposition to it. The gulf between Judaism and Christianity became broader and deeper, and feelings of mutual antipathy eventually prevailed. On the other hand, the Roman authorities for a time seem to have adopted an attitude of detached indifference toward the new religion, apparently regarding it merely as a special form or denomination of Judaism. And since the missionary activities of the apostolic preachers were being conducted within the bounds of the Roman empire, it was obviously of great practical importance

---

[10] This work probably ought not to be dated earlier than the fourth century: see *The Apocryphal New Testament* (ed. M. R. James), pp. 94ff.

for the church that its message should be set forth in such a way as not to offend the susceptibilities of those who represented the imperial government.[11] Hence the exponents of the historical content of the gospel were at pains to show that, although the crucifixion followed a procuratorial trial, it was really through the unwarranted hostility of his own countrymen that the Messiah was put to death: the Jewish hierarchs maliciously engineered the execution of an innocent man.

In view of St. Mark's basic conception of the sufferings and death of Jesus as the divinely ordained prelude to his ultimate exaltation,[12] it is not surprising to find that the story of the passion in the second gospel is primarily a description of the dark passage, so to speak, through which the Messiah must proceed before he can appear to the world with great power and glory. Fundamentally, it is a tragic story in which the cost of the passion, the terrible price which has to be paid for final victory over evil and death, receives the utmost emphasis. But just as the earlier sections of the gospel contain various indications of a tendency to transcend the conception of the Messiah's sufferings as merely the means to an end, so the prevailing gloom of the passion story is relieved by intermittent gleams of a heavenly light. Evidently, St. Mark's faith in the reality of the Messiahship is pressing for some form of overt recognition in the gospel narrative, the consequence being that the essential glory of the Messiah shines forth from time to time amid the obscurity of his incarnate life and occasionally penetrates even the encompassing darkness of his last tragic hours on earth. Thus in 14:37–42 and in 14:62, for example (passages which seem to refer back to certain parts of the great apocalyptic discourse),[13] the life of Jesus, despite all its lowliness and shame, tends to become the

---

[11] Cf. Rom. 13:1–7, where St. Paul exhorts his readers to respect the authority of the state as a divine institution which holds evil in check and facilitates the promotion of good.

[12] Cf. above, Chapter 8.   [13] Cf. above, Chapter 9, n. 45.

actual sphere of his revelation in glory; and in so far as the evangelist adopts an attitude of this kind, there is no need for him to look to the future, since he discerns the reward and justification of the Messiah's amazing condescension in the immediacy of its historical expression.

It may be said that the introduction to the passion narrative in 14:1–11 is eminently characteristic of St. Mark's mode of representation. For verses 1–2, which concern the resolution of external enemies to do away with Jesus, have their natural continuation in verses 10–11, which deal with disaffection among the disciples, the decision of Judas to betray his Master; and we know that the evangelist has a predilection for the insertion of one story into the framework of another.[14] It is reasonable to assume, therefore, that verses 1–2 and 10–11 constituted the introduction to the passion narrative in the form in which St. Mark received it, and that the evangelist himself intercalated verses 3–9, thereby setting the luminous story of the anointing at Bethany on the dark background of malicious scheming and treachery. In verses 1–2 it is made clear to the reader at the outset of the narrative that the Jewish authorities are the prime movers in the action which is taken against Jesus, the general implication being that they must shoulder the burden of guilt for the rejection of their own Messiah; in point of detail we gather from these two verses that the feast of the passover is due to begin after a short interval of two days, that the hierarchs resolve to take Jesus and have him put to death and that an open arrest during the feast must be avoided because it might lead to a popular riot.[15] Thus, for the successful prosecution of the plan, haste and secrecy of action would seem to be called for;

---

[14] Cf. above, Chapter 6, n. 10.

[15] The position of the words ἐν δόλῳ in v. 1 (before the participle and the finite verb) suggests that the stress should be placed on them: the plan is to be carried out "stealthily" or "by stratagem." Cf. Turner in *J.T.S.*, XXV (1924), 384f.

and, as is explained in verses 10–11, these two requirements are met in an unexpected way through the disloyalty of one of the twelve, who goes to the conspirators and offers to help them.

The story of the anointing in verses 3–9 stands in dramatic contrast to such terrible hostility and faithlessness. The scene is set in the house of Simon the leper,[16] where the Lord is reclining at table; an unnamed woman makes a sudden appearance and lavishly anoints the head of Jesus with a precious ointment. This generous action seems to be set forth as a concrete representation of genuine Christian devotion,[17] and it is not impossible that the story reflects a controversy between certain Christians who maintained that the claim of almsgiving are subordinate to those of worship and others who contended that the relief of the poor should be regarded as the more important concern of the church.[18] On this hypothesis, the Lord's defence of the woman's action in verse 6 would signify that worship ought to occupy a preeminent position in the Christian scale of values; and perhaps the story ended there at one stage of its development, verse 7 having been added later to guard against a possible misunderstanding. It is not to be thought that the demands of worship are so important that they leave no room in

[16] This Simon is introduced as though he were a well-known person; perhaps he was known to St. Mark's readers as one who was cured of his leprosy by Jesus; cf. the reference to the sons of Simon of Cyrene in 15:21.

[17] Cf. 3:31–35, where the true family of the Messiah receives concrete representation in the form of an attentive audience.

[18] Cf. Bertram, *op. cit.*, pp. 16ff. For the motif, cf. Luke 10:38–42; it is noteworthy that the fourth evangelist associates Mark 14:3–9 with Luke 10:38–42 in John 12:1–8. In an interesting paper on Mark 14:9 (*Z.N.T.W.*, XLIV [1952–53], 103ff.—cf. *Z.N.T.W.*, XXXV [1936], 75ff.) J. Jeremias argues that the story as it stands, in view of its manifold semitisms and the distinction it may draw between almsgiving (*tsĕdāqāh*) and acts of charity (*gĕmīlūth chăsādhīm*), should be regarded as being of Palestinian origin; there is rabbinic evidence for the view that charity is superior to almsgiving, since it can benefit the dead as well as the living (Tos. Pea. 4, 19).

the life of the church for the practice of almsgiving. Indeed, the argument seems to be that the goodness of the woman's deed derives not from any abstract superiority of acts of worship to acts of practical benevolence (such as the relief of the poor), but simply from the finitude of the period during which such a deed could be performed, namely, the period of the Messiah's incarnate life. The days of his flesh are numbered, whereas the poor are always with us, and the woman is to be commended because she makes the most of a fleeting opportunity for the direct expression of her intense personal devotion to Jesus. It appears, therefore, that verse 7, like 2:19b–20, gives the sanction of the Lord to an established practice of the church (in this case, the practice of almsgiving, in the other, the practice of fasting) on the basis of a saying which might be construed in an opposite sense.[19] Finally, verses 8–9 may have been appended by St. Mark himself when he brought the story into the framework of the passion narrative.[20] With this conclusion the woman's action comes to have significance in relation to the

[19] Cf. above, Chapter 6, n. 35.

[20] On the other hand, in the paper already referred to Jeremias argues that v. 9 is original to the story and that it refers not to the church's mission to the Gentiles, but to the last judgment, a suggestion already made by Ernst Lohmeyer in his commentary on the gospel (1937). Jeremias makes three main points in support of an eschatological exegesis: (1) The phrase εἰς μνημόσυννον as in Acts 10:4 (to which Lohmeyer drew attention) or εἰς ἀνάμνησιν (Hebrew, *lĕzikkārōn*) as in the LXX not infrequently refers to the favorable remembrance of a person on the part of God. (2) The word ὅπου (like *wo* in German) can have a temporal meaning, as in Mark 9:18. (3) The term εὐαγγέλιον may have the signification it possesses in Rev. 14:6f., where the phrase εὐαγγέλιον αἰώνιον denotes the triumphant announcement made in mid-heaven by an angel at the commencement of the hour of judgment, and addressed "to them that dwell on the earth, and to every nation and tribe and tongue" (corresponding to St. Mark's εἰς ὅλον τὸν κόσμον). Jeremias would therefore render Mark 14:9 as follows: "Amen, I say to you, When [the angel of God] shall proclaim to the whole world the last triumphant announcement, then [the angel] shall also relate [in God's presence] what she has done, whereupon [God] will graciously remember her [in the final judgment]." But while such an eschatological

approaching burial of Jesus, and the evangelist seems to hold
that it is primarily because her action possesses such significance
that she will be remembered wherever the gospel is preached.
Possibly, the reference in verse 8 is specifically to the story of the
empty tomb, with which St. Mark brings his gospel to a close.
For, according to 16:1ff., the women who go to the tomb on
the first Easter morning fail to fulfill their purpose of anointing
the body of Jesus since he is already risen when they arrive,
and perhaps the evangelist construes the anointing at Bethany
as a sort of anticipatory compensation for their failure. However
this may be, 14:8–9 make it clear that Jesus is fully aware of the
terrible fate which awaits him; though his enemies conspire
against him in private, yet they cannot take him by surprise.
Moreover, regarding the general signficance of the story, the
woman's act of devotion is probably meant to stand out not only
against the surrounding context of hostility and treachery,
but also against the spiritual insensibility of the bystanders who
think that the ointment has been wasted. Her deed reveals something of the great love which early Christian piety bestowed
upon the Messiah, and when seen in the light of that love it
evokes a deep feeling of aesthetic satisfaction. The woman lavishly anoints the head of Jesus with precious ointment, and her
act is good or beautiful because of its sheer appropriateness,[21]

---

interpretation is not impossible as far as the original form of the story
is concerned, it seems unlikely that St. Mark and his Gentile readers
would have construed the passage in that sense. It might be noted in
passing that Jeremias also thinks that the phrase "in remembrance of me"
in the eucharistic saying (Luke 22:19; I Cor. 11:24f.) has reference to
God's remembering; but cf. the criticism of W. C. van Unnik in
Nederlands Theologisch Tijdschrift, IV (1950), 369ff.

[21] Cf. I Sam. 10:1, where Samuel anoints Saul (by pouring oil on
his head) as the first king of Israel; in later Jewish expectation the Messiah is God's Anointed par excellence for he is commissioned to rule
over the consummated kingdom. In the third gospel, as in the fourth,
the story seems to lose much of its eschatological significance, since the
woman (identified by St. John with Mary) anoints the feet of Jesus: cf.
Luke 7:38; John 12:3.

whereas in the eyes of those who do not know the mystery it is only extravagance. Thus, as in the story of the triumphal entry, the secret of the Messiahship is apparently straining after a mode of open expression which, however, it cannot yet receive save in the form of a symbolic action.[22]

In the following passage (vv. 12–16), which is evidently at variance with the chronological implications of verse 2 of the same chapter,[23] we are presented with the first of a series of three pericopes dealing with the last supper.[24] These pericopes exemplify St. Mark's fundamental doctrine that the passion story concerns the historical realization of the mysterious meaning of the Messiahship, and yet they have something of a Johannine flavor about them. In verses 12–16 Jesus sends two of his disciples into the city to make preparations for the eating of the passover; he knows in advance that a man bearing a pitcher of water will meet them, that this man will lead them to a house whose occupier will at once understand their request for the Master's guest chamber, and that a large upper room, suitably appointed, will be set at their disposal. Thus, as in 11:1–6, the Lord seems to be acting in accordance with a predetermined scheme which has been drawn up even to the minutest detail. Indeed, the story suggests not merely that Jesus is thoroughly conversant with the provisions of an overruling purpose, but that his own will is completely at one with the creative principle which governs all earthly events. He speaks as the disposer of the course of history, who actually determines the shape of things to come by the mysterious potency of his voluntary decisions; and from this point of view he does not suffer as an ordinary man might suffer, since everything which hap-

---

[22] Cf. above, Chapter 9.

[23] For further discussion of this matter, see below, Chapter 11.

[24] Thus vv. 12–25 illustrate St. Mark's liking for groups of three; cf. vv. 27–31, where there is a series of three predictions, and vv. 32–42, where Jesus comes to the three sleeping disciples on three successive occasions; cf. above, Chapter 6, n. 16.

pens to him is, in the last resort, an affirmation of his own transcendent will.

The same kind of impression is conveyed by the pericope which follows in 14:17–21, where Jesus announces that one of his table companions is destined to betray him.[25] The betrayer is not mentioned by name, but this indefiniteness only serves to heighten the dramatic effect of the scene. The pronouncement has all the solemnity of an oracular utterance, and it seems to represent an inscrutable and irrevocable decision on the part of the Messiah himself. The divine word has been spoken, and, frightful though it is, what has been spoken must needs come to pass. Thus the betrayer, whoever he might be, is in the wretched plight of being confronted by a terrible fate from which there is no escape; and hence the disciples, on hearing the malediction, make no professions of loyalty as they do in 14:31 (after the prophecy of Peter's denial), but ask Jesus one by one: "Surely it is not I?" They are smitten with grief, and each of them can only hope and pray that the dreadful role of betrayer has not been assigned to him. But the Lord does not satisfy their anxious curiosity, for it may be that the identity of the betrayer is a divine mystery which cannot yet be divulged. He simply repeats in different language what has already been stated: "It is one of the twelve, he who dips with me into the dish." [26] He then goes on to emphasize the necessity of the betrayal by making a general appeal to the scriptures: "For the Son of Man departs even as it is written concerning him," and this implies that the traitor (who stands utterly helpless in face of the compulsive might of his Master's word) is a mere instru-

[25] St. Mark probably has Ps. 41:10 (E.T. 41, 9) in mind; cf. John 13:18, where there is a quotation of Ps. 41:10b.

[26] Bultmann (*Die Geschichte der synoptischen Tradition*, p. 284) sees an earlier form of the pronouncement in Luke 22:21 ("Behold, the hand of him that betrays me is with me on the table"). But is it not more likely that this passage is an example of St. Luke's skill as a literary artist?

ment in the hands of a transcendent power over which he has no control. But the report ends on a characteristic note of paradox. For the concluding part of Jesus' ominous pronouncement suggests that the disciple referred to is morally responsible for his act of treachery; apparently, the punishment he must endure will match the heinousness of his crime, and therefore it may be said that it would have been good for him had he never been born.[27]

In the last of the three pericopes dealing with the supper (14:22–25) Jesus is presiding at table as a host in the presence of his assembled guests, and his words again make it plain that he is already aware of his impending death. Evidently he is gifted with supernatural foresight, and this enables him to comprehend his passion as a necessary moment in the fulfillment of God's redemptive purpose. But, as in the two preceding pericopes, the mode of presentation suggests that a deeper truth is intended. Thus it is fitting that in the course of the supper he should give the bread and the wine as tokens of his own body and of his outpoured blood, for he is about to give his physical life as a sacrifice for the redemption of many (cf. 10:45; 14:24; Isa. 53:12); it is fitting, too, that he should declare with confidence that he will never again drink of the fruit of the vine until that day when he drinks it new in the kingdom of God (v. 25), for he is the Messiah and as such he must forever remain the master of his fate. Accordingly, the narrative seems to imply that the passion, though a necessary eschatological occurrence, is yet a sacrificial act of self-humiliation, a direct expression of the Messiah's will; and just as he has decided upon his departure in shame, so he may decide upon his return in glory.

It appears, then, that the evangelist takes this supper to mark the end of the period of fellowship between the disciples and

[27] Cf. 11:12ff., where the fig tree is condemned in spite of the fact that it is not the season for figs; cf. above, Chapter 6, n. 14, and Chapter 9, n. 19.

their incarnate Lord; it is a valedictory gathering at which Jesus takes leave of his followers before he goes to his death. On the other hand, the sadness naturally associated with such an occasion is offset by the knowledge that the Messiah's departure is ultimately of his own choosing and by the assurance that fellowship with him will be renewed on the day of the kingdom's consummation.[28] But it would be an error to suppose that the crucifixion means an absolute break in the continuity of the fellowship or that the period between the "here and now" of this meal and the "there and then" of the expected meal in glory could be adequately represented as the desolate period of the Messiah's absence from his followers. For this meal is not only the last earthly meal of Jesus; it is also the first celebration of the Christian eucharist.[29] The disciples receive the bread and wine as the body and blood of their Master, and thereby they anticipate the fellowship of the Lord's table as it is to be realized in the life of the apostolic church. Hitherto the society of the elect has been held together by the bodily presence of the Messiah, the focal point of the community; henceforth, so it would seem, the same kind of function is to be performed by the communal experience of his mystical presence in the bread and wine of the church's sacramental meal,[30] and thus, in spite of the passion, the elect will maintain the continuity of their fellowship with the Lord until the day of his awaited appearance in glory. If we may use the phraseology of the fourth evangelist,

[28] In Jewish writings the final blessedness of the redeemed is frequently represented in terms of table fellowship with the Lord; cf. S.-B., IV, 1154ff. The term "new" (v. 25) has eschatological associations; cf. Isa. 43:19; 65:17; Rev. 21:5.

[29] Apparently Jesus does not partake of the bread and wine (14:12 evidently represents an independent tradition), and hence this part of the meal is "without him" in a material sense, but it could be "with him" in a mystical sense if the disciples had the spiritual insight which comes with the resurrection.

[30] Cf. Lohmeyer's illuminating observations in *Das Evangelium des Markus*, pp. 306f. Also, see below, pp. 258ff.

235

Jesus does not leave his disciples in a state of desolation (John 14:18), since those who eat his flesh and drink his blood know that they abide in him and he in them (John 6:56).

The supernatural foreknowledge of Jesus receives further demonstration in the next pericope (Mark 14:26–31). According to verse 26, after the singing of a hymn or hymns,[31] Jesus goes out with the disciples to the Mount of Olives and, according to the subsequent verses, he proceeds to make a series of three predictions. In verse 27, which prepares the reader for the account of the arrest in 14:43ff., he tells his disciples that they will all be caused to stumble and gives force to his announcement by citing a passage from the scriptures.[32] In verse 28, however, the Master evinces complete confidence in his ultimate triumph over suffering and death by declaring that after his resurrection he will precede his disciples into Galilee—a promise to which reference is made in the angel's command to the women in the story of the empty tomb.[33] Lastly, in verses 29–31 atten-

---

[31] This notice, if it is meant to refer to the *hallel*, may be due to a doctrinal tendency to represent the last supper as a passover meal; cf. 14:12–16.

[32] Zech. 13:7; cf. Jesus' general reference to scripture in 14:49b, which is immediately followed by the report that they all left him and fled.

[33] See 16:7. The Fayoum Fragment (see *The Apocryphal New Testament*, ed. M. R. James, p. 25) omits 14:28. Dibelius (*op. cit.*, pp. 160f., 181, n. 1) holds that the fragment represents a collection of sayings of Jesus which were supplied with chronological data; he notes that Peter's reply is condensed and given only in the genitive absolute, everything being subordinated to the prediction of the denial. Hence he calls it "a Chria-like abbreviated reproduction of a bit of tradition" and maintains that 14:28 "is only in place in a connected description." But even if the fragment is taken to represent 14:27–30, there are still reasons for thinking that 14:28 is a genuine part of the text of the gospel: (1) all the other extant authorities for the text of the work include 14:28 (2) it is almost certain that 14:28 was part of the Markan text as St. Matthew knew it; and (3) the insertion of a "luminous" passage between two "sombre" passages is characteristic of St. Mark's style; cf. 14:1–11, 53–72. Wellhausen explained 14:28 as a justification (by an express command of Jesus) of the disciples' cowardly

tion is again directed to the stern realities of the immediate situation by a direful prediction which prepares the way for the story of Peter's threefold denial, presented in verses 53–54 and 66–72 of the same chapter; and it should be noticed that the professions of loyalty here made by Peter and his colleagues help to bring out the completeness of their failure in the impending hour of crisis.[34]

---

flight to Galilee. On the other hand, there is no attempt to defend the disciples in this way in 14:50 (though it was held, of course, that their flight was ultimately a provision of the divine purpose). It is possible that 16:7, but not 14:28, was interpolated by St. Mark. Thus in Dibelius' judgment (*ibid.*, pp. 181, 183, 189ff.): (1) the pre-Markan passion narrative contained one or more resurrection appearances to Peter and the other disciples (cf. I Cor. 15:5); (2) 14:28 originally referred to those appearances; (3) St. Mark decided to end his work with the story of the empty tomb, but he wished to point forward to the christophanies, hence retained 14:28 and interpolated 16:7; and (4) since the story of the appearance to Peter would tell of his reconciliation to the Lord, the thought of the postresurrection meeting in Galilee would be associated with the thought of Peter's denial, and this explains why the prediction of 14:28 is immediately followed by the prediction of 14:29–31. On the other hand, Lohmeyer (*Galiläa und Jerusalem*, pp. 10ff.) sees in 14:28 and 16:7 a reflection of St. Mark's doctrine of Galilee, in contradistinction to Jerusalem, as the land of divine revelation and eschatological fulfillment; that is, these passages refer not to transitory appearances of the risen Jesus, but to the parousia of the Son of Man. But perhaps it would be safer to hold that 14:28 and 16:7 refer to some resurrection appearance in Galilee *and* beyond all such transitory appearances to the parousia in glory and finality; cf. Lightfoot, *Locality and Doctrine*, pp. 73ff., and below, Supplementary Note E.

[34] For the expression "before the cock crows twice" (v. 30), cf. Rawlinson, *op. cit.*, pp. 208f. The Romans divided the night into four watches, the third of which seems to have been popularly known as "cock-crow" (cf. 13:35); and it has been suggested (by C. H. Mayo in *J.T.S.*, XXII [1921], 367ff.) that the reference was originally to a military signal called *gallicinium* (which would be sounded by the Roman garrison occupying the Castle Antonia) for the changing of the guard at the end of the third watch. Goguel (*H.T.R.*, XXV [1932], 1ff.) thinks that the story of Peter's denial is a construction based on a prediction made by Jesus, but never actually fulfilled. He questions the his-

In the following pericope (vv. 32–42) the idea of the cost of the passion, the terrible price which has to be paid for the Messiah's final victory over sin and death, receives the utmost emphasis. Jesus proceeds to a place called Gethsemane and tells the majority of his disciples to sit where they are. And he takes with him Peter, James, and John and begins to be greatly amazed and distressed. He tells them that his soul is exceedingly sorrowful even unto death and bids them to remain where they are and to watch. He then goes forward a little and falls on the ground and prays that, if it were possible, the hour might pass away from him, and saying:

Abba, Father, all things are possible unto thee; remove this cup from me. Yet, not what I will but what thou wilt.

On returning, he finds the three disciples sleeping and he says to Peter:

Are you sleeping, Simon? Could you not watch for one hour? Watch and pray [all of you] that you may not enter into temptation. The spirit is willing, but the flesh is weak.[35]

He goes away again and prays in the same words as before, and on returning he once more finds the disciples asleep, for their

---

toricity of the story on various grounds such as: (1) according to 14:50 all the disciples take flight; (2) the denial is not mentioned in Gal. 2:11ff.; and (3) discipline in the early church was very strict—cf. Acts 5:1ff. But these arguments are not convincing: 14:50 is not necessarily inconsistent with 14:54, and by force of contrast the deficiency of Peter prior to his experience of the risen Lord would probably tend to enhance, rather than to detract from, his reputation in the apostolic communities.

[35] Peter seems to be mentioned as the representative of the three (notice the sudden change from the second person singular to the second person plural). It is evidently because of the weakness of the flesh that the Messiah exhorts the three (and through them, presumably, the readers of the gospel) to pray that they may not enter into temptation; such weakness is well illustrated in 10:17ff. where, as it appears, the rich man fails to inherit treasure in heaven because he succumbs to the temptation to retain his material possessions.

eyes are heavy; and they do not know what to answer him. Then he comes for the third time and tells them to sleep on and take their rest as the hour has come and the Son of Man is betrayed into the hands of sinners. Thus it is shown that the Messiah is obedient even unto death on a cross (cf. Phil. 2:8) and that his obedience is learned in and through the bitter experience of extreme spiritual stress (cf. Heb. 5:8). But the disciples do not penetrate the mysterious meaning of their Master's anguish of soul; and it is significant that they are distanced from the actual scene of his prayer, for they are not yet in a position to know the fellowship of his sufferings (cf. Phil. 3:10; Col. 1:24). Even the intimate three, who go further than the others, are unable to share his vigil; their spiritual sight is dim, and the importance of the hour is beyond their powers of comprehension.

This story, then, stands in remarkable contrast to the three preceding pericopes concerning the last supper. Jesus no longer acts and speaks as the disposer of the course of history who determines the shape of things to come by the marvelous potency of his voluntary decisions. On the contrary, he comes to represent the purpose of God only by overcoming the weakness of his human nature through the mediation of an agonized effort of will. From one point of view, indeed, the story may seem to imply that Jesus is temporarily inclined to deviate from the purpose of God, such an inclination being a presupposition of his spiritual agony. From another point of view, however, the story is wholly the record of a fulfillment of the divine purpose, since, as the early Christians believed, the Messiah's anguish is indicated beforehand in the psalms of suffering.[36] The same kind of paradox is evinced in Mark 15:34,[37] where the last articulate

---

[36] See Pss. 22:25 (E.T., 22:24); 31:23 (E.T., 31:22); 69:2–4 (E.T., 69:1–3). Cf. the LXX rendering of Ps. 43:5.

[37] Cf. Dibelius, *op. cit.*, pp. 193f., and Lightfoot, *History and Interpretation*, pp. 157ff. There are reasons for thinking that St. Mark attaches special importance to the so-called cry of dereliction: (1) The cry is transliterated (from Hebrew or Aramaic) as well as translated. (2) In what follows some of the bystanders think that Jesus is calling

utterance of Jesus is presented in the form of a citation of the opening words ("My God, my God, why hast thou forsaken me?") of what appears to have been the church's favorite passion psalm (Ps. 22). For, if attention is concentrated solely on the content of the utterance, it seems that Jesus has finally given way to despair, whereas the evangelist would presumably regard the citation as a proof that the Messiah's earthly life to the very last moment was a realization of the will or purpose of God; and in the following verse (15:35) a contrast is perhaps intended between the ignorance of the bystanders, who infer that Jesus has been making an appeal to Elijah, and the implied knowledge of the initiated reader who is familiar with the inspired source of the Lord's last words.[38] Furthermore, while the Gethsemane

---

to Elijah for help; thus attention is drawn to the cry by contrasting its true significance with a misinterpretation of it; its true significance is taken for granted—that is, the contrast presupposes that the reader is conversant with Ps. 22 and its messianic application (cf. the fourth gospel, where the misunderstanding of a saying is often used to bring out the importance of that saying; see John 3:3ff.; 4:10ff.; 11:23ff.). In 15:34f. there are some interesting western readings which Turner (*N.C.H.S.*, pt. 3, pp. 117f.) considers to be genuine: (1) D and k transliterate the cry of dereliction from Hebrew (not Aramaic), and Turner thinks that the use of the sacred language would be natural here. (2) D and k (with two other old Latin MSS) give (instead of "forsaken") "reproached," and Turner holds that the substitution (in all other authorities) of "forsaken" was due to the combined influence of Matt. 27:46 and the LXX. (3) k gives not "Elijah" ('Ηλίαν) but "sun" ('Ηλιον), and Turner suggests that the bystanders were Gentiles who associated the cry with the reappearance of the sun at the ninth hour (cf. 15:33) and interpreted it as an appeal to the sun-god. But it is possible that 15:34f. did not appear in the old pre-Markan record of the passion, for the cry in v. 34 may be a secondary interpretation (made in the light of the classic passion psalm) of the death cry in 15:37; the phrase "loud voice" occurs in each of these verses.

[38] St. Luke and St. John seemingly find the paradox intolerable: in Luke 23:46 the cry of dereliction is replaced by a quotation from Ps. 31:6 (E.T., 31:5), and in John 19:30 it is replaced by the simple affirmation: "It is finished."

story affords a most impressive illustration of St. Mark's fundamental conception of the Messiah's afflictions as the painful prelude to his future glorification, it betrays the tendency we have
noticed elsewhere to transcend the category of means and end
by interpreting the passion directly in terms of its awaited outcome in glory. Thus, in the first place, the form and content of
verses 37–42 are reminiscent of the conclusion of the great eschatological discourse (13:33–37); and, as was suggested in the
foregoing chapter,[39] we should perhaps discern in the parallelism
between these two passages an approach to the Johannine doctrine of the passion as the hour of the Messiah's glorification. In
the second place, the Gethsemane story shows a remarkable resemblance in certain of its features to the account of the transfiguration in Mark 9:2ff., where Jesus temporarily appears in the
glory of his messianic nature. In each instance the three closest
disciples are privileged to behold their Master in a new and mysterious aspect and in each instance they utterly fail to understand the significance of their strange experience; in 9:6 it is
reported that "he [Peter] did not know what to answer" and
in 14:40 that "they did not know what to answer him." [40] Such
parallelism is no mere accidental phenomenon, but is sympto-
matic of the evangelist's dissatisfaction with his primary doctrinal position and arises from his desire to bring the notions of
suffering and glorification into a more intimate relationship than
that which obtains between means and end.[41]

[39] Cf. above, Chapter 9, n. 45.

[40] It is interesting to find that St. Luke introduces the sleep motif into
his account of the transfiguration, for this seems to show that he is associating Mark 9:2ff. with Mark 14:32ff. Cf. Luke 9:32a with Mark
14:40.

[41] The commands in 14:41 are evidently at variance with the imperative and cohortative subjunctive in 14:42. Admittedly, commentators
usually argue that Jesus' opening words in 14:41 are really a question:
"Are you still sleeping, then, and taking your rest?" But a forced translation of this kind does not seem to be necessary. In 14:41 St. Mark is
apparently thinking of the "hour" as the hour of glorification; and when

The next pericope (vv. 43–52), which concerns the arrest of Jesus, is followed by the account of Peter's threefold denial (vv. 53f., 66–72) and the intercalated story of the nocturnal trial before the sanhedrin (vv. 55–65). The last-mentioned story raises certain historical difficulties, and these will be considered at a later stage.[42] But it should be recalled at the present juncture that verse 62 is the second of the two passages in the passion narrative which are apparently meant to refer back to the great apocalyptic discourse of the thirteenth chapter. Forsaken by his followers, disowned by the chief of the twelve, and confronted by his enemies in all their worldly might, Jesus publicly affirms the fact of his Messiahship and confidently declares that his judges shall see the Son of Man coming with the clouds of heaven. Thus something of the supernatural glory of the parousia momentarily lights up the darkest depths of the humiliation and shame to which the passion narrative bears witness; and we are presented with what is, from one point of view, the most striking exemplification in the entire gospel of the evangelist's tendency to move away from the general conception of the Messiah's incarnate life as the period of obscurity and secrecy. It is true that in 9:2ff. Jesus undergoes a metamorphosis and for a fleeting moment actually appears in the glory of his essential status, whereas in the present instance he retains his human form and mediates the revelation merely by word of mouth. On the other hand, only the three chosen disciples are permitted to behold their Master in his transfigured state, whereas in the passage before us the truth concerning the office and destiny of Jesus is openly proclaimed to the world and so the requirements of secrecy are

---

that hour has arrived, presumably there will be no further need for vigilance; cf. 13:32ff. On the other hand, in 14:42 the evangelist's attention has shifted to the exigencies of the immediate historical situation, and Jesus is represented as a hero who would go forward to meet his enemies with courage and confidence.

[42] See below, Chapter 12.

defied in a manner which does not apply to the case of the transfiguration. Accordingly, St. Mark's apostolic faith, which seems to be pressing for direct and open expression in the story of the anointing at Bethany, here subjects the doctrine of the secret to a strain which it cannot withstand; all barriers are broken down, and for a brief interval there is a public disclosure of the fact of the Messiahship.[43]

The remainder of the passion narrative, extending from 15:1 to the end of the gospel at 16:8, falls into five sections, each of which is characterized by a notice of time; in 15:1–20 the hierarchs meet early in the morning (cf. 16:2), or in the fourth watch of the night (cf. 13:35), and decide to hand the prisoner over to Pilate, whereupon Jesus is tried and condemned to death; in 15:21–32 the sentence is carried out, and it is noticed (v. 25) that the crucifixion begins at the third hour; in 15:33–41 darkness covers the whole land from the sixth hour to the ninth, and soon afterwards Jesus expires; in 15:42–47 the burial takes place at eventide, that is, apparently, toward sunset which marks the end of the preparation and the beginning of the sabbath; and in 16:1–8 three women go to the tomb very early in the morning on the first day of the week and make the amazing discovery that Jesus has already risen from the dead. The first two of these

[43] It has sometimes been argued that the account of the nocturnal trial could not have formed part of the first edition of the gospel, since it contradicts St. Mark's theory of the messianic secret. But there are reasons for thinking that this argument is quite unsound: (1) The gospel contains many indications that St. Mark does not work out his theory of the secret with perfect consistency and that he is feeling his way after a more satisfying doctrine. (2) St. Mark is fond of intercalating one story between the earlier and later parts of another. (3) The story of the anointing is to the account of the nocturnal trial as the story of the triumphal entry is to the parable of the wicked husbandmen. For in 14:3–9, as in 11:1–10, St. Mark's faith in the Messiahship is pressing for a mode of open expression, and in 14:62, as in 12:12, the pressure (reinforced by the desire to ascribe responsibility to the Jews) becomes too great for the doctrine of the secret. Thus 14:62 has a significant precedent in the third main section of the gospel.

five sections bear certain striking resemblances to each other and to the preceding section (14:53–72). All three sections are introduced by notices of change of place; [44] in all three sections Jesus is subjected to mockery; [45] and all three sections are to a greater or less extent designed to bring out a contrast.[46] Accordingly, 14:53–72; 15:1–20 and 15:21–32, which set forth the processes leading directly up to the Messiah's death, may be said to form a triad of sections; and 15:33–41; 15:42–47 and 16:1–8, dealing with the connected historical themes of the apostolic message of salvation (cf. I Cor. 15:3f.), may be said to form a second triad of sections. It is evident, therefore, that to the end of the gospel St. Mark continues to betray a decided predilection for series of three in the arrangement of his material.[47]

[44] See 14:53 (from Gethsemane to the high priest); 15:1 (from the high priest's court to Pilate); 15:21f. (from Pilate's court to Golgotha).

[45] See 14:65 (mocked as a prophet by certain members of the sanhedrin); 15:16–20 (ridiculed as a king by Roman soldiers); 15:29–32 (taunted by passers-by, derided by chief priests with scribes, reproached by those crucified with him). The emphasis on the motif of mockery was probably due in some measure to scriptural influence; cf. Pss. 22:7f. (E.T., 22:6f.); 69:10 (E.T., 69:9). Regarding Loisy's view that Jesus was crucified as a mock king in a pagan ritual, and regarding Reich's view that the soldiers mocked Jesus as the hero of a popular mime "The King with the Crown of Thorns," see Rawlinson, *op. cit.*, pp. 229f., and Winter, *op. cit.*, pp. 100ff. For the mishandling and spitting in 14:65; 15:19, cf. Isa. 50:6. Regarding the mode of expression in 14:65b, Hubert Pernot (*Ex.T.*, XXXVIII [1926–27], 105) observes that it is still customary for the Greek peasant to say "to take somebody by the blows, the stick" for "to box his ears, to beat him."

[46] In 14:53ff. the courage of the Master is set over against the cowardice of the chief disciple; in 15:6ff. the innocent prisoner is set over against the criminal Barabbas; and in 15:26f. the King of the Jews is set over against the two robbers.

[47] Notice, too, the division into three-hour intervals in 15:25, 33, the three classes of mockers in 15:29–32, and the three women named in 15:40.

Realization of the Meaning

As we should expect, the first constituent section of the second triad (15:33–41) reflects something of the tremendous eschatological and soteriological significance which the apostolic church assigned to the Messiah's death. The darkness, which covers the whole land (or earth) from the sixth hour to the ninth, suggests that the world of nature is profoundly disturbed at the shameful sufferings of the Creator's Son.[48] It is possible, however, that we are meant to discern here not only a form of testimony to the divine status of Jesus but also a miraculous indication that the passion marks a decisive moment in cosmic history: it is an eschatological event and as such portends the dissolution of the present order of existence when the sun and the moon and the stars shall finally cease to shine and the celestial powers shall be shaken.[49] At the ninth hour, as we have seen, Jesus gives utterance to the opening words of the twenty-second psalm, and certain of the bystanders mistakenly suppose that he

[48] In talmudic literature there are reports of miraculous events accompanying the death of certain rabbis, and there is an interesting midrash which explains the darkening of the heavenly luminaries in Joel 2:10 as a sign of mourning on God's part; see S.-B., I, 1040ff. The idea that the world of nature mourns the passing of godly men is also to be found in pagan literature; see Klostermann, *Das Markusevangelium*, p. 166. The third evangelist expressly refers to an eclipse of the sun (Luke 23:45a); but it is perhaps unlikely that he is thinking of an ordinary eclipse, for this would not last for three hours and would not occur at the time of the (paschal) full moon.

[49] Cf. 13:24f., and Amos 8:9; Isa. 34:4; Joel 2:10. If St. Mark has 13:24f. in mind here (15:33), there are three passages in the passion narrative which refer back to the great apocalyptic discourse. But in this case there is no close linguistic parallelism. Nevertheless, it is noteworthy that the testimony of nature, unlike the testimonies of the temple (15:38) and of the centurion (15:39), is given before the Messiah's death actually takes place, and (with great reserve) it may perhaps be suggested that this is due to the sequence of events in 13:24–27: the darkening of the sun and the moon and the stars precedes the parousia of the Son of Man in glory, and so in this case the darkening of the sun at noonday precedes the manifestation of glory in the Messiah's death.

is appealing to Elijah. Someone offers him a sponge soaked in vinegar, but Jesus apparently does not taste of it; he cries out with a loud voice and expires.[50]

Thus the days of his flesh are at an end; and the completeness and effectiveness of his sacrifice at once receive recognition in the rending of the temple veil (v. 38) and in the Roman centurion's confession (v. 39). Passers-by have been mocking at the dying Jesus for his alleged pretensions to destroy the temple and to build it in three days (15:29; cf. 14:58), and now in a supernatural fashion the temple itself sets the scoffers at naught by bearing witness to the doom to which it is condemned. For the rending of the veil probably belongs to the same category of ideas as the automatic opening of the temple doors, which according to Jewish traditions occurred as a miraculous portent of the catastrophe which was to take place forty years later.[51] Thus, by the juxtaposition of verses 37 and 38, the evangelist apparently means to imply that the Messiah's death and the destruction of the old religious order of Judaism are inseparably bound up together—an idea which seems to lie behind the account of

[50] Turner (*N.C.H.S.*, pt. 3, p. 118) argues that in v. 36 one of those who suppose that Jesus appeals to Helios (cf. above, n. 37) offers the vinegar out of sympathy for the sufferer; but there was some word or movement on the part of the others to discourage their companion's act of mercy, and he answers (in jest or in earnest) in the sense: "Let me alone, let us keep life going in him in case after all the sun-god is coming to deliver him." Thus the vinegar is a refreshment; cf. Num. 6:3; Ruth 2:14; S.-B., II, 64. But perhaps the drink is a torment, as in Ps. 69:22 (E.T. 69:21), and the man may intend to intensify the sufferings of Jesus and thus to give Elijah or Helios more reason for coming. Also, the words: Ἄφετε ἴδωμεν may mean simply: "Let us see" (cf. Moulton and Milligan, *Vocabulary of the Greek Testament*, pt. 1, p. 97; Moulton, *Prolegomena*, pp. 175f.). It is possible that vv. 34f. are due to St. Mark, v. 34 being an interpretation of v. 37 and the form of the misunderstanding in v. 35 having been suggested by v. 36b.

[51] Cf. S.-B., I, 1045f. It is unlikely that such traditions would be in circulation prior to the destruction of the temple, and so St. Mark wrote probably after 70 A.D. Cf. Dibelius, *op. cit.*, p. 195, n. 3.

the cursing of the fig tree and the intercalated story of the cleansing of the temple; the Messiah condemns Israel and thereby brings about his own death as well as the ruin of the nation to which he belongs.[52] It is possible, however, that the evangelist sees in the rending of the veil [53] something more than a portent of approaching disaster and construes it in a positive sense as signifying that a barrier to the divine presence has been brushed aside. For, in the belief of the apostolic church, the Messiah's death not only marks the end of the old dispensation founded on the Sinaitic covenant, but also represents the basis and condition of a new dispensation which comes to light in and through the Messiah's resurrection after three days. To use the language of the author of the epistle to the Hebrews, the high priest after the order of Melchizedek opens up for men a new and living way within the veil by passing into the holy of holies on their behalf and offering the all-sufficient sacrifice of his own blood (Heb. 6:19–20; 10;19–20). The old covenant is superseded by a new one, sealed by the blood of Jesus, which is shed for many (14:24). That such a positive significance should be seen in the passage under consideration, seems to be corroborated in the next verse.[54] For the centurion's words are not merely a typical martyrological motif; [55] adjudged in the light of the work as a whole,

---

[52] Cf. above, Chapters 6 and 9.

[53] The reference is probably to the inner curtain before the holy of holies; cf. Heb. 9:3; S.-B., I, 1043ff.

[54] Turner (*J.T.S.*, XXIX [1927], 12f.) maintains that in 15:39 the original reading is preserved in k (". . . saw that he so cried out, he said. . . .") and makes the following observations: (1) All the authorities except B, L support κράζω. (2) The κράξας of Matt. 27:50 was probably derived from Mark 15:39. (3) κράζω is not used of Jesus elsewhere in the synoptics (though three times in the fourth gospel), and it is the sort of indication of violent emotion that Alexandrian critics would have liked to modify. (4) The reading of A etc. looks like a combination of the readings of k and of Cod. Sin. etc.

[55] The centurion's confession has become such a typical motif in Luke 23:47; for references to parallels, see Bultmann, *op. cit.*, p. 306, n. 1.

they stand out as a fitting complement to the words of Peter in
8:29. Jesus has been secretly acknowledged to be the Messiah
by a Jew at Caesarea Philippi,[56] and now, in consequence of the
passion, he is publicly acknowledged to be the Son of God by
a Gentile. Thus the gospel of Jesus, Messiah, Son of God (1:1)
receives its due confirmation as such within the framework of
the narrative and, in making his testimony, the centurion appears
as the prototype of Gentile Christianity and as the symbol of
Christian universalism.[57] If we may use the words of St. Paul,
the middle wall of partition has been broken down through the
cross of Christ, and therefore Jews and Gentiles alike have access
in one Spirit unto the Father (Eph. 2:11–22).

The section is brought to a conclusion in 15:40–41 with a
notice regarding certain women who witness the death of Jesus
from a distance. Among them are Mary Magdalene, Mary the
mother of James the less and of Joses, and Salome, who attended
Jesus when he was in Galilee. Only two of these women witness
the burial of Jesus (15:47), but all three go to the tomb on the
first day of the week and are evidently the first human beings
to discover that the resurrection has taken place.[58] Thus in the

---

Lightfoot (*History and Interpretation*, p. 85, n. 2) notices that the absence of the Greek article from the phrase "Son of God" in Mark 15:39,
as in Matt. 14:33, may be due to the fact that the expression is a predi-
cate. The probability is that the words have the full Christian meaning
which they have in Mark 1:1.

[56] Strictly speaking, of course, actual Israel cannot bear witness to the
Messiahship, since, in St. Mark's view, the Messiah was rejected by his
own people; hence Peter in 8:29 represents the true Israel; similarly,
in 15:38 the temple seems to symbolize the Jewish religious ideal from
which the people themselves have fallen short; cf. above, Chapter 6,
n. 6.

[57] For the bearing of 15:39 on the general question of the ending of
St. Mark's gospel, cf. above, Chapter 7, n. 13.

[58] 16:1ff. It must be noted, however, that the western authorities
D k n omit the names of the women in 16:1, and according to Turner
(*J.T.S.*, XXIX [1927], 13f.) the omission is right. He maintains that the
ordinary text arose through the influence of the text of the first gospel.

last three pericopes of his work the evangelist betrays a pronounced interest in eyewitnesses, and this is not at all surprising in view of the importance of the Messiah's death, burial, and resurrection in the apostolic gospel. Admittedly, the same kind of interest seems to be evinced elsewhere in the passion narrative, for, as Dibelius pointed out, the young man, who flees without his cloak in 14:51–52, and Simon of Cyrene, who carries the cross in 15:21, may find mention in the record because the narrator wishes to draw the reader's attention to actual eyewitnesses, upon whose testimony the story of the arrest and execution may have been based.[59] The women, however, are expressly referred to as eyewitnesses on two occasions (15:40; 15:47), and yet in 16:8c it is stated that they said nothing to anybody, that is, presumably, they told no one of their amazing experience at the empty tomb. This statement is especially significant since it suggests that the evangelist's interest in the women is not of a purely biographical character; for, from a biographical point of view, what value would attach to witnesses who failed to report on the events they had seen and heard? To some extent, therefore, the evangelist's interest in the women may be governed by doctrinal considerations.

As previously suggested,[60] St. Mark makes a fundamental distinction between the period of the Messiah's incarnate life, which is characterized by lowliness and obscurity, and the period of postresurrection enlightenment, in which the gospel is openly

---

St. Matthew mentions the women three times: in Matt. 27:56 (from Mark 15:40), in Matt. 27:61 (from Mark 15:47), and, because he has interpolated the story of the sealing of the tomb, the names of Matt. 27:61 are repeated in Matt. 28:1. The interpolators felt that since St. Matthew had the names three times, St. Mark ought to have them three times also (though in St. Mark's gospel there is no interval); and with their characteristic liking for fullness, they make the insertion (in Mark 16:1) not of the two names of Matt. 28:1 but of the three of Matt. 27:56/Mark 15:40.

[59] Cf. Dibelius, *op. cit.*, pp. 182f.   [60] Cf. above, Chapter 7.

proclaimed to mankind. Such a distinction implies that the resurrection of Jesus is a turning point in the history of the world and that the appearances of the risen Lord to Peter and the others (cf. I Cor. 15:5–8) signify the dawning of a new age, the age of the church with its mission to the Gentiles and its unfailing hope in the future. Accordingly, since the evangelist is primarily concerned with the period of the incarnate life, he may regard the resurrection christophanies as falling outside the scope of his work, and perhaps it was for this reason that he decided to bring his gospel to a conclusion with the story of the empty tomb. It is not unlikely that the last-mentioned story had but recently come into circulation, and 16:8c may have been partly meant to explain why that story, unlike the stories of the appearances, did not establish itself in Christian tradition from the beginning of the church's existence.[61] Furthermore, according to 14:50 all the disciples are dispersed in cowardly flight on the occasion of the arrest, and in consequence of their complete failure Jesus is poignantly alone at the end. He is rejected by his own nation and utterly forsaken by his closest followers. To use words derived from the scriptures, men have all turned aside from the truth; they have together become unprofitable (cf. Rom. 3:12).

Thus there is a significant break in the continuity of the disciples' fellowship with the Lord, and their contact with him is not restored until the christophanies take place at the dawning of the new age. It would seem, however, that St. Mark does not wish his readers to regard the interruption as an absolute one, for the women are apparently meant to represent a sort of subsidiary connecting link mediating the transition from the period

---

[61] That 16:8c should be understood in this sense, was first suggested to me in private conversation by M. Goguel. But it was not until I read the article by J. M. Creed in *J.T.S.*, XXI (1930), 175ff., that I came to realize that 16:8c affords reason for thinking that St. Mark deliberately chose to end his work at 16:8d.

of obscurity to the period of enlightenment. The connection backwards with the Messiah's incarnate life is established in 15:41, where it is reported that the women followed Jesus and ministered to him while he was in Galilee; and in 16:7, which seems to have been interpolated by the evangelist,[62] we may discern an effort to establish the connection forward with the life of the church: the women are enjoined by the angel to remind the disciples of the promised reunion in Galilee (cf. 14:28). But with the introduction of 16:7 into the story, 16:8c ("and they said nothing to anyone") comes to imply that the women are disobedient. The heavenly injunction is left hanging in the air, and the required connection forward is not really established. St. Mark could easily overlook the discrepancy, because he concluded his work at 16:8d ("for they were afraid"). But had he chosen to continue the narrative beyond that point, the probability is that he would have removed the discrepancy, as the later synoptists removed it, by suppressing 16:8c and allowing the women to carry out the angel's command.[63]

[62] Dibelius (*op. cit.*, p. 192, n. 1) argues that the flight of the women in 16:8 is not the consequence of comforting words promising an explanation, as in 16:7, but of a puzzling event, as narrated in 16:6. Cf. above, n. 33.

[63] For the relation of the Messiah's resurrection to his glorification, see above, Chapter 7.

SUPPLEMENTARY NOTE E: GALILEE AND JERUSALEM

It has been contended by E. Lohmeyer and R. H. Lightfoot that St. Mark sets Galilee in radical opposition to Jerusalem; to use Lightfoot's own words:

Galilee and Jerusalem . . . stand in opposition to each other, as the story of the gospel runs in St. Mark. The despised and more or less outlawed Galilee is shewn to have been chosen by God as the seat of the gospel and of the revelation of the Son of man, while the sacred city of Jerusalem, the home of jewish piety and patriotism, has become the centre of relentless hostility and sin. Galilee is the sphere of revelation, Jerusalem is the scene only of rejection.[1]

It is not possible in this note to give a full appreciation of the position thus outlined, but a few comments on it may be made in the light of the discussions of the foregoing chapters:

1. In view of St. Mark's preface, can it be upheld that Galilee is the sphere of revelation and the land where the divine fulfillment begins? The inspired witness of John the Baptist, the appointed forerunner of the Messiah, is made in the wilderness, presumably near the southern fords of the Jordan (1:4f.); and if it is pointed out that the second testimony of the heavenly voice (9:7) is located on a mountain in the Galilean region, it should also be pointed out that the first testimony of the voice (1:11) is located somewhere on the river outside that region.

2. Apart from 13:10 and 14:9, where the reference is obviously to the missionary activity of the church, the term κηρύσσειν

---

[1] *Locality and Doctrine*, pp. 124f. For Lohmeyer's position, see his *Galiläa und Jerusalem*, pp. 5ff. For some observations on Lohmeyer's theory that Christianity had its oldest roots in north Palestinian territory, see M. Black, *The Scrolls and Christian Origins*, pp. 81ff.

("to proclaim") does not occur after 7:36; but can it be inferred from St. Mark's use of the term that there is no present proclamation of the gospel elsewhere than in Galilee and its environs? The term is used of the Baptist's preaching in 1:4 and 1:7, and of the Messiah's preaching only in 1:14; 1:38–39; and 1:45 (?). In 4:1 Jesus teaches the multitude by the sea, and the same verb (διδάσκειν) occurs in 10:1; having passed over the Jordan, he comes to the territory of Judaea and in accordance with his custom he again teaches the multitude. The word κηρύσσειν is used of the preaching of the disciples in 3:14 and 6:12, but in the latter instance, as well as in the former, the evangelist seems to be thinking of the disciples in their future capacity as apostles of the church; for the mission of the twelve, following on the story of the rejection in the *patris*, may well be a representation in advance of the church's mission to the Gentiles. Elsewhere, at the conclusion of certain miracle stories, κηρύσσειν is used of the publishing abroad of Jesus' great power as a worker of miraculous cures; the term occurs with this meaning in 1:45 (?); 5:20 and 7:36, but since it does not occur in 1:31; 2:12; 3:6; 5:34; 5:43; 7:30; 8:26 and 9:29, there is nothing surprising about its absence from 10:52, that is, from the conclusion of the one healing story which the evangelist assigns to the closing period of the ministry.[2]

3. Is not Galilee to a considerable extent the scene of hostility? The controversy stories in 2:1–3:6 resemble those in 12:13–44, and perhaps they were all derived by the evangelist from the same written source. In 3:20–35 a parallel seems to be drawn between the kinsfolk of Jesus, who declare that he is beside himself and apparently seek to prevent him from continuing his work, and the scribes from Jerusalem, who attribute his supernatural power to the inspiration of the prince of the demons; in 6:1–6a there is the story of the rejection in the *patris*,

[2] Cf. Lightfoot, *op. cit.*, pp. 117f., and N. B. Stonehouse, *The Witness of Matthew and Mark to Christ*, pp. 43ff.

which ought perhaps to be understood as an anticipation of the final rejection at Jerusalem; in 7:1–23 Jesus meets the adverse criticism of the Pharisees and certain of the scribes by enunciating the principle of inward purity; and in 8:11–12 Jesus refuses to comply with the demand of the Pharisees for a sign from heaven. It is true that in 3:22 and in 7:1 the opposition proceeds from Jerusalem; on the other hand, in 3:7–8 the great multitude, attracted by Jesus' supernatural power to heal, is drawn from Judaea and from Jerusalem (cf. 1:5) as well as from the Galilean region.[3]

4. In a certain measure, is not Jesus well received in Jerusalem? From 11:18; 12:12; and 14:2 we gather that the Jewish religious authorities cannot take open action against Jesus because the people generally are favorably disposed toward him; and in 12:37 it is noticed that the multitude likes to listen to the Lord's teaching. Admittedly, the multitude becomes definitely hostile in 15:13–14, but this is only because it has been stirred up by the chief priests (15:11).

5. In view of the distinction made in 11:18; 12:12 and 14:2, may it not be that St. Mark associates Jerusalem with hostility only in so far as he thinks of it as the seat of the religious authorities?

6. Apart from the healing of blind Bartimaeus and the cursing of the fig tree, no miracle is ascribed to Jesus in the sections devoted to the Jerusalem period. But this may be due simply to the evangelist's preoccupation with the passion: in the eleventh chapter the desire to illustrate the grounds of the conflict between Jesus and the religious leaders has become greater than the desire to offer proof of the Messiah's power as a worker of miracles.

7. Perhaps St. Mark does not mean to restrict the Jerusalem ministry to a period of two days.[4] He may even think of the

---

[3] Of course Lightfoot recognizes the presence of the note of disaffection or hostility in St. Mark's Galilean section (*op. cit.,* p. 130); but he does not seem to place sufficient stress upon it.

[4] See above, Chapter 9, n. 19; cf. Lightfoot, *op. cit.,* pp. 125f.

Lord as teaching daily in the temple for a week or two. If this
is so, only a sample of such teaching is presented in 12:13ff. (cf.
the wording of 12:35a).

8. No confession by a demon is assigned to the last two main
sections of the gospel. But such a mode of supernatural testimony to the Messiahship is hardly required after Peter's confession at Caesarea Philippi (8:29) and the divine confirmation
of it at the transfiguration (9:7).

9. According to St. Mark's doctrine of the secret, there can
be no open revelation of the Messiahship and therefore no public
proclamation of the gospel in Galilee or elsewhere prior to the
resurrection. But, as we have seen, the evangelist does not apply
the doctrine consistently, the consequence being that there is a
temporary disclosure of the fact of the Messiahship from time
to time. And it is of interest to notice that the most impressive
example of the tendency to overstep the limits of secrecy occurs
not in the account of the Galilean ministry but in the passion
narrative at 14:62.

10. There are reasons for thinking that the promise of a postresurrection reunion in Galilee [5] primarily refers to one or more
appearances of the risen Lord in that region, not to the final

[5] 14:28; 16:7. Cf. above, Chapter 10, n. 33. In his paper in *J.T.S.*, n.s.,
V (1954), 3ff., C. F. Evans proposes that the promise in 14:28 should
be taken to mean "I will lead you out into the Gentile world"—that
is, the primary reference is to the church's world-wide mission, a point
made explicit in Matt. 28:19 and Luke 24:47. In Mark 16:7, however,
it is the fact that the disciples will see the Lord (not that they will proclaim the gospel) to which attention is drawn, and this suggests that the
evangelist has christophanies in mind. Nevertheless, it is possible that
the universalism of the apostolic faith (in contradistinction to the religious nationalism which had its headquarters in Jerusalem) was not
far from St. Mark's thought when he wrote 14:28 and 16:7. He may
well have held that certain experiences of the risen Lord in Galilee constituted the source whence effective Christianity proceeded to spread
among the nations of the world; and it may be recalled that in his accounts of the confession and the transfiguration he may be associating
the Galilean area or the region beyond Galilee with the universal character of the apostolic faith; cf. above, Chapter 7, n. 1.

manifestation of the Son of Man with great power and glory:

a) The first evangelist takes the promise to refer to an appearance of the risen Lord (Matt. 28:7ff.).

b) The verb "to see" is used in the active voice, as well as in the passive, of experiences of the risen Lord (see I Cor. 9:1; John 20:18).

c) If the promise refers directly to the parousia, its wording is somewhat strange. Why should it be said that the Lord will *go ahead of* his disciples into Galilee?

d) It is likely that St. Mark would connect the final manifestation of the Son of Man with any particular locality on the earth? In early Christian eschatology the parousia is a tremendous cosmic event which is evidently commensurate with the creation of the heavens and the earth; it means the termination of the present order of existence and the commencement of a new and transcendent order. Hence all the people of the earth, whatever the region of their habitation, will be at once aware of its occurrence (cf. Rev. 1:7). There is no mention of any particular locality of the earth either in 13:26 or in 14:62; and, according to 13:24–25, the parousia will be immediately preceded by what appear to be celestial signs of the dissolution of the universe.

e) It is possible that St. Mark regards the so-called triumphal entry as the fulfillment of the popular Jewish belief that the Messiah would make his appearance on the Mount of Olives, which is before Jerusalem on the east.[6] But if this is so, St. Mark's doctrine does not differ from that of T. Zeb. 9:8b as regards topography.[7]

---

[6] See Zech. 14:4. Cf. above, Chapter 9.

[7] It should be observed that in his later work, *The Gospel Message of St. Mark*, pp. 106ff., Lightfoot presents a modified interpretation of Mark 14:28; 16:7. These passages, so it is there argued, indicate that the risen Lord will take up again the ministry started in Galilee; but he will then operate in and through his disciples as a spiritual power unrestricted by his physical body, and the disciples themselves will pro-

claim the gospel with understanding and authority. Thus Lightfoot came to renounce the view that Mark 14:28 and 16:7 refer to the parousia, and in this matter, as he admits (*ibid.*, p. 106, n. 2), he was influenced by T. W. Manson, whose ideas on the subject are summarized in his study *The Servant-Messiah*, pp. 93ff. But Lightfoot continued (rightly, as I think) to hold that the object of the women's fear in Mark 16:8 was the divine revelation, whereas according to Manson they were afraid of human hostility, particularly on the part of Herod Antipas. A big city like Jerusalem was a safe hiding place, while in Galilee members of the new movement would have been immediately exposed and liquidated; and these considerations are alleged to provide sufficient explanation of the women's failure to deliver the message about returning to Galilee: the disciples did not go north because they had not been told, and therefore the resurrection christophanies took place in the Jerusalem region. Such an interpretation, however, is open to serious objections: (1) As far as St. Mark's own position is concerned, the message would seem to have already been delivered in 14:28. (2) It is unlikely that 14:28 and 16:7 would have been retained in the tradition if Peter's experience of the risen Lord (however we understand it) had not taken place in Galilee. (3) In 16:8 we read that the women said nothing to *anybody*, and this suggests that the passage does not admit of an ordinary rationalistic explanation of the sort proposed by Manson; for if they had really not said anything to anyone the story would not have been included in the tradition; in Markan usage "fear" can be a quasi-technical theological term; see above, Chapter 8, n. 2. (4) The story of the empty tomb probably was not included in the earliest form of the passion narrative; it finds no mention in the extant writings of St. Paul, and it has all the appearance of being a legendary development based partly on the Jewish doctrine of the resurrection of the body; thus the dramatic announcement of the young man and the women's reaction to it can scarcely be treated as items in a plain historical record.

II

The Last Supper

THE introduction to St. Mark's passion narrative raises a grave historical difficulty, since the chronological implication of 14:2 seems to be at variance with what is expressly stated in verses 12–16 of the same chapter. As previously suggested,[1] it is not unlikely that verses 1–2 once had their immediate sequel in verses 10–11 and that these four verses constituted the introduction to the passion narrative in the form in which St. Mark received it. Moreover, those who were responsible for the tradition would scarcely have any direct cognizance of the private deliberations of the hierarchs or of the intentions of Judas, and hence the information contained in verses 1–2 and 10–11 was probably the result of an inference from events as they actually took place. To use the words of Dibelius:

It was known that the Sanhedrin had got Jesus into their power before the feast by a *tour de force* and that the arresting party had made use of Judas a disciple of Jesus in the undertaking. Thus they must have decided upon the former and agreed upon the latter; and

---

[1] See above, Chapter 10.

258

there is nothing else in those four verses. They . . . only offer what could be deduced.[2]

But if Jesus was arrested before the feast began, the last supper could not have been a paschal meal; he was already dead when the passover was eaten. On the other hand, in verses 12–16 it is assumed that the last supper *was* a paschal meal, and we may reasonably suppose, therefore, that verses 12–16 were not part of the passion narrative as it was constituted when verses 1–2 were composed to provide it with an introduction. Perhaps, like verses 3–9 (the story of the anointing at Bethany),[3] verses 12–16 owe their place in the narrative to the evangelist himself, who overlooked the fact that the last supper could not have been a passover meal on the chronology implied in verses 1–2.[4]

For the sake of clarity, some reference should be made at this point to contemporary Jewish procedure in connection with the feast of the passover.[5] Soon after midday on the fourteenth Nisan (the first month of the Jewish year) the slaughter of the passover animals began in the temple and went on almost till sunset. This period was known as the preparation. After sunset, that is, on Jewish reckoning, during the evening of the fifteenth Nisan, the paschal victims were consumed at a special meal. This meal was no longer held in the temple area, but it had to take

---

[2] *From Tradition to Gospel*, p. 186; cf. Wellhausen, *Einleitung*, pp. 43, 133, and Lightfoot, *History and Interpretation*, p. 132.

[3] We are inclined to think that the account of the nocturnal trial (14:55–65) and the story of the empty tomb (16:1–8) also owe their presence in the framework of the passion narrative to St. Mark; cf. below, Chapter 12, n. 19.

[4] The variant reading of D in 14:2 (". . . lest haply during the feast there shall be a tumult of the people") may be understood as the result of an attempt to remove the inconsistency in question; for it explains why the hierarchs contemplate secret action in a way which suggests that the arrest of Jesus is to take place during (rather than before) the feast.

[5] Cf. Lightfoot, *op. cit.*, pp. 132ff., and G. B. Gray, *Sacrifice in the Old Testament*, pp. 384ff., 393ff.

place somewhere in Jerusalem. The fifteenth Nisan was also the first complete day of the feast of unleavened bread, which according to the requirements of scripture lasted for seven days. But for some time there had been a growing tendency to regard the preparation as an integral part of the celebrations, and, despite the fact that the paschal rites were over by midnight of the fifteenth Nisan, the terms "passover" and "unleavened bread" could be applied indifferently to the whole of the festal period from noon of the fourteenth Nisan onwards (cf. Mark 14:1). Thus no real difficulty is raised by the wording of the opening statement of Mark 14:12 ("On the first day of unleavened bread, when they sacrificed the passover [6] . . ."). As is well known, the written law emphasizes that the paschal meal is a commemoration of the providential emancipation of the children of Israel from their bondage in Egypt, but by the time of Jesus it had also come to acquire a pronounced eschatological significance; the meal celebrated a deliverance in the past which was the pledge of a mightier deliverance to take place in the future. During the afternoon of the fourteenth Nisan, then, the passover animals were slain, no leavened bread was eaten, and it was usual to abstain from ordinary work. During the whole of the fifteenth Nisan all "servile work" was forbidden by scripture (see Num. 28:18), and this had come to cover most ordinary occupations. It should also be noticed that sometime before midday on the sixteenth Nisan the sheaf of firstfruits was offered in the temple.

On turning to the fourth gospel, it is interesting to find that its evidence is consistently in line with the tradition which seems to be represented in Mark 14:1-2, and with the Jewish paschal customs just outlined. Thus in John 13:1-2 the last supper takes place before the feast of the passover; in John 13:29 some of those present at the last supper suppose that Judas goes out in order to buy what is needed for the feast; in John 18:28 the

[6] In Jewish usage, too, the term "passover" could be applied to the victim consumed at the paschal meal as well as to the festival itself.

Jews who bring Jesus to Caiaphas do not enter the praetorium lest they should incur ceremonial defilement, which would prevent them from partaking of the paschal meal; in John 19:14 it is the preparation of the passover and about the sixth hour when Jesus is handed over to be crucified; and in John 19:42 Jesus is buried during the preparation, the following day (as it happened that year) being a sabbath (cf. John 19:31). According to the fourth gospel, therefore, the Lord was crucified in the course of the afternoon of the fourteenth Nisan, when the passover animals were being slaughtered in the temple, and St. John discerns in this coincidence an important symbolic significance: the crucified Messiah is the paschal Lamb of the new dispensation (John 1:29) whose legs must not be broken (John 19:31, 33, 36; cf. Ex. 12:46; Num. 9:12). And St. Paul seems to have the same coincidence in mind in I Cor. 5:7, where he writes that "our passover also has been sacrificed, [even] Christ." Moreover, if the discovery of the empty tomb was made at an early hour on the day after the sabbath (John 20:1), that is, on Sunday the sixteenth Nisan, the resurrection on the third day evidently took place on the same morning as the offering of the firstfruits in the temple; and St. Paul may be thinking of this coincidence in I Cor. 15:20–23, where he describes the risen Lord as "the firstfruits of them that are asleep."

On the other hand, we gather from Mark 14:12–16 that the last supper was a paschal meal, and from a historical point of view this is somewhat surprising. For it means that the betrayal, arrest, and crucifixion all fell on the fifteenth Nisan, a day on which the Jews were required to suspend all ordinary work and activity. But nowhere else in St. Mark's passion narrative is there any certain evidence that the last supper was a passover. For we cannot be sure that the hymn sung at the conclusion of the last supper (14:26) was the paschal *hallel*; [7] and it should be noticed that there is no reference to the eating of a passover animal in

[7] Cf. above, Chapter 9, n. 13.

14:17–25, and that, apart from 14:12–16 and the corresponding passages in the gospels of St. Matthew and St. Luke, there is nothing in the synoptic tradition which definitely implies that the last supper took place in Jerusalem.[8]

It is plain, therefore, that two conflicting traditions were current in the apostolic church concerning the date of the crucifixion in relation to the passover. The fourth evangelist and, as it appears, St. Paul take the view that the Lord was crucified during the preparation, himself being the paschal Lamb of the new dispensation, and in this respect they seem to be supported by the synoptic tradition, apart from Mark 14:12–16 and its parallels. In the last-mentioned passages the opposing view is taken that the last supper was a passover meal, from which originated the Christian eucharist.

Many attempts have been made to explain this contradiction on historical grounds,[9] but no such explanation has won general acceptance among scholars. Thus Chwolson puts forward the interesting argument [10] that the phrase "between the two evenings" in Lev. 23:5; Ex. 12:6; Num. 9:3 was interpreted strictly in the time of Jesus and was taken to mean "during the period of evening twilight," and so, if the fifteenth Nisan fell on a sabbath, it could be maintained that the preparation of the paschal victims, if it took place at the usual time, would contravene the laws of the sabbath. Chwolson therefore suggests that, when the fifteenth Nisan fell on a sabbath, the slaughter of the lambs was put back twenty-four hours and that this gave rise to two conflicting judgments regarding the proper evening for eating them. Jesus followed the Pharisaic ruling that they should be eaten on the Thursday evening, whereas the Sadducean ruling, which was followed by the Jewish authorities who took part

---

[8] In the fourth gospel it seems to be implied that the last supper did take place in Jerusalem; see John 12:12; 18:1.

[9] Cf. Rawlinson, *St. Mark*, pp. 262ff.

[10] See his *Das letzte Passamahl Christi und der Tag seines Todes*.

in the trial of Jesus (cf. John 18:28), was that they should still be eaten on the Friday evening, the fifteenth Nisan, as the scriptures required. It is probable, however, that Chwolson is mistaken in supposing that the phrase "between the two evenings" was interpreted in a strict sense during the lifetime of Jesus, for there is good contemporary evidence [11] that the preparation of the passover began soon after midday on the fourteenth Nisan, in which case the work entailed by the cooking of the paschal victims could be carried out without any infringement of the laws relating to the sabbath. And, apart from this consideration, it is always possible that when the fourteenth or the fifteenth Nisan coincided with a sabbath, the passover was regarded as abrogating the sabbath laws. Moreover, as we have already seen, the fourth evangelist expressly refers to the (Friday) afternoon on which the crucifixion took place as the time of the preparation.

Billerbeck seeks to avoid such difficulties as these and argues that the correct solution of the problem is to be found in a dispute between the Boethusians, an influential Sadducean family, and the Pharisees, respecting the proper interpretation of Lev. 23:9ff.[12] The former held that the offering of the firstfruits in the temple should always be made on the day immediately following the sabbath which fell in the feast of unleavened bread, that is, always on a Sunday; the latter, on the other hand, contended that the offering should always be made, irrespective of the day of the week, on the second day of unleavened bread since the first day of the feast counted as a sabbath. The first Nisan, which was fixed by observation of the moon, was officially determined by the calendar commission of the sanhedrin, and there is evidence that disputes sometimes arose regarding the validity of the official determination of the new moon, more particularly with reference to its bearing on the position of the

[11] See Philo, *De Septenario*, 18; cf. S.-B., II, 847.
[12] Cf. S.-B., II, 846ff.

fourteenth Nisan relatively to the sabbath. The Boethusians, in the interests of their interpretation of Lev. 23:9ff., were anxious that the fifteenth Nisan should fall on a sabbath, and Billerbeck argues that in the year of the crucifixion this was secured by means of a corrupt understanding with the calendar commission. The Pharisees raised objections, maintaining that the month really began a day earlier. The result was a compromise whereby the reckoning of the calendar commission was upheld for official purposes, while it was conceded that the Pharisees might, if they so desired, observe the passover on the day which, according to their reckoning, was the right one. Jesus and his disciples sided with the Pharisaic party, whereas the priesthood and the Jewish leaders who accused him before Pilate, being predominantly Sadducean, kept the official day.

Despite its erudition and ingenuity, however, Billerbeck's argument is no more convincing than that put forward by Chwolson. For, as Goguel pointed out,[13] it is unlikely that the judgment of the Pharisees on the matter in question would have had any practical value. The Sadducees were the masters of the temple and as such would control all that had to do with the sacrificing of the passover animals. Hence, even if the Pharisees had unanimously considered that the feast ought to be celebrated on a different day from that which had been fixed by the Sadducees, they would scarcely have had the opportunity to follow their convictions. In such a situation as Billerbeck contemplates, that is to say, the probability is that the Pharisees would have been obliged either to celebrate the passover at the official time or else to abstain from celebrating it altogether; and we may safely say that their devotion to the law would have rendered the latter alternative quite unacceptable to them. Furthermore, Biller-

---

[13] See *The Life of Jesus*, p. 433. But it should be noted that Goguel wrongly implies that the objection about to be made can be applied to Chwolson's hypothesis as well as to Billerbeck's. In Chwolson's view, there was agreement regarding the preparation.

beck's approach to the problem is governed by what appears to be an erroneous preconception. He thinks it incredible that there should be a real divergence of view in the tradition concerning the day of the death of Jesus and assumes that the correct solution must yield the result that the synoptists are right and that St. John is right.[14] Such an assumption, however, seems to be founded on a misunderstanding of the nature of the gospels, for the evangelists were not historians in the modern sense of the term, and the aim of those who were responsible for the preservation of the constituent gospel traditions was not to provide material for an accurate biography of Jesus, but to commend a doctrine of salvation. It may well be, therefore, that the divergence of view under consideration was a consequence of the church's doctrinal interpretation of the eucharistic rite.[15]

[14] See S.-B., II, 845. Two remarks ought to be made here: (1) Billerbeck apparently overlooks the fact that Mark 14:1f. seems to be in line with the tradition evinced in the fourth gospel. (2) There is no evidence for Billerbeck's assertion that the divergence of view regarding the day of the crucifixion existed in the earliest form of Christianity. The divergence is, as it seems, already present in the second gospel; but the second gospel does not represent the tradition in its earliest form.

[15] In Mlle A. Jaubert's article in *R.H.R.*, CXLVI (1954), 140ff. (cf. her later publication *La date de la cène: Calendrier biblique et liturgie chrétienne;* also, M. Black, *The Scrolls and Christian Origins*, pp. 199ff.) a renewed attempt is made to explain the early conflict respecting the date of the last supper on historical grounds. Mlle Jaubert points to the tradition common to the *Didascalia Apostolorum*, Epiphanius, and Victorinus, according to which Jesus was arrested on the Tuesday night preceding the Friday of the crucifixion; she also refers to the old sacerdotal calendar attested in the Book of Jubilees, which was upheld by certain priests who rejected the authority of the Hasmoneans, and which was preserved by the community at Qumran. This calendar, disregarding the phases of the moon, provided that the paschal meal should always be eaten on a Tuesday evening, and Mlle Jaubert conjectures that Jesus followed it in this connection. Hence there is no chronological discrepancy between St. Mark and St. John, for the former alludes to the passover of the old priestly calendar, the latter to the passover of the official system. This argument, however, is open to the same order of objections as those already raised against Billerbeck's; and other objec-

If, as we have already suggested, there was nothing corresponding to Mark 14:12–16 in the earliest form of the passion narrative, Jesus was probably arrested shortly before the Jews began to celebrate their feast of the passover.[16] It may be that the crucifixion, as St. John states, actually took place when the

---

tions which may be made against it are: (1) The evidence furnished by the *Didascalia* is confused and very late, belonging to the third century A.D. (2) The four evangelists are unanimous that the last supper and the arrest took place on the eve of the crucifixion. (3) Mlle Jaubert is inclined to be arbitrary in her treatment of the gospel material; for example, in the interests of her theory she is prepared to accept the historicity of Matt. 27:19 (the dream of Pilate's wife), though it has all the appearance of being a legendary development, but she discounts the historical value of John 18:28 (the Jews did not enter the praetorium lest through defilement they should be unable to eat the passover).

[16] It can hardly be said that J. Jeremias succeeds in establishing that the last supper was a passover meal in his scholarly study *Die Abendmahlsworte Jesu* (for a summary of his arguments, see his paper in *J.T.S.*, L [1949], 1ff.). (1) His rendering of μὴ ἐν τῇ ἑορτῇ (Mark 14:2) —"not in the presence of the festival crowd" is extremely forced: Luke 22:2 indicates that the third evangelist took the phrase in the usual sense (cf. below, n. 18). (2) Jeremias seeks to explain the synoptic inconsistencies with paschal laws (the carrying of arms, the meeting of the sanhedrin, the rending of the high priest's garments [a judicial formality], the purchase of linen, the burial, the preparation of spices) by reference to necessities of life or extraordinary circumstances covered by rabbinical pronouncements; but these rabbinical rulings may not all have been operative in the earlier part of the first century, and when the same line of argument is repeated time and time again it inevitably loses much of its original forcefulness. (3) Jeremias takes too easily for granted that what Jesus said at the last supper is authentically reproduced in the extant records: for instance, he contends that red wine (a paschal requirement) was used, since it is made to symbolize the Lord's blood; but it is unlikely that Jesus did in fact make the utterance ascribed to him in Mark 14:24 (cf. below, n. 26). (4) Jews should not have participated in the Roman trial at the passover (cf. John 18:28), and the argument that a Roman demand overruled the paschal regulations scarcely meets the difficulty; for certain Jewish leaders evidently took the initiative in the action against Jesus and could have arranged for the arrest to take place at a time convenient to them.

passover animals were being slain in the temple and that this coincidence was the immediate occasion of the analogical doctrine, already expressed in the writings of St. Paul, that the crucified Messiah is the paschal Lamb of the Christian dispensation. In any case, at a very early date in the history of the church the Messiah's death was interpreted in terms of the soteriology of sacrifice, and, in view of its great significance and the month of its occurrence, it is not surprising that it should have been thought of specifically as a paschal sacrifice and that the eucharist itself should have been construed as the Christian equivalent of the Jewish passover; for the bread consumed at the church's communion rite was taken to represent the body of the sacrificed Lord. Moreover, according to apostolic belief, the eucharist was a repetition of what took place at the last supper, and hence the last supper was not only the last earthly meal at which Jesus presided in the company of his disciples, but was also the first celebration of the Christian passover. This doctrine, however, involved an obvious difficulty, for the paschal Lamb of the new Israel was not yet sacrificed when the last supper took place. The crucifixion still belonged to the future and so, strictly speaking, the last supper could not have been the celebration of the Christian paschal feast. Perhaps it was precisely in order to avoid this difficulty that St. John decided not to include an account of the institution of the eucharist in his gospel, and perhaps it was partly for the same reason that St. Mark in 14:12–16 was induced to identify the last supper with the Jewish paschal celebration. Such an identification, we may presume, would be facilitated by the fact that the eucharist, like the paschal meal of the old dispensation, commemorated a saving event in the past which was interpreted as the pledge of God's expected deliverance of his people at the end of the existing historical order. Indeed, as Lightfoot suggested,[17] a desire to bring out the eschatological significance of the Messiah's death may have been

[17] See *op. cit.*, pp. 140f.

the principal motive behind St. Mark's emphasis on the paschal character of the last supper in 14:12–16; and seeing that the Christian passover was not yet sacrificed when the eucharist was instituted, the evangelist came to represent the last supper as a Jewish paschal meal, not realizing, as it seems, that this mode of representation was inconsistent with the traditional introduction to the passion narrative.[18]

It would appear, then, that in the earliest form of the tradition the last supper was not a passover celebration, and Dibelius was probably right in insisting that the essential feature of the proceedings is indicated by the words "and they all drank of it" in Mark 14:23, the fundamental idea being that all drink of one cup, just as they have all eaten of one loaf.[19] For on the assump-

[18] St. Luke evidently recognized this inconsistency and avoided it in his own narrative by excluding from Luke 22:1f. (/Mark 14:1f.) all reference to the decision not to take action during the feast. It ought also to be observed that in Luke 22:14–16 St. Luke provides a most ingenious connecting link; referring to these verses, Lightfoot (*op. cit.*, p. 168) writes; "We may almost describe these words as the despair of commentators. They appear to support the view of the preceding verses (Luke 22:7–13/Mark 14:12–16) that the last supper was a passover, and thus serve to bind the narrative together; but at the same time they certainly suggest that our Lord did not partake of it, and in this way they help to explain the absence of any passover reference in the story of the meal itself." Luke 22:17f. would seem to form part of this suture composed by the evangelist: as Jesus did not eat of the passover lamb, so he did not drink of the passover cup. For further evidence of St. Luke's concern to present a connected and coherent narrative, cf. below, Chapter 12, n. 27.

[19] Cf. Dibelius, *op. cit.*, p. 206. The church soon came to esteem St. Matthew's gospel more highly than St. Mark's, and, as in other instances, it is possible that the text of Mark 14:22 in most MSS has been affected by the corresponding passage in the first gospel (Matt. 26:26). For, as Turner pointed out, while in the account of the institution of the cup St. Mark's text differs sensibly from St. Matthew's, in the case of the institution of the bread their texts are almost identical, save in the Codex Bobiensis (k), the unique fragment of the earliest Latin version as used by St. Cyprian; its text of Mark 14:22ff. runs: ". . . he took bread and blessed and brake and gave to them, and they all ate of it; and he said to

tion that the distribution of the bread and the dispensing of the cup are primarily communion rites, it is not difficult to understand how the eucharist came to possess the relatively complicated significance which it already has in I Cor. 10:16–17 and 11:23–26.[20] It may be, as Otto maintained, that the custom of holding communion or fraternal meals was fairly widespread among the Jews of the period.[21] Presumably, such a custom

---

them, This is my body. And he took a cup and blessed and gave to them, and they all drank of it; and he said to them, This is my blood. . . ." If this is the true text of Mark 14:22ff., St. Mark recorded the institution of the bread and that of the cup on precisely the same lines, and St. Matthew made the same alteration in both, replacing the statement that "all ate" / "all drank," by the command, "Take, eat" / "Drink" (see N.C.H.S., pt. 3, p. 107). Thus the k reading in Mark 14:22 ("and they all ate of it") may be correct, and this lends support to the suggestion made by Dibelius.

[20] I Cor. 11:23–25 and Mark 14:22–25 seem to represent variants of the same aetiological account of the eucharistic rite, which was handed down in the cultus as an independent tradition. In view of Mark 14:18a ("And as they reclined and were eating"), Mark 14:22a ("And as they were eating") is hardly required by its context in the gospel; hence it may have constituted the introduction to the tradition as St. Mark received it.

[21] See R. Otto, *The Kingdom of God and the Son of Man*, pp. 277ff. There is evidence that already in the Greek period Jews were attaching much importance to consecrated common meals, which, for increasing numbers, were replacing sacrifices (so Oskar Holtzmann in *Die Mishna, Traktat Berakot*, p. 80). According to Josephus, *Ant.* 14, 10, 8, certain Jews should be allowed to hold communal suppers as their customs require; cf. Josephus, *Bell.* 2, 8, 5 for the great significance ascribed by the Essenes to their table fellowship. In connection with food and eating the rabbis came to distinguish "associates" (*chaberīm*) from "the people of the land"; and A. Geiger (*Urschrift und Übersetzungen*, pp. 121ff.) argued that the "associations" (*chabūrōth*) originated as priestly brotherhoods which celebrated their unity in fraternal meals, the most sacred of these meals being the passover which, according to Josephus (*Bell.* 6, 9, 3), was eaten in a *phratria* of some ten to twenty persons. Cf. I. Elbogen, *Festschrift zu Israel Lewy*, p. 180, and *Der jüdische Gottesdienst*, pp. 107ff., by the same scholar; cf. also the thesis of Lietzmann set forth in his *Messe und Herrenmahl*. On the other hand, A. Büchler (*Der galiläische 'Am-ha-'Ares*) contended that the *chaber*,

would bear witness to the survival of the ancient Semitic notion of the bond of salt, which is elucidated in the following passage from Robertson Smith's classic work:

If I have eaten the smallest portion of food with a man, I have nothing further to fear from him; 'there is salt between us', and he is bound, not only to do me no harm, but to help and defend me as if I were his brother.[22]

The same general conception seems to be exemplified in I Cor. 10:17, where St. Paul writes:

Because there is one loaf, we who are many are one body, for we all partake of the one loaf.[23]

---

separated from the mass of people as a strict observer of the regulations for levitical purity, did not appear on the scene until after the failure of the revolt in 136 A.D. But the evidence does not seem to justify this view, and it is reasonable to suppose with Billerbeck (S.-B., II, 507) that at the latest in the first century of our era certain elements in Pharisaic circles were moved to form *chabūrōth* whose members, in the interests of ceremonial purity, pledged themselves to limit their dealings with the so-called people of the land. The argument of Jeremias (*op. cit.*, p. 26) that such associations did not hold ordinary meals together (but see E. Gaugler, *Das Abendmahl im Neuen Testament*, p. 30) would seem to have no bearing upon the question of the nature of the last supper, for those who partook of it certainly were not *chaberīm* in the technical rabbinical sense. Accordingly, when due attention is paid to certain features of the cultural environment, one is constrained to conclude that Jesus and his disciples may well have formed a religious confraternity whose solidarity and distinctive sense of divine mission were confirmed and promoted in habitual table fellowship of a sacred character; and it is noteworthy that the word κοινωνός (cf. I Cor. 10:16) was the Greek equivalent of the Hebrew term *chaber*—cf. the article by G. V. Jordan in *J.B.L.*, LXVII (1948), 111ff. For an interesting account of a formal meal in ancient Judaism, see S.-B., IV, pt. 2, 611ff.

[22] See *The Religion of the Semites*, p. 270. T. W. Manson was of the opinion that the saying of the Lord in Mark 9:50b should be understood in the light of this old Semitic notion; see his essay in *Christian Worship* (ed. Micklem), pp. 48f.

[23] For this rendering, cf. H. H. Rowley's review of the work by Ernst Percy (*Der Leib Christi in den paulinischen Homologumena und An-*

However this may be, there can be little doubt that in the milieu of primitive Christianity the bond of table fellowship had a much deeper significance than it normally has in modern western civilization. It was only natural, therefore, that the last occasion on which Jesus ate and drank with his disciples should have been regarded as an event of special importance, which marked the termination of an epoch of communion between the Lord and his followers.

But as we have previously observed,[24] besides being a valedictory meal, the last supper had also come to be regarded as the occasion of the first celebration of the Christian eucharist, and this rite served to compensate in some measure for the Messiah's absence from his followers during the interim period extending from the time of the passion to the awaited meal of reunion in the consummated kingdom. After the crucifixion had taken place, although the disciples could no longer eat and drink with their Master, yet, thanks ultimately to the postresurrection christophanies, they felt that their fellowship with him was preserved and extended. They continued to take part in a fraternal meal, and hence we might say that they formed one body in the eucharistic bread (cf. I Cor. 10:17). As a definition of their fellowship, however, such a description would be unsatisfactory, since it could be applied equally well to other religious confraternities. What distinguished the church from all other associ-

---

tilegomena) in *Ex.T.*, LVIII (1946–47), 221. The Dead Sea Scrolls provide further evidence of the importance which Jews of the period attached to sacred meals of fellowship, and in this case the ritual eating and drinking have an eschatological setting. But as with the Qumran baptismal rites (cf. Chapter 1, n. 21), there are significant differences which make it quite unlikely that the Christian eucharist was derived from the Qumran community; for example, there is no suggestion in the recently discovered texts that the consecrated bread of the communal meal was identified with the body of a messianic and saving Lord of the cultus. In general, cf. M. Black, *The Scrolls and Christian Origins*, pp. 102ff., 169.

[24] Cf. above, Chapter 10.

ations was the fact that its members were united by a common faith in the Messiahship of Jesus, to whom they had committed themselves in loyalty and obedience. They belonged to the Lord by faith, and hence we might say that they formed one body in the Messiah (cf. Rom. 12:5). Moreover, during the period of the earthly ministry the community of the disciples had its rallying point or tangible center in the bodily presence of the Master, and subsequently the corporate life of the church had its tangible center in the bread of the holy table. Thus the eucharistic bread served as an agency of integration in the society of the elect, and therefore its function was analogous to that of the Messiah himself, and, more particularly, to that of the Messiah in his incarnate form. It is this analogy, as it seems, which is brought out in the formula "This is my body" (Mark 14:22), where, indeed, it is emphasized to the point of identification, the bread being actually assimilated to the corporeal life of its distributor. Such a formula would naturally suggest that every celebration of the eucharist testified to a mystical continuation of the Messiah's incarnate life. The essential spirit of the Messiah resided in the blessed bread just as it had previously resided in the physical body of Jesus of Nazareth; and since the bread was consumed by believers, it would be felt that the bodies of the elect were dwelling places of the Lord; and, as St. Paul sought to make clear, such a conception had its ethical implications (see I Cor. 6:13, 19f.). But the church itself no less than the eucharistic bread was thought to be the body of the Messiah, and so it would be felt not only that the Lord abode in the bodies of the faithful, but also that the faithful, as members of his body, dwelt in the Lord (cf. I Cor. 6:15; John 6:56). In the light of these considerations, therefore, we may safely state that the institution of the eucharist represented not so much the founding of a fellowship as the provision of tangible means for its continuance and extension in the new situation brought about by the Messiah's death.

The Last Supper

The development of a sacrificial interpretation of the crucifixion would tend to confirm the doctrine that the eucharistic bread was one with the Messiah's body. For, in the first place, the Lord gave the bread to his disciples when he was about to give his physical life for the redemption of many; and, in the second place, under the old dispensation the flesh of the paschal victim was eaten at a special meal, and this would suggest that the flesh of the paschal Lamb of the new Israel was eaten at the eucharist, the Christian equivalent of the Jewish passover celebration. It is important to observe, however, that there is no reference to the sacrificial doctrine in St. Mark's version of the utterance accompanying the distribution of the bread, whereas in I Cor. 11:24 the words "which [is] for you" are added to the formula "This is my body"—and presumably this addition would be meant to imply that the Messiah's body had been sacrificed for the salvation of all Christian communicants. On the other hand, there is no reference to the soteriology of sacrifice in St. Paul's version of the utterance accompanying the dispensing of the cup, whereas in Mark 14:24 we read of the blood that is "poured out for many"[25]—a phrase which is reminiscent of Isa. 53:12, where it is written of the suffering Servant that "he poured out his soul unto death" and that "he bore the sin of many" (cf. Mark 10:45).

Thus our two earliest accounts of the institution of the eucharist have the idea of sacrifice in different places, and this suggests that the idea perhaps made no appearance at all in the common tradition from which I Cor. 11:23–25 and Mark 14:22–25 may have ultimately been derived. Furthermore, it is possible that the person who was responsible for introducing the sacrificial interpretation into Mark 14:24 (it may have been the

[25] St. Matthew adds "unto remission of sins" (Matt. 26:28) and does not allude to the remission of sins in connection with John's baptism (Matt. 3:1ff.; cf. Mark 1:4); cf. Heb. 9:22 ("apart from shedding of blood there is no remission").

second evangelist himself) transformed the whole utterance accompanying the dispensing of the cup, for it is most unlikely that a member of a primitive Jewish-Christian community would have identified the wine in the cup with the blood of the Lord.[26] On the other hand, the form of the utterance in I Cor. 11:25—"This cup is [representative of] the new covenant [which is sealed] by my blood"[27]—raises no such difficulty and was probably formulated as a fulfillment of Jer. 31:30 (E.T., 31:31), where the prophet envisages a new covenant which Yahweh will make with the house of Israel and with the house of Judah (cf. II Cor. 3:1ff.). But the person who made the supposed transformation seems to have been influenced partly by the report in Ex. 24:8 that Moses ratified the Sinaitic covenant by sprinkling the blood of sacrificed oxen on the people (cf. Heb. 9:11ff.), and partly by an aesthetic tendency to bring the account of the institution of the cup into close parallelism with the account of the institution of the loaf.[28] Accordingly, we may reasonably infer that the early tradition at the basis of I Cor. 11:23–25 and of Mark 14:22–25 had "This is my body" without

[26] Cf. Dibelius, *op. cit.*, p. 207. The eating of flesh with blood in it was, according to Jewish belief, a monstrous offence, for the commission of which a person was liable to extirpation from among the people of God: see Klausner, *Jesus of Nazareth*, p. 329; Montefiore, *The Synoptic Gospels*, I, 332; Moore, *Judaism*, II, 74. V. Taylor (*Jesus and His Sacrifice*, pp. 134f.) argues that Jesus invited his followers to drink wine not as symbolizing his blood but as representing the life he surrendered; it remains, however, that in Mark 14:23f. the equivalence between the Lord's blood and the contents of the cup (which they all drink) is plainly involved, and it is difficult to believe that such an idea actually came to expression in the upper room.

[27] That is, presumably, by the Lord's death.

[28] For this tendency, cf. above, n. 19. It is already evident in I Cor. 10:16, which may imply that St. Paul was free from the characteristic Jewish aversion to the idea of drinking blood. It is possible, however, that the "communion of the blood of Christ" signified a mystical participation in the Lord's sufferings and death; cf. Rom. 6:5; 8:17; Phil. 3:10.

"which [is] for you" and "This cup is the new covenant in my blood" rather than "This is my blood of the covenant which is poured out for many." As for the commands, "Do this in remembrance of me" (I Cor. 11:24) and "Do this, as often as you drink [it], in remembrance of me" (I Cor. 11:25), the probability is that they were absent from the primitive tradition since, like the words "which [is] for you," they do not occur in St. Mark's recension.

That the institution of the eucharist had its *raison d'être* in the Messiah's imminent departure from this life is indicated in Mark 14:25, where Jesus declares that he will never again drink of the fruit of the vine until that day when he drinks it new in the kingdom of God. This saying, with its typically Jewish turn of phrase, probably belonged to the old tradition of the rite.[29] Presumably it meant that the disciples would continue to drink wine together and that Jesus would not rejoin them in their drinking before his parousia in glory.[30] But though the interim table fellowship of the elect would be "without the Lord" in a physical sense, it was believed that it would be "with him" in a mystical sense. For the bread was distributed as the body of the Messiah, and this implied that the eucharist was

[29] It is true that the declaration does not appear in St. Paul's recension, but the comment which he makes in I Cor. 11:26 ("For as often as you eat this bread and drink the cup you proclaim the Lord's death until he comes") suggests that the eucharistic tradition with which he was acquainted gave some form of expression to the eschatological expectation that the rite would have its fulfillment in the fellowship of the consummated kingdom. Doubtless the term *new* would here be understood by St. Mark in an eschatological sense (cf. above, Chapter 10, n. 28); as S. E. Johnson puts it, "everything in the coming age will be a new creation" (*A Commentary on the Gospel according to St. Mark*, p. 232). On the other hand, as I. Rabinowitz informs me, it could be that the καινόν in this case arose from a mistranslation of an Aramaic original *běchedwěthā'* ("joyously"), which was confused with *běchadtūthā'* ("newly").

[30] The idea of a reunion in the consummated kingdom is made explicit in Matt. 26:29, where the words "with you" are added.

founded to provide outward and visible means for the continuation of the disciples' fellowship with their Lord after the days
of his flesh had come to an end. Moreover, since the communion
acts of the institution presuppose the imminence of the passion,
it was only natural that they should come to be construed as
symbolic preenactments of the crucifixion. The breaking of the
bread, for example, came to signify the breaking of the Messiah's body in violent death; [31] but in this instance, as the fourth
evangelist perhaps wished to point out in John 19:36, such a
mode of interpretation did not harmonize very well with the
paschal symbolism.[32]

Accordingly, whether or not it was a *kiddush*,[33] the last supper,
simply as the last of a series of consecrated meals which Jesus
had enjoyed in the fellowship of his disciples,[34] would acquire
a special significance. It was a valedictory supper held in dramatic circumstances, and it could hardly have failed to impress

[31] Cf. the variant "which is *broken* for you" in I Cor. 11:24.

[32] In St. Luke's account of the last supper (Luke 22:14–20) the part
which deals with the institution proper (vv. 19f.) seems to betray a development in the tradition beyond the points reached in the Pauline and
Markan recensions. For example, the notion of sacrifice is evinced in
the utterance concerning the loaf ("which is given for you") as well as
in the utterance concerning the cup ("which is poured out for you").
Of course this does not necessarily mean that St. Luke was acquainted
with I Cor. 11:23–25, but only that he presents a more elaborate variant
of the eucharistic tradition than St. Paul or St. Mark. Vv. 14–18 seem to
be a connecting link composed by St. Luke (cf. above, n. 18); v. 16,
like v. 18, probably has its basis in Mark 14:25. The evangelist appears
to have introduced the passover lamb and the passover cup into this
elaborate suture, the result being that his account of the meal includes
four ritual acts. And on this view the elaborate variant readings in our
textual authorities for Luke 22:15–20 may be described as attempts to
lessen the number of the four acts either by changing the arrangement
or by deletion; see Dibelius, *op. cit.*, p. 211.

[33] See, for example, W. O. E. Oesterley, *The Jewish Background of
the Christian Liturgy*, pp. 167ff.

[34] Cf. Luke 24:30f., where the risen Jesus is discerned in the act of
breaking bread; cf. also Mark 6:41; 8:6, 19.

itself with particular forcefulness upon the minds of the faithful who were privileged to be present on such a momentous occasion. But if we may trust Mark 14:25 the celebration was something more than a communion signifying a valediction; it was meant to prefigure a promised reunion in the glory of the consummated kingdom. So, after the postresurrection christophanies, when fellowship among the disciples was renewed in the eucharist of the primitive church, the sacred meal, besides being retrospective as a memorial of the Messiah's voluntary humiliation, retained an eschatological meaning; and such a combination of ideas helps to explain how it should have come to be regarded as the Christian counterpart of the Jewish passover, for the latter also combined a backward with a forward reference, being at once a reminder of a saving event in the past and of a still more glorious event that would take place in the future. On the whole, however, it is perhaps of greater importance to notice that, on the basis of the chronology of the fourth gospel (a chronology which may also be implied in Mark 14:2), the crucifixion took place at the time of the preparation when the passover lambs were being slain in the temple; for such a coincidence would naturally suggest that Jesus was the passover Lamb of the new dispensation (I Cor. 5:7; John 19:31, 36).

As we understand the matter, therefore, the eucharist was primarily a religious meal of communion; the members of the holy fellowship were all one body as they partook of one loaf and of one cup. But paschal associations soon complicated thought on the subject, a remarkable consequence being that the eucharistic bread came to be construed as the body of the Lord. Thus in apostolic belief the Messiah came to fulfill a dual role: besides presiding over the celebration, he is also one with the sacred bread which is consumed by Christian communicants. A second factor which may have been involved concerns the parallelism between the unifying function of the physical presence of Jesus (his corporeal existence) during his earthly life and the unifying function performed by the eucharistic bread. In I Cor. 10:17, as we have seen, St. Paul gives expression to the idea that the solidarity of believers comes about through their togetherness at the holy table; their oneness is somehow realized through their partaking of the one loaf. Thus, just as the bodily presence of the Messiah had been the rallying point of the fraternity of the disciples prior to the crucifixion, so in the interim period between the crucifixion and the parousia in glory the bread of the holy table is the center and focus of Christian fellowship. A third factor which ought to be mentioned in this connection is the analogy between the Messiah's act of giving the bread and his act of giving himself sacrificially for the redemption of humanity (Mark 10:45; 14:22; I Cor. 11:24; Gal. 2:20): as the loaf is broken and given to communicants, so the Lord had surrendered his physical life in the fulfillment of his saving mission in the world.

Even if red wine was used, its identification with the blood of the Messiah is perhaps not so easy to understand as the identification of the bread with his body—at all events, on the basis of current Jewish ideas and practices. Hellenistic influence may have made itself felt at this point. It should be observed, however, that the identification could have come about partly through a natural urge within the early Christian communities to bring the eucharistic cup into line with the eucharistic bread. In Mark 14:24 the saying over the cup runs, "This is my blood of the covenant which is shed for many"—an utterance which was probably meant to refer back to the blood with which Moses sealed the Sinaitic covenant; then follows in verse 25 the eschatological pronouncement envisaging the ultimate reunion. On the other hand, in I Cor. 11:25 the wine is not equated with the Lord's blood; it is affirmed, "This cup is the new covenant in my blood"—an utterance reminiscent of Jeremiah's doctrine of a new covenant and intended to indicate that the death of Jesus established the spiritual life of the new Israel.

Although speculation of this kind can be dangerous, it may perhaps be tentatively suggested that these three sayings over the cup reflect three distinct stages of a not-unnatural liturgical development which took place in primitive Christianity. The eschatological pronouncement would represent the first, the utterance about the new covenant the second, and the affirmation identifying the contents of the cup with the Messiah's blood the third stage of the process. The collateralism between the two kinds of consecrated elements becomes still more perfect in the fourth gospel where the more specific term "flesh" is used instead of the word "body." [35] For "flesh" and "blood" are coordinate as signifying the solid and liquid constituents of the Lord's physical organism, whereas the term "body" should properly include both constituents in its signification. Thus St. John's symbolism may be regarded as representing the fourth and final stage of the liturgical development contemplated, a development in which an aesthetic desire for balance or symmetry had an important part to play.

[35] See, for example, John 6:54: "He who eats my flesh and drinks my blood has eternal life."

The Trial of Jesus

IT has sometimes been argued that the account of the nocturnal trial before the sanhedrin in Mark 14:55–65 could not have formed part of the first edition of the gospel, since the confession at verse 62 conflicts with the evangelist's doctrine of the messianic secret. But as we have previously seen,[1] the gospel affords ample indications that St. Mark is not completely satisfied with his general theory of the secret and that he is feeling his way after a mode of representation in which the Messiah's humiliation and glorification are synthesized in the unity of a single conception. Indeed, the story of the nocturnal trial may owe its present position, if not its elaboration, to St. Mark himself. For, in the first place, his faith in the reality of the Messiahship is already pressing for some form of direct or open expression in 14:3–9 (the account of the anointing at Bethany), and in 14:55–65 the pressure seems to be strongly reinforced by his desire to ascribe full responsibility for the crucifixion to the Jewish authorities. And, in the second place, grave historical difficulties are involved in 14:55–65 which make it hard to believe that the story of the

[1] Cf. above, Chapter 8; Chapter 10, n. 43. For some general information concerning the Jewish court, see my article "Sanhedrin" in *The Interpreter's Dictionary of the Bible* (ed. G. A. Buttrick), IV, 214ff.

nocturnal trial appeared in the early record of the passion, especially as a further meeting of the sanhedrin takes place, according to 15:1, at an early hour on the following morning. That such difficulties should be involved in the story is not altogether surprising when we remind ourselves that the followers of Jesus, who were all dispersed in cowardly flight at the time of the arrest (14:50), are not likely to have had any accurate information regarding the deliberations of the hierarchs and the grounds on which they decided to hand the prisoner over to the imperial authority. Accordingly, the report which St. Mark presents in 14:55–65 ought perhaps to be understood as a piece of Christian interpretation rather than as a plain statement of fact: the Jews condemned Christianity because of its affirmation of the Messiahship of Jesus, and, reasoning by analogy, certain sections of the apostolic church came to suppose that the sanhedrin condemned Jesus to death simply because he made claim to messianic dignity.[2]

The first historical difficulty to which attention may be drawn is of a chronological character. In 14:53 it is reported that the arresting party leads Jesus away to the high priest, and in 14:55 the trial before the sanhedrin immediately ensues;[3] according to the ruling of the Mishnah, however, a capital charge may not be tried on the eve of a sabbath or festival, nor may it be tried at nighttime (San. 4, 1). And there are other respects in which the proceedings fail to comply with the legal requirements laid down in the Mishnah and in the Tosefta.[4] Thus in 14:55 the

---

[2] See H. Lietzmann, "Der Prozess Jesu," *S.B.A.* (1931), pp. 310ff. Cf. Dibelius, "Das historische Problem der Leidensgeschichte," *Z.N.T.W.*, XXX (1931), 193ff.; Lietzmann, "Bemerkungen zum Prozess Jesu I," *Z.N.T.W.*, XXX (1931), 211ff., Lightfoot, *History and Interpretation*, pp. 142ff.; P. Winter, *On the Trial of Jesus*, pp. 20ff.

[3] That St. Mark takes the night session to be a formal trial, not merely a preliminary investigation, seems to be shown by 14:64b.

[4] Cf. S.-B., I, 1020ff.; Bultmann, *Die Geschichte der synoptischen Tradition*, p. 291, n. 2.

hierarchs take an active part in the prosecution by seeking out witnesses to give evidence against the prisoner, but thereby they disqualify themselves as judges (Tos. San. 7, 5). The witnesses are not punished for giving false evidence, as they ought to be (San. 11, 6); and a verdict of conviction is arrived at on the day of the trial, as it ought not to be (San. 4, 1). In 14:63–64 Jesus is condemned to death for committing blasphemy, but his confession in verse 62 is not blasphemous, since it contains no express mention of the divine name (San. 7, 5). Moreover, the presiding judge is not entitled to be the first to proffer an opinion regarding the verdict (San. 4, 2); and unanimity should be taken to nullify a verdict of conviction (San. 4, 1).

It must be recognized, however, that such contradictions constitute no proof that the trial described in 14:55–65 did not take place or even that its procedure was irregular, for it is improbable that the Mishnah supplies us with a legal code which was in force during the lifetime of Jesus.[5] The sanhedrin, as a political institution with duly constituted legislative, executive, and judicial powers, came to an end at the fall of Jerusalem in 70 A.D. The sanhedrin which succeeded the political body was essentially a rabbinical school which also came to function as a sort of ecclesiastical court whose powers were derived solely from its moral influence over those who remained loyal to Judaism. Thus there was a fundamental difference in status between the two institutions; and, as far as the composition of the council is concerned, it should be borne in mind that the priesthood ceased to exist with the destruction of the temple, the result being that the Pharisees became the unrivaled leaders of the people. But since the rabbis firmly believed in the historical continuity of Judaism, they tended to think of the old political council in terms of the academical institution with which they

[5] Cf. H. Danby, "The Bearing of the Rabbinical Criminal Code on the Jewish Trial Narratives in the Gospels," *J.T.S.*, XXI (1919), 64ff.

were acquainted and to overlook the great changes brought about by the catastrophe of 70 A.D. Thus, judging from such passages as San. 2, 1, the high priest is of no more importance than any other member of the council, whereas from non-rabbinical sources we gather that he is the president and enjoys special powers.[6] Also, the jurisprudence set forth in the Mishnah is generally of such an abstract and nonpractical character that it could hardly have been framed with the exigencies of a working judiciary in view. The incessant disputations over legal minutiae and the extreme lengths to which the principle of mercy is taken (cf. Makk. 1, 10) afford ample illustration of the academical outlook of those responsible for the mishnaic codification.

It ought not to be assumed, therefore, that the legal provisions of the Mishnah can supply us with a faithful representation of the correct procedure of the sanhedrin as it existed during the procuratorial period. Nevertheless, it is likely that many ancient rulings were handed down and preserved in the tractates of the Mishnah; and hence the fact that the account of the Jewish trial of Jesus in Mark 14:55–65 fails to comply with the mishnaic regulations on so many points at least suggests that the historicity of the evangelist's story should not be taken for granted.

The story raises a difficulty of another kind in 14:55–56. It is reported that the chief priests and the whole sanhedrin fail to secure evidence against Jesus, for while many bear false witness against him, their evidence does not agree. The implication seems to be that members of the sanhedrin actually arrange for certain witnesses to come forward with false evidence, but the conspiracy proves unsuccessful since, when the suborned witnesses come to make their statements, they contradict one another. In the circumstances, however, the incoherence of the

[6] See Acts 5:21; 7:1; I Macc. 14:44; Josephus, *c. Ap.* 2, 22; *Ant.* 20, 10, 5 etc.

testimonies is hard to understand; had there really been collusion between members of the sanhedrin and the witnesses, surely the statements to be made by the latter would have been determined beforehand so as to avoid all possibility of disagreement at the trial. And, in any case, if all the judges had been conspiring against the prisoner, would any incongruity in the evidence have deterred them from passing judgment forthwith? Again, toward the end of the story in 14:65a certain members of the sanhedrin seem to take the initiative in the maltreatment of Jesus, spitting on him and covering his face and striking him; for the τινες ("some") can scarcely refer to any other persons than to some of the πάντες ("all") of 14:64b, the police officers not being mentioned until 14:65b. But that magistrates of the supreme court would engage in undignified action of this kind at the close of a session is most improbable. It should be noted, too, that in 14:65a, besides being mishandled, the prisoner is mocked by being commanded to prophesy, whereas he has just been condemned, not as a false prophet, but for committing blasphemy in making claim to messianic status. But this is a minor difficulty which may be overcome by the consideration that the Messiah was sometimes thought of as the prophet par excellence (cf. Deut. 18:15, 18).

It has been contended that the high priest's question in 14:61b is of doubtful authenticity because its wording is characteristically Christian, not Jewish. The occurrence of "the Blessed One" as a pious circumlocution of God's name is quite in accordance with Jewish usage; but the expression "the Son of God" as a designation of the Messiah, though widely current in the early church, was not in general use, so it is argued, among the Jews and probably would not have been employed by the high priest.[7] This argument, however, is not altogether convincing. It is true that "the Son of God" does not occur as a

---

[7] See Dalman, *The Words of Jesus*, pp. 271f.

messianic designation in rabbinic literature, except in certain passages where its use in that sense is directly dependent on scriptural usage. On the other hand, God sometimes speaks of the Messiah as "my Son" in pseudepigraphic literature, and hence it is unsafe to conclude that the expression "the Son of God" was not commonly used of the Messiah by the Jews during the early decades of the first century A.D. Indeed, it is possible that the rabbis came to avoid the use of "the Son of God" as a messianic designation because the expression had become a favorite messianic title in Christian circles.[8] Furthermore, the argument under consideration concerns only the form of the high priest's question as it appears in the text of St. Mark's story. Thus the view could be taken that Jesus was asked simply if he were the Messiah, and that the additional phrase "the Son of the Blessed One" was appended to the question in the process of the story's transmission in the apostolic communities. Nevertheless, it would be a mistake to suppose that the high priest's question raises no historical difficulty, for it is introduced in the story as the immediate occasion of the messianic confession, which is set forth not only as the climax of the scene but as the sufficient reason of the court's decision to pass a sentence of death on the prisoner. And, as we shall see more clearly at a later stage of the discussion, there are good grounds for suspecting that this is Christian interpretation rather than an informed statement of the facts of the case. In the meantime the evidence brought forward by some of the false witnesses and the taciturnity of Jesus must receive consideration.

In 14:57–58 certain people bear false witness against the prisoner and allege that they have heard him say:

I will destroy this temple, made with hands, and in three days I will build another, made without hands.

[8] Cf. S.-B., III, 20.

Although these mysterious words are not directly ascribed to Jesus anywhere in the second gospel and despite the fact that the witnesses are said to be testifying falsely, the evangelist probably holds that the words were actually uttered by the Lord. For the doctrine which they seem to represent, besides being an important article of belief in the apostolic church, apparently comes to expression elsewhere in the gospel. Thus in 11:12ff., by intercalating the account of the cleansing of the temple between the earlier and later parts of the story of the cursing of the fig tree, St. Mark perhaps wishes to show that the Messiah's condemnation of the people for misusing the temple brings about the ruin of his own physical life on the cross, as well as the ruin of the religious life of the old Israel "after the flesh"; [9] in 13:2 the Master informs one of his disciples that the time is coming when there shall not be left one stone of the temple upon another which shall not be thrown down; [10] and in 15:38 the rending of the veil may be intended to suggest not only that the temple is doomed, but also that a barrier to God's presence has been removed; the crucifixion means the end of the old dispensation with its material sanctuary and the beginning of the new dispensation of the spirit which comes to fruition through the resurrection on the third day. [11] We might also compare such passages as Acts 7:48 and 17:24, where emphasis is laid on the inadequacy of a temple "made with hands" as a dwelling place of the sovereign and ubiquitous spirit of God—or Heb. 9:11 and 9:24, where Christ is said to enter the holy place of a tabernacle not "made with hands" and, by the sacri-

[9] Cf. above, Chapter 6.

[10] It should be observed that at the end of 13:2 some western authorities add: "and in three days another [temple] shall rise up [made] without hands" (cf. John 2:19).

[11] Cf. above, Chapter 10. In Mark 11:17 it may be implied that the spiritual temple of Christianity, unlike the material temple of Judaism, is open as a place of communion with God to people of all nations; cf. above, Chapter 9, n. 22.

fice of his own blood, opening up for men a new and more perfect way to communion with God.

Accordingly, it would seem that St. Mark regards the declaration attributed to the prisoner in 14:58 as a genuine saying of the Lord; and hence he reports that the witnesses testify falsely and that their evidence proves incoherent (14:59), not because their allegation is a misrepresentation of what they actually heard, but because they are opposed to the accused and are unable to grasp the mysterious import of his words. If this is so, St. Mark's attitude in this connection is not unlike that of the fourth evangelist in John 2:18ff., where, after the cleansing of the temple, the Jews ask Jesus to show them a sign. The Lord responds to their request by telling them to destroy the temple and declaring that he will raise it up in three days. The Jews, however, misunderstand the significance of his utterance. They suppose that he is referring to the material sanctuary which took forty-six years to build; but, as the disciples were destined to realize after the resurrection had taken place, he is really referring to the temple of his body, that is, presumably, to the elect community of the new Israel which is sustained by the creative spirit of the risen Christ (cf. Rom. 12:5; Eph. 1:22–23; 2:21–22). Thus St. Mark's treatment of the evidence of the false witnesses in 14:57–59 seems to be largely governed by doctrinal considerations.

It is noteworthy that, after the account of the arrest, St. Mark ascribes only three articulate utterances to Jesus (14:62; 15:2; 15:34), and, as Lightfoot pointed out, this is strong evidence for the general excellence, historically, of the passion narrative as it appears in the second gospel.[12] But we must be careful to guard against the assumption that the relative silence of the accused in St. Mark's accounts of the two trials is merely a

[12] See *op. cit.,* p. 145, n. 1. Lightfoot adds that if we contrast St. Mark's passion narrative in this respect with the later gospels, canonical and apocryphal alike, we shall be the more impressed by his reticence.

confession, so to speak, of the evangelist's ignorance concerning the actual details of the proceedings. There is a certain abruptness about the introduction of the high priest's question in 14:60 ("Have you no answer to make?"), for, in view of the incoherence of the evidence in 14:59, the situation does not seem to call for a reply on the prisoner's part; and in 15:5 it is expressly observed that Pilate is amazed at the prisoner's refusal to make any attempt to refute the many charges which have been brought against him. Thus the evangelist appears to be anxious to emphasize the reticence of Jesus, and perhaps this is because he has a scriptural parallel in mind: the prisoner is the suffering Servant of the Lord who humbles himself and opens not his mouth (Isa. 53:7; cf. Od. Sol. 31:8; T. Ben. 5:4). Moreover, it may have been felt that the contrast between the fewness of the prisoner's words and the multifarious statements made by his accusers would serve to bring out the moral greatness of Jesus by making it plain that he retained his composure throughout the shameful proceedings.

In the next part of the story (14:61b–64) the high priest asks the prisoner if he is the Messiah, and to this direct question Jesus gives an equally direct reply:

I am; and you shall see the Son of Man sitting at the right hand of the Power and coming with the clouds of heaven.

The high priest at once concludes that there is no further need for witnesses, adjudging the confession to be blasphemy; the sanhedrin agrees and unanimously condemns the prisoner to death. As we have seen, this judgment conflicts with the ruling of the Mishnah which requires the use of the divine name in a case of blasphemy. Admittedly, such a ruling may not have been in force at the time of the trial of Jesus. But there is no evidence (outside the gospels) that any of the numerous pretenders to messianic or royal dignity, who arose during the troubled period extending from the death of Herod the Great to the fall of Jerusalem in 70 A.D., was condemned for committing the religious offence of blasphemy; it seems that they were generally dealt with by the Roman authorities as disturbers of the peace or as potential or actual political revolutionaries.[13] And we may observe that the Jesus, son of Ananus, whose strange activities are described by Josephus in *Bell.* 6, 5, 3, was not prosecuted on a religious charge, although he prophesied against Jerusalem and against the temple; the Jewish authorities intervened only to hand him over to the procurator, who had him scourged and, after conducting a cross-examination, concluded that he was a madman and released him. Exactly seventy years later, Bar Kokhba, the leader of the great revolt of 132–136 A.D., claimed to be the Messiah, and his pretension was deemed to be valid by no less a person than R. Akiba. In the light of these considerations, therefore, it is difficult to believe that in 14:61b–64 St. Mark sets forth a trustworthy historical explanation of the condemnation of Jesus.

But if it is allowed that a messianic claim as such was not blasphemy in the sense of the law, the question immediately arises: How did certain members of the apostolic church come to believe that their Lord was condemned to death for committing blasphemy in making pretension to Messiahship? The most satisfactory answer to this important question seems to be that they interpreted the situation anachronistically; they assumed that what applied to themselves in their relationship to the Jewish authorities applied to Jesus in a similar relationship. But an assumption of that kind ought not to have been made, for in the meantime Jesus had been crucified, and, on Jewish presuppositions, this meant that he had been made the curse of God (cf. Deut. 21:23; Gal. 3:13); and hence, as St. Paul knew from bitter experience, the cross of Christ was a stumbling block to the Jews (I Cor. 1:23; Gal. 5:11). Accordingly, many lawyers may have regarded the doctrine of the crucified Messiah as

---

[13] Cf. Josephus, *Ant.* 17, 10, 5–7; 20, 8, 6; *Bell.* 2, 13, 4; 6, 5, 2.

blasphemy in the legal sense; they may well have argued that the upholders of that doctrine were guilty of attempting to reverse the very judgment of God himself in seriously affirming that one whom God had manifestly cursed was none other than God's beloved or only Son. Such an argument, however, could not have been brought forward when Jesus was standing for trial before the sanhedrin since he had not yet suffered the disgrace of crucifixion, and this is the important point which seems to be overlooked in Mark 14:61b–64.

Furthermore, St. Mark's story evidently conflicts with a significant implication of the indubitable fact that Jesus was put to death on a cross. For crucifixion does not appear to have been employed as a method of execution among the Jews of the period. It was a characteristically Roman form of punishment; hence from the fact that Jesus was crucified it is legitimate to infer that he was sentenced to death by the procurator. Had he really been condemned for blasphemy in a Jewish court, he would have been put to death by stoning (cf. Lev. 24:16; San. 7, 4). In face of these considerations one might endeavor to save the historicity of St. Mark's story by appealing to John 18:31, where it is stated that the Jews reminded Pilate that it was not lawful for them to put any man to death. It might then be argued that the sanhedrin, though competent to pass sentence in capital cases, had not the power to carry out such a sentence; execution could take place only after the sentence had received ratification at the hands of the procurator. But the argument ought to go further, for Pilate did not merely confirm a sentence which had been passed by the sanhedrin; otherwise Jesus would have been put to death by stoning. Hence it must be argued that the sanhedrin was not competent to carry out a capital sentence even when the sentence had the approval of the procurator, this being the meaning of the statement in John 18:31.

In such circumstances, however, it is far from easy to understand why the proceedings described in Mark 14:55–65 should have taken place at all; a Jewish trial could have no legal validity, and would members of the sanhedrin have left their homes during the night in order to take part in a sort of mock trial at which they might make pretence of condemning a prisoner whom in reality they could only prosecute? But there are strong reasons for doubting the authenticity of the statement in John 18:31. In the first place, according to the inscription discovered by Clermont-Ganneau in 1871, the Jewish authorities were entitled to inflict penalty of death on any Gentile who might be found trespassing on a particularly sacred area of the temple.[14] And, in the second place, it is unlikely that the Jews would have reminded Pilate of the limits of their authority, and it is no less unlikely that the procurator would have needed any such reminder. Thus John 18:31 provides a very insecure basis for the argument under consideration and has all the appearance of having been designed by the evangelist with apologetic aims in view. It is not impossible that the passage was directed against the Jewish people and that the statement addressed to Pilate was intended to show that the limitation of the constitutional powers of the sanhedrin was the only thing which prevented the Jews from actually putting their own Messiah to death. But, as the following verse suggests, the idea which seems to have been uppermost in the evangelist's mind was of a more definitely theological character; the crucifixion, as a provision of the divine purpose, was foreseen by Jesus, and in the light of that overruling purpose it could even be said that the Jews told Pilate of the limits of their authority in order that the Messiah's prediction concerning the manner of his death might be fulfilled.[15]

[14] For further details concerning this inscription, see Supplementary Note F, below.

[15] See John 12:32–33; 18:32. Is not the wording of John 18:32 such as to suggest that the evangelist may be indifferent to the question whether the Jews are speaking the truth in John 18:31b?

Attention should now be drawn to the account of the condemnation of Stephen in Acts 6:8ff., which at certain important points shows striking similarity to St. Mark's story of the nocturnal trial. St. Luke reports that the opponents of Stephen, being unable to withstand the wisdom of his arguments, suborn men to declare that they have heard him speak blasphemous words against Moses and against God. In this way the people are stirred up, and Stephen is arrested and taken before the sanhedrin. False witnesses are brought forward who testify that they have heard the prisoner say that Jesus of Nazareth would destroy the temple and change the customs handed down by Moses. The high priest asks if these allegations are true, and Stephen proceeds to defend himself with a prolonged speech [16] which infuriates the audience. When he finally affirms that he sees the heavens opened and the Son of Man standing at the right hand of God, the people cry out loudly and stop their ears and, rushing upon him with one accord, they cast him out of the city and stone him to death.[17] Thus, as Stephen is accused of saying that Jesus would destroy the temple, so the prisoner in St. Mark's story is accused of saying that he would destroy the temple; and in each instance the accusation is made by false witnesses.[18] Also, as Stephen's fate is sealed by his tacit identifica-

---

[16] In this respect the report differs from St. Mark's story of the nocturnal trial, which, as we have seen, shows preference for the motif of reticence on the part of the prisoner.

[17] St. Luke nowhere states that the stoning of Stephen is due to an outbreak of mob violence. Presumably, the sanhedrin adjudges that Stephen commits blasphemy when he implies that the crucified Jesus is the exalted Son of Man. Hence the people stop their ears at his words and, in accordance with the requirements of the law, proceed to stone him to death.

[18] No certain answer can be given to the question whether the charge made in Mark 14:58/Acts 6:14 is ultimately based on a genuine saying of the Lord. According to one tradition (Mark 13:2), Jesus predicted the destruction of the temple, and Goguel argues that the prediction is an authentic saying on the ground that the words "there shall not be left

tion of Jesus with the exalted Son of Man, so the prisoner in St. Mark's story is condemned to death for making a messianic confession in which he refers to the Son of Man as sitting at the right hand of the Power and coming with the clouds of heaven. In other words, the principal features of the nocturnal trial as it is presented in Mark 14:55–65 correspond to the main elements in St. Luke's account of the condemnation of Stephen; and this seems to corroborate the view that St. Mark's story is not so much a historical record of a trial which actually took place as a piece of Christian interpretation made in the light of the church's experience of conflict with the Jews and designed to emphasize Jewish responsibility for the outrage of crucifying the Son of God.

Accordingly, there is warrant for supposing that the passion

---

here one stone upon another which shall not be thrown down" excludes the possibility of destruction by fire (see his article, "A propos du procès de Jésus," *Z.N.T.W.*, XXXI [1932], 297). But this argument is not convincing (see above, Chapter 9, n. 38), and in any case it is one thing for a person to say that a building will be destroyed, but quite another for him to say that he will destroy it. According to another tradition (Mark 11:15–19), Jesus condemned his people (or some of them) for their misuse of the temple, and the so-called cleansing of the temple may have been a symbolic act originally meant to foreshadow the radical renovation of the existing order, which was expected to take place at the parousia of the Son of Man. In current Jewish eschatology it was thought that in the messianic era there would be a new and more glorious temple in a new and more glorious Jerusalem (see Bousset and Gressmann, *Die Religion des Judentums,* pp. 238ff.), and in the view of some apocalyptic writers this implied that the existing temple would have to be destroyed (cf. I En. 90:28f.). It may also be noticed that in Mandaean eschatology the idea is expressed that the temple would be destroyed on the appearance of the celestial Man (see Reitzenstein, *Das mandäische Buch des Herrn der Grösse,* pp. 67ff.). It is not impossible, therefore, that Jesus uttered some saying, alleged to show disrespect for the temple, which was mentioned by those members or agents of the sanhedrin who conducted the prosecution. But the evidence at our disposal is such as to allow of no more than a tentative judgment on the matter.

narrative in its earliest form did not include any record of a nocturnal session of the sanhedrin; [19] and hence we may presume that events after the last supper really took the following course: Jesus was secretly arrested on the Mount of Olives by officers of the sanhedrin who received assistance from one of the disciples; he was held in custody at the high priest's residence during the remaining hours of the night; and he was handed over to the procurator after a meeting of the hierarchs early the next morning. The notice of the matutinal meeting of the sanhedrin is given in 15:1,[20] and an account of the trial before Pilate follows in verses 2–5. The sketchiness of these two reports seems to betray that they are not based on information derived from an eyewitness of the proceedings, but are the result of an inference drawn from the well-known facts that Jesus was arrested at the order of the sanhedrin and executed at the order of the procurator. The story concerning Barabbas follows in verses 6–15 and, with its emphasis on the unwillingness of Pilate to condemn the prisoner, affords further illustration of the doctrine that the Messiah's shameful death on a cross was brought about through the unwarranted hostility of his own countrymen.[21]

[19] Perhaps the story of Peter's threefold denial also was absent from the passion narrative in its earliest form, though it may have been present in the narrative as St. Mark received it. We are inclined to think that 14:3–9 (the anointing at Bethany), 14:12–16 (the preparations for the last supper), 14:55–65 (the trial before the sanhedrin), and 16:1–8 (the empty tomb) are the pericopes which are most likely to owe their presence in the framework of the passion narrative to St. Mark himself.

[20] This verse does not seem to refer back to 14:55–65; as Lightfoot noted, there appears to be no real justification for the suggested translation "the chief priests . . . confirmed their resolution" (*op. cit.*, p. 143, n. 1). Turner compares Acts 25:12 (where συμβούλιον means "council") and proposes the translation "formed themselves into an assembly" (*N.C.H.S.*, pt. 3, p. 113). The term συμβούλιον occurs elsewhere in the second gospel only at 3:6; both in 3:6, and in 15:1 there is uncertainty regarding the accompanying verb. On the whole, the R.V. translation in 15:1 ("held a consultation") seems to be as good as any.

[21] Cf. above, Chapters 6 and 10.

It is noteworthy that in 15:1ff. the title "the King of the Jews" suddenly comes into prominence. The expression is used by Pilate on three occasions: in 15:2, before any accusation has been made, he asks the prisoner if he is the King of the Jews; in 15:9 he asks the multitude if they would like him to release the King of the Jews; and in 15:12, after the chief priests have incited the people to make request for the liberation of Barabbas, he asks the multitude what he should do to him whom they call the King of the Jews. In 15:17–19 the soldiers mock Jesus by dressing him in purple, putting a crown of thorns on his head, hailing him as King of the Jews, and doing obeisance to him. In 15:26 the words THE KING OF THE JEWS form the titulus on the cross, advertising the charge on which Jesus was sentenced to death. And in 15:31–32 the chief priests with the scribes make fun of Jesus, taunting him as the Messiah, the King of Israel. The last-mentioned passage serves to show that St. Mark regards the two titles "the King of the Jews" (or "of Israel") and "the Messiah" as equivalent to each other, and this is quite natural, seeing that, in current Jewish expectation, the promised Messiah was frequently represented as the ruler of the divinely restored kingdom of Israel. Accordingly, in view of 14:55–65, it may be assumed that the evangelist takes the inscription on the cross in 15:26 to signify that Jesus was executed because he made claim to Messiahship. Indeed, in Bultmann's opinion,[22] 15:26 is a direct outcome of the erroneous belief that Jesus was condemned for his messianic pretension (the principal question at issue in the Jewish-Christian controversy) and, like the story of the nocturnal trial, is a legendary accretion to the old record of the passion; and if 15:26 is without foundation in fact, the same is true of the other passages in which Jesus is referred to as his nation's King.

Such a hypothesis, however, offers no explanation of certain striking points of difference between 14:55ff. and 15:1ff. In the

[22] See *op. cit.*, pp. 291, 293f., 295.

first place, there is the sudden change in terminology; in 15:2–32 Jesus is referred to as the national King on no less than six occasions, and yet the title "the King of the Jews" (or "of Israel") is not applied to him anywhere else in the gospel; it appears that the evangelist uses the expression "the Son of God" as the normal Gentile equivalent of "the Messiah" (cf. 1:1; 8:29; 15:39). In the second place, in 14:63–64 the prisoner is found guilty of blasphemy and is sentenced to death in accordance with the requirements of the law of Moses, but there is no mention of any religious crime in 15:2–5. In the third place, in 14:61b–62 Jesus volunteers a definite affirmative answer to the high priest's question ("Are you the Messiah, the Son of the Blessed One?"), whereas in 15:2 he gives the obscure reply "You say" to the procurator's question ("Are you the King of the Jews?"). It should also be observed that in 14:55–65 the evangelist is dealing with what is evidently a closed session of the sanhedrin, but 15:26 concerns a public announcement, and hence there is no presumptive reason for doubting its historical validity; as we have already seen,[23] it is possible that the account of the crucifixion is ultimately based on the firsthand information of an eyewitness, namely, Simon of Cyrene, who according to 15:21 was compelled to carry the cross and whose two sons, Alexander and Rufus, are mentioned as though they were well-known figures in certain sections of the apostolic church.

But if it is granted that 15:26 belongs to the earliest stratum of the passion narrative, the probability is that its original meaning was quite independent of the Christian belief that the Lord was condemned for blasphemy. As we gather from the writings of Josephus, leading Zealotic revolutionaries of the tetrarchical period were wont to make claim to royal dignity, and from this we may reasonably infer that they were often fired with an intense religious enthusiasm, imagining that they were actually anointed of God or divinely commissioned for the sacred task of

[23] Cf. above, Chapter 10, n. 59.

finally delivering their people from the yoke of their Gentile oppressors.[24] Thus it may well be that 15:26 originally signified that Jesus was sentenced to death by the procurator on a political charge, as a nationalist leader whose activities were deemed to be subversive of the authority of the imperial government. Such an interpretation is perhaps corroborated in 15:6ff., where Jesus is associated with Barabbas, who, as it is reported in verse 7, was held in custody with the rioters who had committed murder during the insurrection.[25] And it seems to receive further corroboration not only in the fact that there is no reference to any religious offence in 15:1ff., but also in the prisoner's indefinite reply to the procurator's question in 15:2. As Dibelius pointed out,[26] if Jesus had given a definite affirmative answer to the question, Pilate would have had to bring the trial to an abrupt conclusion by passing sentence forthwith, whereas the indefinite reply "You say" admits of a continuation of the scene. And we may presume that the writer was particularly anxious that the scene should be continued, because he desired to show that it was only through the malicious intrigues of the hierarchs that Jesus was sentenced to death, thereby making it plain to the reader that the Lord was not really an opponent of the imperial government.[27]

---

[24] Cf. above, n. 13. Josephus naturally wished to present Judaism in a favorable light to the Romans; hence some allowance should be made for his tendency to minimize the importance of the religious factor in Jewish revolutionary movements of the first century A.D. Cf. Goguel, *The Life of Jesus*, pp. 81f.

[25] Regarding the historical basis of the Barabbas story, see above, Chapter 10, n. 9.

[26] See his article, "Herodes und Pilatus," in *Z.N.T.W.*, XVI (1915), 117.

[27] It appears from Luke 23:2 that, to St. Luke's mind, there was a disparity in the second gospel between the high priest's question concerning Messiahship and the procurator's question concerning Kingship; he evidently saw that whereas the former had a theological, the latter had a political, meaning; hence, in accordance with his desire to present a

We are thus led to the conclusion that Jesus was handed over to the procurator after the matutinal meeting of the sanhedrin, that he was prosecuted on the basis of a political charge or charges, and that he was condemned to death by the procurator as a dangerous aspirant to royal power. No certain answer can be given to the question why the hierarchs did not deal with the case themselves.[28] One possibility is that they did not wish to assume responsibility for the execution of a prisoner who had many supporters among the common people. But it may be that Jesus had not committed an obvious capital offence against the law of Moses, and it may be that certain members of the sanhedrin were not unfavorably disposed toward him.[29] In such a situation those who desired the removal of Jesus would naturally feel that they might encounter serious difficulties of a technical character in any attempt to prove, to the satisfaction of the full council, that the prisoner was worthy of death; hence they decided to put the matter into the hands of the procurator and to prosecute on political grounds. We have no definite knowledge of the evidence on which the accusations were based. One possibility is that the so-called cleansing of the temple aroused the Sadducean priesthood to active opposition against Jesus. Even if it was originally intended to have only a religious or eschatological significance, a violent action of that kind might easily have had serious political consequences.[30] Apparently it required but little provocation to excite the patriotic passions of

---

smooth and consistent narrative, he introduces his account of the trial with an introduction in which a claim to Messiahship is equated with a claim to Kingship, this being construed politically as a challenge to the authority of Caesar; cf. Lightfoot, *op. cit.*, pp. 168ff.

[28] The view that the sanhedrin (during the procuratorial period) was not competent to deal with capital cases seems to be erroneous; see Supplementary Note F, below.

[29] Perhaps he had Pharisaic support in the matter of the cleansing of the temple; see above, Chapter 9, n. 20.

[30] Cf. E. Meyer, *Ursprung und Anfänge*, II, 451.

the multitudes that assembled in Jerusalem at the time of the passover, and the Sadducean leaders possibly thought that, as a precautionary measure, Jesus must be put out of the way before the feast began. Thus they may have acted, partly at all events, from quite disinterested motives, for they would be well aware of the violence with which the procurator was wont to suppress popular risings.[31] Without making very close inquiries they may have concluded that Jesus was a Zealotic or Cananaean national-ist who made pretensions to messianic or royal dignity. Accord-ingly, it is not unreasonable to suppose that, soon after the in-cident in the temple, some of the Sadducean magistrates (who generally sought to uphold friendly relations with the Roman authorities) resolved to have Jesus secretly arrested and pro-ceeded to make arrangements for a procuratorial trial at which the prosecution was to be conducted on the basis of a charge of sedition.[32]

[31] Cf. Luke 13:1; Josephus, *Ant.* 18, 4, 1.

[32] In John 18:3, 12, Roman soldiers are evidently present at the arrest; hence, seeing that the general tendency of the tradition was to assign more part to the Jews and less to the procurator, Goguel (*Z.N.T.W.*, XXXI [1932], 292, 298f.) argues that the Jewish and the Roman au-thorities actually cooperated throughout the proceedings, though on the initiative of certain Jewish leaders. But it seems unlikely that a cohort and a chiliarch would have been required at the arrest of Jesus, and per-haps the references to these in John 18 should be understood in the light of Ps. 2:2 (cf. Acts 4:23ff.). It is possible that the story of the trial be-fore Herod in Luke 23:8ff. should be understood in the same light; cf. the article by Dibelius in *Z.N.T.W.*, XVI (1915), 113ff. On the other hand, that there was some cooperation between the two authorities can scarcely be doubted; cf. Winter, *op. cit.*, pp. 44ff., 136ff., and his article on Mark 14:53b, 55–64 in *Z.N.T.W.*, LIII (1962), 260ff.

SUPPLEMENTARY NOTE F: THE COMPETENCE
OF THE SANHEDRIN [1]

The arguments that have been brought forward in support of
the view that the sanhedrin during the procuratorial period had
not the power of inflicting capital punishment are unconvincing.
They may be conveniently considered under five headings.

1. According to St. Mark's gospel (where the passion narrative is evidently presented in its earliest extant form), Jesus
was arrested at the order of the Jewish authorities and executed
at the order of Pilate. And he had to be handed over for trial to
the procurator, so it is argued, because the sanhedrin was not
competent to deal with capital offences. It is quite possible,
however, that the prisoner was handed over to Pilate because
he had not committed an obvious capital offence against the
law of Moses (cf. above, Chapter 12), and that St. Mark's account of the nocturnal trial before the sanhedrin (14:55–65) is
basically a reflection of the fact that certain Christians had been
put to death at the order of the Jewish authorities for committing blasphemy in identifying the crucified Jesus with the
promised Messiah (cf. below, n. 4). On the other hand, despite
the internal and external incongruities of Mark 14:55–65, G. D.

---

[1] Cf. J. Juster, *Les juifs dans l'empire romain*, II, 132ff.; H. Lietz-
mann, "Der Prozess Jesu," *S.B.A.* (1931), pp. 310ff.; F. Büchsel, "Die
Blutgerichtsbarkeit des Synedrions," *Z.N.T.W.*, XXX (1931), 202ff.;
H. Lietzmann, "Bemerkungen zum Prozess Jesu II," *Z.N.T.W.*, XXXI
(1932), 78ff.; F. Büchsel, "Noch einmal: Zur Blutgerichtsbarkeit des
Synedrions," *Z.N.T.W.*, XXXIII (1934), 84ff.; R. H. Lightfoot, *History
and Interpretation*, p. 147, n. 2.; H. J. Ebeling, "Zur Frage nach der
Kompetenz des Synedrions," *Z.N.T.W.*, XXXV (1936), 290ff.; P. Benoit,
"Jésus devant le sandhédrin," *Angelicum*, XX (1943), 162f.; P. Winter,
On the Trial of Jesus, pp. 1ff., 21ff., 186ff., 192ff.

Note on the Sanhedrin

Kilpatrick (see his lecture, *The Trial of Jesus*, pp. 9ff.) thinks that the narrative represents a credible historical tradition which consists essentially of two sections: the first section concerns a successful attempt on the part of the prosecution to secure the unanimous support of the sanhedrin by showing that the prisoner was guilty of blasphemy in a strict sense; the second section concerns an examination of the accused with a view to his appearing before the procurator on a political charge, the sanhedrin being incompetent to deal with capital cases.

a) Kilpatrick (*op. cit.*, p. 9) argues that the high priest Caiaphas was astute enough to avoid the sort of mistake which, according to Josephus (*Ant.* 20, 9, 1), Ananus committed in 62 A.D.: he saw to it that Jesus was unanimously condemned by the sanhedrin on a religious charge, and so no important element of public opinion could be outraged by the prisoner's condemnation at the hands of the procurator.

But would Caiaphas have needed to resort to such a complicated procedure in order to secure the support of the more influential Jewish parties? His position was much more secure than that of Ananus, and he was probably on very good terms with the procurator; he held office for a longer period (18–37 A.D.) than any other high priest in the first century, and it is perhaps significant that he came out of office only a short while after Pilate's return to Rome (*Ant.* 18, 4, 3). Moreover, while it is not impossible that Jesus had some Pharisaic support in the matter of the cleansing of the temple, there is evidence that Jesus had aroused the hostility of certain Pharisees through his persistent criticisms of their religious point of view.

b) Kilpatrick (*op. cit.*, p. 16) observes that in the later part of St. Mark's report, as it is an account of a preliminary examination of a prisoner before trial, the prisoner is questioned directly and no witnesses are called, whereas in the earlier verses, where witnesses are employed, we have the appearance of a trial.

But there is no such break in the narrative as it now stands. After the confession in 14:62 the high priest concludes that there is no further need of witnesses, the suggestion being that up to that point it had been expected that witnesses would have to be called in again.

c) In Kilpatrick's view (*op. cit.*, p. 10) those who testified that Jesus had said that he would destroy the temple (vv. 56ff.) were not really false witnesses; perhaps the ascription of falsity to them was due to St. Mark's writing before 70 A.D. (when the temple was still standing) or to the Christian idea that all witnesses against Jesus were *ipso facto* false witnesses.

But it may be that Jesus foretold merely the destruction of the temple (cf. 13:2) and that such a prediction later gave rise to the tradition that he himself would destroy the temple, the allusion being, however, not to the material building as such, but to the religion of the old dispensation which was destined to be superseded by the *corpus Christi* with its universalist transcendence of racial distinctions. In this connection the reference to a house of prayer for all nations in 11:17 may be significant, and also the reference to the rending of the temple veil in 15:38 (cf. above, Chapter 10 and Chapter 12, n. 18).

d) Kilpatrick (*op. cit.*, pp. 11ff.) contends that, although there is nothing in rabbinic literature which indicates that speaking against the temple was blasphemy and deserving of the death penalty, there is Old Testament evidence for treating such a saying as blasphemy, and this mode of interpretation may have persisted into the first century A.D. In support of his contention Kilpatrick cites *inter alia* Acts 6:11–14, where it is alleged that Stephen spoke blasphemous words against Moses and against God: "This man does not cease to speak against this holy place and the law; for we have heard him say that this Jesus of Nazareth shall destroy this place and shall change the customs which Moses delivered to us."

As we understand the matter, however, it is most unlikely that a prediction of the destruction of the temple would have been generally regarded as blasphemous in the technical sense by Jewish authorities during the first century A.D. Would such a passage as Micah 3:12 have been retained in a canonical text if the sort of prediction in question had been strictly blasphemous? Also, the temple was not really confused with the Being of God in Jewish belief—such a confusion, indeed, would have been sheer idolatry in Jewish eyes, and it is noteworthy that, according to Josephus (*Bell.* 6, 5, 3), the divine Presence quits the sacred precincts before their destruction at the hands of the Romans. And as far as the case of Stephen is concerned, his accusers do not allege merely that he spoke against the temple. Furthermore, a careful reading of Acts 7:54ff. suggests that it is the tacit identification of Jesus with the exalted Son of Man which constitutes the main determining factor in Stephen's condemnation. We might compare a passage from Justin Martyr (*Apol.* 1, 31, 6—a text cited by Kilpatrick) where it is reported that during the persecution of 132–136 A.D. the leader of the Jewish revolt made the essential demand that Christians should deny the Messiahship of Jesus, the central tenet of the new religion; from the Christian standpoint, it would be blasphemous for a member of the church to make such a denial—and, we seem entitled to infer, the assertion of the Messiahship of Jesus was frequently held to be blasphemous in a strict sense among Jewish authorities.

e) Assuming that the later part of the nocturnal proceedings were meant to secure grounds for a political charge which would carry weight with Pilate, Kilpatrick argues (*op. cit.,* p. 15) that the high priest put the question: "Are you the king of Israel?" and that Jesus replied in the affirmative; either St. Mark's report is incomplete or the original question was transformed into the question which now stands in 14:61—"Are you the Messiah, the Son of the Blessed?"

But in view of the improbability that any of the disciples were present at the trial of Jesus, would it not be more reasonable to take the view that St. Mark's brief account of the Roman trial represents an inference from the titulus on the cross, and that the question ascribed to the high priest in 14:61 is really a translation of the royal title into Jewish religious terms, a translation made in the light of the apostolic belief that Jesus was the Messiah, the Son of David and the Son of God?

2. According to John 18:31 the Jews informed Pilate that it was not lawful for them to put any man to death. But it is historically improbable that the Jews would have reminded the procurator of the limitations of their legal powers; and the passage has all the appearance of having been designed by the fourth evangelist with apologetic aims in view (cf. above, Chapter 12).

3. In the Jerusalem Talmud we read:

A Baraita states: Forty years before the destruction of the temple the power to pass capital sentence was taken away from the Jews [San. 1, 1; 7, 2].

But, as Juster pointed out, that this statement is of doubtful historical accuracy is soon seen when it is considered in relation to two passages in the Babylonian Talmud. The first of these passages reads:

It is taught [by the Tannaites]: Forty years before the destruction of the temple the sanhedrin left the temple-chamber and held its sessions in the bazaars. And, according to R. Isaac b. Evidemi, this means that the sanhedrin no longer judged criminal cases. But why criminal cases? Say rather that it no longer judged capital cases [San. 41a].

Thus the Baraita cited in the Jerusalem Talmud is apparently based on a tradition which did *not* assert that the sanhedrin was deprived of the power to deal with capital offences some forty years before the destruction of the temple. The other passage in the Babylonian Talmud reads:

R. Ishmael b. Josse [who flourished toward 200 A.D.] says: My father said . . . forty years before the destruction of the temple the sanhedrin moved from the temple and established itself in the bazaars [Ab. Zar. 8b].

It would seem, therefore, that the Baraita under consideration belongs to the later half of the second century. According to information supplied by R. Ishmael, the sanhedrin ceased to hold its sessions in the temple chamber forty years before the destruction of the temple and, according to a rule which was apparently not laid down before about 150 A.D., the sanhedrin could pass a capital sentence only when sitting in the temple chamber. Hence the inference was drawn that the power to deal with capital offences was taken away from the Jews about forty years before the destruction of the temple. It should be noticed, however, that Kilpatrick (*op. cit.*, p. 17) raises two objections to an interpretation of this kind:

(i) The Baraita of the Jerusalem Talmud belongs to the period before 200 A.D., and so can hardly derive from an inference made by one of the Amoraim after 200 A.D., and perhaps not earlier than 250 A.D.

But the tradition concerning the sanhedrin's change of location, no less than the Baraita regarding the restriction of the sanhedrin's competence, finds attestation in the second century; and the fact that the Babylonian Talmud ascribes the inference to R. Isaac b. Evidemi by no means excludes the possibility that the same kind of inference had previously been made by another rabbi belonging to a different school.

(ii) Kilpatrick's second objection is based on a statement made by Hermann Strack to the effect that, for information respecting the Judaism of Palestine, the Jerusalem Talmud contains more trustworthy data than the Babylonian Talmud.

This generalization is undoubtedly true, but it does not seem to be relevant to the matter under discussion. The Babylonian Talmud does not disagree with the Jerusalem Talmud on the point that the authority to deal with capital offences was withdrawn from the sanhedrin forty years prior to the destruction of the temple; it simply preserves a fuller tradition which serves to indicate how the opinion expressed in the Baraita may have been arrived at. There is no evidence elsewhere that such a constitutional change took place in 30 A.D., and we suspect that the tradition concerning the removal of the sanhedrin to the bazaars belongs to the same circle of ideas as the tradition (referred to above, Chapter 10, n. 51) that the doors of the temple were miraculously opened as a portent of the destruction of the sacred precincts, which was to take place forty years later in 70 A.D. Moreover, if the crucifixion occurred in 27 or 28 A.D., as Goguel argued (see his *Life of Jesus*, p. 228), a constitutional change which took place in 30 A.D. could have had no bearing on the trial of Jesus; and it is of interest to notice that Joachim Jeremias in his paper "Zur Geschichtlichkeit des Verhörs Jesu vor dem hohen Rat (*Z.N.T.W.*, XLIII [1950–51], 147f.) contends that the power to deal with capital cases must have been taken away from the sanhedrin, not forty years but sixty-four years before the destruction of the temple—that is, in 6 A.D., when Judaea became a procuratorial province of the empire. Such defiance of the text (by a scholar in general agreement with Kilpatrick on this whole question) can scarcely be said to increase one's confidence in the Baraita as a piece of reliable historical information.

4. Jeremias (*op. cit.*, pp. 148ff.) adduces the *Pericope Adulterae* (John 7:53ff.) in support of the hypothesis that the sanhedrin could not execute capital sentences.

a) His argument proceeds on the assumption that this pericope is a trustworthy historical record, despite the fact that it has all the appearance of being a paradigm or pronouncement story, perhaps constructed in one of the early Christian communities to provide a setting for a traditional saying of the Lord. There is no evidence that the story was known to any of the canonical evangelists; it is a "western" interpolation in the text of the fourth gospel, and in a group of Greek cursive MSS it is found appended to Luke 21:37. It may have originated in the interests of a party that advocated leniency in the treatment of an offender against ecclesiastical discipline. Like the controversy stories in Mark 2:1ff. and 12:13ff., the pericope illustrates the Master's skill in debate and his ability to silence his opponents (cf. Mark 11:27ff.).

b) Jeremias argues that the verdict (which in his view cannot be carried out) has already been passed, for a jeering crowd rather than scribes and Pharisees would have been accompanying the woman if she were being taken to court.

But may not the reference to the scribes and Pharisees be purely conventional, as so frequently appears to be the case in the controversy stories contained in St. Mark's gospel? Like "the Jews" in the fourth gospel, they seem to be introduced as the agreed enemies of Jesus.

c) Jeremais holds that if the adulteress were being taken to court, the question put to Jesus (v. 5) would be historically improbable, the provisions of the law (Deut. 22:23f.) being quite explicit and leaving no room for doubt.

But the question would not be historically improbable if the scribes and Pharisees are seeking to bring out the folly of Jesus' moral teaching concerning the necessity of love and forgiveness (see, for example, Luke 6:27ff.): if his law of love were strictly applied in actual life, evil would have a free course, and flagrant acts of sin—such as the one recently committed by the wretched woman before him—would multiply till organized social life became impossible.

d) Jeremias thinks that the answer of Jesus (v. 7) presupposes that the verdict has been given; the wording is not "let him first accuse her" but "let him first cast a stone at her."

But since the woman had been taken in the very act of adultery (v. 4), the condemnation could easily have been treated as a foregone conclusion. Moreover, what would have been the point of taking legal proceedings against the woman if the sanhedrin was not competent to deal with capital offences?

e) Jeremias' account of the dilemma is not new; it accords with that given by A. E. Brooke (Peake's *Commentary*, p. 765), for example: if Jesus pronounced against the carrying out of the Mosaic law he would be discredited by the people, whereas if he counseled action contrary to the imperial decrees his enemies would secure material for accusation against him.

But this exegesis would seem to imply that Jesus had shown himself inclined to commend action that was contrary to the decrees laid down by the Roman authorities, and the gospels hardly justify such a view. The likelihood is, as we have already suggested, that the essential reference is to the Master's own commendation of the way of love and forgiveness. The scribes and Pharisees regard a moral doctrine of this kind as ridiculously impracticable, and, assuming that they have a dilemma in mind, it could be: if Jesus declares that the woman should be released he is contravening the law of Moses, whereas if he declares that the Mosaic ruling should be applied he stands condemned by his own moral teaching.

f) In support of Jeremias' mode of interpretation T. W. Manson (*Z.N.T.W.*, XLIV [1952–53], 254f.) draws attention to verse 6b—"But Jesus stooped down and with his finger wrote on the ground"—and argues that it is to be understood in the light of the fact that it was a Roman practice for the presiding judge at a trial to write down the sentence and to read it out from the written record. Jesus defeats the scribes and Pharisees "by going through the form of pronouncing sentence in the best Roman style, but wording it so that it cannot be executed."

But there is no suggestion in the narrative that Jesus is deliberately pretending to write; he *does* write on the ground. And there are reasons for holding that he is not reading out what he has written when he makes his reply. In the first place, he does not reply immediately to the question that is put to him, so the scribes and Pharisees persist in demanding an answer (v. 7a); surely if he were writing his verdict on the ground they would have been able to read it for themselves. In the second place, when he has made answer he stoops down again and continues to write on the ground (v. 8); that is, he does not follow the Roman custom of writing the verdict down and then, having finished the writing, proceeding to read the sentence aloud. In the third place, the answer he gives is not really a form of sentence upon the prisoner; it represents rather a refusal to pass sentence, for he does not declare the woman to be either guilty or not guilty (cf. Luke 6:37). We suspect that the writing on the ground is in fact a motif intended to stress the imperturbableness of Jesus in face of the aggressiveness of his opponents: his careless doodling serves to indicate his complete mastery of the situation (cf. the motif of sleep in St. Mark's story of the stilling of the storm in 4:38 and the motif of silence in his accounts of the trial scenes in 14:61 and 15:5).

5. Jeremias (*op. cit.*, p. 150) also brings forward a passage from the *Megillat Ta'anit*, a document which probably originated during the great rising of 66–70 A.D. and which gives a list of national Jewish feasts characterized by a prohibition of fasting. According to a statement in the sixth section, five days after the withdrawal of the Roman occupation troops, on the twenty-second of the month of Elul (66 A.D.), the Jews were again able to put evildoers to death.

But who are the evildoers the writer would primarily have in mind? In the eyes of the Zealotic revolutionary, the greatest sin was committed by members of the chosen race who betrayed Israel by giving active support to the Roman government in Palestine; and the passage under consideration may well mean that, soon after the removal of the occupation forces from Jerusalem, true Jews were free to deal with traitors and apostates after the manner required by divine justice. No one doubts that during the procuratorial period the imperial power represented the supreme legislative and judicial authority; but this does not mean that the Romans did not respect Jewish customs sufficiently to allow the sanhedrin to deal effectively with religious offences according to the prescriptions of the Mosaic law.

We are thus led to conclude that Mark 14:55–65; John 18:31; Jer. San. 1, 1/7, 2; John 7:53ff.; and Meg. T. 6 do not warrant the hypothesis that at the time of the trial of Jesus the sanhedrin was incompetent to inflict and execute a capital sentence. Moreover, there are other pieces of evidence which seem to support the contrary view, and these may be conveniently considered in six sections as follows:

1. In the writings of Josephus there are certain passages which appear to imply that during the procuratorial period the Jews enjoyed constitutional autonomy as far as the practice of their religion was concerned:

a) According to *Bell.* 2, 8, 9, the Essenes were extremely accurate and just in their trial of cases, and they punished any blasphemer of Moses with death.

It should be observed, however, that Kilpatrick (*op. cit.*, p. 19) thinks that this passage should not be adduced in support of the view we are defending, as "in some ways the Essenes resembled a secret society, and secret societies, such as the Mau Mau of today, are not in the habit of referring to established governments their decisions for life and death."

But while the Essenes constituted a distinctive religious sect, it seems very rash to compare them with the Mau Mau of East Africa. There is no evidence that action was ever taken against them for contravening an imperial decree, and Josephus (*Vita*, 2), besides mentioning them alongside such highly respectable parties as the Pharisees and the Sadducees, shows no reticence in declaring that he himself had made trial of the sect as a young man.

b) According to *Ant.* 18, 3, 5, a Jew who had been accused of transgressing their laws (that is, presumably, the laws of the Jews) fled from his own country because he feared the punishment which might be inflicted upon him.

c) According to *Ant.* 13, 10, 6, the Pharisees were lenient as judges; and, according to *Ant.* 18, 1, 4, the Sadducees, when they acted as magistrates, addicted themselves to the notions of the Pharisees, for otherwise the public would not have tolerated them. Thus public opinion, which was predominantly Pharisaic, exercised a restraining influence on the Sadducean magistrates; but there is no mention of any restrictions imposed by the imperial authority.

d) According to *Ant.* 20, 9, 1, James and certain others were put to death at the order of the sanhedrin, and objection was taken to the action. In Juster's opinion, only the earlier part of the passage is authentic; it reads:

Caesar [Nero], on hearing of the death of Festus [62 A.D.], sent Albinus to Judaea as procurator. . . . The younger Ananus, who now, as we have stated, took over the high priesthood, was a rash and very audacious man; he belonged to the sect of the Sadducees, who, as we have already explained, are more ruthless when judging offenders than all the rest of the Jews.

Juster considers that the sequel is unauthentic; it reads:

Such was the character of this Ananus, who, thinking that a favourable opportunity now presented itself—Festus being dead and Albinus still on the way—summoned the judicial court of the sanhedrin, brought before it the brother of Jesus who was called Christ—James was his name—with some others, and after accusing them of transgressing the law, delivered them over to be stoned to death.

In Juster's opinion, this part of the story is inconsistent with the point already made by Josephus that it was the influence of the Pharisees, not the authority of the procurator, which prevented the Sadducees from being as severe in judgment as they would have liked to have been. The passage continues:

This action aroused the indignation of all citizens with the highest reputation for fairness and strict observance of the laws; and they sent a secret message to King [Agrippa] petitioning him to restrain Ananus, who had been wrong in what he had done already, from similar behavior in future. Moreover, some of them went to meet Albinus on his way from Alexandria and explained that it was illegal for Ananus to convene a meeting of the sanhedrin without his consent. Albinus was persuaded by their arguments and wrote an angry letter to Ananus threatening to punish him. King Agrippa, on his side, for this action deposed Ananus from the high priesthood, when he had held office but three months, and appointed Jesus, son of Damnaeus, in his place.[2]

But, asks Juster, would Albinus have been so easily convinced? Would not some official have been temporarily in charge of the imperial administration during the absence of the procurator? Would not Albinus have already known what the rights of the high priest were? And would Jews have informed a Roman official that their own supreme court could not be convened without his consent? Juster considers that the situation described is as historically incredible as that presented in John 18:31, and he concludes that the latter part of the story in its present form is the work of a Christian apologist who, like the fourth evangelist, held that the Jews had not the power to inflict capital punishment.

Such an interpretation, however, is open to various objections: (1) In a Christian interpolation one would have expected to read that Jesus was the Messiah, not merely that he was said to be the Messiah. (2) If Juster's interpretation were correct,

---

[2] It may be noticed that, according to *Ant.* 20, 9, 7, Agrippa II was entrusted with the care of the temple by the Emperor Claudius, and this evidently included the authority to appoint and dismiss the high priest.

would not the notice of James have been more laudatory? (3) A subordinate official may have been temporarily in charge of the imperial administration during the procurator's absence, but the likelihood is that he would not command the same degree of respect as the procurator himself. (4) Since Albinus had but recently been appointed to the office of procurator, it could hardly be expected that he would be thoroughly acquainted with the details of constitutional procedure in Judaea. (5) The parallel between the story before us and John 18:31 is not so close as Juster suggests; according to John 18:31 the Jews informed Pilate that it was not lawful for them to put any man to death, whereas in the complaint made to Albinus it is explained that Ananus acted illegally in convening a meeting of the sanhedrin without procuratorial consent.

Nevertheless, even if we accept the authenticity of the received text of the story, the complaint made to Albinus does not necessarily imply that the court of the sanhedrin was formally incompetent to deal with capital cases. Ananus, the Sadducean high priest, saw in the absence of the procurator an opportunity for taking action against certain people of whom he disapproved, the result being that James and some others were put to death at the order of the sanhedrin. But a number of citizens, probably belonging to the Pharisaic circles, at once raised their voices in protest against an action which, in their view, had no legal justification. Presumably, they argued that James and the others had committed no crime against the national religion for which the law of Moses required the infliction of capital punishment; and they drew the attention of Agrippa to the matter. Moreover, on the basis of such an argument they could go on to complain that Ananus ought not to have convened the sanhedrin without procuratorial consent. Presumably, they contended that, if James and the others had committed any crime at all, they must have committed a political crime, and offences against the state came under the jurisdiction not of the sanhedrin but of the procurator. Hence it was arranged that a deputation should meet Albinus with the complaint that Ananus acted unconstitutionally in assembling the sanhedrin to try a case which properly came under the jurisdiction of the imperial authority. Accordingly, when the story is understood in this way, one may infer from it that the sanhedrin was formally competent to pass and execute a capital sentence in certain cases of religious offence.[3]

2. According to Acts 6:8ff., Stephen was condemned to death by the sanhedrin (cf. above, Chapter 12). There is no indication in the text of the story that the proceedings were irregular; and if they were irregular, why did not the Roman authorities intervene? Feelings doubtless ran high; and after the implied identification of Jesus with the glorious Son of Man (7:55f.), the people cried out loudly, stopped their ears, and rushed upon the prisoner as one man. But such reactions were probably all meant to prevent their hearing further blasphemies from Stephen's lips; their shouting would drown his words, while their rushing upon him would make further utterance on his part extremely difficult; also, the witnesses' act of laying their clothes at the feet of a prominent member of the council is in accordance with San. 6, 4, and the people observe the precept of Lev. 24:14 in taking the prisoner out of the town to be stoned (7:58). Thus the court evidently found Stephen guilty of blasphemy and the required penalty of death by stoning was duly inflicted.[4] And

[3] It may be noted here that there is only one passage in the New Testament (Acts 22:30) where it is stated that a meeting of the sanhedrin was convened by a Roman officer.

[4] It appears that certain representatives of Pharisaic opinion came to question the validity of the judgment, which was perhaps commonly upheld by the Sadducees, that those who identified the crucified Jesus with the Messiah were guilty of blasphemy in the sense of the law and merited capital punishment; cf. Gamaliel's warning in Acts 5:34ff., and the passages in Josephus (*Ant.* 13, 10, 6; 18, 1, 4; 20, 9, 1) referred to in the preceding section.

elsewhere in the Acts of the Apostles (as, for example, in 4:1ff. and 5:17ff.) it seems that the sanhedrin was quite free to try religious offences.

But while agreeing that the proceedings taken against Stephen were not irregular, Jeremias (*op. cit.*, pp. 146f.) supposes that they were made possible by the fact that the procurator had strengthened Jewish power specifically against the Christians at the instigation of the high priest; in support of this hypothesis he points out that permission would have had to be obtained for the extension of the persecution (cf. Acts 8:1ff.) beyond the frontiers of Judaea (cf. Acts 9:1ff.), and that Caiaphas, who was on good terms with Pilate (remaining in office for the record period of some twenty years), would not have had much difficulty in securing a special dispensation.

This line of argument, however, is far from being compelling. If the high priest could get the procurator to strengthen the power of the sanhedrin against the Christians, why could he not have also persuaded him that the sanhedrin ought to be made competent to try other offences for which the Mosaic law still more obviously required the death penalty? Perhaps Jeremias supposes that Caiaphas stressed the political danger inherent in the new religion, but in that case why did not Pilate himself take action? We know that the procurator was quite capable of violently suppressing seditious movements when occasion arose (cf. Luke 13:1; Josephus, *Ant.* 18, 4, 1). Moreover, if concerted action (or at least Jewish action with Roman backing) against Christianity had definitely been decided upon, it is strange that the apostles were allowed to remain active in the capital (cf. Acts 8:14) and that the persecution was so sporadic and half-hearted (cf. Acts 8:25; 9:31). Also, it is noteworthy that Ananus, during the dispute of 62 A.D. discussed in the foregoing section, evidently made no appeal to any ruling given by Pilate.

3. In San. 7, 2 of the Mishnah (where the correct method of burning a condemned person is being discussed) we read:

R. Eliezer b. Zadok said: It happened once that a priest's daughter committed adultery and they encompassed her with bundles of branches and burnt her to death [cf. Lev. 21:9]. They said to him: Because the court at that time had not the right knowledge.[5]

This passage may afford trustworthy evidence for the view that the sanhedrin during the procuratorial period had the power to inflict capital punishment. But the date of the execution to which it refers is disputed. Some scholars think that it took place during the reign of Agrippa I (41–44 A.D.), when the procuratorial system of government was temporarily suspended. Thus, in a letter to Lietzmann (*Z.N.T.W.*, XXXI [1932], 81f.) Jeremias argues that the available data all but compel us to conclude that the incident took place in Agrippa's reign. For, according to Bab. Yeb. 15b, the younger Eliezer, son of Zadok, was studying the torah while still very young during "the arid years"—that is, so we may infer, during the famine of 47–49 A.D. And, according to San. 9, 11 of the Tosefta, Eliezer declared that he had actually witnessed the execution of the priest's daughter from the vantage point of his father's shoulders. Evidently, he was a little boy at the time, and his father carried him to prevent his being crushed by the crowd or to enable him to see the spectacle. Accordingly, if Eliezer was, say, twelve years of age in 48 A.D., he would be between five and eight years old during Agrippa's reign, and it would be natural for a child between five and eight years of age to ride on his father's shoulders in a crowd. This interpretation, however, is only one of many possible interpretations of the data adduced. Thus Eliezer need not have been more than six years old in 48 A.D., for some rabbis commenced their talmudic studies at a very early age; and it is not impossible that he was carried on his father's shoulders when he was a child of ten or eleven. Hence the priest's daughter may have been executed at as late a date as 53 A.D.

[5] According to the Babylonian Gemara (San. 52b) the court was composed of Sadducees.

4. As Winter has pointed out (*op. cit.*, pp. 67ff.), in San. 7, 1 of the Mishnah strangling is mentioned as one of the four authorized modes of capital punishment, although this punitive measure is nowhere referred to as a recognized Jewish practice either in the Old Testament or in the Greek sources. It seems to have been introduced by the rabbis before 100 A.D., perhaps in an effort to avoid official detection of the fact that they continued to exercise judicial authority in some measure after 70 A.D., when the sanhedrin was deprived of all constitutional power. The court had now to carry out its executions of capital sentences in secret, and this evidently implies that prior to the collapse of the state such executions were quite in order.

5. In Agrippa's letter to Caligula (cited by Philo in his *Legatio ad Gaium*, 39) we read:

If any Jew, I will not say of the common people, but even of the priestly families, and those not of the lowest order, but those who are in the rank next to the first, should enter [the holy of holies] either by himself or with the high priest, and if the high priest himself should enter [the holy of holies] on two days in the year, or three or four times on the same day [the day of atonement], he would be inevitably punished with death.

This passage plainly shows that the sanhedrin during the procuratorial period enjoyed the competence to punish certain religious offences with death.

6. The inscription discovered by Clermont-Ganneau in 1871 definitely shows that the Jewish authorities were formally entitled by the imperial government to put any Gentile to death if he ventured to pass into the sanctuary beyond the second enclosure of the temple. It reads:

No foreigner may enter within the balustrade and enclosure surrounding the sanctuary. And whoever is caught so doing will have himself to blame that his death ensues.[6]

[6] For allusions to this ordinance, cf. Josephus, *Ant.* 15, 11, 5; *Bell.* 5, 5, 2; 6, 2, 4; Philo, *Leg.* 31; Acts 21:29; Eph. 2:14. For a photograph of

This ordinance doubtless implies that a special dispensation had been granted by the Roman government to the Jewish authorities. Generally, the sanhedrin would be competent to deal only with religious offences committed by Jews. The procurator would be responsible for the maintenance of public order; all political cases would come under his jurisdiction, and he would be kept informed of proceedings at the Jewish court. But it ought not to be inferred from the special character of the ordinance that the inscription has no bearing on the general question whether the sanhedrin was formally competent to inflict the penalty of death on Jews convicted of capital offences against the law of their religion. For if in certain circumstances the Jewish authorities could put a Roman citizen to death, a right which was not even enjoyed by the procurator himself, surely they would be formally empowered to pass and execute a capital sentence on any ordinary Jewish citizen who was found guilty of a religious offence for which the law of Moses required the infliction of the death penalty.

---

the inscription, see Deissmann, *Light from the Ancient East*, p. 75. Deissmann notes that when he saw the slab in 1906 the characters seemed to him to show traces of paint. Cf. also J. Armitage Robinson, *St. Paul's Epistle to the Ephesians*, pp. 59f., 160f.

Conclusion

ST. MARK'S gospel is not an essay in scientific biography, but a religious document which was written for the edification of believers. As we gather from its superscription, the evangelist is concerned to depict the life of Jesus as the earthly career of the Messiah, the Son of God, and it is interesting to find that the declarations of the heavenly voice and the confessions of the demons are supplemented in the later part of the gospel by a Jew's testimony to the Messiahship at 8:29 and by a Gentile's testimony to the divine Sonship at 15:39. Despite the fundamentally divine character of its central figure, however, the gospel story is not an epic of unrelieved triumph and continuous success, for it relates how Jesus was rejected by his own people and crucified by the Gentiles, and St. Mark evidently seeks to overcome the difficulty thus raised by holding that the true status of Jesus was a predetermined secret. The Master was not accepted as the Messiah, and the evangelist maintains that it was an integral part of the divine purpose that he should not have been so accepted. Hence in the second gospel Jesus is represented as deliberately concealing the truth from the public by the in-

319

junctions to silence and by the cryptology of parabolical teaching.

Accordingly, Christianity was (as it remains) essentially a paradoxical religion which had to make room in its total interpretation of Messiahship for the shame of the crucifixion. The situation demanded that the church should reconcile the indubitable fact of the humiliation of Jesus with its ardent faith in his ultimate supremacy as the plenipotentiary of God. Indeed, it was precisely the task of synthesizing such opposing conceptions in a coherent scheme of thought that constituted the main problem of apostolic christology. The earliest solution, which finds characteristic expression in the writings of St. Paul, appears to have been that the Messiah's sufferings were a necessary prelude to his final manifestation in glory. St. Mark, however, refuses to regard the messianic glory purely as an object of anticipation to be realized in the future and, in some measure, he considers that it is already evident amid all the lowliness and shame of the Master's life on earth. But in so far as the church's historical traditions concerning the career of its founder are evaluated from such a standpoint, the difficulty raised by the rejection of Jesus becomes all the more acute; and this helps us to understand why the evangelist emphasizes the secret character of the Messiahship.

Broadly speaking, St. Mark seems to distinguish four principal stages or periods in the historical realization of God's plan of salvation: the period of preparation, which comes to an end with the imprisonment of the appointed forerunner; the period of the incarnate life, which is characterized by suffering and obscurity; the postresurrection period of enlightenment, in which the gospel of the crucified Messiah is publicly proclaimed by the church; and the period of eschatological fulfillment, which will be gloriously inaugurated by the Son of Man at his awaited parousia. It is not to be supposed, however, that the evangelist presents us with a systematic body of doctrine concerning these periods and the manner of their interconnection. He is much less a master of his material than the fourth evangelist, for example, and this is not surprising seeing that he was apparently the first writer to respond to the church's increasing need for a connected account of the ministry.

But there can be little doubt regarding St. Mark's fundamental attitude. Convinced that Jesus is the Messiah, he takes the view that the Lord's humiliation represents the pledge or guarantee of his triumph in glory which is subsequently to be made manifest. It is as though the soteriological process were governed by a principle of divine retribution which ultimately effects a reversal of the situation existing during the period of the earthly ministry. Heavenly exaltation is the reward of self-abnegation. The evangelist therefore contemplates the sufferings of Jesus and the tribulations of the church in the light of a revelation in glory, and yet, since the reward always comes after the humiliation, there is a break or rift in the soteriological process. Thus, in an important sense, St. Mark's thought is basically bipolar. The sufferings and the glory belong to different epochs, and the relationship between them has the appearance of being no more intimate than that which obtains between means and end. They are not brought together in the unity of a single conception as they are, for example, in the fourth gospel, where the notion of the cost of the passion has almost disappeared.

On the other hand, there is a countertendency at work which militates against the bipolarity of the evangelist's fundamental position and induces him to represent the life of Jesus as the locus of secret revelation. Apparently, he is not completely satisfied with the doctrine that the humiliation of the Messiah is the appointed means to his future triumph, and thus he comes to attach a greater degree of intrinsic importance to the incarnate life than seems to be allowed in the epistles of St. Paul, who betrays little or no interest in the actual details of the Lord's earthly ministry. Probably the delay in the arrival of the parousia helped to bring about the new emphasis. But in whatever manner the change is to be accounted for, St. Mark undoubtedly goes some way toward closing the gap, as it were, between the notion of the Messiah's humiliation and that of his supremacy, or toward overcoming the bipolarity of what appears to be his primary philosophical position. In the story of the transfiguration, for instance, the veil of the flesh is temporarily withdrawn, and the three most intimate disciples are privileged to behold their Master as he really is and in the form in which he will be made manifest to the world when he comes again finally to establish the kingdom of God with great power and glory.

But the countertendency in question is more pronounced in some passages than in others, and, whenever it becomes particularly strong, St. Mark is inclined to overstep the limits prescribed by his doctrine of the secret and to delineate the incarnate life openly in terms of the apostolic faith. Hence certain passages convey the impression that the true nature of Jesus is reaching out for some definite form of articulate expression which, however, it cannot yet receive; in the stories of the triumphal entry and of the anointing at Bethany, for example, the evangelist's belief in the reality of the Messiahship is apparently pressing for overt recognition in the narrative, thereby putting great strain on the requirement of secrecy. And, notably, in the account of the nocturnal trial the pressure exerted by the evangelist's conviction subjects his doctrine of the secret to a strain which it cannot withstand, the result being that in 14:62 there is actually a disclosure of the fact of the Messiahship outside the circle of the initiated. Forsaken by his followers and confronted by his enemies in all their worldly might, Jesus gives open confession to his messianic status and confidently declares that his judges shall see the Son of Man coming with the clouds of heaven. Thus something of the supernatural glory of the parousia lights up the darkest depths of the humiliation to which the passion narrative bears witness; and we are presented with what is, from one point of view, the most striking exemplification in the entire gospel of St. Mark's inclination to move away from the conception of the incarnate life as the period of obscurity toward a characteristically Johannine mode of representation.

In the last-mentioned passage, however, the urge to set forth the earthly ministry directly in terms of the apostolic faith seems to be reinforced by the motive to ascribe responsibility for the crucifixion to the Jews as represented by their leaders. For, although St. Mark believes that the passion was provided for in God's sovereign purpose, he none the less wishes to show that the crucifixion really took place through the unwarranted hostility of the Lord's own countrymen and hence that the burden of guilt for that most terrible crime is borne by a people whose God-given privileges only serve to make their conduct the more reprehensible. The operation of such a motive naturally makes for a certain inconsistency in the evangelist's treatment of his material. As we should expect, in so far as he is concerned to emphasize the culpability of the Jews, he tends to contravene the requirement of secrecy by allowing the true nature of Jesus to come out, so to speak, into the light of day. Consequently, in St. Mark's representation Jesus does not always address the public in the cryptology of parables, as he is said to do in 4:34, and he does not always seek to perform his miracles in private, as he does, for example, in 5:40. On the contrary, in certain passages the fact of the Messiahship is to a greater or less extent exposed to public view, and so it could be maintained that the Jews were in an inexcusable position, since they had perpetrated their crime not in ignorance but with a cognizance of that for which Jesus stood.

In St. Mark's interpretation, then, the life of Jesus, despite its outward show of tragic frustration, is really a continuous fulfillment of God's plan of salvation. The failure of the public to recognize the fact of the Messiahship and the failure of the disciples to understand its meaning are alike provisions of the divine purpose for the redemption of humanity. But it is important to notice that the two instances of failure do not make their historical appearance in the same way. For, while the fact of the Messiahship is concealed from the public by the injunctions to silence and by the teaching in parables, it is discovered by Peter at Caesarea Philippi, whereupon its implications are expounded to the twelve and something of its essential glory is made manifest to the privileged three on the occasion of the transfiguration. The veil is withdrawn in the presence of the chosen few, but they are not yet in a position to grasp the significance of the *mysterium* revealed to them. Their spiritual sight is dim, and so it must remain until the time of the Messiah's resurrection, which marks the end of the period of obscurity and the beginning of the period of enlightenment. Thus the confession at Caesarea Philippi is of importance in the evangelist's thought because it serves as a basis for further instruction which, besides preparing the mind of the reader for a right appreciation of the passion narrative, enables the disciples to receive the saving truth of the gospel from the Lord himself. For, although they cannot understand the divine word when it is communicated to them, they can retain it as authentic tradition and can thus equip themselves for their future role as apostles and pillars of the church.

Select Bibliography

Abrahams, I. *Studies in Pharisaism and the Gospels.* 2 vols. Cambridge, Eng., 1917–1924.

Bacon, B. W. *The Beginnings of the Gospel Story.* New Haven, Conn., 1909.

——. *The Gospel of Mark: Its Composition and Date.* New Haven, Conn., 1925.

——. *The Story of Jesus and the Beginnings of the Church.* London, 1928.

Barth, M. *Das Abendmahl: Passamahl, Bundesmahl und Messiasmahl.* Zurich, 1945.

Bartsch, H. W., ed. *Kerygma and Myth.* London, 1953.

Bauernfeind, O. *Die Worte der Dämonen im Markusevangelium.* Stuttgart, 1927.

Beasley-Murray, G. R. *Jesus and the Future—An Examination of the Eschatological Discourse, Mark 13, with Special Reference to the Little Apocalypse Theory.* London, 1954.

Bertram, G. *Die Leidensgeschichte Jesu und der Christuskult.* Giessen, 1922.

Bevan, E. *Hellenism and Christianity.* London, 1921.

Black, M. *An Aramaic Approach to the Gospels and Acts.* Oxford, 1954.

Black, M. *The Scrolls and Christian Origins.* New York, 1961.

Blinzler, J. *The Trial of Jesus.* New York, 1959.

Boobyer, G. H. *St. Mark and the Transfiguration Story.* Edinburgh, 1942.

Bornkamm, G. *Jesus of Nazareth.* New York, 1960.

Bousset, W. *Die Religion des Judentums im späthellenistischen Zeitalter.* 3d ed. rev. by H. Gressmann. *(L.H.B.)* Tübingen, 1926.

——. *Kyrios Christos.* Göttingen, 1926.

Brandon, S. G. F. *The Fall of Jerusalem and the Christian Church.* London, 1951.

Branscomb, B. H. *The Gospel of Mark.* *(M.N.T.)* London, 1937.

Büchler, A. *Der Galiläische 'Am-ha-'Ares.* Vienna, 1906.

Bultmann, R. *Jesus.* Berlin, 1926.

——. *Die Erforschung der synoptischen Evangelien.* Giessen, 1930.

——. *Die Geschichte der synoptischen Tradition.* Göttingen, 1931.

——. *Theology of the New Testament.* 2 vols. London, 1952–1955.

Burkitt, F. C. *The Earliest Sources for the Life of Jesus.* London, 1910.

Bussmann, W. *Synoptische Studien.* 3 vols. Halle, 1925–1931.

Buttrick, G. A., ed. *The Interpreter's Dictionary of the Bible.* 4 vols. New York and Nashville, Tenn., 1962.

Cadbury, H. J. *The Peril of Modernizing Jesus.* New York, 1937.

——. *Jesus—What Manner of Man?* New York, 1947.

Cadoux, A. T. *The Sources of the Second Gospel.* London, 1935.

Cadoux, C. J. *The Historic Mission of Jesus.* London, 1941.

Carrington, P. *The Primitive Christian Calendar: A Study in the Making of the Marcan Gospel.* Vol. I: "Introduction and Text." Cambridge, Eng., 1952.

——. *According to Mark: A Running Commentary on the Oldest Gospel.* Cambridge, Eng., 1960.

Causse, A. *L'évolution de l'espérance messianique dans le Christianisme primitif.* Paris, 1908.

Charles, R. H., ed. *Apocrypha and Pseudepigrapha of the Old Testament.* 2 vols. Oxford, 1913.

Chwolson, D. *Das letzte Passahmahl Christi und der Tag seines Todes.* Leipzig, 1908.

Cranfield, C. E. B. *The Gospel according to Saint Mark.* Cambridge, Eng., 1959.

Cross, F. M. *The Ancient Library of Qumran and Modern Biblical Studies.* London, 1958.

Cullmann, O. *Urchristentum und Gottesdienst.* Basel, 1944.

———. *The State in the New Testament.* London, 1957.

———. *The Christology of the New Testament.* London, 1959.

Dalman, G. *The Words of Jesus.* Edinburgh, 1902.

———. *Jesus—Jeshua.* London, 1929.

Danby, H., ed. *The Mishnah.* Oxford, 1933.

Daniélou, J. *The Dead Sea Scrolls and Primitive Christianity.* Baltimore, 1958.

Davies, W. D., and D. Daube, eds. *The Background of the New Testament and Its Eschatology.* Cambridge, Eng., 1956.

Deissmann, A. *Light from the Ancient East.* London, 1910.

Dibelius, M. *From Tradition to Gospel.* London, 1934.

———. *Jesus.* Philadelphia, 1949.

Dodd, C. H. *The Parables of the Kingdom.* London, 1935.

———. *The Apostolic Preaching and Its Developments.* London, 1936.

———. *New Testament Studies.* Manchester, 1954.

Ebeling, H. J. *Das Messiasgeheimnis und die Botschaft des Marcus-Evangelisten.* Berlin, 1939.

Elbogen, I. *Der jüdische Gottesdienst in seiner geschichtlichen Entwicklung.* Leipzig, 1913.

Elbogen, I., and M. Braun. *Festschrift zu Israel Lewy.* Breslau, 1911.

Eltester, W., ed. *Neutestamentliche Studien für Rudolf Bultmann.* Berlin, 1954.

Enslin, M. S. *The Prophet from Nazareth.* New York, 1961.

Epstein, I. *The Babylonian Talmud.* 35 vols. London, 1935–1952.

Farrer, A. M. *A Study in St. Mark.* London, 1951.

———. *St. Matthew and St. Mark.* London, 1954.

Fascher, E. *Die Formgeschichtliche Methode.* Giessen, 1924.

Fenner, F. *Die Krankheit im Neuen Testament.* Leipzig, 1930.

Fiebig, P. *Antike Wundergeschichten zum Studium der Wunder des Neuen Testaments*. (*L.K.T.*) Bonn, 1911.

Foakes-Jackson, F. J., and K. Lake, eds. *The Beginnings of Christianity*. 5 vols. London, 1920–1933.

Fridrichsen, A. *Le problème du miracle dans le Christianisme primitif*. Strasbourg, 1925.

Gaugler, E. *Das Amendmahl im Neuen Testament*. Basel, 1943.

Geiger, A. *Urschrift und Übersetzungen der Bibel in ihrer Abhängigkeit von der innern Entwicklung des Judenthums*. Breslau, 1857.

Gloege, G. *Reich Gottes und Kirche*. Gütersloh, 1929.

Goguel, M. *The Life of Jesus*. London, 1933.

——. *La foi à la résurrection de Jésus dans le Christianisme primitif*. Paris, 1933.

——. *L'église primitive*. Paris, 1948.

——. *The Birth of Christianity*. London, 1953.

Gore, C., H. L. Goudge, and A. Guillaume, eds. *A New Commentary on Holy Scripture including the Apocrypha*. London, 1929.

Grässer, E. *Das Problem der Parousieverzögerung in den synoptischen Evangelien und in der Apostelgeschichte*. Berlin, 1957–1960.

Grant, F. C. *The Earliest Gospel*. New York, 1943.

Grant, R. M. *Miracle and Natural Law in Graeco-Roman and Early Christian Thought*. Amsterdam, 1952.

Gray, G. B. *Isaiah 1–39*. (*I.C.C.*) Edinburgh, 1912.

——. *Sacrifice in the Old Testament*. Oxford, 1925.

Guénin, P. *Y-a-t-il eu conflit entre Jean-Baptiste et Jésus?* Geneva, 1933.

Guignebert, C. *Jesus*. London, 1935.

——. *The Jewish World in the Time of Jesus*. London, 1939.

——. *Le Christ*. Paris, 1943.

Gunkel, H. *Zum religionsgeschichtlichen Verständnis des Neuen Testaments*. Göttingen, 1903.

Guy, H. A. *The Origin of the Gospel of Mark*. London, 1954.

Héring, J. *Le royaume de Dieu et sa venue*. Paris, 1937–1959.

Herzog, R. *Die Wunderheilungen von Epidaurus*. Leipzig, 1931.

Higgins, A. J. B. *The Lord's Supper in the New Testament.* London, 1952.

——, ed. *New Testament Essays: Studies in Memory of Thomas Walter Manson 1893–1958.* Manchester, 1959.

Hirsch, E. *Das Werden des Markusevangeliums.* Tübingen, 1951.

Holtzmann, O. and H. von Beer, eds., *Die Mishna, Traktat Berakot.* Giessen, 1912.

Huxley, A. *The Devils of Loudun.* London, 1952.

James, M. R., ed. *The Apocryphal New Testament.* Oxford, 1924.

Jaubert, A. *La date de la cène: Calendrier biblique et liturgie chrétienne.* Paris, 1957.

Jeremias, J. *Jesus als Weltvollender.* Gütersloh, 1930.

——. *Die Abendmahlsworte Jesu.* Göttingen, 1949. (E.T., Oxford, 1955.)

——. *The Parables of Jesus.* London, 1954.

Johnson, S. L. *A Commentary on the Gospel according to St. Mark.* London, 1960.

Juster, J. *Les Juifs dans l'empire romain.* 2 vols. Paris, 1914.

Kent, C. F. *The Sermons, Epistles and Apocalypses of Israel's Prophets.* London, 1910.

Kilpatrick, G. D. *The Trial of Jesus.* Oxford, 1953.

Kittel, G., ed. *Theologisches Wörterbuch zum Neuen Testament.* 6 vols. Stuttgart, 1933–.

Klausner, J. *Jesus of Nazareth: His Life, Times and Teaching.* London, 1925.

Klostermann, E. *Das Markusevangelium.* (L.H.B.) Tübingen, 1936.

Knox, W. L. *Some Hellenistic Elements in Primitive Christianity.* London, 1944.

——. *The Sources of the Synoptic Gospels—I: St. Mark.* Cambridge, Eng., 1953.

Köhler, L. *Das formgeschichtliche Problem des Neuen Testaments.* Tübingen, 1927.

Kümmel, W. G. *Verheissung und Erfüllung.* Basel, 1945.

Lagrange, M. J. *Evangile selon Saint Marc.* Paris, 1929.

Lake, K. and S. *An Introduction to the New Testament.* London, 1938.

Leenhardt, F. J. *Le sacrement de la sainte cène.* Neuchâtel, 1948.

Lietzmann, H. *Messe und Herrenmahl.* Bonn, 1926.

——. *Der Prozess Jesu.* (*S.B.A.*) Berlin, 1931.

Lightfoot, R. H. *History and Interpretation in the Gospels.* London, 1935.

——. *Locality and Doctrine in the Gospels.* London, 1938.

——. *The Gospel Message of St. Mark.* Oxford, 1950.

Lohmeyer, E. *Galiläa und Jerusalem.* Göttingen, 1936.

——. *Das Evangelium des Markus* (with *Ergänzungsheft*). (*M.K.E.K.*) Göttingen, 1951.

Loisy, A. *Les évangiles synoptiques.* 2 vols. Paris, 1907–1908.

——. *L'évangile selon Marc.* Paris, 1912.

Major, H. D. A., T. W. Manson, and C. J. Wright. *The Mission and Message of Jesus.* London, 1937.

Manson, T. W. *The Teaching of Jesus.* Cambridge, Eng., 1935.

——. *The Servant-Messiah.* Cambridge, Eng., 1953.

Manson, W. *Jesus the Messiah.* London, 1943.

Marxsen, W. *Der Evangelist Markus: Studien zur Redaktionsgeschichte des Evangeliums.* Göttingen, 1956–1959.

Masson, C. *Les paraboles de Marc IV.* Neuchâtel, 1945.

McCasland, S. V. *By the Finger of God: Demon Possession and Exorcism in Early Christianity.* New York, 1951.

McGinley, L. J. *Form-Criticism of the Synoptic Healing Narratives.* Woodstock, Md., 1944.

Meyer, E. *Ursprung und Anfänge des Christentums.* 3 vols. Stuttgart, 1921–1923.

Micklem, E. R. *Miracles and the New Psychology: A Study of the Healing Miracles of the New Testament.* Oxford, 1922.

Micklem, N., ed. *Christian Worship: Studies in Its History and Meaning by Members of Mansfield College.* Oxford, 1936.

Milik, J. T. *Ten Years of Discovery in the Wilderness of Judaea.* London, 1959.

Montefiore, C. J. *The Synoptic Gospels.* London, 1927.

Moore, G. F. *Judaism in the First Centuries of the Christian Era.* Cambridge, Mass., 1927–1930.

Select Bibliography

Moulton, J. H. *A Grammar of New Testament Greek.* Vol. I: "Prolegomena." Edinburgh, 1906.

Moulton, J. H., and G. Milligan. *The Vocabulary of the Greek Testament.* 8 parts. London, 1914–1929.

Nineham, D. E., ed. *Studies in the Gospels: Essays in Memory of R. H. Lightfoot.* Oxford, 1955.

Oesterley, W. O. E. *The Jewish Background of the Christian Liturgy.* Oxford, 1925.

Otto, R. *The Kingdom of God and the Son of Man.* London, 1938.

Parker, P. *The Gospel before Mark.* Chicago, 1953.

Pernot, H. *Etudes sur la langue des évangiles.* Paris, 1927.

Rawlinson, A. E. J. *The Gospel according to St. Mark.* (*W. Comm.*) London, 1925.

Reitzenstein, R. *Poimandres: Studien zur griechisch-ägyptischen und frühchristlichen Literatur.* Leipzig, 1904.

———. *Hellenistische Wundererzählungen.* Leipzig, 1906.

———. *Das mandäische Buch des Herrn der Grösse.* Leipzig, 1919.

Riesenfeld, H. *Jésus Transfiguré.* Copenhagen, 1947.

Robinson, J. A. *St. Paul's Epistle to the Ephesians.* London, 1903.

Robinson, J. M. *The Problem of History in Mark.* London, 1957.

Rohde, E. *Psyche: The Cult of Souls and Belief in Immortality among the Greeks.* London, 1925.

Ropes, J. H. *The Synoptic Gospels.* Cambridge, Mass., 1934.

Schmidt, K. L. *Der Rahmen der Geschichte Jesu.* Berlin, 1919.

Schniewind, J. *Das Evangelium nach Markus.* Göttingen, 1949.

Schweitzer, A. *The Quest of the Historical Jesus.* London, 1911.

Sharman, H. B. *Son of Man and Kingdom of God.* New York, 1943.

Sjöberg, E. *Der verborgene Menschensohn in den Evangelien.* Lund, 1955.

Smith, W. R. *The Religion of the Semites.* 3d ed., with an introduction and additional notes by S. A. Cook. London, 1927.

Steinmann, J. *Saint John the Baptist and the Desert Tradition.* London, 1958.

Stendahl, K., ed. *The Scrolls and the New Testament.* London, 1958.

Stonehouse, N. B. *The Witness of Matthew and Mark to Christ.* Philadelphia, 1944.

Strack, H., and P. Billerbeck. *Kommentar zum Neuen Testament aus Talmud und Midrasch.* 5 vols. Munich, 1922–1928.

Streeter, B. H. *The Four Gospels: A Study of Origins.* London, 1926.

Sundwall, J. *Die Zusammensetzung des Markusevangeliums.* Turku, 1934.

Taylor, V. *The Formation of the Gospel Tradition.* London, 1933.

——. *Jesus and His Sacrifice.* London, 1937.

——. *The Gospel according to St. Mark.* London, 1952.

——. *The Life and Ministry of Jesus.* London, 1954.

Thackeray, H. St. J. *Selections from Josephus.* London, 1919.

Tödt, H. E. *Der Menschensohn in der synoptischen Überlieferung.* Gütersloh, 1959.

Torrey, C. C. *The Four Gospels: A New Translation.* London, 1933.

Vermes, G. *Scripture and Tradition in Judaism.* Leiden, 1961.

Vielhauer, P., ed. *Festschrift für Günther Dehn.* Neukirchen, 1957.

Weinreich. O. *Antike Heilungswunder.* Giessen, 1909.

Weiss, J. *The History of Primitive Christianity.* London, 1937.

Wellhausen, J. *Das Evangelium Marci.* Berlin, 1903.

——. *Einleitung in die drei ersten Evangelien.* Berlin, 1911.

Wilamowitz-Moellendorf, U. von. *Reden und Vorträge.* Vol. II. Berlin, 1926.

Wilder, A. N. *Eschatology and Ethics in the Teaching of Jesus.* New York, 1950.

Winter, P. *On the Trial of Jesus.* Berlin, 1961.

Wrede, W. *Das Messiasgeheimnis in den Evangelien.* Göttingen, 1901.

——. *Vorträge und Studien,* ed. by A. Wrede. Tübingen, 1907.

Index

Abrahams, I., 198 n.20
Ananus, 311ff.
Anointing, 228ff., 243, 259
Anti-Romanism, 93 n.12
Anti-Semitism, 15, 117ff., 153, 201ff., 224ff., 294
Apostles, 140 n.49
Arrest, 236, 299 n.32
Authority, 34f., 200

Bacon, B. W., 161 n.19, 193
Baptism, 12ff., 270 n.23
Barabbas, 225, 244 n.46, 294, 297 n.25
Bar Kokhba, 289
Barrett, C. K., 212 n.4
Bartimaeus, 184ff., 188ff., 195
Bauernfeind, O., 76ff., 86ff.
Beare, F. W., 134 n.37
Beasley-Murray, G. R., 207 n.40
Beelzebul:
    in general, 47ff., 154 n.11
    controversy, 75, 84 n.22, 136f.
Benoit, P., 300 n.1
Bernadin, J. B., 159 n.15
Bertram, G., 222 n.4, 229 n.18
Betrayal, 228, 233f., 258f.
Bevan, E., 50 n.7
Billerbeck, P., see Strack, H., and P. Billerbeck
Bipolarity, St. Mark's, 177ff., 208f.

Bisexuality, 203 n.32
Bishop, E. F., 191
Black, M., 22 n.21, 252 n.1, 265 n.15, 270 n.23
Blasphemy, 282, 288ff., 314f.
Blind man of Bethsaida, 149, 190
Blood, 274
Boldly, 172f.
Boobyer, G. H., 19 n.15, 107 n.7, 132 n.33, 157 n.13, 160 n.17, 161 n.18
Bousset, W., 292 n.18
Branscomb, B. H., 198 n.20, 206 n.39
Brooke, A. E., 308
Büchler, A., 269 n.21
Büchsel, F., 300 n.1
Bultmann, R., 2 n.1, 17 n.12, 32, 39 n.21, 52 nn.10, 12, 56 n.17, 72, 81 n.20, 82 n.21, 86 n.1, 93 n.12, 101 n.3, 123 n.16, 133, 136 n.42, 137 n.43, 138 n.48, 146 n.1, 160 n.17, 182 n.24, 185 n.28, 199 n.21, 200 n.23, 205 n.35, 233 n.26, 247 n.55, 281 n.4, 295
Burkill, T. A., 2 n.1, 280 n.1
Bussmann, W., 141 n.51
Buttrick, G. A., 280 n.1

Cadbury, H. J., 6 n.4, 210
Caesarea Philippi, 146
Campbell, J. Y., 165

333

Index

Carrington, P., 61 n.27, 82 n.21, 133 n.35, 135 n.40
Centurion, 117 n.3, 119 n.6, 246ff.
Chaburoth, 269 n.21
Christology, St. Mark's, 19f., 156ff., 160 n.16
Christophanies, 156ff., 223f., 255ff.
Chwolson, D., 262
Clermont-Ganneau, C., 291, 317
Cock-crow, 237 n.34
Collingwood, R. G., 4 n.3
Communion, 234ff., 268ff.
Confession of Jesus, 242f., 280, 288
Controversy stories, 123ff., 203ff.
Counterquestions, 131, 133, 200
Covenant, 273ff., 278
Cranfield, C. E. B., 217 n.5
Creed, J. M., 157 n.13, 165, 250 n.61
Curse of God, 289
Cycles of tradition, 140 n.49

Dalman, G., 284 n.7
Danby, H., 282 n.5
Daniélou, J., 22 n.21
Darkness at noon, 239 n.37, 245
Daube, D., 35 n.14, 98 n.1
Davies, W. D., 133 n.35
Dead Sea Scrolls, 22 n.21, 203 n.32, 265 n.15, 270 n.23
Deissmann, A., 56 n.16, 59 n.22, 73, 225 n.9, 317 n.6
Demoniac:
    in the synagogue, 33ff., 62ff., 71ff.
    Gerasene, 63, 86ff.
Demonology, 47ff.
Demons, confessions of, 62ff.
Dereliction, cry of, 239f.
Dibelius, M., 19 n.16, 52ff., 80 n.18, 91 n.8, 94 n.13, 123 n.16, 146 n.1, 185 n.28, 204 n.34, 221 n.2, 222 n.5, 236 n.33, 239 n.37, 246 n.51, 249, 251 n.62, 258, 268, 274 n.26, 276 n.32, 281 n.2, 297, 299 n.32
Disciples:
    calling of, 31f., 135, 205 n.36
    obtuseness of, 103ff., 168ff., 184ff.
Dodd, C. H., 165ff.
Dove, 17f.

Ebeling, H. J., 300 n.1
Elbogen, I., 269 n.21
Eliezer, 315f.

Elijah, 11ff., 147, 177 n.13, 180f., 183, 239 n.37, 240, 246
Eltester, W., 152 n.8
Empty tomb, 236, 249ff., 256 n.7, 259 n.3
Ending at Mark 16:8, 157 n.13, 248 n.57
Ephphatha, 61 n.27
Eschatological discourse, 177ff., 205ff., 241
Eucharist, 232ff., 258ff.
Evans, C. F., 255 n.5
Exorcisms, 47ff., 62ff., 86ff.

Faith, 57ff., 139
False witnesses, *see* Witnesses
Farrer, A. M., 24ff.
Fascher, E., 152 n.8
Fasting, 132f.
Fear motif, 169 n.2, 256 n.7
Feeding of the multitudes, 106f.
Fenner, F., 61 n.25, 190 n.2
Fig tree, cursing of, 121f., 197f., 234 n.27, 246f., 286
Firstfruits, 260f.
Flesh, 279
Foakes-Jackson, F. J., 9 n.3, 128 n.25, 180 n.18
Foreknowledge of Jesus, 223, 232ff.
Forgiveness of sins, 129ff.
Form-criticism, 6 n.4
Fraternal meals, 269 n.21
Fridrichsen, A., 59 n.21, 75, 84 n.22, 95, 130, 136 n.42
Fulfillment, 10, 30ff., 222ff.

Galilean reunion, 236, 255ff.
Galilee and Jerusalem, 236 n.33, 252ff.
Gamaliel, 314 n.4
Gaugler, E., 269 n.21
Geiger, A., 269 n.21
Gerasene, *see* Demoniac
Gethsemane, 238ff.
Glorification of Jesus, 156ff., 241 n.41, 242
Godsend, 160 n.16
Goguel, M., 22 n.21, 160 n.17, 174 n.11, 237 n.34, 250 n.61, 292 n.18, 297 n.24, 299 n.32, 306
Gospel, 9, 28, 230 n.20
Grant, R. M., 61 n.27
Gray, G. B., 113, 259 n.5

Index

Grenfell, B. P., and A. S. Hunt, 138 n.48
Gressmann, H., 17, 72, 292 n.18
Guénin, P., 17 n.12
Gunkel, H., 17, 23 n.23
Guy, H. A., 132 n.33

Hallel, 236 n.31, 261
Helios, 246 n.50
Héring, J., 128 n.25, 204 n.34
Herodians, 123 n.15, 135 n.38, 203
Higgins, A. J. B., 212 n.4
Holtzmann, O., 269 n.21
Holy of holies, 247
Holy Spirit, 16ff.
Hostility, 117ff., 188ff., 218ff., 252ff., 258f.
Hour, the, 208 n.45, 238f., 241 n.41
Hunt, A. S., *see* Grenfell, B. P., and A. S. Hunt
Huxley, A., 61 n.27

Inconsistency, St. Mark's, 29, 69ff., 122, 128, 155f., 202f., 243 n.43
Injunctions to silence, 62ff., 182
Intercalations, 121 n.10, 228

Jahnow, H., 127 n.23
James, M. R., 226 n.10, 236 n.33
Jaubert, A., 265 n.15
Jeremias, J., 134 n.37, 229 n.18, 230 n.20, 266 n.16, 306ff., 309f., 315, 316
John, St., 14ff., 67, 70, 110, 116 n.17, 130, 160 n.16, 164 n.23, 176, 192, 195f., 208 n.45, 224 n.7, 240 n.38, 241, 260, 262, 276, 287, 290f., 304
John the Baptist, 9ff., 21 n.19, 22 n.21, 28, 147, 175f., 182f., 200
Johnson, S. E., 275 n.29
Jordan, G. V., 269 n.21
Juster, J., 300 n.1, 311f.
Justin, 12 n.6

Kent, C. F., 113 n.14
Kiddush, 276
Kilpatrick, G. D., 300ff., 310
Kingdom of God, 28ff.
King of the Jews, 117 n.1, 244 n.46, 295ff.
Kittel, G., 158 n.14
Klausner, J., 198 n.20, 274 n.26

Klostermann, E., 47 n.3, 88 n.3, 131 n.32, 200 nn.23, 26, 245 n.48
Krauss, S., 127 n.23

Lagrange, M. J., 92 n.9
Lake, K., 6 n.4, 9 n.3, 128 n.25, 180 n.18
Last supper, 232ff., 258ff.
Law, Jesus' attitude toward, 119f., 184f., 203f.
Leaven, 106
Legion, 93 n.12
Leper, cleansing of, 37ff., 82ff., 125
Lietzmann, H., 269 n.21, 281 n.2, 300 n.1, 316
Lightfoot, R. H., 20 n.18, 39 n.20, 84 n.22, 90 n.7, 138, 149 n.6, 157 n.13, 160 n.16, 196 n.15, 212 n.4, 236 n.33, 239 n.37, 247 n.55, 252ff., 259 nn.2, 5, 267, 268 n.18, 281 n.2, 294 n.20, 297 n.27
Lohmeyer, E., 31 n.7, 35 n.15, 89 n.6, 123 n.16, 135 n.38, 142 n.52, 147 n.3, 158 n.14, 161 n.20, 163 n.22, 173 n.8, 180 n.18, 181 nn.19, 20, 195 n.14, 199 n.22, 230 n.20, 235 n.30, 236 n.33, 252ff.
Loisy, A., 116, 127, 197 n.18, 244 n.45
Lord, 11 n.5, 141 n.51
Luke, St., 138 n.47, 163f., 195f., 201 n.24, 233 n.26, 240 n.38, 241 n.40, 245 n.48, 268 n.18, 276 n.32, 292 n.17, 297 n.27

Mandaean eschatology, 292 n.18
Manson, T. W., 14 n.8, 15 n.9, 32 n.10, 47 n.3, 110 n.11, 114, 128 n.25, 133 n.35, 170 n.3, 185 n.28, 256 n.7, 270 n.22, 308f.
Marriage, 203 n.32
Marxsen, W., 219 n.1
Matthew, St., 108ff., 138 n.47, 163f., 192 n.7, 195f., 200, 248 n.58, 268 n.19
Mayo, C. H., 237 n.34
McCasland, S. V., 61 n.27
Melchizedek, 247
Messiah crucified, 220ff., 267
Meyer, E., 47 n.3, 51 n.8, 225 n.9, 298 n.30
Micklem, E. R., 61 n.26
Micklem, N., 270 n.22
Milligan, G., 128 n.24, 246 n.50

Miracles:
  in general, 41ff.
  classification of, 52ff.
Mockery, 244 n.45
Montefiore, C. J., 111 n.12, 274 n.26
Moore, G. F., 14 n.8, 16 n.11, 23 n.22,
  133 n.35, 274 n.26
Morgan, C. Lloyd, 43 n.2
Moses, 180f., 184
Motivation, 6 n.4, 210
Moulton, J. H., 128 n.24, 246 n.50

New, 275 n.29
Nineham, D. E., 110 n.11
Nocturnal trial, 242f., 259 n.3, 280ff.

Oesterley, W. O. E., 195 n.13, 276
  n.33
Openly, 172f.
Otto, R., 60, 61 n.26, 73, 269

Parables, 96ff., 137, 202
Parallelism, 136f., 137f., 182f., 241, 245
  n.49, 274, 277f.
Paralytic, healing of, 126ff.
Parousia, 156ff., 165ff., 208f., 242,
  255ff., 292 n.18
Paschal:
  Lamb, 261, 267, 277
  regulations, 266 n.16
Passion narrative:
  in general, 218ff.
  early form of, 236 n.33, 259 n.3, 294
  n.19
Passover, 232f., 258ff.
Paul, St., 2 n.1, 28, 42, 115f., 118, 130,
  160 n.16, 162f., 174f., 179, 192 n.7,
  221, 256 n.7, 261ff.
Percy, E., 270 n.23
Pericope Adulterae, 306ff.
Pernot, H., 113 n.13, 128 n.24, 244 n.45
Peter:
  confession, 119 n.6, 145ff., 248 n.56
  denial, 236 n.33, 237 n.34, 242, 294
  n.19
Philosophy, St. Mark's, 1ff., 69ff.,
  173ff., 227ff., 239ff., 249ff., 319ff.
Pilate, 226, 243, 294, 299
Predestinarianism, 110ff., 151ff., 171ff.,
  187, 197 n.19, 207 n.41, 222ff.
Predictions of the passion, 151ff.,
  168ff.
Preparation, 259f.

Procuratorial trial, 243f., 294ff.
Psalms of suffering, 222 n.5, 239

Rabbi, 171 n.4
Rabinowitz, I., 61 n.27, 275 n.29
Rawlinson, A. E. J., 206 n.39, 225 n.9,
  237 n.34, 244 n.45, 262 n.9
Redemption, 185, 212, 273, 278
Reitzenstein, R., 72, 78 n.16, 292 n.18
Rejection in the *patris*, 58, 137ff., 201
  n.24, 253
Remembrance, 230 n.20, 275, 277
Remission of sins, 273 n.25
Resurrection:
  of Jesus, 160ff., 165ff., 248ff.
  on the third day, 174 n.11, 286f.
Retribution, 121 n.9
Riesenfeld, H., 134 n.37, 158 n.14, 169
  n.2, 181 n.19
Robinson, J. A., 317 n.6
Rohde, E., 73
Rowley, H. H., 270 n.23

Sabbath observance, 133ff.
Sacrifice, 273ff., 278, 286f.
Salt, 270
Sanhedrin:
  in general, 280 n.1, 282ff.
  competence of, 298, 300ff.
  seat of, 304ff.
Satan, *see* Beelzebul
Schwartz, E., 197 n.19
Seeley, J. R., 41 n.1
Sharp, D. S., 128 n.24
Sign from heaven, 30, 142
Simon of Cyrene, 249, 296
Simon the leper, 229 n.16
Sjöberg, E., 2 n.1
Skinner, J., 113 n.14
Sleep motif, 241 n.40
Smith, M., 101 n.3, 116 n.16
Smith, W. R., 270
Son of David, 190ff., 204, 304
Son of God, 10, 16, 18 n.13, 20, 63ff.,
  88, 156ff., 181, 247 n.55, 284f., 296,
  304
Son of Man, 2 n.1, 30, 70, 128, 151ff.,
  156ff., 183, 185, 204 n.34, 242, 288,
  292f., 314
Sower, parable of, 111f.
Spirit, Holy, 16ff.
Spitta, F., 23 n.23
Steinmann, J., 22 n.21

Index

Stephen, stoning of, 292f., 303, 314f.
Stonehouse, N. B., 19, 157 n.13, 253 n.2
Strack, H., 305
Strack, H., and P. Billerbeck, 14 n.8, 15 n.9, 16 n.11, 18 n.14, 22 n.20, 30 n.5, 32 n.10, 35 n.14, 37 n.18, 47 n.3, 48 n.4, 49 n.6, 51 n.9, 57 n.19, 59 n.23, 73, 93 n.12, 106 n.6, 129 n.27, 133, 152 n.7, 180 n.18, 190 n.2, 191 n.6, 197 n.19, 198 n.20, 199 n.21, 200 n.23, 201 n.25, 202 n.26, 205 n.35, 206 n.38, 235 n.28, 245 n.48, 246, 247 n.53, 263ff., 269 n.21, 281 n.4, 285 n.8
Strain on secrecy, 188ff., 243 n.43, 280
Strangling, 317
Streeter, B. H., 141 n.51, 161 n.21
Suffering Servant, 160 n.16, 185, 212, 222 n.5, 273, 278, 288
Sully, J., 43 n.2
Syrophoenician woman, 118, 141

Tabernacles, 181
Taciturnity of Jesus, 287f.
Taylor, V., 101 n.3, 210ff., 274 n.26
Teacher, 171 n.4
Temple:
    cleansing of, 121f., 196ff., 246f., 286f., 292 n.18, 298
    destruction of, 206, 285ff., 292 n.18
    portents of the destruction of, 246, 306
Temptation, 20ff.
Threes, see Triads
Time, notices of, 161 n.19, 174 n.11, 243, 244 n.47, 254f.
Titulus, 212, 222 n.5, 295, 304
Torrey, C. C., 154 n.10, 194 n.12
Transfiguration, 16, 20, 156ff., 180ff., 241 n.40
Triads, 123 n.16, 203, 205, 205 n.36, 232 n.24, 236, 243ff.

Triumphal entry, 193ff., 243 n.43, 256
Turner, C. H., 9 n.1, 10 n.4, 16 n.10, 33 n.11, 38 n.19, 52 n.11, 65, 81 n.19, 125 n.17, 141 n.51, 148, 154 n.11, 157 n.13, 169 n.1, 170 n.3, 174 n.11, 182, 199 n.21, 228 n.15, 239 n.37, 246 n.50, 247 n.54, 248 n.55, 268 n.19, 294 n.20
Typology, 24ff.

Universalism, 199 n.22, 248, 255 n.5, 286 n.11
Unleavened bread, 259f.
Unnick, W. C., van, 230 n.20

Vegetarianism, 203 n.32
Veil of the temple, 119 n.6, 246f., 286
Vermes, G., 212 n.4
Vielhauer, P., 2 n.1
Vigilance, 207ff., 241 n.41
Vinegar, 246 n.50
Voice from heaven, 16, 19, 20, 181

Weiss, J., 4 n.2, 9 n.3
Wellhausen, J., 13, 19, 93, 101 n.4, 127 n.23, 128, 181 n.20, 236 n.33, 259 n.2
Wenham, J. W., 133 n.36
Wicked husbandmen, 201ff., 243 n.43
Wilamowitz-Moellendorf, U., von, 157 n.13
Winter, P., 16 n.10, 93 n.12, 134 n.37, 135 n.38, 141 n.51, 203 n.32, 217 n.5, 222 n.5, 224 n.7, 225 n.9, 244 n.45, 281 n.2, 299 n.32, 300 n.1, 317
Witnesses, 244 n.47, 248ff., 283ff., 296
Women, 244 n.47, 248ff.
Word, the, 172f.
Wrede, W., 2 n.1, 71, 91 n.8, 100 n.2, 102 n.5, 173, 190, 192, 204 n.34, 210ff.

Zebedee, sons of, 31f., 184f.